2_

the
escape artist

HELEN FREMONT

Gallery Books
New York   London   Toronto   Sydney   New Delhi

Gallery Books
An Imprint of Simon & Schuster, Inc.
1230 Avenue of the Americas
New York, NY 10020

First Gallery Books hardcover edition February 2020

GALLERY BOOKS and colophon are registered trademarks of Simon & Schuster, Inc.

For information about special discounts for bulk purchases, please contact Simon & Schuster Special Sales at 1-866-506-1949 or business@simonandschuster.com.

The Simon & Schuster Speakers Bureau can bring authors to your live event. For more information or to book an event, contact the Simon & Schuster Speakers Bureau at 1-866-248-3049 or visit our website at www.simonspeakers.com.

Interior design by Davina Mock-Maniscalco

Manufactured in the United States of America

10   9   8   7   6   5   4   3   2   1

Library of Congress Cataloging-in-Publication Data

Names: Fremont, Helen, author.
Title: The escape artist / Helen Fremont.
Description: First Gallery Books hardcover edition. | New York : Gallery Books, 2020.
Identifiers: LCCN 2019022576 (print) | LCCN 2019022577 (ebook) | ISBN 9781982113605 (hardcover) | ISBN 9781982113612 (paperback) | ISBN 9781982113629 (ebook)
Subjects: LCSH: Fremont, Helen. | Fremont, Helen—Family. | Children of Holocaust survivors—United States—Biography.
Classification: LCC E184.37.F74 A4 2020 (print) | LCC E184.37.F74 (ebook) | DDC 940.53/18092 [B]—dc23
LC record available at https://lccn.loc.gov/2019022576
LC ebook record available at https://lccn.loc.gov/2019022577

ISBN 978-1-9821-1360-5
ISBN 978-1-9821-1362-9 (ebook)

For Donna

the
escape artist

author's note

This memoir, as well as its predecessor, *After Long Silence*, attempts to make sense of the secrets that underlie the family in which I grew up. In both books, I have changed many names, locations, and other identifying details to provide a measure of privacy to my family and others, and to underscore that this is my story. I have been careful in making changes to select settings that are consistent with the actual events described. Because different events are considered in this volume, readers of both works will notice that I have changed the geographic setting and other details from those provided in my first volume to better maintain this consistency with the actual events described in this book.

This book also considers aspects of my relationship with my sister and our personal difficulties that did not appear in my first book. Some events recounted had already occurred; some had not. I turn to them now because I have come to understand the extent to which they inform my story.

I have relied on my journals and memories spanning decades in setting out what I have come to remember, believe, and understand about my life. Like all personal narratives, mine is inherently subjective. However intertwined my life is with the lives of others, I can only speak my own truth; I recognize that their memories may vary from mine, no matter how many experiences we share and how much I love them.

predeceased

The light started to seep into the foothills of the Berkshires, the outline of trees barely visible against the dark sky. February 2002: I was driving the Mass Pike to Schenectady to meet with an estate lawyer. My dog, who had come along for support, sat in the backseat with his tongue hanging out, filling my rearview mirror with his blocky golden head.

I'd grown up in a town near Schenectady and had driven this road hundreds of times, with its old-fashioned tollbooths and Pilgrims' hats on green signs. My mother had taken me and my older sister, Lara, to Jiminy Peak on this road when I was barely old enough to hold a ski pole in a mittened fist. She'd taken us to the Clark Art Institute to gape at giant paintings of satyrs and nymphs. Later she'd driven me to Williamstown to see Bertolt Brecht's *Mother Courage* and *Arturo Ui*, and other plays my father refused to see because they were about war and suffering, and he had already seen too much war and suffering. Later still, I'd driven the Mass Pike to college and law school in Boston. The road to the Atlantic Ocean always returned home to Schenectady, like a fishing line cast out and reeled back in, over and over.

The last time I had driven this road was in November—three months before—to attend my father's funeral. It had seemed, at the time, a transformative reunion. My mother, sister, and I had spent hours talking, crying, laughing, and catching up, and in my little ballroom of wishful thinking, I believed we had regained our footing. But now, heading to the lawyer's office, I had trouble figuring out what had really happened.

Just six weeks after Dad's funeral—the letter arrived on Christmas Eve—I found out that I had been disowned by my family. My father had signed a last-minute codicil to his will, declaring me to have "predeceased" him. I'd responded like a dead person: I took to my grave. I made no attempt to contact my mother or sister, and they made no attempt to contact me.

For more than forty years, our family had been closer than fused. My parents and Lara were my cell structure and membrane, my very identity. Yet so much had been hidden from me—shadows and illusions that I'd never understood. I'd spent most of my life trying to decipher the mystery of my family, and I was still at a loss. Perhaps loss was precisely the point of our story.

———

When I was growing up, my mother said that our family was held together by the great glue of suffering. World War II had shattered my parents, and they had emerged from the charred remains of Europe with pieces missing. Around these holes they had built our family of four. We loved each other like starved people: we always wanted more.

A Sad and Difficult Time for All of Us

On the day I found out I was disowned, I woke before dawn as usual, slipped quietly out of bed, and stepped over my dog who lay on his side like a toppled Sphinx. I pulled on my gym shorts and T-shirt, laced up my sneakers, zipped up my parka, and went down the three flights of stairs. The streets were empty as I walked to the Y. It was the day before Christmas and the students who often made my building feel like a frat house were gone. Boston was between storms, so the sidewalks were clear, and the wind didn't hit me till I crossed Huntington Avenue. It was too early for traffic, a nice time to be out in the city, a little before 5 a.m.

I was forty-four years old and feeling optimistic: there was good reason to think that the three-year rift in my family was starting to heal. In 1999, I had published a memoir revealing my family's true identity and history. The book's unexpected success proved catastrophic for my mother, and her distress, of course, wreaked havoc for the rest of us. But now, over the past six weeks since the funeral, my mother had started writing to me again, handwritten letters telling me how she was managing now that Dad had died, and hoping that we could repair our relationship. And I wrote her too, telling her about my own grief, and that I loved her, and that I was so relieved to have her back. It was not the first time my mother had cut me off, but it had been the longest and most searing of our separations, and I felt grateful and relieved and lucky and sad all at the same time. At eighty-six, my father had been suffering from Parkinson's for a dozen years. Although he and I had always been close, Mom's refusal to speak to me had meant I was not permitted to see him for the last years of his life when he lived at home with her.

During those three years, my older sister and I had also not spoken, and the longer I had been cast off from my parents, the closer she had grown to them. And so, although I felt the enormity of my loss of my father, and although I didn't know whether my sister and I could mend our relationship, I felt heartened that my mother was finally emerging from her silent rage, and we could begin to be friends again. She was, I thought, starting to soften; she was letting in a little light and warmth through the cracks that my father's death had opened in her, and I wanted to stand in that sunshine and drink in all the warmth I could. I wanted to beam it back to her tenfold; I wanted her to know how much she meant to me.

———

When I got home from the gym, I took the dog out and picked up the mail. Among the bills, I saw a fat business-size envelope from my mother, addressed in her familiar European handwriting. I looked forward to her letters. But when I opened the envelope, I found a typed cover letter on legal letterhead from a lawyer. The letter, addressed to my mother, began, *As you know* . . . and went on to say something about signing my father's will. I pushed it aside and turned to a ten-page stapled document, a photocopy of my father's last will and testament. I'd never seen this before, and with growing unease, I turned the pages. The paper felt stiff and kept buckling in my hands—it had been folded into thirds, and now seemed to want to fold itself up again. It was a standard form will, and although I had trouble taking any of it in, I recognized my name here and there, together with my sister Lara's and my mother's, sprinkled among the numbered paragraphs of legalese.

I didn't want to read this document; it seemed a violation of my father's privacy somehow, and I was disturbed by this cold, impersonal evidence of his death. But I forced myself to skim a few pages, and I saw that everything in my father's estate was to be distributed through a family trust equally to my sister and me; my mother was the executor, my sister and I were trustees, and various distributions were to be made . . . *equally to my children Lara and Helen . . .* and *in equal shares to Lara and Helen . . .* and so on. The will was signed and dated October 1998.

And then I came to the last page, a single sheet not stapled to anything. The word CODICIL was written at the top in bold letters, and as my eyes trailed down the page, I saw my name in capital letters, repeated in a series of paragraphs that stated: *Delete HELEN FREMONT from each paragraph, and replace her with . . .* The final sentence read: *For the purposes of this my Last Will and Testament, my daughter, HELEN FREMONT, and her issue, if any, shall be deemed to have predeceased me.*

And there, at the bottom of this piece of paper that removed me from his life, was my father's shaky, Parkinsonian signature. He could barely hold a pen by then; my mother must have helped him. It was dated July 2001, soon after he'd suffered a near-fatal collapse and four months before his death. My mother had now sent me these documents with her own attached handwritten note, saying simply, *It is a sad and difficult time for all of us.*

Because of the new names of Lara's partner and, improbably, of her swim coach that "replaced" Helen in the codicil, I felt sure that my sister had been complicit. She was now declared my parents' only daughter.

It would take me a long time to understand how my sister could have participated in this. I have no doubt that she did so out of a sense of loyalty to my parents. Our family was built on lies to protect one another from what we believed to be more painful truths. In the end, we got tangled up in our own fictions. Our stories had sharp edges; I was sliced off.

part one

Sisters are a setup. Shot from the same cannon, you're sent on a blind date for the rest of your lives.

My sister, Lara, and I had a script we were supposed to follow. My mother and her sister, Zosia, had written it, and they were our role models, which is pretty scary when you consider what they'd been through. During the war, Zosia had saved my mother's life. Or maybe it was the other way around. The stories were twisted and my mother and aunt were bound together in ways that Lara and I didn't begin to understand, but we did our best to follow for most of our lives. Although Zosia lived in Italy and we lived in upstate New York, Mom and Zosia's love was formidable, the stuff of legend, built on a mythic past. One day, they told us, my sister and I would have what they had.

But unlike our mother and aunt, Lara and I didn't have any real wars to test our bond; we had to make up our own. From our earliest years, we liked to go to extremes with each other. We tested our limits, pushed ourselves and each other a little further, a little harder, to see how much we could take. To prove how much we loved each other.

Usually these tests of strength took place in the wilderness, far from the comforts and complications of our everyday lives.

In 1990, when I was thirty-three and Lara was thirty-six, we went ski mountaineering in the remote Battle Range of British Columbia. A helicopter dropped us off on a mountain ridge above a wall of ice. The pilot would come back for our group of ten a week later, weather permitting.

Forty feet of snow had fallen in the last three months, and they'd had to dig down to find the entrance to the hut we would use as our base. We hustled our gear inside and went back out for avalanche practice. We were going to learn how to save each other's lives. After clipping on our skis, Lara and I followed our guide into an unannounced blizzard. The storm had come out of nowhere, and we weren't going far—just far enough to feel like an avalanche was possible. Then we began the drill, making an imaginary grid in the snow and finding the buried "victim" using our transceivers. The guide timed us. It was hard to see in the swirling snow, and we struggled against the wind, holding the transceivers in front of us as we walked back and forth in the deep powder trying to locate the signal. We weren't very good at search and rescue, and I could see that the real purpose of the drill was to teach us that we would never survive an avalanche. The guide had come through a few, but despite our years of exercising poor judgment in the mountains, Lara and I had never tripped one.

It was Lara who had talked me into this trip, and I was a little anxious about skinning up a few thousand vertical feet each day. The next morning under clear skies we trekked single-file up a steep ravine, skirting a series of heart-stopping crevasses—freakish blue gashes in the snow that dropped hundreds of yards into darkness. Sweat poured from our faces. Not a sound—just the whistle and whip of the wind, the huff of our breathing, and the hushed swish of our skis moving through deep powder, like giant silencers on our feet.

I liked to follow behind Lara, and imagined that our legs were connected by the same body. When she pushed her right leg forward, mine slid forward automatically, as if invisible strings attached my ski boot to hers. I could sink into her rhythm without using any of my own energy; I could siphon off her. You can really lose yourself like this. Your *self* actually disappears. Your body is there, a huffing, puffing, pounding machine that slides along with your sister's. But your mind stretches out, and your spirit soars, and there is nothing that binds you to the earth. A giddy feeling of floating high above the thousands of miles of mountains around you, and for a moment you feel as if you have touched God, that you dwell in the bodiless land of the spirit, whether it's the wind on your cheek or the blue in the sky or the sharp knives of the peaks in the distance, surrounded by emptiness and snow and the simplest of elements. It's a kind of rapture, a sort of passionate love affair with the universe.

This was the heady bond Lara and I had shared since childhood. You have to climb to the end of the earth because the middle of your life is too weighed down by trinkets of the mundane, the alarm clock with its rigid hands, the same twelve numbers arranged in the same circle, the same wheels that carry you to this street or that; to this desk or that; to this bed or that. I had found my true north. It was the world away from everything. Lara had brought me here, above the trees, above life. It was as cool and creamy and thrilling as death itself.

Back then, there was no doubt that if an avalanche had come for my sister, I'd have leapt in front of it and pushed her to safety.

But that was a long time ago.

one

Lara and I grew up outside Schenectady, near the snow belt of upstate New York. Winter moved in for good by November and didn't really start to lose interest until well into April. Summers were short, crisp, and businesslike, so brief as to seem a false memory. By mid-August, you could already feel the air changing, sharpening its teeth. In October, the ground frosted and hardened. Winter storms swooped down from the northwest with a thrilling blast of cold air that you had to bite into, just to breathe.

While our father saw patients at his office and made hospital rounds, our mother cleaned the house and everything in it. And I spent my earliest years stumbling after Lara, who seemed to be in constant motion—flying down the hills behind our house on a sled or a cart, running through the woods, and leaping off the ledges of my mother's rock garden.

It was obvious to anyone that she owned me. Like most big sisters and mob bosses, she ordered me around, insisted on my participation in her schemes, and, if I balked, she could use brute force to get me to comply. Through her, I absorbed galaxies of information—about climbing trees and Indian wrestling, stick fighting, rock throwing, berry picking, and igloo building. Most importantly, I learned that resistance was pointless.

We were allies: we both loved adventure and action, tests of strength and courage.

We were enemies: we hated each other. I was half her size and a crybaby; she could throw me to the ground with one hand while eating an ice cream cone with the other.

Home Movies, 1956–61

The movies begin in Italy in 1956, before I was born: two-year-old Lara and Mom and her older sister, Auntie Zosia, are walking through the gardens at the Villa d'Este in Tivoli, outside Rome, where Auntie and Uncle live. Mom is walking briskly—short dark hair, very trim; she cuts a smart figure. Auntie Zosia is a curvy redhead, with high cheekbones and an alluring, mysterious face. And there's Uncle Giulio, daintier than the women, a small gem. He smiles sweetly at my father, who holds the movie camera. An authentic Italian count, Uncle is conspicuously beautiful, slim and sophisticated in his tailored linen slacks, yellow polo shirt, and sporty ascot.

Now Dad must have given Mom the movie camera, because here he is, striding toward us: freakishly tall compared to the rest of them, athletic. His hair is striking—white with a single dark stripe down the middle, combed straight back off his forehead like an exotic animal. He towers over the world, his legs crazy long, his chest and shoulders broad, his waist trim. He looks like some bizarre exaggeration of the ideal male body.

Trailing behind is my cousin Renzo, a gangly thirteen-year-old, dark and handsome with hooded eyes and a bored look on his face. Thirty-five years later, Lara and I would realize that things were not always as we'd been told. Renzo looks more like my mother than like anyone else in these movies, and he certainly doesn't look like Giulio. For my mother, identity was slippery, and history was a vast game board on which the pieces could be moved, exchanged, and transformed at will. My mother's survival of the war had depended on such sleights of hand and shifts in identity. For the rest of her life she would continue to rely on the stories she told to stay alive, long after the need for lies was apparent.

My father focuses the camera on Lara now. Here she's running toward him, stumbling about, exploring everything. She's curious, fearless, a live wire. She wears a little white dress over her diaper.

Cut back to my mother, who looks severe and unhappy. She barely glances at my father.

In the next scene, it's the summer of 1957, and there I am, hidden from view inside my mother's giant belly. She sits, very pregnant, on a lawn chair in Evans Mills outside the clapboard house with peeling paint that my parents rented as their first home and medical office. Despite her belly, she looks hollowed out, cold, devoured.

Suddenly it's Christmas 1957, and it's all Lara, all the time. My father cannot get enough of her. She's opening presents, pure delight. And now a quick glimpse of me in the crib—holding on to the bars, stunned and wide-eyed, which is how I look in the movies for the next several years. A blob with big dark eyes, sort of in a daze, trying to make sense of all these characters.

And now my parents are working outside the rakish brick house they bought near Schenectady six months after I was born. The house was a full-fledged member of our family, and it had its own problems. Built on a hill, surrounded by woods, it was all sharp angles and soaring ceilings. The whole thing was made of mistakes. Its walls, inside and out, were a patchwork of partially exploded bricks, scarred by the kiln but not completely destroyed, and we liked them for their character. As a child I often had bruises in the shape of those bricks, whenever my sister shoved me against them. Even the floors were made of brick, shellacked and bumpy on our bare feet.

Then there was all that glass: an entire wall of giant floor-to-ceiling glass slabs running the length of the loft-style living room. If you leaned with all your weight and some of your father's, you could slide one slab past the other along an extended track, and open the living room onto the screened-in porch.

I loved the house for its soaring self-confidence and the explosion of sky-splitting light, the way the land and woods seemed to be part of our living room. It had great flair, despite all its broken-brick bones. Everyone else I knew lived in ordinary homes with the rectilinear promise of solidity, propriety, and order. Our house, like our family, was dangerous and unpredictable, a wild adventure.

Here in our home movies, my parents are hauling rocks and building the slate steps from the driveway up the steep hill to the front door. And there's Mom in a green surgeon's cap, raking leaves in the fall, and in winter she's out there shoveling paths through two feet of snow up those slate steps and around the house. Then it's spring again, and she's lugging boulders and heaving the earth like a steam shovel.

Together with my father, she pummeled the wilderness into lush hills of honeysuckle and pachysandra. This was where they put all the parts of themselves that they couldn't put into words. All of their losses and betrayals and grief and rage went into the ground and rocks and trees around us. And unlike my sister and me, the house and grounds accepted everything they did without question or objection, and reflected back the best of them.

In all these home movies, there isn't an ounce of play in either of my parents. They have work to do, hard, knuckle-breaking work, and there is a sense of great productivity and drive.

By 1959 they've already turned the house into a jewel of lawns and gardens in the middle of a forest. The isolation is striking. You could run through those woods, but you would not find another human being for what seemed like miles. In fact, there were a couple of houses some distance away, but they were hidden, childless, equally isolated.

That nowhere-ness of home. The sense of being apart from the rest of the world. No relatives or extended family, just us. And I was on my own planet, apart somehow from this family.

———

After I was born in 1957, my mother and aunt set up a schedule so that the two sisters could be together as often as finances allowed. Like the Summer Olympics, we went to visit Zosia every four years. On an alternating schedule, Zosia came to visit us in Schenectady. Renzo, already a teenager by then, was off in the parallel universe of girls and motorcycles.

Zosia and Mom would spend their days in Schenectady cooking and baking and inviting friends for dinner and bridge, and going for walks, and always talking, talking, talking in Italian. Once, Uncle Giulio came along with Zosia, and nearly froze to death because the Schenectady summers were so cold. Another year, Renzo—already an engineer—came and built Lara and me a superb underground fort in a field behind our house. But the main event was always my mother and aunt, who immersed themselves in a bubbling stream of Italian.

The two sisters endured the years between their summers together by writing letters to each other every day. When the mail arrived each afternoon, Mom made herself a ritual cup of tea and settled down to read Zosia's letter. She typed her response on a blue aerogram, licked and folded down the flaps, and left it for my father to post the next morning. Lara and I learned not to disturb her during her reading and writing of Zosia's letters. Even Dad must have realized by then that my mother's heart belonged to her sister, and not to him.

Aside from this daily communion between the two sisters, my family was on its own in the New World—free of context, as far as Lara or I could tell. My father had no surviving relatives. Whatever possessions my family had once owned had been lost or destroyed in the war. There were no existing photographs of my parents until after the war, when my father's hair was already white and my mother was sharp-angled and serious. As a child, I had trouble believing that my parents had ever actually been children, since no evidence supported this. I knew that my father had spent six years as a prisoner in Siberia during the war, but aside from that, my parents wouldn't talk about the past, and everyone who'd known them was dead. In my mind, they had always been adults and always would be—hardworking, long-suffering, and serious. I was determined never to let adulthood happen to me, and by and large, I succeeded.

————

When my parents moved to our brick house outside Schenectady in the late 1950s, my father developed a small circle of doctor friends who worked at the local hospital. Their wives took turns hosting dinner parties followed by a couple of tables of bridge. Every few months when it was my mother's turn, she dutifully followed the elaborate recipes of Julia Child, set the dining room table, and made sure the bar was stocked with sherry and vermouth. By the time my father came home from work and changed into his navy-blue suit, my mother had already zipped herself into one of her Italian dresses, combed and shaped her eyebrows, and glossed her lips red. Lara and I stared, amazed at the transformation.

Around the house, Mom wore no-nonsense slacks for her daily housecleaning rampages. Armed with scouring pads, rags, and cleaning solutions, she was a veritable cleaning dynamo—furiously dusting, vacuuming, and mopping up after us. She washed the windows inside and out, scrubbed the toilets, tubs, and sinks, and vacuumed not only the dog hair from the carpets but also the dog himself. The surfaces of our house sparkled, especially when she was upset or anxious or angry. "Cleaning is my outlet," she said. The worse things got at home, the better our house looked. The minute you put something down—a book, a sweater, a pair of glasses—it was swept up, dusted under, and dispatched to your room.

But she had a number of elegant dresses from her years in Rome, when clothes had been bartered and tailor-made in a perpetual recycling of prewar garments. In 1946, she'd married my father on her lunch break in Rome wearing a wool business suit that had been made out of one of Uncle's black Fascist uniforms. Her shoes, too, were Italian, and every Sunday, when she dressed to take us to St. Pius, our local Catholic church, she looked stylish and sophisticated.

When she stood next to my father in her Florentine high heels, my mother's head, with its defiant waves of thick, dark hair, barely grazed my father's armpit. You could fit three of her into his chest alone. My father's shoulders rose like a mountain range above her. His head, too, was large and majestic, with a chiseled nose, ice-blue eyes, and white hair combed straight back. While my mother was quick, lithe, and impossible to catch, my father was tall, powerful, and impossible to move.

But their attachment was more intellectual than physical. They liked each other's minds, and they were closely matched in the areas of self-confidence and stubbornness. I never saw them kiss or hold hands; they rarely touched each other with affection.

When their guests arrived, it sounded like a home invasion— women screeching their hellos, heels clattering on the brick floor, pots and pans banging in the kitchen. In the safety of the television room, Lara and I hunkered down with the dog, listening to the adult voices rising and falling like boats on the ocean, here a crescendo of chatter and laughter, there the tinkling of ice in cocktail glasses, now the booming laughter of one of the men, and above it all my mother's animated voice, lively, bright, filled with theater.

Careful to keep quiet, Lara taught me various kung fu moves that she invented on the spot. We practiced in the hallway, flying through the air, folding ourselves into pretzels. In her Wrangler jeans and Fruit of the Loom T-shirt, she looked like a loose-limbed boy with wild brown hair. We had matching short haircuts, but mine was darker and more obedient.

At some point after the guests had been fed and tamed and seated at their bridge tables, Lara and I would be trotted out to say hello to them. Then we disappeared into the kitchen, stunned by the mess that adults could make: stacks of dirty dishes, decapitated hors d'oeuvres, and a scattered graveyard of cigarette butts stained with garish pink lipstick. It was the Lebanese lady who smoked. She took only a few puffs from each cigarette, then stubbed it out and lit another. Her lips were everywhere.

By morning, my mother had already scrubbed everything clean. The bridge tables had been folded up and rolled back into their boxes; pots and pans glistened like cairns of stainless steel rising from the dish rack.

My mother acquitted herself of such social obligations quite well, offering genuine warmth to her friends without burdening them with too much intimacy. Later I came to understand that my mother did not have close friends on purpose. She was a chameleon, effortlessly blending in everywhere, attuned to everyone, but trusting no one. Whenever I saw her with others, I marveled at her complete fluency in the world, the ease with which she displayed her many colors. She dazzled me.

My father was less adept at social skills. His idea of conversation was cornering one or two people at a party and telling them the intricate details of something he had just read about—cold fusion, perhaps, or gravitational collapse. He could never read the glazed-over faces of his victims, who were too polite to extricate themselves.

His most successful relationships were his chess friendships. He had become something of a chess champion in the Gulag, where playing chess was punishable by death, so he had developed a lightning-quick technique that he still deployed. While his opponents contemplated their next move, my father would busy himself by cracking open and eating all the nuts in the bowl on the table, or getting up and stretching his legs. The second his opponent had completed his move, Dad would pounce, snatching his own chess piece and slamming it down on another square, leaving his opponent once again to study the board and ponder the possibilities.

———

Of my parents, Mom was the one you wanted to be with. She was strict, but warmer, more patient. Dad, on the other hand, waited for no one and accepted no excuses. His word, he always told Lara and me, was *iron*, and whenever he said this, he made a powerful fist with his right hand. He had a sharp wit and a sly sense of humor, but his bitterness ate into everything he did. While he was in Siberia, fellow prisoners had broken his left elbow while trying to steal his clothes. Years later, surgeons in Italy removed the calcified joint and sewed him back together, but he never recovered full use of his arm. My father tried not to speak of his years as a prisoner, but he acted like a man who had lived with beasts. He wolfed his meals in seconds, and nothing my mother said or did could get him to slow down. "I can't," he'd say helplessly. "It's food."

He kept ferociously busy, saw patients day and night, built rock ledges behind the house, planted bushes, mulched trees, chopped wood. One year he bought a thousand evergreens and planted them across the grounds, along the driveway, all over the lawn. He was a colossus of efficient, if furious, energy. At night, his shrieking nightmares jolted us awake. The next morning my mother would dismiss them with a weary shrug, saying, "The Gulag again," as if genocide were just one more annoyance that kept intruding into our lives.

———

We never knew when an image or a sound or a fight between my sister and me would trip the invisible wire, and my father would blurt out a horrifying incident from the camps, or my mother would cry, "I should have died with my parents! Don't you understand? We shouldn't be alive!" My sister and I would freeze—the whole planet froze—as we watched our parents being stolen from us by the past.

These moments would never be spoken of afterward. Our family circled them with a thick layer of silence, around which my sister and I tiptoed, magically thinking that if we were careful, we could avoid sparking another explosion.

Through such experiences Lara and I laid down the framework of our own story. We absorbed their secrets and turned them into our own drama. Maybe it wasn't an exact translation of our parents' war, but it was the best we could do with what we had. To Mom and Dad's unspoken past we added our own hunger, the rapacity of children who have everything and still want more—love, attention, adoration. Lara and I fought each other as if battling for the last scrap of oxygen in the house, as if there were room in our parents' hearts for only one child.

———

By the time I was in second grade, I decided that Lara's usefulness as an older sister had expired. She had become baggage. Her socks sagged at different heights. She buttoned her blouses right up to her chin, and wore braces on her buck teeth. She was flat-footed, with long narrow feet that didn't seem to match her solid body. Even the clothes my mother sewed for us looked all wrong on her—her legs were too long and her waist too wide. She had no friends. She got straight As. In class, she was obedient, polite, and brilliant. And she had a gift for math and music and science, and she later learned Russian—all the skills and talents my father had—ensuring a lifelong competition between them.

Although her teachers loved her, her classmates at Glenwood Elementary School laughed at her for her geeky height, her chipmunk cheeks and weird hair. Every day she ran home in tears. "Why are they so mean to me?" she cried to my mother.

I was exactly the opposite. Perhaps I had learned something from watching her, or perhaps I was just plain lucky, but from the moment I set foot in school, I began my conquest of friends. Although I wore Lara's hand-me-down clothes, I wore them at a raffish angle and thought I looked cool. I had no time for Lara now. Without so much as a backward glance, I shucked my sister like an old T-shirt, and courted my classmates. Lara watched this parade of little kids in and out of our house, and saw me laughing and goofing off with Jill and Pam and Lori and Freddie, and it made her want to break my smile over her knee.

————

One day I came home from second grade to find Lara writhing on the floor in the doorway to the kitchen. She was screaming that she would never go back to school again. Her eyes had a wild look to them, and her teeth were clenched. When she saw me standing in the entranceway, she shouted, "I hate you!" and started hissing. Her hair, thick and tangled, flared from her head. On the other side of my sister, a safe distance away, my mother tried to reason with her. Mom glanced up at me. "Helen," she said in her most ordinary voice. "How was school?"

I decided to take her cue and pretend Lara wasn't there. "Can I get a glass of milk?" I asked.

"Of course," Mom said.

I tried to step over Lara, but she emitted a snarl, then a gurgling sound deep in her throat. Her eyes widened, and for a moment it seemed she would leap from the floor and sink her teeth into my leg. I backed off. At ten, she was already bigger and stronger than my mother.

"She won't let me in," I said.

My mother considered this. "Lara, let her into the kitchen."

"Make me!" Lara shouted. "You make me!" She planted her foot against the doorjamb for leverage.

My mother looked disappointed.

"Mom," I pleaded.

"I'll get you a glass of milk," she said. She took a step toward the refrigerator, but Lara kicked at Mom's ankles. My mother backed away. "All right, never mind, Helen." Mom was not in the mood to fight. "Change your clothes. You can have a glass of milk later."

My father came home from the office two hours later. By then my mother and sister were murmuring softly in each other's arms in Lara's bedroom. I watched them from the hallway, jealous. I heard the quiet of my father's entrance, the way the air shifted around his body. He always entered the house as if on a stealth mission—ears pricked, eyes alert, every muscle tensed. He and I were hooked up to the same radar. He seemed to weigh the valence of electrons in each room. I met him at the top of the stairs. He cocked his head.

"They're in Lara's room," I said.

———————

I steered a wide berth around my sister after that. It took nothing to set her off. She would slam me against the brick wall if she happened to pass me in the hallway. An elbow to the jaw, a knee in my ribs. I quickly learned to fight back: whenever I was safely out of reach, I would snicker and call her a weirdo, or laugh at her for being such a creep. I delighted in seeing her face turn red, even though I already knew I was toast. Because that was my trump card; Lara could beat the living crap out of me, but I knew she feared being different, freakish. I did my best to remind her of it every chance I got. And so we went to war.

My parents couldn't do much about this. We fought offstage, while my mother was cleaning the house or writing her sister, and my father was at the office or the hospital. Our fights did not compare to the more pressing concerns of earning a living and running a household. In the annals of competitive suffering, Lara and I knew from an early age that we were lucky to be irrelevant. But on the scorecard of our daily lives as children, we wanted to matter.

And of course we did matter very much to our parents, as long as we did our jobs as blue-chip children and straight-A students.

"My life is over," Mom often told us. "My life ended in the war. You are all that matter."

We were small shoots now, perhaps, but with care and feeding and sunlight, with green vegetables and vitamins and snowsuits in winter and sunblock in summer, with French lessons and piano lessons and ballet lessons and swim lessons, we would grow strong and cultured and smart, and we would redeem all that had been taken from her, restore reason in the world.

And, oh my, the love. Our parents loved Lara and me with such a ferocity, it was hard to remain standing in the face of it. They loved us with cyclone force. They loved the arms right out of our sockets. My friends were loved with the casual American ease of prairie love, of cows grazing in a fenced-in field. My sister and I were loved with the blazing heat of immigrant love. The scorched-earth love of a people hunted down, displaced, and resettled countless times before clawing their way to the topsoil of upstate New York.

————

Overlooking our increasingly frequent fights, Mom seemed gratified to see how closely Lara and I mirrored our mother and aunt. "You're just like me," Mom always told me. "You were an easy child." I opened my mouth and words came to me. I closed my eyes and sleep embraced me. I went to school and children played with me. For Lara, nothing came easily. She was in constant battle with herself and the world. "Lara is so much like Zosia," Mom would say. "Always in motion, always restless." She assured me that Lara and I would be closer than anyone else in the world. Sisters shared each other's secrets and saved each other's lives. It sounded good. But by the time I was in the second grade, I started to think I had the wrong sister for that. I brought this up with my mother. "I don't think Lara is right for me," I said. Mom smiled. "Just wait. You'll see when you get older."

But with time, things only got worse. Night would fall, and Lara's eyes snapped open with the certainty of danger. Enemies filled her room, hid in her closet, slipped between the sheets of her bed, stole behind the radiator, leaked under the windowsill. If she closed her eyes, they would spring out to get her.

The voices began as whispers, then grew louder, she would tell me years later. Everything buzzed. Her bed began to move. She leapt from it and stared at it—but of course, now it was still. The curtains fluttered. She lifted one corner and traced the pattern of movement across the fabric, a wave on the beach. So elusive, the shadows. The creatures had no shape or form, but only a function—to hurt her, to laugh at her, to twist her into knots.

While Lara was fighting her demons in her bedroom, my father was back in Siberia, and my mother was having her own nightmares of being taken by the "police" from her home, as she would tell us in the morning. I knew nothing of this at the time, but now I wonder if Lara's voices were coming to her through the walls of our parents' unspoken memories.

———————

When she was eleven, Lara finally went crazy in a way that perhaps our whole family had been waiting for. Every night after our mother had turned out our lights and retreated to the living room, Lara would start.

I could hear her get out of bed and flick the light switch in her room on and off rapidly, dozens, maybe hundreds of times. My room shared a wall with hers, and I could hear the sharp *click-clack-click-clack*, like a rapid-fire machine gun. I'd hear her snapping the curtains back and forth along their runners the length of the room: *Zhiiiiing! Zhiiiiing! Zhiiiiiing!* Then back to the light switch—*click-clack-click-clack*. Then a muffled rummaging sound, when she must have dropped to the floor and scanned under her bed. Then the curtains sang again. Now she was rustling in her closet, sweeping the skirts and blouses back and forth on their hangers.

I didn't understand what she was doing, and I didn't care. As far as I could tell, most of the things Lara did were intended to irritate me, and I wasn't about to give her the satisfaction. Out of vengeance, I fell asleep.

But her rituals got even longer and more elaborate. I would wake in the middle of the night to the sound of my sister's drapes flying across their runners. I would listen for what would come next. Midnight, one o'clock, two. The rest of the house was dead, and only Lara's room was alive with sound. Her Concerto for Lights and Drapes.

It never occurred to me to tell my parents about this. One night, though, I tiptoed down the hall to the bathroom. Lights blazed in my sister's room, and I could hear the murmur of my parents' voices. Just as I walked past the door, I heard my mother say, "psychologist," and the door to Lara's room swung shut. The hairs stood up on my neck.

Lara's gone psycho, I thought with a chill. Like those wide-eyed freaks in the horror movie reruns on TV, arms outstretched, lurching robotically. All of a sudden, I realized that stuff like that didn't just happen to people on TV; it was happening to *my sister*.

The implications were terrifying. If such a condition could strike Lara, it was only a matter of time before I too succumbed. She'd given me everything—measles, chicken pox, mumps—and I'd catch this from her too. I hovered outside Lara's closed door, transfixed by the seam of light glowing under it. I could not make out my parents' words, just their hushed mumbling voices.

After that night, Lara skulked around the house under a dark cloud of dread. I was careful not to get too close to her, but I studied her for signs of craziness. Her hair had always been thick and unruly, and now it looked even worse. She had dark hollows under her eyes, and her fingernails were picked to bloody stumps. When she caught me looking at her, she bared her teeth and growled wolfishly. My parents spoke Polish all the time now in hushed tones.

A few days later, my mother carried the skinny fold-up cot from the basement and set it up in Lara's room. Mom assured my father it would only be for a night or two, but it turned out to be three nights and then four, then a week, then two weeks, and then we just pretended it was normal that my mother slept in Lara's room.

———

Soon after she moved into Lara's room, my mother told me that Lara was going to start seeing a psychologist who would help her feel better. "You cannot mention a word of this," she said in a low voice.

I nodded. Mom looked hardened, like metal.

"I want you to take a vow," she said. "You must promise never to say a word about this to anyone."

"Okay," I said.

"This is a private matter," she said. "A family matter."

I knew what that meant. Our family had many things we were not allowed to speak of. We didn't speak about my parents' war, or about their parents, or about anything that had happened Before.

When I went to school the following morning, the secret of my sister's illness weighed on me. I saw my eight-year-old classmates as if from a great distance, and I felt a strange gap open up between us. They were still my friends, but suddenly they seemed so young and free. They were unaware of the enormity of danger in the world, and although I myself didn't understand what that danger was, I knew that our family had it, that it was in our house. A deep, unspeakable line separated me from everyone outside my family.

two

I was in the kitchen one afternoon after grade school when my father came home to take Lara to the psychologist. "Make me!" she shouted, throwing herself to the floor. "Go ahead, make me!" My father grabbed her by the wrist. Lara kicked and clawed and spat at him as he dragged her to his car and planted her in the front seat. He had a hard time of it. My father had been a world-class athlete before the war, and although he seemed to rise above everyone in the state of New York, he really only had the use of his good arm. Lara, however, seemed to have a dozen arms. He finally got her in the car and gunned it down the driveway.

An hour and a half later, he brought her home. Lara burst into the kitchen shouting that she hated the psychologist, and she hated my parents, and most of all she hated me. As if the idea had just occurred to her, she lunged and knocked me to the floor. My mother had been cooking dinner, and the kitchen smelled of mashed potatoes, which I hated, and I remember a splotch of potato on the green linoleum. It was my father who pulled her off me, and while Lara was screaming that she would kill me, my father hustled me out to his car. Even before I'd closed the passenger door, he had started the engine. I was still sniffling, rubbing my elbow where I'd hit the linoleum. "Fasten your seat belt," he ordered. I understood that my crying was grating on his nerves, so I clicked in and shut up.

He turned onto Natchaug Road. "Are you hungry?" he asked. I shook my head.

"Let's get a hot dog," he said. We drove to a fast-food place near his office, and he gulped his down in two bites.

"I hate her guts," I said.

My father looked at me sternly. "Don't say that."

"Well, it's true."

He said nothing. We drove through the seedier part of State Street to his office, where he let me hang out in one of his exam rooms while he did his bookkeeping. Neat jars of sterile gauze and long Q-tips, bottles of ammonia and medicines gleamed on the Formica counters. In his kitchen he had beakers and test tubes and a centrifuge and an autoclave so he could do his own lab work and minor surgery. He even had his own X-ray equipment down the hall, a monster of a machine that filled the entire room, and a separate little glassed-in booth where my father worked the controls like the Wizard of Oz. He was a family doctor, and his patients were mostly immigrants and working-class people who came to him because he didn't charge much, he worked around the clock, and he cut his patients some slack if they couldn't pay him right away.

Being with my father made me feel safe (he was big) and proud (he was successful), but he was not my mother, whose warmth we all craved. When I was younger, I used to crawl into her lap while she was reading on her chaise longue, and she would absentmindedly stroke my hair and tuck it behind my ear. But after a moment she would tell me to find something to do with myself and I would climb down and go to my room, feeling that I had gotten something precious—a small package of warmth from the one I adored.

My father, by contrast, was all sharp edges and modern efficiency, like a chrome-framed chair to my mother's chaise longue. When he finally drove me home late that night, I could hear my mother in my sister's room, murmuring over and over that she loved her, she forgave her, it wasn't her fault at all.

My jealousy caught flame and heated my face as I crawled into bed. I kicked off the covers, hating my sister for taking my mother away from me. I wanted Lara out of the house; I wanted her dead. The feeling was mutual; we were exactly alike in that regard.

———

In the all-or-nothing language of childhood memories, by the time I was eight years old, I saw Lara as two separate identities—sometimes she was my beloved big sister, and other times she was a wild animal, unpredictable and vicious. But of course the reality was much more complicated. The Lara who helped me herringbone up a ski slope when I was five, who calmed my fears and planted her poles in the snow to prevent me from slipping downhill, was the same Lara who taught me to eat lemons (rind and all) to gross out the babysitters my parents hired when they went out to the movies; the same Lara who taught me how to swallow the giant penicillin pills Dad prescribed for my ear infection. (She demonstrated by using M&M's.) And it was the same Lara who later taught me to dribble a basketball, switching hands as we ran through an obstacle course of sneakers she'd thrown down on the driveway. My sister and I had always been teammates, coconspirators. But something happened in 1965 that changed our relationship—it was then that my sister seemed capable of turning suddenly into this other Lara, a terrifying creature whom I could neither recognize nor reason with. Decades later, when we tried to talk about those times, our feelings were still too brittle, and in order to preserve our adult bond, she and I inevitably switched to safer topics. To this day, I think, both of us preserve within us the inconsolable core of an injured child, each certain of our own innocence—convinced that it was the other who caused such irreparable damage, the other who deserved whatever justifiable rage we unleashed on each other.

But maybe Lara and I were just set up by history—the war, the secrets, the silence. Or perhaps we were set up by the perfect sisterhood of Mom and Zosia. Sometimes Lara and I felt that we could never fulfill their expectations; sometimes we felt we weren't even supposed to be alive. More than once our mother told us that surviving the war had been her biggest mistake.

History Lesson

From the time Lara and I were little kids until we went to college, my mother had told us bits and pieces of her life before we were born— partial truths, incomplete stories that didn't always fit together. She, Dad, and Zosia were the only ones from their city in eastern Poland who had survived the war, she said. Although they were Catholic—or so they said— their parents, friends, and entire community had been killed by bombs.

Zosia, seven years older than Mom, had left Poland before the war.

Zosia had gone to graduate school in Italy in the 1930s, fallen in love, and eventually married my uncle Giulio, an Italian count and high-level lawyer in Mussolini's government.

Mom, in the meantime, had remained in Poland during the war and stayed alive through her wits, enormous luck, and a daring born of desperation. She told us that after her parents were killed in 1942, she escaped the Nazis by cutting her hair short, dressing as an Italian soldier, and marching out of Poland with the Italian Army. She had grown very close to an Italian officer named Luigi, who helped her escape. "He risked his life for me," Mom told us. "I was trying to reach Zosia in Rome, and without Luigi, I would never have gotten out of Poland." Mom was arrested at the Italian border and presumed to be a spy, but with Zosia's and Giulio's help, she was miraculously saved from the firing squad and imprisoned in a camp instead. Afterward she lived in Rome with her sister, her brother-in-law, and their baby, Renzo. Mom got a job as a translator with the American Red Cross and married my father after the war; finally, in 1950, she and Dad emigrated to the States.

In 1953, the postwar relief services sent my parents to Evans Mills, a tiny outpost in upstate New York not far from the Canadian border, where my father replaced the country doctor who had just died. It was there that my thirty-five-year-old mother became pregnant with Lara and fell into an all-consuming depression. In the emptiness of Evans Mills, separated from her sister and nephew by an ocean, the sheer weight of Mom's losses crushed her.

My father, on the other hand, was on fire to build his new life and start a family. Nearly forty years old, he'd lost half his twenties and thirties to the war. Imprisoned for six years in forced labor camps in Siberia, he'd miraculously escaped in 1946 and made his way back to his hometown. There he learned that everyone had been killed except his sweetheart—my mother—who, he was told, had escaped to Italy to live with her sister. He spent the next several months walking across Europe by night as a fugitive until he reached Rome, found my mother, and married her in November 1946, ten years to the day after they'd first met.

Within months, he had learned Italian and passed his Italian medical boards. But jobs were scarce in postwar Rome, and my mother, now a translator for the new government, was the sole supporter of her sister's family. The only work my refugee father could find was at a tuberculosis sanitarium in the Italian Alps. So for three years in the late 1940s, the newlyweds were once again separated. They saw each other once a month, when my mother made the long journey north to spend a weekend with Dad. Often (to my father's consternation) she brought along her five-year-old nephew, Renzo, who could not bear to be separated from her.

It wasn't until 1950 that my parents were finally allowed entry to the United States. My mother immediately got a job at an import-export firm in New York City, while my father worked as a resident at Mount Sinai Hospital. It took him another two years to gather sufficient evidence of his medical credentials to be allowed to sit for the New York State medical boards. (His first medical diploma, the Polish one, was in the hands of the Russian police; his second, the Italian license, was unacceptable in America.) Finally, after passing his medical boards in America, he was hungry for the happiness—or at least the freedom and productivity—for which he had struggled for so long. Instead, in 1954, at the age of thirty-nine, he found himself starting a medical practice in an impoverished town a few hours from Schenectady, while his baby screamed in the other room and his wife stared at the ceiling of her bedroom, sunk in a state of despair so profound she could not rise from bed.

———————

My mother later told me that in Evans Mills, after a brief stint as my father's receptionist and bookkeeper, she told him that she would never again have anything to do with his medical practice. "I couldn't stand him telling me what to do," she told me. "I was a women's libber before the word was even invented." Headstrong as my father was, it turned out Mom was even more so. "That's when I laid down the rules of our marriage," she told me. "I told Dad he could have sole authority over his medical practice, and I would have sole authority over the household and the children. I wouldn't interfere with his business, and he wouldn't interfere with mine."

By the end of my father's first year as a struggling self-employed physician, my parents had managed to save a few hundred dollars by scrimping on their own food and necessities. It still wasn't enough to cover the cost of a plane ticket for my mother to visit her sister, so instead, my mother bought the newest American invention- -a washing machine—and shipped it to Zosia in Italy, where no one had heard of such a thing. Two years later, in 1956, my mother could finally afford the round-trip airfare for herself, my father, and Lara. This was the trip to Rome that my father captured with his first movie camera.

———————

It wasn't until Lara and I were in our thirties that we tried to find out more about our family history. Lara sent letters to various international organizations, and one day in 1992 she received a packet of documents from a rabbi in Israel. *Jackpot,* he wrote. He enclosed pages of testimony from survivors describing how each of our relatives had been shot or gassed or starved in ghettos and camps by Germans, Ukrainians, and Poles during the war. Lara and I were stunned to discover that we were not Catholic but Jewish, and our parents were Holocaust survivors with huge families—dozens and dozens of aunts and uncles and cousins we'd never even heard of—all of whom were Jews, and all of whom had been killed.

Ironically, just as Mom and Zosia had been bound together by their lifelong vow of secrecy, Lara and I now forged our bond as the younger pair of sisters determined to discover what the older pair were hiding. Over the next few months, we interviewed hundreds of survivors and historians and rabbis and shrinks and anybody else who could shed light on our family.

At first we kept our research a secret from our parents, who, by then, were in their midseventies. But in May 1992 Lara and I sat down with them and told them about our discovery, and as anticipated, they didn't want to talk about it. Or at least, not at first. Two months later they finally acknowledged that we were Jewish and told us more about how they had survived. The revelation was a watershed in our family; we began to dismantle the walls between us and see each other in a new light. Lara and I finally began to understand the unspoken forces that had been acting on us all our lives.

But throughout our childhood and into our thirties, before we learned the truth of our past, Lara and my parents and I seemed locked in a script of madness from which we were helpless to escape.

1965

A few weeks after Lara started seeing a psychologist, my mother told me they'd made an appointment for me to see the psychologist too.

"Why me?" I asked.

"Well, the doctor felt that he should do some tests on you too."

"But I'm fine," I said.

"Of course you're fine!" My mother smiled unconvincingly. "Dr. Johnson just wants to learn as much as he can about our family," she said. "So that he can help Lara."

"What if he thinks I'm crazy?"

"No one's crazy," my mother said. "How could you say such a thing?"

"Well, Lara's . . . um . . ."

My mother's face turned fierce. "Don't ever use that word!" she said. "Where did you hear that?"

I shrugged.

"We're trying to help her," my mother said in a kinder voice. "Don't you want to help?"

Lara wanted to maim me, and "help" wasn't exactly what I wanted to offer her in return.

"She's sick, darling. We all have to help her."

———

My mother drove me downtown to Dr. Johnson's office and sat in the waiting room while I went into his office. He had a round, moist face with thick caterpillar eyebrows above horn-rimmed glasses. His hair was slicked back with Brylcreem. I tried not to look at him because he was definitely creepy.

"Have a seat." He smiled nervously, running one hand over a pad of lined paper on his desk. "I just want you to relax." He picked up a pen and put it down.

"Now, to start with, I'm going to show you some pictures, and I want you to tell me the first thing that pops into your head. Okay?"

I nodded. My heart was pounding so hard I was afraid he could hear it.

He pulled out a stack of white boards with black splotches all over them. He held one out on the desk for me. "Now, just look at this, and tell me what you see."

I knew exactly what I saw. "A monster," I said.

He nodded. "Uh-huh." He placed the board facedown and scribbled something on his pad. "Okay," he said. He held up another picture. This time the monster was even bigger and scarier.

"A monster," I said.

One of his giant eyebrows shot up. "Mm-hmm." Again he wrote something on his notepad.

When he held up the third card, the monster was practically leaping off the board at me. I bit my lip. This was not looking good. I figured three monsters in a row meant I was certainly very disturbed, possibly crazy. "A house," I said.

His lips twitched as if he might speak, but then he clamped his mouth shut. I was afraid he might be on to me. "A house," he finally said.

I began sweating. The monster had an enormous hairy head and sharp ears. Its mouth was open, and it seemed to know I was lying.

"Can you show me the house?"

"Right there," I said vaguely, pointing to the picture.

"Where? What do you see?"

"Um, here's a door," I said, pointing to a part of the monster that was clearly a foot and not a door. "And, um, here are the windows."

"Okay," Dr. Johnson said. He laid the card facedown and wrote on his pad before holding up the fourth card.

I couldn't believe he was showing me another monster. No one saw so many monsters. They would lock me up for sure.

"It's an Easter basket," I said.

He must have shown me a dozen cards, and every one of them was a different-shaped monster. I told him I saw a sunny day, a boat on a lake, a tree with songbirds, a friendly dog romping in a meadow, anything to sound happy and well-adjusted.

Finally it was over. He got up and opened the door to the waiting room where my mother was reading her latest *New Yorker* magazine. She stood and smiled at the doctor, who said he'd call her later.

She thanked him and we walked out. My scalp felt tingly and my mouth was dry. My mother took me home. I never heard about Dr. Johnson again; Lara stopped seeing him too, and in all the years since then, we've never talked about him. I wonder sometimes what Lara saw in those Rorschach images, and I wonder what I would see in them today. I never found out how I did on the test. At the time, I was afraid Dr. Johnson would pronounce me unfit to be my parents' child and I would be taken away. I didn't dare ask my mother; I just waited to see what would happen next.

————

What happened next was family therapy, but that's not what it was called. We called it Taking Lara to the Hoffman Children and Family

Center, where we were all going to help her get better. We were all ferociously unhappy, and incurable, of course, but the psychiatrists kept working on us with their trowels, trying to make us grow up properly in the garden of mental health.

My father directed all of this. I have no idea how he shopped for our shrink or how he found the Hoffman Center. Mainly, I think, he wanted to send my mother and sister to therapy, but he didn't trust them to do it right; he needed to be there to get the record straight. And they said I had to be there too, which bothered me. I hadn't done anything wrong, why did I have to go? "You're part of the family," my mother explained. At the age of eight, I bit down hard on that nut of indisputable fact, and did as I was told.

Every Friday afternoon my mother picked me up from Glenwood Elementary School. I had been granted a weekly early release for "dental" reasons, my mother told me in a hushed tone. *Under no circumstances*, she said, was I to divulge the real reason for my absence from the third grade on Friday afternoons. To my amazement, my teacher, a fierce woman with flaming orange hair, never so much as batted an eye at my dental excuse. No one in Glenwood Elementary School went to therapy, I was quite certain.

My mother always dressed up for our Hoffman Center appointments. She wore one of her tailored Italian dresses from the forties. She'd also combed her eyebrows, powdered her cheeks, and applied her Cherry Blossom lipstick. I wore whatever my sister had outgrown: the boxy jumpers my mother had sewn, Lara's old button-down blouses, her pathetic socks. I carried my books and baseball glove under my arm and climbed into the backseat of my mother's Dodge Dart.

We drove to St. Mary's, a private girls' school where my parents had enrolled Lara in the seventh grade, to protect her from the cruelty of public school kids. Now she trudged out from the stone building in her navy-blue uniform, plaid book bag thrown over her shoulder like a sack of bones. She flopped onto the front seat and brooded the whole ride downtown.

Schenectady was a hardscrabble town back then. Ragged apartment buildings leaned against one another, windows boarded up, doors hanging off hinges. People sat on the front stoops with empty eyes, smoking and drinking from bottles in paper bags. I stared out the window of our car as my mother steered us through the broken streets. I was shocked by this other world, dark and dismal and foreign. Surely these people needed help more than we did?

My mother parked behind my father's blue Chrysler New Yorker at the Hoffman Center. Entering the building seemed to drain the color from our cheeks and the strength from our bodies. My father, in his usual gray business suit, was already pacing slowly up and down the waiting room, staring at the drab carpet as if measuring the weight of each footfall. My parents exchanged a few words in Polish.

When the door swung open, we traipsed in, heads bowed. The social worker, Miss Jameson, tall and pear-shaped, with hips that looked pneumatic, closed the door behind us. Mom and Lara sat together on a little couch in the middle of the dimly lit room, and the rest of us sat in chairs around them. Our psychiatrist, Dr. Grokle, was a shriveled woman with dark whiskers. She sat calmly in a wingback chair, her long black-and-gray hair wound up in a frizzy beehive. It wobbled slightly when she turned from my father to my mother and Lara, and it looked a little sinister, as if it might be concealing something.

At first I thought family therapy might work to my benefit: I was hoping that a professional psychiatrist would remove my sister from our house and lock her up somewhere. My mother, of course, would sooner drink lighter fluid than lose Lara to an institution, so I did not voice my hopes to her. Between my father and me, I sensed an illicit understanding, but once when I mentioned that I wished Lara were gone, he said nothing. No one ever asked me my opinion in family therapy.

My father started each session by recounting the family's transgressions of the past week. He had memorized the entire chronology of misery—our mopiness, our disrespect, our bickering, our violent outbursts, our personal failures. Nothing got past him. Sometimes he consulted his notes scribbled on blue-lined paper from Woolworth's. But most of the time he could recite the entire week's melodrama from memory. I was usually missing from my father's list of psychological crimes, which I attributed to my deceptively angelic character. He focused primarily on Lara, whose outbursts were our ignition switch, and on my mother, who couldn't hit the brakes. Mom and Lara must have felt like a car wreck, to hear their behavior reduced to my father's score pad. Although we knew it was coming, his recital still felt like a fresh crash every week.

"Now," my father said at the beginning of one session, crossing his legs so that one of his size-twelve shoes dangled just above the other. "Last Friday night, Lara picked a fight with Helen. When Maria intervened, Lara started fighting with her. This went on till after midnight. Lara would not take a Valium. And Maria would not put her foot down; she would not send Lara to her room. I had to be the one to—"

"That's not true!" Lara said. She burst into tears. My mother leaned over and stroked Lara's shoulder. My father glanced at the shrink, his eyebrows raised as if to say, *See what I mean?*

Dr. Grokle maintained her look of quiet concern.

"He hates me!" Lara said. Her face was red and contorted, like one of those twisted gourds at Halloween.

My mother leaned closer to Lara, the two of them in a huddle. "He doesn't hate you, darling—"

"He hates me!" Lara said. "He doesn't understand!"

"What doesn't he understand?" Dr. Grokle's voice was so quiet that no one paid any attention to her.

"I love you," my father said haughtily. "But I will not tolerate your manipulative behavior."

"All right, Kovik," my mother said. "That's enough."

"I am simply stating the facts," my father said. "I am a realist."

"You don't even know what's going on!" Lara said.

"I know what I see."

"Kovik, let her speak."

"He's a bully!" Lara said. "I hate him!"

My father sat straight in his gray suit, dwarfing the chair.

"What is it that you hate?" the shrink said to Lara in a gentle voice.

"You have to admit that you refused to practice the piano Monday night," my father said.

"I had a stomachache!"

"And you refused to practice the piano on Wednesday."

"That's not true!"

"She did practice on Wednesday," my mother said.

"Not for the entire half hour," my father corrected. "She barely started the Chopin before storming off—"

"That's because you yell at me every time I make the slightest mistake!" Tears streaked Lara's face.

"I never yell," my father said. "But we are paying for your lessons, and you're just wasting it! If you don't play the piano, that's fine—no more lessons! But as long as you want private lessons, you have to practice."

"Kovik, let her speak."

"Why do you always defend her?" my father said. He turned to Dr. Grokle. "She always takes Lara's side. This is a typical pattern. I try to point out a problem, but Maria always undermines me. Instead of supporting me, she caves in to Lara. And Lara takes advantage of it. She—"

"You don't know a thing!" Lara said.

My mother passed Lara a tissue. Tissues were free at the Hoffman Children and Family Center. You could have as many as you wanted.

To my dismay, no one paid any attention to me. Sitting in my chair next to the social worker, feet dangling, I could have been on Mars, for all they knew. Even more disturbing, no one seemed to think that my life was in danger. My father's reports to Dr. Grokle mentioned Lara's attacks on me as if they were mere pretexts for a larger battle—as if I were simply the lure that Lara used to get at my mother, and therefore irrelevant.

I didn't dare speak of my own terror, because I was ashamed of it. My parents always told me that I was overreacting when I tried to tell them about Lara's assaults, and I hated myself for being such a chickenshit. I knew that whatever Lara did to me was nothing compared to what the Russians had done to my father in the war.

Dr. Grokle was a complete disappointment to me, with her furrowed brow and high-rise hair. And Miss Jameson, in a candy-colored dress, just scribbled notes on a steno pad balanced on her eye-popping thighs. I realized that these two experts were never going to figure out how to send Lara anywhere.

So I kept my mouth shut. My life was directly linked to the outcome of these sessions—who would win and who would lose at therapy, and by how much. I simply hoped that whoever won would be good to me. In my experience, you never got what you wanted by asking for it. You were better off waiting to see what you were going to get, and then figuring out how to deal with it.

———

Recently I gave a reading at a college. In the women's room, notices were posted on the walls. The questions were simple and direct: *Do you feel safe in your home? Have you ever been struck by someone you live with? Are you afraid that you may be hurt by someone in your home?*

You were supposed to call a confidential hotline if you answered yes to any of the questions. You were not supposed to tolerate living in fear. This was considered domestic abuse, and there were agencies to help you. The idea seemed so strange to me. If I had seen such a sign in my school, would I have called for help? Of course not. Like most kids, I would never have admitted to anyone what happened in our home. Speaking out would be a deadly betrayal of my parents. Besides, they were all-powerful: if they could do nothing, then there was nothing to be done.

———

It was always dark when we got out of therapy. The four of us marched into the cold night in stony silence. My mother and father consulted briefly about dinner before climbing into their separate cars. Sometimes we went to the cafeteria at Macy's for dinner, but usually we went to Sears. The food was not as good at Sears, but my father was the store doctor, and we got a 10 percent discount.

Lara always rode with my mother, but I went with my father because I felt sorry for him; no one would ever choose my father's company over my mother's. He was too stiff and awkward, too painfully needy. As we drove through the city streets after those exhausting sessions, neither of us could think of anything to say. My father's despair was like an animate being riding between us. I always wanted to make him feel better, but the pressure was too great and I remained silent.

Occasionally, as we sat at a traffic light, he might ask, "Tell me how you are. How is school?" By this, I took him to mean, *Are you happy? Am I a good father?* I would reply that I was happy and doing well. He always accepted this information at face value, with great relief.

As we glided north, I would mull over what had gone on in the session. My parents and Lara always tore into each other, and then my parents assured Lara they loved her, and then they'd all rip each other apart some more. Mom and Dad kept batting the word *love* back and forth like a shuttlecock in a game of badminton. I, for one, was ready to concede the point.

But I learned not to say this. If I so much as expressed doubt as to whether I loved my sister, my mother would come down on me like rain. "Don't ever say that!" she would snap. "Lara is your sister. Of course you love her!"

Her fury always alarmed me. "It's just that—"

"She's your sister!" my mother said.

I could see I wasn't going to win this. I kept my angry love to myself.

———————

My father and I parked outside the shopping mall and went into the Sears cafeteria, where we waited for Lara and my mother, who was a dangerously cautious driver. The cafeteria was empty; no one else in the world ate dinner there. We'd never gone there before we started family therapy, and three years later, after we finally quit therapy, we never again ate at Sears.

I stayed close to my mother as we slid the plastic trays along the steel rails and selected our food. We sat at a table in the far corner lit by orbs of orange lights that hung like giant insects from the ceiling. The whole place was creepy and dark, and even our food had a radioactive orange glow to it.

We ate in silence. Lara brooded through dinner, picking at her food and looking away. I pushed the meat around my plate until it looked tired and beat-up. Then I dug into my chocolate cake. My father, as always, had engulfed his entire meal before the rest of us had even unfolded our paper napkins. He sat nervously across from us, jiggling one leg under the table, causing his body to tremble as if an electric current were running through him. He had the patience of a fruit fly. We were all nursing our wounds, replaying the awful things that had been said in the session. We were stung by the injustice of our roles as father, mother, daughter, sister. None of us saw any escape, and this realization was so depressing and infuriating, we sat in our chairs and ate until we could leave.

We didn't fight till we got home. Then the dam burst. Even before our jackets were off, we lost our heads and were swept up in the torrent of our rage. Sometimes Lara jumped me, sometimes she ransacked my room; sometimes she threw herself on the floor in the doorway to the kitchen, and kicked and clawed at anyone who tried to get past her. My parents fought with each other about how to handle Lara—my mother insisting on patience, and my father on discipline—and I shrieked bloody murder whenever Lara came near me.

———————

But the thing about Lara was that she could also be really, really fun. You just never knew when. "Let's pig-pile Mom," she whispered to me one Sunday morning later that fall, her green eyes sparkling with excitement. As usual, my father had gotten up at six, and now, at eight, he was still at the hospital doing rounds. My mother was the sleepyhead of the family, and Lara and I tiptoed into my parents' dark bedroom. Mom was crashed on her side of the bed as always, lying on her belly like a little kid, arms flung up on either side of her head. You couldn't see her face for the cloud of thick brown hair, roots graying between monthly visits to the beauty parlor.

Lara and I drew closer, suppressing giggles—completely unnecessary, since Mom's relationship with sleep was passionate and exclusive.

"Now!" Lara whispered, and we jumped onto the bed, shouting, "Pig pile! Pig pile!"

A groan emerged from somewhere under my mother's hair. Her voice came as if from a deep cave. "Oh, let me sleep."

Lara and I set to tickling her.

"Ohhhhh," Mom said louder, a note of sorrow and sleepy joy in her voice. "Give me five minutes. Just five more minutes."

Lara laughed. "Come on, you lazy bum! Get up!"

My mother curled into a ball. "I'm a lazy bum," she said pleadingly. "Let me sleep."

But in my mother's Eastern European accent, it came out "la-*zee* bum," which sent Lara and me into peals of laughter.

"She's a la-*zee* bum!" Lara crowed. I chimed in, and we chanted, "A la-*zee* bum with a potbel-*lee*!"

"What?" my mother said. "A what?"

"A potbelly!" I said. "A potbel-*leee*!"

My mother laughed. Her stomach was flat as a pastry board. There wasn't an ounce of unnecessary flesh on her.

"I'm a la-*zeee* bum with a potbel-*leee*," she agreed, pleading.

We tugged on her arms now, and got her to sit up. We poked at her belly. "Look at the potbel-*lee*," Lara said.

My mother puffed her belly out so it would look round. Then she grabbed me suddenly and flopped back on the bed, pulling me down with her. In an instant, Lara and I were tickling her again, but Mom had come to life, and she tickled us back, and the three of us rolled around on the bed, a mother with her two cubs, our delight in each other as natural and easy as the sun streaming through the trees behind the pulled curtains.

I don't know how or why these windows of joy opened and closed in our lives. They seemed to come without warning, like sudden changes in the weather. No one ever came up with a diagnosis for Lara. There was plenty of mother-blaming going around in the sixties, and in our double sessions at the Hoffman Center, my father and the shrink seemed to think that Mom's depression during her pregnancy with Lara had caused the problem. The way I understood it, my mother's unhappiness had surrounded Lara when she was still in Mom's womb. It seeped into Lara's body through her skin, so Lara "caught" a mental illness, the way you caught a cold. By the time I came along, my mother was in a better mood, so I came out okay.

––––––––

I don't remember my mother ever being depressed. She possessed a colossal history and big emotions compacted into a body the size of a small vacuum cleaner. She had enormous energy, she sucked everyone into her vortex, and she was virulently anti-dirt. You could not tire her out. She had been through everything—the war, the ghetto, camps, prison, poverty, humiliation, as well as bridge parties, garden clubs, the Women's Auxiliary. And she tended the grounds and raised the children and got a graduate degree and taught German and sewed the drapes and still had time to read world literature. My mother was a giant. At five foot three and 110 pounds, she had the confidence of a world leader and an even more amazing ability to bluff. She figured that if she was still alive, the world was a very stupid place, and it was not hard to outwit it.

––––––––

Over the following weeks, our fights got worse. Lara started going on eating binges and tore through the kitchen, devouring boxes of crackers and cookies. My mother followed her. "Please, Lara," she begged. "Talk to me." Mom seemed to be as dependent on these fights as my sister— as if she needed to prove her devotion to Lara over and over. Sometimes my mother would fall to her knees and sob that she should have died with her parents, and Lara would start crying and they would hug and console each other for hours. I didn't understand it at the time, but I think that my mother was fairly drowning in grief and rage; the weight of her secrets and losses was almost too much for her to bear. And Lara had always been the sensitive one in our family. She and my mother seemed to be acting out a drama of love and war and loss and death.

One time Lara grabbed a carving knife and backed my mother out of the kitchen, before ransacking the cabinets for flour and sugar to make a batch of cookies. Mom marched back in and stunned Lara by pouring half a gallon of milk down the sink. For Mom, throwing away food was like slashing open a vein; it was as if the milk going down the drain were her own blood.

"You want to bake cookies?" my mother shouted. "You want to eat more?" She slammed the empty carton down on the counter. "There. No more milk. No cookies. No baking."

Lara stared at Mom in horror. "I'm sorry, Mommy," she said. "I'm sorry!"

I cowered just outside the door. I pictured the police coming afterward to photograph the bodies and wipe up the blood and gather the bloody knife and milk carton and chocolate chips as evidence, and I would be able to testify for Mom. I would be able to tell someone what had happened to our family.

My father lived at his office during most of these fights. He could not break the grip Lara had on Mom, nor Mom on Lara. He could not compete with Mom in his own house. And so he paced up and down the world outside, fuming over his lack of access. In his office late at night, he wrote in his journal, transcribing his arguments with my mother, his frustrations with my sister, his discussions with the shrink. Hundreds of pages of meticulous record-keeping of how our family had gone so wrong. Years later, he would show them to me when I was home from college. "These will be for you," he told me. "I am writing them for you so you will have them after I die. Then you will understand."

It was so like my father to offer intimacy after he was dead, as if life were no time for explanations or understandings. I felt special being the daughter he trusted, but I knew it wasn't enough. He needed what he'd never had—a happy childhood, the love of his life, the years the Soviets had stolen from him. And all those journals that he'd written for me, that he put in boxes with my name on them—all of his journals now belong to my sister.

Americans already had human rights, he said. Just look at the Soviet Union for comparison. What I was really doing as a public defender, he scoffed, was obstructing justice. My father's moral compass was flawless—of this he was certain.

It was his certainty that was most annoying, more so than his morals. He was not a particularly pious man, but his confidence was almost too much to bear. He was always right, and this seemed unfair. My sister and I were eager to find him wrong on something, but it never happened—at least, not until much later.

Like my colleagues, I felt at home on the side of the lowly and despised, crusading for civil rights. I took everything personally. But the adrenaline rush of trial work—the whiplash of highs and lows—got to me. When I lost, my guilt at having failed my clients was overwhelming. I couldn't bear to see them handcuffed and led off to prison. I thought of my father, sentenced to ten years of hard labor without the right to defend himself. It was complicated—he was at once authoritarian and ruthless, a force against whom I fought, and also a man who had been unjustly condemned, a man I wanted to rescue.

"Daddy's little defender," he used to call me when I was little, because I stood up for him in family fights. Despite his size and strength, he didn't hold much power in our household. It was my mother and sister who called the shots. I sided with him so he wouldn't be outnumbered.

Given his disdain for lawyers, it's ironic that in the final months of his life, my father relied on a lawyer to create a legal instrument—a codicil to his will—to disown me. And it's also ironic that in order to find out what had happened, I had to hire a lawyer myself. Through my attorney I learned of my mother's role in seeking out the lawyer

three

2019

I work in the public defender office in Boston. From the minute I started in 1985, I knew I belonged here—everyone is committed to equal rights and justice, and more to the point, we all have a huge problem with authority. We revel in tripping up cops on the witness stand, and crow about our victories over the state's attorneys with a glee that could be considered . . . well, undignified.

When I was growing up, both my parents ruled my world, but it was my father who had always represented unassailable authority. Dad was a man of principle. He was a man of honor. He was a man of his word. He had impressed upon us that these were rare commodities, and he had all of them. He always obeyed the law, but he was also quick to point out that the law was often misapplied, misinterpreted, and even mistaken. Lawyers, he said, were slippery opportunists who capitalized on other people's misfortunes. He was not particularly thrilled when I became a lawyer, and he was even more disappointed when I chose a field of law in which I made no money at all. "But I'm fighting for human rights and justice," I told him.

who wrote the codicil for both of them. It was Mom—and perhaps Lara—who drove my father to the lawyer's office four months before his death, and who helped him hold the pen to sign the codicil. My parents' final words to me were executed by law. The man they'd hired to eliminate me shared my profession.

1966

Lara felt great sensitivity to animals, and grieved for weeks when one of our pet turtles or mice died. I recovered from such losses within the twenty minutes it took my mother to drive us to the pet store to get a new one. But I had an unseemly devotion to things—*my* things—and I kept everything I owned in a pristine, OCD state of unblemished perfection. I worshipped my collection of shiny Matchbox cars that I took out to play with (indoors only) and returned to their special carrying case, fitting each car into its corresponding numbered compartment. And I was devoted to my collection of little souvenirs from various trips—a small wooden skier from Vermont, a miniature seal from Canada, and so on. I dusted them every Saturday and replaced them in precisely the same configuration on the display shelf my father had built for me. My prize possession was a diary my parents had given me in 1965. I wrote in it every day, and carefully hid it in a box in my desk drawer. I recorded various important facts about my life, like what we did in gym class that day, or what the weather was like. And with the knowledge that I was committing a subversive act, I wrote about how much I hated Lara. Writing was dangerous, and my diary reflected the fact that I lived in the country of Big Sister. Discovery meant certain death.

When I was eight, I begged my parents for a lock for my bedroom door. I would be able to lock myself in my room, I explained, so that Lara couldn't get me. And I would be able to leave my room without worrying about Lara wrecking my things in my absence. To my surprise, my father agreed and went to Sears, purchased a doorknob and lock, and installed it in my door. He kept one key for himself and gave me the other.

From then on, I always locked my door whenever I stepped out— even for a moment—when I walked to the bathroom, or to the kitchen, or to ask my mother a question. It drove Lara crazy, because she had always counted on being able to jump me in my room, or to get at my diary, or to ransack my belongings when I was out. As long as I was vigilant, I could keep the contents of my room safe from her. I carried the key in the front pocket of my jeans, and miraculously, Lara never succeeded in getting it away from me. I was prepared to die for that key.

On Easter Sunday 1966, we were invited by the Palowskis to an afternoon cocktail party. Unlike my parents, who typically observed the Easter holiday by cleaning the house and eating matzos, the Palowskis were real Polish Catholics who had fled Kraków to escape the Communists. That morning, Lara refused to get out of bed. My mother sat at her bedside, pleading with her to get dressed and come with us. Mom pushed a strand of Lara's hair behind her ear, and Lara swatted it away. My father strode down the hallway in his dark-blue suit and polished shoes. "We'll leave her here," he said. "It's time to go." This is what the experts at the Hoffman Children and Family Center had told us to do when Lara refused to participate in family outings. She was almost twelve, capable of making her own decisions and staying home if she chose not to go. Lara hated being left alone, but wouldn't budge from bed. "It's all right, darling," my mother assured her as we left. "We'll be home in a few hours."

The Palowskis' house sat on a hill like an exotic gem on green velvet. It had a grand entrance and powder-blue Oriental carpets in the living room. I went out to the yard with the children of other guests, all of us painfully overdressed in Easter outfits, ruling out the possibility of any real fun. The grown-ups drank cocktails and laughed and spoke in Polish. After a few hours, my parents called for me. We put on our coats and walked down to the car, my patent-leather shoes clacking on the asphalt and my mother's high heels making little bird-pecking sounds. We drove home in silence.

As usual, my father slowed the car to a crawl as we approached our driveway so that we could admire the grounds. I could see him mentally comparing his work to that of the Palowskis' professional landscapers. The blue spruce and fir trees he had planted years before were already taller than I was, and the forsythia bushes were starting to burst open.

It was eerily quiet when we came in the house. There was no sign of Lara. My mother went to the closet to hang up her coat. I went to my room to take off my stupid dress, but for some reason my key wouldn't fit in the door. I looked closer and saw that nails had been hammered into the keyhole. From her bedroom, I could hear the low rumble of Lara's laughter.

The assault felt visceral, as if she had hammered nails into my own flesh. I let out a scream. The sound was terrible, but I couldn't stop. My father and mother came running. When they saw the doorknob, they rolled their eyes. "Oh, Helen, it's nothing," my mother said. "Nothing happened." They were tired and battle-weary, and they wanted to take off their formal clothes and relax and get a look at the Sunday *Times*, and maybe have a cup of tea and unwind. They did not want to deal with what they always dealt with: their children fighting childish wars.

My father went down to his workbench in the basement and returned with a hammer and pliers and a screwdriver. He set to work and yanked and pulled and twisted and banged. Eventually he was able to remove the ruined knob and open the door.

What lay before me was even more devastating. It looked as if a bomb had exploded: everything I owned had been flung across the room. Matchbox cars, games, figurines, socks, underwear—all ripped apart and scattered. My clothes had been clawed from their hangers and shelves and tossed in all directions. The desk drawers were yanked open, shredded papers and pens and books everywhere. And on the upended desk chair, my diary—torn open, pages fluttering.

It took a moment for me to grasp what had happened. My windows had been pried open with a screwdriver, and the screen had been removed from the frame. My sister had come in through the windows. I began shrieking with new horror. It was the end, I thought. I could not live here anymore. I wanted her dead; I wanted her sent away, locked up, thrown out.

My father spent the rest of the day repairing my window, replacing the screen, and removing the nails from the doorknob. The key still worked, after a fashion. I locked myself in my room and sat on my bed, rocking and crying and folding my clothes. I would never be the same, I thought. Nothing would ever be the same.

———

But I was wrong. Everything was exactly, precisely the same. As always, my father left for his evening office hours at four forty-five, right after our fifteen-minute dinner. For the next several months, as soon as his blue Chrysler slipped down the driveway, my sister would begin. She waited until I emerged from my room, and knocked me into the wall as I tried to reach the bathroom. She threatened to kill me and called me a crybaby if I made a sound.

Over time I learned not to react. I learned that to cry was to play into her hands, to give her what she most wanted: proof of my terror. I began to learn that my best defense was passive resistance. The pretense of unruffled composure. She could bang me around, she could knock me down, but I swallowed my fear and presented only a calm, bland exterior. This drove her nuts, of course, and I liked that. I sensed my power. Sometimes I even whistled a tune, to really drive her over the edge. Then she had to go to even greater lengths to get a rise out of me. She was training me to ignore pain, and I was learning, but I was also keeping score.

How did we manage to keep this up day after day? There were no broken bones, no trips to the emergency room. We trafficked in terror and shame, strictly small-time stuff. I remember thinking, *This is how I learn to hurt someone. I can do it all by myself, without lifting a hand. I can go numb*—and this numbness was my sharpest sword of all.

I practiced on Lara, and she practiced on me, and we maximized our tolerance for inflicting and receiving pain. And every few weeks, between bouts of murderous rage, like some sort of diabolical interval training, we played well together, swimming at the local pool, playing basketball, collecting stamps, and inspecting insects.

Our parents stayed out of it as much as possible. They knew, of course, that sibling rivalry was to be expected, and my mother had an uncanny ability to see only what she wanted to see. And so I learned how to fight at home. I learned how to hate, and how to do harm. Sometimes, after long hours of combat, after my mother and sister had collapsed in tears in each other's arms, I went outside and stood on the lawn, staring up at the stars. Everything dark, silent, mysterious. I wanted to strike the match that would explode the sky.

four

In the weeks following the receipt of my father's will in the mail, I tried to follow the path of my daily life as best I could: I went to the gym; walked the dog; walked my wife, Donna, to the health-care center where she worked, and then took the T to my office downtown. I could do almost everything but sleep. At night I padded around our apartment and wrote in my journal, recording everything I knew about my family, trying to make sense of my father's last words in his codicil.

Donna had known my family back when all of us had been close; she had watched our implosion over the years. Now, as I moved restlessly around our apartment, I was careful not to wake her. But I could hear her voice in my ear, a warm, slow-rolling Alabama accent that made you feel that all would be well. She was tall and lithe, with honking red toenails and dark almond eyes that tilted slightly on her thin face. When I'd first met her eight years earlier in my backyard—the neighbors had set us up!—her eyes had been so strangely beautiful, I'd run inside and changed my T-shirt, as if that might improve my chances. It did. Two months later I moved into her apartment, and two years after that we exchanged rings. It wasn't yet legal, but we knew not to expect much of the law, and therefore we were not disappointed.

That winter of 2002, Donna was still recovering from ten months of chemotherapy after a recurrence of cancer. We had been through a hard year. She had managed to sidestep a literal death sentence just as I was dealt a figurative one.

———

I was nine when my parents started talking about divorce during our Children and Family sessions, and they went on talking about it at home behind closed doors, when they thought Lara and I weren't listening. Of course, Lara and I were always, *always* listening, especially when they spoke in Polish, a language neither of us understood. All the dangerous, important discussions between our parents were in Polish, and Lara and I translated them into our worst fears.

Lara's worst fear was that they'd send her to a mental institution. My worst fear was that they would not.

I didn't really understand what divorce was. I had classmates whose parents had died, but none who had divorced. This was back in the days before divorce spread through the suburbs like color TVs.

It was my father who first brought it up one Friday night at the Hoffman Children and Family Center that spring of 1966. He was sitting with one knee over the other in the chair across from me, his maroon striped tie slightly askew under his dark suit jacket. He sounded very businesslike. "After we get a divorce, I could move into my office."

A divorce sounded like something that you bought, like a coffin in which you put your discarded marriage. As I understood it, once my parents went out and got one, Dad would visit us from across town, which made sense, because he mostly worked all the time anyway.

My mother didn't say anything, but sat very rigid, her back straight and knees together, her mouth a thin line. I stole a glance at Lara, who looked bug-eyed. For once she wasn't even picking at her fingers; she was barely breathing.

Dr. Grokle also sat motionless, but her beehive of hair quivered. It was my father who could no longer live with us, he said icily, because he was a realist and my mother was not. Mom, I could tell, was angry— she didn't say a word, but stared at him as if he were a stack of dirty dishes. I said nothing, believing that things were more likely to go away if I ignored them.

Now I wonder. What if my father had a girlfriend? Or perhaps he wanted a girlfriend, but felt constrained by the vows of marriage? "My word is like iron," he used to say proudly. He would not break his word for all the nooky in the world.

But perhaps he would break his marriage for just one big, buxom blonde. Decades later, Lara reminded me that Miss Jameson, the social worker at the Hoffman Center, mysteriously disappeared from our therapy sessions at some point in the midsixties, and was never spoken of again. "She was hitting on Dad," Lara told me. "She kept calling the house. That's why we got an unlisted number, remember? Mom went apeshit over it."

Dad and Mom were always fighting over the correct use of a word, or the proper translation of a phrase from Latin or German or Italian into English. They ran for the dictionary and gloated when they got the

expression right. But what came between them was far more treacherous than grammar or syntax. Mom depended on the illusion of a happy
family, and could not admit that ours was broken. She would never
have agreed to divorce. My father, on the other hand, could not tolerate pretense.

Lara's problems were the field on which they fought, but their
troubles went deeper. There was something about my mother's all-
consuming bond with her older sister that my father resented. He
complained that my mother's attention was never on him; instead she
lavished her love on Zosia and Renzo in Italy. "It's not normal," he said.
I don't think it ever occurred to him that Mom and Zosia might be
keeping a secret from him. He only knew that, despite appearances, he
was left out of his own marriage. Divorce would be more honest.

They didn't get divorced.

———————

Something shifted the fall after I turned eleven and Lara was fourteen—
at first it seemed that Lara had simply gone on a diet and lost weight,
but then it turned out that she'd more or less stopped eating. We had
been on a two-year reprieve from family therapy for good behavior, but
now we went back. Anorexia was sort of a parole violation.

At dinner now, Lara would cautiously tap at her food with the
tines of her fork, as if a green bean might suddenly leap from the plate
and strangle her. She slowly pushed a piece of steak to the left of her
plate, then to the right. She turned it ninety degrees. She lifted her
glass of water and took a few sips, then returned it to the counter and
stared at it, exhausted by the effort.

My mother started cooking special meals for her: steamed vegetables, tiny portions of New York sirloin, lettuce with vinegar, fish with lemon. Lara ate less and less and grew tiny before our eyes. My mother became desperate. My father threatened hospitalization. Dr. Grokle at the Hoffman Center continued to bob her beehive at us.

None of this concerned me too much. What rocked my world was that Lara was no longer a physical threat to me. As I grew taller and stronger, she grew thinner, more frail, twig-like. For the first time in my life, I felt completely safe.

But within a month or two, Lara had risen to a new kind of power over our family—by disappearing before our eyes. I didn't see what the big deal was. Let her starve herself, I thought—at least she didn't bother me anymore. To my surprise, it looked like anorexia might actually get her hospitalized. Even Dr. Grokle started talking about it. Only my mother held out.

"Please, Lara, you have to eat," Mom begged at every meal. Please, darling. Try."

Lara would slouch so low over the counter you couldn't see her plate for her hair.

"I'm too fat!" More of a moan than words.

My father, sitting next to me at the opposite end of the counter, had just finished my potatoes and pork chop for me. I was not a big eater in those days, and my father was always hungry. When my mother wasn't looking, I'd broom my leftovers onto his plate. He hoovered them up before anyone noticed. Sometimes I wondered whether he even realized that the food had come from my plate.

"But you're skin and bones, darling! Look at yourself! Do you know how many times I've had to take in your school uniform? It's hanging off of you."

"Well, I'm not hungry," Lara said. "You can't make me eat when I'm not hungry."

"Oh yes we can," my father said in a low voice.

Lara leaped up, sending her chair crashing to the floor. "No you can't!" she shouted. "You can't make me do anything!"

"They'll do it at the hospital," he said coolly. "If you don't eat, they'll insert a food tube and force the food directly into your stomach."

"Oh, you'd like that, wouldn't you? You'd love to see—"

"Lara, please—" My mother held out her arms, but Lara swatted them away.

"Get away from me!" she shouted. "Why do you hate me so much?"

"We don't—"

"Leave me *alone!*" She ran to her bedroom and slammed the door.

At the time I had no sympathy for Lara, and even less curiosity about what she might be going through. Looking back now, it occurs to me that she was given an impossible role as my older sister—everything was riding on her. All of my parents' losses—their broken hopes and dreams, the heartbreak of our murdered grandparents—landed on Lara's shoulders. There was no way she could repair the past, and the weight of our parents' needs must have been crushing. Perhaps Lara fought against the burden, thrashing and kicking and bucking them in the only way she could—with her body. I was luckier: I came after her, and while she commanded everyone's attention, I was able to slip by relatively unnoticed. At least for a while, until I grew old enough to engage in the battle with our family's past as a full-fledged participant.

———

Hospitalization was my father's ace in the hole. Even my mother knew she couldn't keep Lara at home if she didn't eat. Deadlines were set, weigh-ins established, calories counted. Cheating, broken promises, threats to call the police. New bargains, new deadlines, more fights. Lara ate enough to stay out of the hospital, and we settled into a sort of detente. Time slipped by, and Lara got better, apparently all by herself. By the time she was seventeen, Lara was feeling good enough to switch from the safety of St. Mary's to the raucous regional public high school for her senior year.

I didn't realize it at the time, but I was learning from a master. Years later, when I was in college, I would follow in Lara's dangerous footsteps and engage in my own food wars. But back in 1969, when I was twelve, food was my friend. The bigger I grew, the safer I felt around Lara. Our mutual hatred was alive and well, but now our skirmishes became more strategic.

"Helen is going out with boys," she told Mom when I was thirteen.

This was a stroke of genius on Lara's part, because Mom considered my interest in boys evidence of my lack of allegiance to our household. At the time, I would rather have been almost anywhere than attached to the flypaper of my family. And it was this apparent desire of mine to escape from home that most angered my mother. To her, family was sacrosanct and friends were suspect. Boys—the entire gender—were just plain off-limits.

"You are not to date," my mother informed me.

"I'm not *dating* anyone," I lied. "I hang out with my friends. We go to parties." This was true. I didn't mention that we also paired off and necked with the lights out.

"All right, no more parties then," my mother said. "Weekends are for family." To Mom, I was worse than crazy or violent like Lara: I was *disloyal*.

Lara had never had a boyfriend in her life, and her standards were even more Victorian than my mother's. I couldn't fight both of them. And to be honest, it wasn't that much of a sacrifice—I didn't really care that much about boys or partying to begin with. I just wanted to be loved by everyone.

––––––––––

During the fall of 1971, Lara was applying to colleges, and brochures were spread across the dining room table—Williams, Amherst, Middlebury, Smith. All those glossy scenes of swirling autumn leaves, students tossing Frisbees and reading books under giant oak trees. My mother had done her homework, and I could see the excitement growing in her eyes. College, I realized, was where I needed to focus my energy. I tagged along with Mom and Lara on their tours of prospective schools all over New England. As we strolled across the leafy campus of Wellesley College, I recognized immediately what my mother's eyes said: they said, *I want*. She wanted the luxury of time and books and immersion in the world of academia. I decided to give her Wellesley. She'd worked hard to make college material of me, and she deserved to have me go to the college of her choice.

I began amassing my credentials. I threw myself into the student government, the school newspaper, varsity sports. I performed in a talent show at the old-age home. I was aiming high—for the beam in my mother's eye. Even my dad started noticing me—I had finally risen to his line of vision. This was wealth. I would soar into the stratosphere for my parents.

I asked my teachers for extra-credit assignments in addition to my schoolwork, in order to inch my grades higher. Now I was spending all my time reading, studying, brownnosing, ass-kissing, teacher-petting, and good-girling. My teachers loved me because their jobs were hard and I was easy. I wanted to please. I followed directions, and only rebelled in the privacy of my own mind, when no one was looking.

Mainly I wanted to prove to my parents how capable I was; I wanted them to beam with pride. I considered that my job description: Perfect Child.

Looking at my photos from that freshman year of high school, I see I was relatively dark-skinned, with long dark hair and brown eyes. I liked myself, or thought I did, and I had a self-confidence that I did not deserve, perhaps, but I believed I would go places and do things that other people would not do. It would take decades to realize that my young confidence covered for a sense of terrifying responsibility to excel, and a life-threatening fear of failure.

My ninth-grade physics teacher, a John Belushi look-alike with muttonchop sideburns and a wreck of rumpled clothes, was the only one who saw this as a problem. One day after class, Mr. Moskowitz grabbed me by a few strands of my hair and said, "C'mere." I thought he was joking (he had a malicious sense of humor that was usually pretty funny), but this hurt, and I had to bend sideways and tilt my head toward him as he pulled me down the hall. Students gaped as we passed by. When we reached the cafeteria, he sat me at a table across from him. My scalp was burning.

"You've got to stop this," he said.

"What?" I still thought this was some kind of joke, but I couldn't figure it out.

"Just cut the bullshit."

"What are you talking about?"

"All this extra credit, all this trying to get into college. You're four-teen! Cut the crap! You're missing out on your own life."

I was stung. I suddenly hated Mr. Moskowitz.

"I am living my life," I snapped.

In retrospect, it's strange that Mr. Moskowitz, the most unlikely person on the planet, had me *nailed*. He just didn't know the half of it, or how to help. Of course, no one could have helped me then; my need to impress my parents trumped my own interests, whatever they were.

———————

The spring of my freshman year, through no fault of my own, a senior named Kevin Flanagan took an interest in me. My sister happened to be in the same homeroom as Kevin, now that she was in the public school system. Lara immediately reported to my mother that Kevin was a thug who smoked dope and mouthed off in class.

This was only partly true. He did smoke dope and mouth off in class, but he was also a voracious reader, passionate about history, philosophy, and ethics. And he was tall and broad-shouldered, with a head of free-flying rust-colored hair, a tanned face from working outdoors, and something like a beard-in-progress. Despite our four-year age difference, Kevin and I were in the same elective French class, where we learned to speak French with a Brooklyn accent like our teacher. One day Kevin ap-proached me after class, introduced himself, and told me he made leather belts and wallets; would I like one? He pointed to his own belt as evidence of his craftsmanship, and I felt a little funny staring at his hips. He was long-waisted and trim, and his faded jeans rode low on his hips.

He pulled his wallet from his back pocket, and handed it to me so I could admire how smooth the leather was, how fine the stitching.

"I'll show you how I make them," he offered.

My mother, with her firm grip on the choke collar of my social life, dropped me off at Kevin's house for the sole purpose of letting me watch Kevin stitch two pieces of leather together. Upon completion of this task, Kevin's father drove me home.

Over the next few weeks, I bought a wallet from Kevin that I didn't need, a belt, and a sort of purse that looked more like a saddlebag, sturdy enough to withstand a stampede of horses. My mother examined and scoffed at each purchase, making it clear that I could throw away my babysitting money however I wished, but I was certainly not going to see Kevin Flanagan for anything other than arm's-length financial transactions.

My sister left for college in the fall of 1972. A mini-flotilla of two long-finned Chryslers filled to the brim with clothes, stereo, and the members of our nuclear family moved solemnly east across the state line to Smith, an ivy-whiskered institution of Gothic sobriety. My father, whose finger was always on the safety lock of his wallet, broke out in a sweat when he saw the manicured lawns of Lara's new campus. He was a provider *par excellence*, and proud of it, but he had grown up in abject poverty, and never felt comfortable with wealth.

By sundown we had transferred the contents of both cars into her dorm room, and left the old green Chrysler with Lara. She stood at the curb, tearfully waving good-bye to us as we receded into darkness. Stretched out in the backseat, I could barely contain my excitement at having gotten rid of my older sister in this perfectly legitimate way. I spent the ride dreaming of my freedom from Lara's surveillance: the escapades I would lead, the days I would spend with my friends in her absence.

I had not yet stumbled upon the addictive quality of misery as Lara had. Every Friday she would drive the hour and a half from college directly to her shrink's office in Schenectady. From there, she drove home to unleash her first downpour, and our family fell into the familiar pattern. It was like getting Lara's Doom in concentrate: a full week's misery condensed to fit a weekend. By midday Sunday, the anxiety in the household had ratcheted up; we were all waiting to see whether she would manage to return to college in time for Monday classes. We tiptoed around her, afraid to start another fight, while she sat slumped over the kitchen counter, anger rising from her like chlorine gas. Sometimes she would leave Sunday afternoon; sometimes she would wander back to bed and not emerge till dinnertime. Sometimes she would leave Sunday night, and sometimes, when our nerves were about to snap, she would brood through the night and not drive back to college until Monday morning.

In the meantime, Kevin Flanagan had enrolled in a nearby college, where his father was chair of the Physics Department. ("He's not a *real* doctor," my mother sniffed, offended that anyone with a mere PhD could appropriate the title of "doctor.") I was fifteen now, and my mother grudgingly agreed to let me play tennis with Kevin on the asphalt courts behind his school. Kevin and I were both sufficiently athletic, competitive, and inept at tennis to keep this interesting.

As my mother feared, I actually liked Kevin. He was much more worldly than I, yet he seemed genuinely interested in what I thought about things like the war in Vietnam and the role of students in overthrowing the government. (I was against war, I said. I didn't know much about overthrowing anything.)

In those days, Mom monitored me closely and allowed daytime activities, as long as I didn't *date*. She defined *dating* in the old-fashioned sense of the word, where the boy comes to the house, picks up the girl, and takes her out to the movies or the basketball game or the school dance. These common uses of boys were *verboten* in my family, or at least for me. So instead, on warm Saturday afternoons, Kevin and I went bicycling on deserted country roads, surrounded by endless fields of wildflowers and woods and wilderness. When the sun grew too hot, we leaned our bikes against a tree and walked into the woods and settled on a grassy knoll and kissed. We were surprisingly restrained, and never lost our heads or clothes or any of the other things we had to lose.

We also kissed in the basement of his house. His parents were upstairs; they'd invited me for dinner. Kevin leaned over me and kissed me full on the mouth and I kissed him back, hard, and we stood there, kissing with necks of steel, pressing against each other like contestants in the World's Strongest Kissing Competition. Then we went upstairs and had dinner with his parents, and his father drove me home.

For me, kissing was a life skill one ought to acquire, like grammar or long division. It never had any effect on me physically. I never stopped to wonder about this.

Some weeks later, while we were once again standing in his basement and kissing (a bit less strenuously), Kevin ventured to touch my breast, so softly, through the cotton of my T-shirt and the polyester padding of my AA-cup bra. I brushed his hand away. "Come on, Kevin. Cut it out." For some reason, alarm signals went off in my head. Kissing was one thing—I used my mouth in public all the time, for talking, for eating; it was right out there for all the world to see. But no one had ever touched my breasts before; they were a part of my body that were, to my mind, an unpleasant encumbrance, twin bumps that I preferred not to think about. His touching them was a reminder of the danger that lay within me that my mother was so afraid of.

Kevin seemed hurt but said nothing, and we continued kissing, like *nice* people.

I'm not sure what Kevin was thinking at the time. I suspect he was actually falling in love, or something like it; he was a hopeless romantic, and he was going to get hurt. Or maybe my intransigence was exactly what made the relationship safe for him. Years later we would talk about our natural affinity for disappointment. Both of us were used to making do with whatever we got—a little attention, some affection, some love.

———

It was after that evening of the Bra Touch that I started to panic. I was clearly doing something illegal behind my mother's back—something my sister would never have dreamed of doing. Lara would have been as outraged as Mom, and would have ratted me out in an instant. I couldn't bear to enter this treacherous uncharted territory of boys against my mother's wishes.

And I knew this meant something was wrong with me. After all, my classmates had boyfriends in plain view, in front of their siblings and parents, as if it were the most natural thing in the world. There was no way I could do that. Maybe I could fudge certain details that Mom didn't really care about, but I absolutely could not break the law of family loyalty. Between Kevin and my mother, there was really no contest. I would choose Mom. I would choose my family.

So I called Kevin in tears. "I have to see you," I said. "I have to tell you something. You're going to hate me, but we need to talk."

It was a chilly Sunday afternoon in late April. I got my mother to give me a ride to his house. Wringing my hands, I walked with him up and down the hills where he lived. "I can't have a romantic relationship with you," I told him. "I want to, and I've tried, but I know my mother is against it, and I just can't make myself go against her wishes. It's driving me crazy."

Kevin murmured reassuring words and tried to calm me down. Why was he being so nice?

"This is my own problem," I said, choking back tears. "If I were you, I'd be really angry, and really hurt."

But Kevin looked incredibly sweet and concerned. "It's okay, Helen," he kept saying.

"You won't want to see me again," I continued, my tears flowing freely now. "And you shouldn't. You should just move on, find a normal girl who will love you and be a proper girlfriend."

To my amazement, he told me it didn't matter. It mattered more to him that we continue our friendship, even if it remained platonic.

I was stunned. This fairly blew me away. It had never occurred to me that Kevin would want to be friends if we couldn't be more than that.

So there it was. At fifteen, I was still too much my mother's daughter to be Kevin's girlfriend. In fact, I was too much my mother's daughter to be *myself*.

five

The summer I turned sixteen, Mom, Lara, and I flew to Rome to stay with Zosia and Uncle in their apartment in the city. Uncle spent his days puttering around his bedroom, which doubled as his office. Stacks of books and papers rose from floor to ceiling: legal documents, genealogical charts, books of heraldry, history, Nostradamus, astronomy, and law. We sneaked a peek now and then when he opened the door a crack, but no one—not even Zosia—ever set foot in it. Zosia's bedroom was as small and tidy as Uncle's was big and unwieldy. Mom, Lara, and I slept in the majestic living room on narrow cots that we folded up each morning before tiptoeing out of the apartment at dawn.

Mom marched Lara and me all over the city. She knew and loved Rome as a native, and blossomed into a new person here, as if she'd stepped into another version of herself, one with color and joy. Her exhilaration was contagious, and Lara and I fell under her spell. This was the city where she and Zosia had reinvented themselves, where they had begun their lives together after Mom had escaped the Nazis in Poland.

Here was the grand Teatro dell' Opera, and here the catacombs of Sant'Agnese, my mother told us, where she'd taken groups of American GIs from the Red Cross Rest Center during the war. And here, the rusticated palazzo of the Ministero dell'Agricoltura where she'd worked as a translator after the war, before handing her job off to Zosia and emigrating to the States with Dad. Lara and I followed her everywhere, enthralled. She introduced us to her Italian friends, who told us stories about how she had bartered for food on the black market; how she'd helped them smuggle cigarettes out of the Red Cross Center.

Years later, my mother would tell me that she had never wanted to emigrate to the States with my father after the war. "I wanted to stay there with Zosia," she said with tears in her eyes. "And with Renzo. He was eight years old when I left." She shook her head. "It was Zosia who forced me to go."

"Why?"

My mother wiped her eyes. "Zosia knew Dad would never fit in in Italy. You know Dad. He would have been so unhappy there."

Remembering this now, I marvel at the guilelessness of my mother's stories. On the surface, her explanations are completely true. My father, with his mathematical certainty of right and wrong, would indeed have been driven crazy in Italy, where the laws of physics are so easily curved to accommodate the needs of personality and politics. But later I would come to realize that Zosia's reasons for sending her sister and brother-in-law overseas after the war were more complicated. After the war was over, the secrets took on a life of their own, and it would be decades before I could begin to piece together the whole story.

That fall, I applied to colleges, eager to launch. Now I looked beyond Wellesley—to Brown, Dartmouth, Bowdoin. My mother pretended that the choice was mine, but she dropped hints in case I made the wrong decision. "A women's college," she said. "You want to get an education, not a husband." In fairness to my mother, Kevin Flanagan wasn't the only boy she wanted gone; she seemed intent on removing the entire gender from my life.

My mother also helped me choose my career that year. Unlike Lara, a science geek, all I cared about was languages. I loved writing stories and dreamed of one day writing the story of my parents' lives. At the time, I didn't realize that my mother had created a fiction of her own life, but I was captivated by what little I knew of her past.

"I want to be a writer," I said. "A novelist."

"A foreign correspondent," my mother corrected. "You'll live in Paris, or perhaps Rome or Heidelberg, and submit articles on art and culture to the *New Yorker* or the *Atlantic* or the *New York Times*."

Clearly, if you didn't write for the *New Yorker* or the *Atlantic* or the *New York Times*, there was no point in writing at all. I was going to be a huge disappointment to my mother, but neither of us knew exactly how huge at the time.

My mother drove me to my college interviews—in the end, I'd obediently applied only to two women's schools: Wellesley and Smith, where Lara was a sophomore now. She had finally settled into dorm life, and was actually sort of fun to be with, and I felt the familiar tug of sisterhood to join her. My mother kept dropping hints about how nice it would be if Lara and I were together. "Lara has a car," Mom pointed out, as she drove me to my interview at Smith. "You and she could come home together on weekends."

As it turned out, while I was being interviewed in the admissions office, my sister was two flights above me in the dean's office, being disciplined for breaking into the cafeteria with some classmates and raiding the ice cream bins. This caper had great appeal to me, and I pictured Lara and me bonding over similar adventures once I enrolled here. But another part of me remembered the volatility of our relationship. The urge to stay away from her was as strong as the urge to join her, and eventually I decided it would be safer for us not to go to the same school.

I was on crutches that fall, thanks to a field hockey injury that had torn my left quadriceps. Apparently, admissions committees could not resist a theatrical entrance; both colleges admitted me immediately, without waiting for me to finish my junior year of high school. And so, two weeks after my seventeenth birthday, in the fall of 1974, I became a high school dropout and college freshman.

———

Wellesley wasn't what I expected. I thought it would be like high school, only more beautiful, with better sports facilities. I'd gone to a semirural regional public school, so it was something of a jolt to find myself in a cerebral New England bastion of WASP privilege. Not that I knew what a WASP was; I only knew I was different. In my sweats and pixie haircut, I felt like an impostor, a kid from the boonies who did not belong with the sophisticated, sharp-dressed students on campus who called themselves "women" instead of girls. I wasn't used to this feeling of being a misfit, and it dawned on me that perhaps this was what Lara had felt like all her life. I felt a creepy shift in allegiance to her now.

Even more unnerving, the workload was killing. In high school, I'd never had to study more than an hour or two to outshine most of my classmates. But here, the syllabus for a single course listed more books than I'd read in the last two years of my life. One of the students in my literature class had read *Beowulf* in the original, and another discussed the political ramifications of nineteenth-century German philosophy over lunch. Cowed, I shackled myself to my desk and studied until the words on the page melted together.

My roommate was from the North Shore of Boston and had gone to a private boarding school. I liked her immediately—a tomboy in an oversize Brooks Brothers shirt, Levi's jeans, and Top-Siders without socks. She tied her limp hair in a ponytail and threw parties in our room for the whole floor, at which she served imported cheeses and bottles of gin. I'd never drunk anything more than a glass of wine in my life. Our room was small, so our classmates piled in, sitting on our beds and desks, on the floor, and even on the bookcases and dressers. Those who couldn't fit inside clogged the doorway and overflowed into the hall. At first, I liked being the social hub of our dorm. I could feel my coolness quotient rising. I passed the cheese and crackers, and quickly shed my unspoken identification with Lara. But after four or five parties in so many days, I started to worry about my studies. I couldn't figure out how to sneak off to the library without looking like a complete dork. So I played along and pretended to sip gin from my plastic cup of tap water, and tried to hide my growing anxiety over losing precious study time. But my affectation of a Fun Person was showing signs of wear.

Soon our parties attracted upperclassmen and students from other dorms. My roommate, flush with success, took periodic head counts of our guests. Later in the evening I would hear her talking excitedly on the phone with Mummy, proudly reporting the number of people who had attended our party.

That's when I understood that she and I were not so different after all. We were both desperate to impress our mothers; the only difference was how our mothers measured our success.

A few weeks later, my roommate and I were approached by some classmates who'd brokered a floor-wide freshman roommate swap to mix things up. I would move to a room at the end of the hall with another misfit, Janet Kairns, a public school kid like me in denim overalls, tube socks, and sneakers, who came from a hick town not far from my own. She and I bonded immediately over our common affliction of homesickness, something we hadn't dared admit to anyone before. And something else about Janet: in her geeky, good-natured way, she was a sweeter, simpler version of my sister. I felt comfortable and safe with Janet; she was like an overgrown eight-year-old boy mixed with a golden retriever. But strangely enough, I also found myself longing for the complicated edginess, the danger and sheer *Laraness* of Lara.

As if a switch had been flicked, I was now flooded with fond memories of skiing and hiking and swimming with Lara, of ganging up on Mom, who always seemed to delight in being the brunt of our silly jokes.

Here at college I was ashamed of this part of me, this childish, homesick Helen. It was time for me to become a successful adult in the world. So I spent my first semester holed up in the library and studied all weekend as if my life depended on it, which, of course, it did. Janet too disappeared into the stacks of the library, while the other women in our dorm smoked dope and drank vodka tonics from giant bowls, and fucked the boys from Harvard and MIT and Dartmouth and whoever else showed up on campus. I now missed my family in a way that took my breath away. I'd always been so self-assured, so hell-bent on getting out of there. But here in the world, I discovered I was more like them than like anyone else.

And now, for the first time in our lives, Lara and I started writing to each other—letters that were funny and self-mocking and oddly reassuring. To my surprise, we actually seemed to *like* each other. Perhaps now that we were both away from home, we began to see the possibility of friendship rather than rivalry. I took a bus to visit her over the Columbus Day weekend, and we had a surprisingly good time together, biking on country roads past tobacco fields and apple orchards, buying giant cookies at the country store. Lara was inexplicably good-natured and laid-back, no longer the dweeb I remembered from home. She nodded knowingly when I confessed to being intimidated by my classmates' erudition. Perhaps she was relieved to see that I was becoming less of an asshole—I could finally admit to cracks in my self-assured façade. In any event, it turned out we were very much alike, Lara and I—two college kids trying to impress our parents, for whom we felt a toxic mix of awe and love, and a sense of crushing obligation.

But over the next few weeks and months, it was precisely this similarity to my sister that began to gnaw at me. The pursuit of perfection was grinding me down. The fact that I'd managed to score straight As my first semester only plunged me deeper into despair. How was I going to keep this up? Now that I'd staked my claim at the top of the alphabet, anything else would feel like a failure.

This sense of implosion was new to me. It followed me everywhere—when I ran the tree-rooted trail around Lake Waban, when I tried to drown my anguish in ice cream sundaes in the dorm cafeteria, even when I shot hoops with Janet on weekends. *I'm sliding down the same chute as Lara*, I thought. Whatever "it" was that had tormented my sister since childhood, I had finally caught it. I was literally *turning into* Lara, or at least the version of Lara that was unglued. Somehow, Lara and I had quietly swapped places that winter. She had emerged the confident one, and I had turned into an insecure mess. I didn't know it then, but this was the beginning of a pattern my sister and I would fall into for decades to come.

————

It wasn't until the spring semester that I stumbled upon rowing. Or rather, first I stumbled upon Emma Dunlap, a tall, blond Californian with a goofy smile and calves the shape of mangoes. She seemed to breeze through campus as if she were on a surfboard—long athletic limbs, silky hair, aquamarine eyes. She and I were lab partners in Biology 100 that winter; we operated on the same frog and examined its tiny heart and kidneys. "He's beautiful," she murmured. This had not occurred to me. I had seen the frog as a speed bump on my way to a high-powered career of some sort; Emma made me see him as a lush country with rivers of life.

Emma was also a rower and had raced in the Head of the Charles in October. She showed me her photos of the regatta. I'd never seen a crew shell before. She'd developed and printed the pictures in one of the darkrooms in the art center. I caught my breath at the high-gloss images, stunned by her talent, her boundless energy, her off-kilter beauty. I imagined what it would feel like to fly across the water in one of those long, sleek racing shells with Emma and a team of women.

"You have to join the crew," she said. "We'll row together."

I pictured the mist rising at dawn as our boat unzipped the surface of the lake.

"Yes," I said.

———

Rowing was unlike any sport I'd ever done. The fastest crews are quiet and smooth, the perfection of power squeezed into as narrow and clean a line as possible, a speed seamstress streaking down the racecourse, stitching each stroke into the fabric of the river, and finishing before the water even knows it's been cut.

From the moment I tried it, I was in love. You take four strong women and blend them into a single motion. You slide together, catch together, breathe together. You lose sense of your boundaries. You become one with the boat, with the other rowers, with the water.

We would roll out of bed and stumble down to the boathouse before dawn, when the lake was just a dark smudge surrounded by the shapes of trees. We launched into darkness, our blades sailing over the water and punching holes in the lake. Now the first rays of sunlight seeped through heavy rags of mist. Behind us the shore was barely distinguishable from the soup of early morning. Soon the second boat joined us and we raced side by side.

The morning flew by as if on time-lapse photography. The sun rose like a gold coin in the sky, and the shore came into focus. The woods sprang up, dark limbs snaking through the sharp green of spring. The lake grew choppy, a slate color that turned blue-black, then gunmetal gray. Out on Route 16, cars began their slow descent into the city.

We spent an hour and a half racing each other from cove to cove, turning quickly at the end of each set and pausing—just long enough to pass the water bottle, wipe our foreheads on our shirtsleeves, and gasp for breath. We sat hunched over, shoulders soaked, legs quivering. Our fingers grew blisters and then calluses, hard and smooth.

By the time we docked, the world had awakened. Breakfast was cooking in the cafeteria. We threw on our sweats and ran up the hill to the dorm. Wet, flushed, stained with oarlock grease, we stormed the dining room, where a handful of our classmates sat slumped in bathrobes, sucking down coffee, stunned by the fact of morning. Flush with endorphins, we filled the room with roars of laughter, heaped our plates with food, and sat down to our meal like the victorious army we believed ourselves to be.

Passions crossed from one boat to another. Attraction was unavoidable. We were teenagers, we moved in sync, and it was all pretty much preconscious—most of us hadn't yet made the connection between love and Lesbos. It was 1975, but I don't think anyone on our crew had even heard of the Stonewall riots six years earlier. I certainly never imagined that the soaring feelings and giddy excitement I felt for some of my teammates could be more than the inevitable camaraderie of a close-knit team of athletes. My anxiety and self-doubt of the previous semester fell away. I grew closer to Emma. In the evenings she and I would sit on the floor of her room and talk about our families and our dreams for our future, as if our lives were a movie that could be previewed and condensed into tantalizing trailers. I barely mentioned my sister, and instead ratcheted up the romance and drama of our family story. After all, my parents had always been the real stars in my life; Lara and I were the tendrils you pushed out of the way to see them more clearly.

In her photos, Emma's parents and two brothers looked youthful and happy, bronzed by the California sun, while my family lurked in the shadow of its dark past. Her father had rowed for Berkeley in the fifties, while my father was still learning English and washing his gray hair in the residents' sinks at Mount Sinai Hospital. I wanted to be just like her. I wanted to grow a second skin like hers—smooth, strong, confident. She and her family hiked in the Sierra Nevada and rock-climbed in Yosemite, and her father was a helicopter pilot in his spare time, when he wasn't handling major financial deals for his bank. I fantasized about being adopted by the Dunlaps and tried not to think too much about my own family.

six

Lara came home from her junior year sunk in a soul-sucking depression. Her head hung to her chest, and she moved as if her feet were shackled together. She barely said hello to me as she shuffled through the door. I was shocked that the Lara of last fall had dissipated into this other Lara, someone I had buried deep in my memory of our unpleasant past.

She had gotten extensions on her final papers. Our family sprang into action, turned the dining room into our war room, and spread Lara's notebooks and research materials across the table. My mother prepared the plan of attack. My father did fact-checks, and I was assigned to editing. Lara perked up and got to work.

She completed her junior year with her fine grade point average intact. Then she fell apart. She disappeared into her room and could not be roused from bed for days at a time. It felt as if our house had closed around a festering wound, and my parents and I moved uneasily from kitchen to living room to bedroom, afraid of what might ooze out.

I'd returned home that May after my freshman year with a broken heart. Emma was transferring to Berkeley to be closer to her family, and we wrote long, passionate, coast-to-coast letters over which I cried and cried. She sent me pressed wildflowers from the High Sierras and invited me to California. To my astonishment, I burst into tears at the mere mention of her name, and read and reread her letters obsessively. My mother thought this was perfectly normal. After all, it was the way she missed her sister, who was about to arrive from Rome to spend the summer with us, as she did every year now. During the winter months when she and Zosia were apart, my mother would run to the mailbox every afternoon for Zosia's letter as if it contained the oxygen she needed to get through the next twenty-four hours.

Now Mom made up the little couch in the television room as Zosia's bed for the summer. It was oddly sweet to see Mom dancing around Zosia like a puppy, bringing her tea, offering her fresh-baked linzer torte, and chattering away in Italian. Zosia was still groggy from the long flight, and it took her a few days to get over her jet lag, put on an apron, and start churning out choux pastry and apfelstrudel and panettone in the kitchen. My father, as usual, was at his office or at the hospital all day, stopping by for supper at four-thirty before rushing off for evening office hours a few minutes later. He seemed to accept that Zosia and his wife were a unit. He would join in their conversation in Italian at times—usually to correct them on some point of politics, history, or grammar, depending on the topic of discussion.

I can't remember exactly what happened to Kevin that summer. When I first came home in May, he'd proposed a summer fling, which I declined, having lost all interest in him. He seemed to be a dull shard from a distant past. I spent that summer of 1975 working the cash register at Herman's World of Sporting Goods. I was about to turn eighteen, still too young to work in a store that sold guns, but the manager was a Rotary Club friend of my father's, so he let it go. The rest of the employees, in their little mustard-colored vests with the World of Sporting Goods logo over the left breast, grumbled behind my back. I took my breaks with the High Adventure guys, who sold pitons and chalks and bright-colored climbing ropes. I listened to them brag about their winter assaults and Class 7 climbs. We sat on folding chairs around the dented table in the employee lounge and ate Clark Bars and Raisinets from the candy machine. Cigarette butts cascaded from a hubcap-size ashtray in the middle of the table. Bolted to the wall was the time clock, and next to it the metal rack with our time cards. If you punched in a minute late, you were docked fifteen minutes.

I spent most of my paycheck on climbing gear they recommended, and one of them, Joe Cantagna, asked me on a date. He had dark wavy hair and an uneven mustache, and he was always touching the calluses on his hands with his fingertips. Although I was in college, my mother still did not allow me to date, and boys did not understand my compliance with this rule. I had no interest in dating Joe Cantagna or any other guy. So I lied and told Joe I already had a boyfriend. It was easier all around. In my experience, going out with boys was not worth the acrobatics involved in lying to my mother. I needed my mother; I did not need boys. I didn't waste time wondering about this.

Lara wasn't able to do much with herself that summer. Mainly she stayed at home under the covers, playing games with the drugs her shrink prescribed—she'd take them, not take them, stockpile them, pretend to take them, fight with my father about them, etc. She would stagger from her room every day or two, dazed and barefoot. She dragged herself to the kitchen, collapsed in a chair at the counter, and picked at her fingers. She wore the same torn white T-shirt all summer, with a faded emblem of her Amateur Athletic Union swim team across the front.

We exchanged scowls. Would it have killed me to be nice to her? I was obviously in better shape than she was that summer, but it only made me more stingy with my tiny quota of kindness.

As soon as she sat down, my mother jumped to her feet. "Oh, Lara!" she said. "Coffee?"

Lara grunted, and my mother poured.

"Darling, would you like some panettone?" Lara picked at the coffee cake, then pushed it away, then picked at it some more. My mother leaned over her and whispered something in her ear. I refused to look at them, annoyed by the dance that bound them together. I did not want to be as miserable as Lara to deserve that kind of attention. But I wanted something too shameful to admit: I wanted my mother to myself. I wanted our long conversations about books and art and movies. I missed her laughter.

And I couldn't have said it at the time, but I also wanted my big sister back, the version of Lara who had reassuringly appeared out of the monster of childhood. I wanted the Lara who patiently listened to me and my problems, who took care of me and inspired me to go on adventures with her. I hated it when she was like this, so aggressively depressed, staring daggers and shoving me aside with a smoldering rage. Not only had this lout of a Lara taken my beloved sister away, but she had also taken my mother with her.

Zosia's presence added a new twist. Until this summer, my mother had managed to keep our family's misery a secret from Zosia. Lara had always been able to pull herself together around Zosia in the past. But by July, Lara had given up any effort at pretense, and she was having her meltdowns in plain view of all of us. Zosia seemed unfazed by this. "I'm tough," she would tell me. "I can take a lot."

"She's very fragile," my mother would say of Zosia. "She cannot take it."

And so we pursued our own ideas about ourselves and each other.

As the summer wore on, my father spent more time at his office. I wasted my days at the cash register, dreaming of someday busting loose. I had visions of running away to California to be with Emma, hiking the spine of the Sierras, climbing out of my life in the suburban Tri-City area. With my employee discount, I bought a backpack, tent, sleeping bag, headlamp, water bottles, everything I needed to get away from everyone and everything.

One day Zosia pulled me aside. "Your mother has her hands full," she said. "She doesn't have time for you. Tell me. I'm the auntie. Tell me what you did today." With her silvery hair and lined face, she seemed much older than last summer, when we had been together in Rome.

"I worked."

"What was it like?"

"I can't stand it," I said. "I can't stand watching Mom pour herself into Lara, day and night. It makes me crazy just seeing them!"

"You have to be patient, darling." Zosia's voice dropped. "Lara is very sick, and your mother is doing the best she can. She loves you very much—"

"Oh, please," I said, turning away.

"No!" Zosia caught my wrist. Her eyes flashed. "You have to help your mother. You have to be as nice to her as you can. What she is dealing with is very, very hard."

Zosia's anger alarmed me. "If Lara's so sick," I said, "then how come she can be raving mad one minute, and then when the phone rings—if it's some friend of hers—she's instantly sweet and funny and fine, as if nothing's happened? Either she's sick or she's not! It's not like some spigot she can turn on and off at will."

"She's sick, darling. You have to understand."

My father agreed with me about Lara. But he took the discussion into dangerous territory that I did not wish to explore. "Mom is deranged," he said matter-of-factly. "She is damaged by the war." His face went solemn, and the creases around his mouth deepened. "She never recovered from the killing of her parents."

I kept silent. I refused to believe that my mother was deranged; I believed Lara was the problem. Remove Lara, I thought, and all would be fine.

I was just as deluded as everyone else.

———

One evening my father was driving Zosia and me down State Street to his office to fetch toilet paper for our house. He ordered it wholesale for his office, and we siphoned off the supplies for home use, keeping careful count for the IRS. We were riding in his new Plymouth Duster, and he recorded the mileage and gas expenditures in a little notebook, so he could monitor the engine's efficiency.

"She can't help it," Zosia was saying.

"Then she should be properly medicated."

I listened from the backseat. All we ever talked about was Lara. All day, every day, all my life. This summer was the first time Zosia was pulled in too.

"You can't just drug her into a stupor," Zosia said. "She has a problem. She needs help. "*Psychotherapy*," she added, coming down hard on the *p*. "She needs intensive *psychotherapy*."

Wrong! I thought. Shrinks had been poking sticks at Lara for the past ten years, and they seemed to be part of the problem here. They could make anyone look crazy, especially someone as messed up as Lara. At least, that was Lara's position, and I was starting to agree with her. The more she saw psychiatrists, the worse she got.

"She needs patience," Zosia said.

"She also needs discipline," my father said. "She needs someone to lay down the law. Maria is too permissive. She gives in to Lara's every wish."

Although I was aligned with my father, his idea of discipline scared me; sometimes it looked a lot like sadism. He had Siberian standards of punishment. Once, when I was fourteen, he asked if I'd like to take a walk with him. It was August; we were on vacation in Maine. I chose to wear my new sandals—Dr. Scholl's knockoffs—of which my father disapproved. "Put on sensible shoes," he said. "But they're comfortable," I assured him. To teach me a lesson, he took off at a breakneck pace, walking as briskly as his long legs would carry him. I had to run to keep up, and by the time we got home an hour later, my feet were pulp, my sandals covered in blood. Neither of us said a word, but I had trouble walking for the rest of our vacation. I suppose I was more like my father than I liked to admit.

"Lara is a sick girl," my aunt said softly. "Kovik, remember, she's a child. She has a mental problem. I never realized it till this summer, you know. Maria didn't want to tell me. But now I see."

"She's twenty-one."

Zosia threw him a cutting glare. "A child."

"She needs to understand there are rules," he said. "And consequences." His hand came off the steering wheel and made a karate chop in the air. "If you separate Maria and Lara," he said, "then you will see."

"What will you see?"

"Without Maria, Lara will have no one with whom to engage. She will see that she gets nowhere with her tantrums and threats, and she will have to learn self-control."

I kept quiet, my default mode when my family talked about Lara. I knew that my voice in these matters was irrelevant, that I was better off listening and keeping my opinions to myself.

The sun dropped off the edge of State Street. In the midsummer dusk that gathered outside the windshield, the neon signs of fast-food joints and convenience stores popped to life. At home, I knew, my mother and sister would be speaking softly to each other. My sister would be in bed, and my mother would be sitting at the edge, stroking her hair, reassuring her of her love. This was their time alone, their moment together when they did not have to justify themselves to the rest of the family. They could love each other as they were meant to love: stubbornly, wholeheartedly, without shame or guilt.

———

August came. In another month, Zosia would be flying back to Rome, I would be returning to college, and if my parents could pull it off, Lara would return for her senior year. Lara had a knack for bouncing back from suicidal depression to successful scholar in no time flat. In retrospect, I can see the enormous pressure she was under, the rigidity of our parents' needs, and how impossible it must have felt to Lara to meet them. But at the time, I considered Lara's versatility in mood swings proof of her resourcefulness, evidence of the calculated power she held over us. Instead of feeling sorry for her, I was furious at her manipulation of us.

In mid-August, Dad and I came up with a brilliant plan.

"You need a vacation," he said when he picked me up from work one day. "You should get out of the house."

We were sitting in traffic on Drake Road. "What about you?" I said. "You haven't had a break all summer."

We were nearing home, the fun-less zone. It made us want to take care of each other.

"When does school start?" Dad asked.

"The day after Labor Day."

"How about the week before, then? We could take a trip."

A wild feeling of danger and hope surged through me. "I don't know about my job—I told them I'd work through Labor Day."

"I'll talk to Conklin," my father said. "I can get you out of it."

And so my father and I ran off together.

———

The great thing about running away with my father was that it was sanctioned by the family. I could get out of the house without having to assume the label of Selfish Child. I could pretend I was doing it for my father, and he could pretend he was doing it for me.

The bad thing about running away with my father was that I

would be stuck with him for ten days. Going on vacation with a sixty-year-old Holocaust survivor and former Gulag prisoner who tends to relive each moment of his six-year incarceration is not for everyone. But consider the alternative. If I had to spend one more minute at home, watching all of us move around Lara like deep-sea creatures, I was sure I would explode.

Dad and I packed a suitcase and two sleeping bags. He picked me up from work the next day and asked to speak with his friend Conklin, the manager. Mr. Conklin was a timid man with thinning hair and a sad little mustache that you had to look at twice to realize it was really there. He wore caved-in shoes and an overall dreariness that made me feel sorry for him. You could see that he revered my father. When Dad appeared before him, Mr. Conklin's face lit up with wonder. He seemed not to mind my father's too-short clip-on tie that swung slightly to the right. Conklin's own fashion sense was not keen either. He wore the same thing he wore every day: a cheap maroon blazer with the Herman's World of Sporting Goods insignia emblazoned on the pocket. His shoulders swam in it.

"I'm sorry to ask this," my father said in a tone that suggested pain and dignity. "The situation at home is . . ." He paused and glanced down at his shoes. "It is extremely difficult. . . ."

I was curious to know what my father would tell my boss about "the situation at home." Conklin looked up at my father with genuine sympathy. You could see he would give my father anything he asked for. He would hand him the keys to the store, to the entire stockroom of goods. He would hand over his wallet, his watch, his wedding ring—*anything*, as long as my father didn't go into details.

"I know Helen agreed to work through the Labor Day weekend," my father said. He drew his lips into a thin line. "But the situation at home . . . I'm sorry that I must ask for Helen to step out of work a week early."

Conklin was already nodding his head before my father had finished his sentence. "Of course," he said. "Of course."

My father didn't stop there. "Someday," he said, looking wistfully over Conklin's head at the fluorescent lights gleaming in the Golf Department, "someday I will tell you about it." He sighed. "But I cannot now." He glanced briefly into Conklin's eyes. "It is too painful."

Conklin patted my father on the arm, a gesture that startled me by its intimacy and sweetness. Conklin barely came up to my father's tie clip, and the sight of him extending his polyester arm toward my father broke my heart. "I'm sorry," he murmured. "I'm so sorry."

My father nodded. "I cannot talk about it," he said quietly.

I was suddenly annoyed that my father spent so much time saying what he could not talk about. Our forced silence about "the situation at home" drove me crazy. I wanted to scream it from the rooftops. Of course, it never occurred to me that maybe I could use some therapy myself. That would mean I was mentally ill, and I would sooner have died than see a shrink.

"If there's anything I can do," Conklin murmured, his small hand on my father's elbow, "please call me." His earnest face, those black horn-rimmed glasses, those broken-down shoes . . . I was embarrassed to see him give my father such support. And I was somehow ashamed of our performance, which was not a performance—our pain was genuine, yet it seemed so ridiculous played out in public. Did we really need to break my promise to my employer? I would never see Mr. Conklin again, but my father, no doubt, would see him at the Rotary

Club luncheons, and would make some sad remark that would tell Conklin nothing and everything, and he would look at Conklin as a man who could not possibly imagine his suffering.

My mother and Zosia seemed relieved to get Dad and me out of the house. Now they could tend to Lara full-time without the nagging interference of my father and me. Lara was all-consuming, and now, at last, they could be fully consumed.

————

I let my father dictate our route. We drove north to the White Mountains and hiked in the Presidential Range, then drove south to Boston, where Dad spent a day in Harvard Square and played the Chess Master for a dollar per game. He kept winning his dollar back for hours, till it was too dark to see the board and they had to quit. Next we went to Cape Cod for lunch at a fish shack, and then to Falmouth, where we boarded the ferry for Martha's Vineyard. Armed with a map of the island, we drove from one cheap motel to another, and I would run into the office, ask the price of a room, and run back to my father. He shook his head if the price was too high. He made a soft whistling sound if the price was completely outrageous. After an hour or so, we found a campground. For ten dollars, they gave us a tent platform with an army surplus canvas tent that was mostly waterproof, albeit mildewed. We had brought our own sleeping bags and unfurled them across the wood-planked platform. Our sweaters and socks were our pillows.

It rained that night, and mosquitoes lined up and bit our necks, our ears, our eyelids. My father snored like a Cossack. I circled the tunnel of my sleeping bag and wondered whether I would ever find my way out of my family. I'd been in such a hurry to grow up and get out of high school, chart my course in the open world. But the world was full of mosquitoes and mildew and crap jobs behind a register. It was hard to choose the world when my family knew my name and the words to my heart. They could open and close it with the twist of a key. Would I ever get away?

Dawn finally broke and we went into town for coffee. A mimeographed sheet tacked to a bulletin board advertised a local chess tournament. The name of the contact person was familiar—I'd read a book about a disastrous climb up Everest by a guy named Woodrow Wilson Sayre. I called the number from a pay phone and said that my father would like to enter the tournament.

"Sorry, it's over," the man said. "I should take that flyer down."

"Um, are you, by any chance . . . Did you write *Four against Everest?*"

The man's voice warmed. "Why, yes," he said. "If you want to come over, I can sell you a copy." I was elated. "And tell your dad I'll play him a game, if he likes."

I hung up and ran back to my father in the car.

"The tournament's over," I said quickly, "but it's the same guy who climbed Everest and wrote a book about it! He said he'd sell me one if we go to his house!"

My father shook his head, unimpressed.

"And he said he'd play you a game, if you like."

At this, my father perked up. "Call him back and get directions," he said.

———

They played most of the afternoon and into the evening, while I reread Sayre's book. He happily sold it to me for fourteen dollars. Given his designer house with wall-to-wall windows, bronze sculptures, and family portraits by artists I'd studied in art history, I suspect he didn't really need my fourteen dollars, but it was well worth it for my father's six hours of uninterrupted chess.

In the evening we strolled the streets of Vineyard Haven staring at rich people who had puttered in from their yachts in the harbor. Art Buchwald waddled down the main street in a short-sleeved button-down shirt and shorts stretched over his round stomach. My father did not like rich people, whom he suspected of not having worked sufficiently hard or suffered enough (in his opinion) to earn their wealth. But he did like funny people like Art Buchwald, and he was willing to forgive certain funny people for being rich.

It was in Provincetown back on the Cape that he started talking about the Gulag. Stories and memories he'd never told me before. He talked about the cold in a way that made the Arctic take shape as an isolated world of blackened toes and endless ice and wind. He spoke of hunger, a constant drilling against the belly and the skull. Men went crazy from hunger. They daydreamed recipes and visualized beef stews. They salivated from memory and imagination. He told me more about himself than he ever had before, and I drank up his words with awe.

"In the Gulag, I learned to be an idiot," my father said. "The others tried to engage me in discussions, but I just shrugged and said, 'I know nothing. I have no opinion.'" My father looked so old to me then, more myth than man. I wanted to rescue him from his past, to absorb his pain and bring him back to life.

"I learned not to trust anyone," he said. "This was the most important lesson I learned. And that is the reason I was able to survive. That, and the fact that I was a doctor. Because as a doctor, I could work indoors. Everyone who worked outside died of starvation and exposure."

I spoke very little during these walks. I did not want my father to stop talking. I hoped he wouldn't notice me sucking up his life with a hunger I could not explain. It was important, I thought, for him to be able to unburden himself, and I wanted to be the one in whom he could confide. By the time I returned to school, I felt about a thousand years old. With zero sense of who I was.

seven

English had always been my favorite subject, but now I decided that the most impressive thing I could do for my father was to become a doctor. Never mind that Dad didn't *like* practicing medicine (he'd always wanted to be a violinist). He had no patience for people who complained; he hated practicing what he called "an imperfect science"; and he felt personally offended when a patient's condition got worse. Even so, he liked helping people, was proud of the status and income that his medical degree afforded him, and believed it was an excellent, if stressful, career choice. At eighteen, I didn't concern myself with the actual job description of being a doctor; I just wanted to pick the direct route to my parents' hearts. My sister was premed, and despite the fact that I'd never had the least interest in math or science, my scholastic achievement suggested I should be premed too. "Be a doctor," my mother had always advised us, "don't marry one."

"What should I take?" I asked Lara over the phone that September. Now that she and I were both back at school, she seemed to have reverted to her big sister role as fellow hunter-gatherer of good grades, and reliable provider of curricular information.

"Load up on chem," she said. "And get your physics out of the way. You'll need calculus too."

It was reassuring to have my sister back, to have her attention and advice. As a senior, she'd already taken this path, and could warn me of the pitfalls. I pictured us both hoisting our course loads like rucksacks and hiking along the precipitous path to an MD, just as we'd hiked across the Alps the summer I was fifteen, Lara in the lead. Only this time, instead of whining with exhaustion, I would embrace the suffering and conquer it.

The first inkling that I might have a problem was chemistry. I'd signed up for the survey course and took notes like a stenographer. I drew diagrams and graphs and charts with colored pencils, and labeled my beakers in the elegant penmanship for which I had won awards in grade school. My lab notebook could have been displayed in the Museum for the Anal-Retentive.

The problem was not my grades, nor my comprehension of chemistry. The problem was new to me: it was a problem of *attitude*. Until now, it had been none of my business whether I liked a subject or not; my job was to study my brains out and get an A. Now, for the first time, I had *feelings* about it. I did not like chem lab. Lab started at one in the afternoon and lasted until nearly five. While I was indoors pouring liquids from one beaker into another, the lake was out there turning its smooth face to the sky, begging to be rowed on. The trails in the woods were just waiting for me to lace up my sneakers and run on them.

Chem lab was, quite simply, a crime against nature. Against *my* nature. I could feel my soul being sucked dry, one drop at a time. I faced a dilemma. I could strip myself of what I loved by turning myself in to the lab each afternoon, or I could skip lab sciences altogether and row my heart across the lake and back.

Within months, I made a decision that suited my soul: I decided not to be a doctor. The immediate pleasure I obtained by this decision: my afternoons would be free of lab for the rest of my life. I had, with the simple dismissal of a career choice, given myself the gift of light in the afternoons. Ironically, the career that had saved my father's life by keeping him indoors and safe from Siberian winters was precisely the career I rejected because it kept me inside a lab in eastern Massachusetts.

That semester I was also taking an English lit class taught by a battle-ax of a Chaucer scholar named Helen Corsa. In the middle of a lively discussion of *Moll Flanders* one day, she stood in front of the class with her fists on her hips and announced, "People always say, 'Don't major in English! What can you *do* with an English major?'" She rocked back on her heels and eyed us through thick glasses on her jowly face. "Well, who the hell cares whether it's *useful*? Major in it because it's *fun*!"

My heart leapt. I made an appointment to see her the following week, and asked her to be my advisor. Would she sign the paper declaring my English major? To my disappointment, she barely glanced at me as she scribbled her name on the document and handed it back to me. "There you go," she said, and returned to the papers on her desk. I felt foolish for having hoped she might take an interest in me, and I was too ashamed to ask for any more of her time. Despite my timidity, I reveled in Professor Corsa's belligerent take-no-prisoners attitude about choosing a field of study for *fun*. Here was someone as strong and opinionated as my parents, but with a completely opposite agenda. Of course, I didn't have the guts to stand up either to Professor Corsa or to my parents, but I was pretty sure that Helen Corsa could kick their butts, at least when it came to championing the importance of Chaucer in my life. The battle between my English professor and my parents took place in my mind, and I needed her in there.

Unfortunately, unlike Helen Corsa, who was a literary genius, I knew I was majoring in English because it was a breeze—only eight English classes and no lab component! How would I explain this to my parents? Taking the easy road was a felony in our family. Living up to my Potential, I understood, required hard work, pain, and suffering. My parents had talked about this magic Potential of mine from grade school on, as if it were some utopia that had been furnished and prepared for me with fresh linens and modern window treatments, and it was my responsibility to climb the stairs to get to this fabulous future of mine, a special deluxe suite at the top of the world. There was no time for dillydallying, as my father liked to say. If I didn't race up those stairs, if I didn't spend every ounce of my time, energy, and concentration on propelling myself upward, my Potential could simply evaporate, leaving me empty, alone, unloved, and worthless in a windowless studio with a Murphy bed.

October 1975

"Hold still," Harriet said, one callused hand on top of my head, the other holding a pair of scissors. I was sitting on a chair in the women's room of her dorm, with half of my hair scattered on the floor.

"You're scalping me!" I said. "Leave me *some*thing, will you? Like an inch?"

Harriet bent over, momentarily choked up with laughter. "I left you way more than an inch," she said, pointing to a tuft of hair above my left ear. She stared at me in the mirror, trying to keep a straight face.

"Just wait till it's your turn," I said.

It was mid-October, six weeks into my sophomore year, and now that Emma had gone to Berkeley, I found myself (in that same cluelessly self-closeted way) crazy about Harriet Goodwin, a big-boned Minnesotan who rowed right behind me in our coxed four. She, in turn, had a crush on Jim, commander of the *Enterprise*—the character that William Shatner played in *Star Trek*. Harriet was a senior and captain of our team, a pure powerhouse of a rower who had been awarded a single racing shell by the U.S. Olympic Development Team. In practices, I could feel her drive with each stroke—she pried the lake open with her oar, propelling our boat forward.

It was her idea that we cut each other's hair. "We'll be more aerodynamic," she said. It was our private joke—we didn't include our teammates. Afterward, we both wore blue bandannas to classes, and laughed when we took them off. Neither of us cared, really, what we looked like. The idea was more of a bonding ritual, cutting our hair short in preparation for the Head of the Charles Regatta, in which we'd be racing in a few days.

I was slated to stroke our varsity boat, with Harriet rowing in the seat behind me. My parents had offered to drive out to Boston to watch me race, and then to bring me home for the long weekend. At eighteen, I was overjoyed that they were coming, and eager to show them off to my coach and teammates. Although Lara and I had been playing on varsity teams all our lives, neither of my parents had ever watched us compete. Girls' sports were not considered important in those days, and Dad certainly never took time off from work to do anything as trivial as watch an athletic event. So I felt I'd scored the attention of the grand duke and duchess of my world. Later I would realize that they had arranged their visit for completely different reasons than I'd imagined. They had more important things on their minds.

I still hadn't broken the news about declaring an English major to my parents; I hadn't even told my sister about my decision to drop the whole premed thing. I was afraid Lara might feel let down. Weren't we supposed to be in this together? She and I hadn't spoken since the beginning of the semester, when she'd told me what science courses to take. In the meantime, I'd spent more time rowing and goofing off with Harriet than studying.

The morning of the regatta was a New England special: blue sky, trees in flame, river sparkling. Magazine Beach was covered with racing shells and men and women sporting muscle shirts and blast-off legs. When it was time for our race, we stripped off our socks and gingerly stepped on slimy rocks, carrying the boat into the water. We locked the oars, climbed in, toweled off our feet, laced them into the foot stretchers, and rowed down to the start.

We fought a brisk wind into the basin. When they called our start, we fairly exploded from the line, oars in sync, coxswain screaming. The crowds on the riverbanks were a blur, their cheers a dull roar. We were flying at an impossible stroke rate, and after a few minutes, I started to panic. *I can't do it*, I thought. *I'm going to let them all down.* I yanked wildly on my oar, my breath ragged. The boat lurched to port. "It's okay, just relax." Harriet's voice drifted over my shoulders. "Just settle down and drive with your legs." Her voice was calm and even, and it cut through my terror.

I found the rhythm again and we were back in the race. But my face burned with shame. What had happened? What was wrong with me? I poured my anger into each stroke. Soon we passed a boat near the Western Avenue Bridge, and another at Anderson. We did all right in the end, seventh in a field of some twenty crews. Seventh was perfectly respectable, but it was small solace for the realization that I could not rely on myself—that in a pinch, when push came to shove, when everyone was counting on me, I could not deliver.

"It's okay," Harriet said after we'd put the boat on slings and wiped it down. She patted my shoulder a bit awkwardly. We started derigging the boat. Despite my bravado, I knew I was weak at the center of my being. I was not reliable; I could not trust myself. It was at times like this that I felt a creeping sense of identity with Lara. She was the symbol of all that was scary and uncontrollable and irrational in our family. I felt myself slipping into that crater, and it was unnerving.

After our team loaded the boats back onto the truck, I found Mom and Dad waiting for me on the dock of the Weld Boathouse. Among the crowds of spectators in jeans and T-shirts, my father stood out in his dark business suit and my mother in a formal pantsuit.

"Do you have everything?" my mother asked, eyeing the small sports bag slung over my shoulder. I'd only packed two textbooks; I didn't feel like studying much over the weekend, and I was looking forward to spending time with my parents. Mercifully, my mother said nothing about my haircut, and I couldn't tell whether she'd even noticed it.

We walked to the car. I knew it was of no consequence to my parents how my team did. My father had been a decathlete on the Polish Olympic team, but instead of competing in the 1936 Olympics, he had chosen to study for his medical exams. "Sports are an excellent outlet," he'd always said, "but a career is what matters."

It was fine if I wanted to row, as long as my studies didn't suffer.

One of my teammates' parents had invited the whole team to dinner at their home in Cambridge, one of those quiet multimillion-dollar houses three blocks from Harvard Square. It never occurred to me to be impressed by these folks. On the contrary, I wanted to show off *my* parents, who, I thought, were so foreign and exotic, so clearly extraordinary, everyone would admire me for my affiliation with them.

"We don't have time to stop," my father said.

"Oh, please," I begged. "Can't we just drop by for a couple minutes to say hi?"

We were the last ones to arrive. Mom and Dad stood stiffly in the foyer, politely declining offers to eat or drink. I felt inexplicably proud, simply because they were my parents. But their awkwardness was obvious, and we left quickly.

Night had fallen. Cambridge was strangely quiet, a planet of empty streets. My mother and I climbed into the Chrysler and my father started the engine. My eyelids closed of their own accord, and in the darkness I saw the racecourse again, the crowds cheering on the riverbank like colorful bits of confetti, crew shells skimming the water, fighting each other through the bridges. I was looking forward to the weekend at home. I would have a chance to rest and recover before returning to classes.

And I also wanted to talk to my mother about what had happened to me during the race. I didn't want to admit my weakness to my father, but I figured tomorrow, when Dad was at work, I could talk to Mom about it. She was better at that kind of stuff.

My father slipped the car into gear and we floated silently through the city and onto the Mass Pike. I began loosening the seat belt, longing to slide across the backseat and fall asleep.

"Helen," my mother said. "We have something to tell you."

I stiffened at the sound of her voice, and studied the outline of her head. Something was wrong. She didn't turn toward me, but stared straight ahead out the windshield. Stars had popped out in the sky, and we seemed to be driving into them, scattering them.

"It's about Lara," she said.

I held my breath.

"Lara has . . . well . . . you know she was having a very difficult time this summer." My mother's voice broke. "She's gone into an institution."

"What?"

"The Institute of Living," my mother said. "It's the best of its kind. Near Hartford, Connecticut."

"Of *Living?*" It made me think of death.

"It was last month. She just couldn't continue—" Mom paused to dab her eyes with a Kleenex. "She was terribly sick."

"But . . ." I gripped the seat as if it were a flotation device.

An institution?! I tried to organize this information into a logical beginning, middle, and end. While I'd been messing around in boats all fall, my sister had gone nuts. Why hadn't they told me sooner?

"She didn't want you to know," my mother said. "And there was nothing you could do anyway. She made me promise not to tell you.

But in another month it will be Thanksgiving, and you would find out then anyway. . . ."

No no no no no. I'd spent a good chunk of my childhood hoping for Lara to get locked up someplace where she couldn't hurt me. But so much had changed since then—I *needed* Lara now. She and I were in this together, this terrible battle to grow up—and I couldn't lose her to the loony bin.

"She finally agreed to go," my mother said in a dead voice. "We took her to the Institute, and she finally agreed to sign herself in."

"There was no other choice," my father said bluntly.

My mother practically leapt out of her seat at him. "Oh, you've been wanting this for years!" she hissed. "You've wanted to send her away since she was a child!"

My father stared straight ahead, the hairs on his head shining in the headlights of a passing car.

"How could you?" my mother shouted. "How could you do this to your own daughter?"

I'd never heard my mother speak like this—it was as if Lara's rage were spilling directly out of my mother's mouth.

I had the sudden impulse to flip open the door, jump to the side of the road, and run back down the highway to my dorm. My teammates would be sitting around in the lounge, laughing and talking about the races.

"You know that's not fair," my father said in a low voice.

I concentrated on sitting perfectly still and making no sound.

"It's true!" my mother cried. "You've wanted this all along!"

I stayed quiet and let my father take the rap, though I was the one who had always wanted Lara sent away when I was little. For a moment in the sixties, when Lara was fourteen and starving herself, my wish had almost come true. There was a hospital in White Plains, and the Hoffman Children and Family Center had made all the arrangements. They were just waiting for my mother to agree. It sounded good to me—I pictured a distant, desolate land stretched across a white expanse of New York State. She would be safely out of reach.

But it had never happened. Week after week, Lara always cleaned up her act at the last minute and ate something. I'd always imagined that with Lara gone, my parents and I could live in peace. It hadn't occurred to me that without Lara to distract us, my parents would turn on each other.

My mother was too angry to speak now. She stared ahead, and we plunged forward into the darkness.

We arrived at home late and my mother put the kettle on for tea. My father walked past us without speaking.

My room seemed so much smaller than I remembered. The blue shelves my father had built held the same childhood collection of figurines, some glued together after Lara's tantrums. They looked forlorn, remnants from a previous life.

Without thinking, I found myself walking into my sister's room next to mine. Her room was dark. I sat on her bed and lost all sense of time. She was gone, and I felt sick. I missed her. Her absence felt physical, a broken shell tumbling in my stomach. This couldn't be happening. I should have done something; I should have helped her.

From the kitchen I could hear my father murmuring and the staccato of my mother's response. The kettle screeched, and as I walked into the kitchen, my father brushed past me. "Good night," he said.

Mom and I sat at the kitchen counter, stirring our tea, staring at our reflections in the window. "It was very hard," my mother said. She unwrapped a hard candy and popped it in her mouth. "Want one?" She held the little bowl out to me. I shook my head.

"The doctor says she is doing better." She took a sip of tea, holding the candy between her teeth. "It was very bad the first few nights."

A light was on in my parents' bedroom, and I had the feeling my father was listening as he read the enormous black tome on psychiatry that he kept at his bedside.

"After Lara signed in, I hugged her good-bye, but when the aides came for her, she got very violent. She pushed them away and started screaming and fighting." My mother took a Kleenex from the cuff of her sweater and wiped her nose. "They had to wrestle her down and put her in restraints. There was nothing I could do. And Lara was yelling at me, 'You did this to me! It's your fault!'" Mom's voice cut off, and she brought the teacup to her mouth. "Eventually," she said, "they sedated her and took her to a room downstairs."

I put my hand on my mother's arm, but I didn't know what to say. I pictured Lara on one of her wild rampages. It must have taken half a dozen guards to bring her down.

"You know," my mother said, shaking her head, "I felt . . . I felt I'd betrayed her. Never again will I let that happen to her. *Never*."

My mother took a sip of tea. She blinked away tears.

A chill crept down my spine. I had conveniently forgotten that Lara could get like that, and it was a jolt to be reminded. Why couldn't I ever hold those two parts of my sister together in my mind—Lara the beloved, and Lara the ballistic? When things were good between us, as they had been the year before, I simply washed her postal periods from my mind. Or rather, I tucked them into some hidden compartment called "the past," a chamber in which our family threw everything that was dangerous and scary. We pretended—no, we *believed*—that nothing from the past could ever return to haunt us. I rarely thought about our childhood fights, and when I did, I shrugged them off. Whatever had happened in the past, I told myself, couldn't have been as bad as I remembered. In any case, it was over and done with. We were fine.

But now part of me felt relieved that hospital staff—*people outside my family*—had seen Lara when she was like that. So it was real. There were witnesses. There was a record.

"The following day, they put her back on the general ward," my mother said. "She called me afterward. She was very angry." My mother lowered her voice. "She demanded that I get her out of there, that it was all my fault."

I said nothing, but my heart broke for my mother, whom I held blameless. *Lara's crazy*, I thought. *How could she guilt-trip Mom like that?* But then again, maybe Mom wasn't so innocent after all. Why was she always catering to Lara's shit?

Sitting at the kitchen counter that night, I felt ashamed that I'd known nothing about Lara's hospitalization—I'd been encased in my own little bubble those past weeks while Lara and my parents had been flying through the woods of mental illness. My own meltdown during my race seemed so insignificant by comparison, it didn't even warrant mentioning. Instead I felt overwhelmed by the larger family drama—angry at my sister, sorry for my mother; angry at my mother, sorry for my sister. I couldn't sort it out.

"How long will she be there?"

Mom shrugged. "It all depends on how she does." Then she added, "You mustn't say a word of this to anyone."

Of course not, I thought. Secrets were the lifeblood of our family. No one must know that Lara was in a mental institution; her future was at stake, her brilliant career as a physician. Not even Zosia would ever be told.

———

It would be many years before I realized the connection between my mother's leaving Lara at the Institute that day, and an earlier separation that had occurred long before Lara was born. It was in October 1942, Mom told us, when she left her parents, cut her hair short, dressed up as an Italian soldier, and escaped to join Zosia in Rome. Her mother had talked her into leaving them and saving herself. Mom never saw her parents again. They were killed in a death camp months later. Mom had been twenty-three at the time—two years older than Lara was when Mom and Dad dropped her off at the Institute. Both separations, thirty-three years apart, were surrounded by secrecy, shame, and a sense of irrevocable loss. Leaving Lara at the Institute, I now realize, must have been excruciating for my mother, and she would never let it happen again, no matter how desperately ill Lara might become in the years ahead.

———

It cost a fortune, Dad told me years later. To prevent any record of my sister's hospitalization, my parents didn't file for insurance; my father footed the entire bill himself. My parents told Lara's college that my father had suffered a heart attack; they made this up as the reason for Lara's leave of absence.

Around the same time, my father installed a single foldout couch in the basement of his office on State Street. Also a refrigerator and a little ice-cube-size shower stall. He drove me to the office to show it to me. "I did this for a reason," he said in a low voice.

I tried to read his face, the deep lines around his eyes, the sharp dagger of his jaw. He looked away from me. "Mom and I are going to get a divorce."

It took a moment for this to sink in. No one had mentioned divorce since I was little, at the Hoffman Children and Family Center. I stared at him now as he turned to face me. His eyes were red. Everyone I loved was falling apart.

It wasn't until Thanksgiving that I saw Lara. She'd gotten a pass from the Institute to come home for the holiday, and she sat hunched over the kitchen counter or in the living room—wherever we were—just picking, picking, picking at her nails. *Look what you've done to me,* she seemed to be saying. It didn't matter that she'd signed herself into the nuthouse; we were all accountable and we were all guilty.

At the end of the weekend, my mother drove Lara and me to Hartford to drop Lara off at the hospital, and then to Springfield, so I could catch the bus back to Boston. The three of us rode the Mass Pike in silence, Mom gripping the wheel at sixty miles an hour, my sister in the passenger seat, face hidden in a duck blind of dark-brown hair. And I sat in the backseat, staring out the window at the trees whizzing by.

What was going through my mother's mind, taking one daughter

to a mental institution, and the other to an elite college, a school similar to one that my mother herself had dreamed of attending—if only
she hadn't been Jewish, if only the war hadn't broken out? And what
was my sister thinking, at the age of twenty-one, sitting in the nuthouse, while fifty miles away her college teammates were doing their
workouts in the pool and snapping each other with towels in the
locker room? It must have pissed her off that her little sister was sitting
in the backseat, blithely returning to her undisturbed life with her
friends and classes and freedom as a Wellesley sophomore.

And I, that lucky little sister, what was I thinking, in the heavy silence of that hour-and-a-half ride to the hospital on a cold gray November day in 1975? I remember only how lonely I felt, how bereft,
how empty and angry, yes—*angry* at the oppressive ruins of my family,
the violence and tragedy of its past, and the hopelessness of its present. My life, such as it was, belonged to them and not to me. I did not
know who I was without them, and I hated myself for who I was with
them.

It was around noon when we arrived at the Institute and went up
to Lara's floor, the solid *clunk-clunk* of doors locking behind us as we
moved down the hall. The air was stifling. Wisps of mental patients in
bathrobes drifted by with empty eyes. The shiny linoleum floors and
the whispering sadness.

Lara showed us her room that she shared with another patient,
who, thank God, was not there. My mother started putting away the
clothes she'd washed for Lara. This made me inexpressibly sad, and I
could not bear to watch. I turned toward the window, but it had black
metal bars, and I could not bear to see that either. Lara didn't belong
here any more than I did, I thought. It was such an obvious mistake—

couldn't everyone see that? She was nothing like those husks of women sitting in front of the TV or standing around the common room like dandelion fluff.

Mom talked quietly while Lara and I stared at the floor. At last it was time to go. Mom left a tin of linzer torte on Lara's dresser and hugged her good-bye. Lara and I exchanged a quick nod, both of us ashamed to be there. Then Mom and I walked to the end of the hall where a nurse buzzed us through the doors, then down the stairs, and out into the exquisite blast of cold November air.

Mom and I said little as she drove me to the bus station. "She's doing so much better," she said when we hugged good-bye.

That night I lay awake in my dorm room, unable to scrub the images of the Institute from my mind. The barred windows. The dead eyes of the women in robes and slippers, sitting like stones on the dreary couch in front of the TV in the common room, staring at *Days of Our Lives*.

———

Another sleepless night, a mounting anxiety, and I felt a growing urge to tell someone. The more I wrestled it down, the more urgent it felt. What was I after?

Attention, I thought, horrified—the most shameful, weak, and egotistic form of self-indulgence in the world. What's more, I wanted attention for problems that weren't even mine! After all, *I* wasn't in the hospital. My parents were right—I was selfish.

At last I broke. In early December, I knocked on Carrie Hanson's door. She was our resident assistant, a slim-hipped psych major and natural-born caretaker of the needy and forlorn. I sat on her neatly made bed and told her my sister was in a mental hospital and my parents were getting a divorce, and I was breaking the rules by talking about it. She held me while I cried, and murmured reassurance. Still, I felt strangely detached from myself, afraid that I was making a big deal out of nothing. I felt vaguely false and guilty—like a well-fed dog scavenging for scraps from the neighbors, when I had it better than most.

"Helen, you know, maybe you should talk to someone at Campus Counseling. They're really good."

I reeled back. "No way!" I said. "That's exactly what got my sister into this mess! The shrinks *totally* screwed her up."

Carrie nodded, her eyes a beautiful blue that made me want to touch her face. "Okay," she said. "It's completely up to you. Anyway, you can always come talk to me."

I thanked her and stood, embarrassed and a bit confused. *What am I doing?* I felt the sharp bones of her shoulder blades as she hugged me again. Then I went out for a walk under the stars. The darkness felt good. But as the days went by, I still couldn't shake it—I felt haunted by my sister and trapped by my parents' insistence on silence. Finally I decided to tell Harriet, although I didn't know what I wanted or expected from her. Did I think she would love me more if I told her? Feel sorry for me? Hug me? At lunch one day I forced myself to say, "There's something I want to tell you."

Harriet cocked her head in the most adorable way—as a puppy might, waiting for what would come next.

"Um, my sister—she's in a mental hospital. I went to see her over Thanksgiving."

Harriet paused, knit her eyebrows together, and said, "I'm sorry."

Then, a silence that was awkward for both of us, and I changed the subject. We never spoke of it again.

————

By mid-December, I had finished reading all 1,534 pages of Samuel Richardson's *Clarissa* for my eighteenth-century English lit class. Now I was chugging through *Pamela; or, Virtue Rewarded*, another overwritten brick about a teenager who gets abducted and locked up and endures repeated attempts at rape, until she falls in love with her captor. My English major exhilaration was wearing thin.

I moved joylessly from class to carrel and back to class. The snows came, rowing season was over, and I didn't go to Harriet's dorm anymore. She and I were both on the basketball team, but I withdrew into myself and she let me be. Mom called to tell me that Lara was improving, and the doctors were very pleased. "It looks like they'll release her in time for Christmas!" my mother said cheerfully.

The prospect of spending Christmas with my parents and Lara made me break out in a cold sweat. I wanted out from my family. I wanted to be free, light, unburdened. Long ago, Emma had invited me to California for winter break, and now Harriet invited me to spend Christmas with her family in Minneapolis.

I did the unthinkable. I wrote my parents a letter saying that I could not face going home, and that I wanted to go to Harriet's for Christmas, and to Emma's for winter break.

My parents let me go. They did not forgive me.

eight

February 2002

Aquarter of a century after refusing to go home to my family for Christmas as a college sophomore, I was driving to Schenectady on the Mass Pike as a disowned daughter. I'd gotten the name of the New York estate lawyer from a friend in Boston who had told me I should contest my father's will. I had never communicated with my family through a lawyer before—but then again, I'd never been legally pronounced dead by my family, so the situation called for adaptation all around.

I paid the toll at the exit ramp and thought about the nearby house in which I'd grown up, the house in which my mother was now sleeping. I no longer had rights to anything in that house—not to the artwork or the sculptures or the Oriental rugs or the Barcelona chairs or the piano that I'd dutifully practiced each day. Everything now belonged to my sister, the beneficiary, trustee, and heir to my parents' kingdom.

I considered following Natchaug Road north to the house. It was still early; the sun would be slanting through the pines outside Mom's

window. I would creep in through the basement and steal up the stairs
and remove the Emilio Greco drawings from their hooks on the walls
and swipe the statues from the immaculate coffee table and leave in silence. My mother, who could have slept through the bombing of Dres-
den, would wake a few hours later and realize slowly that something
had happened. But it would be so quiet, so dark, so free of any sign of
overt violence, that it would all fit precisely into the contours of her
own actions. She did not like to think of herself as an aggressor, but
here it was: she'd effectively killed off one daughter. How fitting for
the dead daughter now to strike before dawn, without a word, without
a drop of blood, and take back what was hers—that is, the right to a
piece of the past, the most beautiful piece, the part of my mother's life
that had offered promise and hope and beauty.

Instead, I continued downtown to the lawyer's office. I arrived
early and let the dog off leash for a romp in Central Park. He found a
tree branch and carried it proudly in his mouth, prancing across the
white expanse of snow. Less than an hour later, I left him in the car at
a ticking meter on State Street, while I met with the lawyer on the
top floor of an office building. His hourly rate was eight times more
than I made as a public defender in Boston. He was terribly civilized,
which, I came to realize, was worth paying for, under such circumstances.

———

1976

Lara managed to get herself sprung from the Institute after three
months, which was sort of a world record at the time, when patients

could linger for years. "That place was straight out of Kafka," she said. She sat slumped at the kitchen counter in her college T-shirt that was torn at the neck. Her arms were tanned and strong, and she sat with an athlete's disregard for space; her legs straddled the chair like separate beings, and although she was not particularly large, her limbs were everywhere. Her face looked thinner than usual, her mouth puckered so her cheeks puffed out. I felt a pang of regret for making fun of her chubby cheeks as a kid.

We were home at the end of my spring semester, sitting side by side at the counter, staring out the window. In the woods next to Mom's rock garden, my father had erected his latest squirrel-proof bird feeder—a giant spaceship-looking contraption suspended from a high tree branch, and draped with curving sheets of aluminum. Squirrels were leaping onto it from nearby trees, but they kept sliding off the aluminum and falling to the ground.

I shifted uneasily. Part of me wanted to pretend Lara's hospitalization had never happened. Another part of me wanted to hear all of it— every gruesome, painful detail—as if by absorbing Lara's experience, I could assuage my guilt for having skipped out on her. I still pictured those shiny corridors of the Institute, the barred windows, the provocative beauty of the landscaped lawns and gardens below. As sisters, we were supposed to get the same servings of meat and potatoes, success and failure, good and bad luck. Perhaps I feared retribution, since I believed—in my medieval sense of sibling justice—that now that she was out, she would make sure I suffered as much as she had.

"How come you signed yourself in?" I asked.

She didn't answer, and picked at a piece of skin on her thumb. "The whole place was a complete crock," she finally said. "I couldn't believe how crazy it was. I went to all their bullshit therapy and 'activities' classes, and just played along. I never told them anything I was really thinking or feeling." She snickered. "I learned to be a good little patient, and just said whatever they wanted to hear."

Lara's bitterness reminded me of my father's. I thought of the stories he'd told me about his years as a prisoner in Siberia, when he too had kept his own counsel. Lara's escape from the Institute sounded similar. She'd outwitted the system, and I admired her for that. She hadn't let them swallow her whole.

"The real problem," she said, "is the shrinks. They have no clue what's going on, but they have all this power. It's like *Cuckoo's Nest*, you know?"

I'd seen the movie with Emma in Berkeley a few months earlier over winter break, and I'd felt as if the walls of the theater were closing in on me. The Jack Nicholson character, a puckish small-time criminal, gradually gets ground down by the rigid rules of the mental hospital. *My sister's in a place like that*, I thought. What right did I have to be at a movie theater in California?

A dull thump startled us; a squirrel had dive-bombed my father's bird feeder and now clung, spread-eagled, to the giant curved sheet of aluminum. The contraption swung wildly, and the squirrel hung on for a second or two before sliding off and hitting the ground. He shook his tail with irritation, then ran up the tree again, preparing for his next attempt.

Just like us, I thought. All four of us were throwing ourselves at one another over and over, desperate to get the goodies. Love, I suppose. Love was the birdseed we all wanted in my family, but we kept slamming into these crazy barriers between us.

"If not for swimming," Lara said, "I would have gone completely nuts."

"They had a pool?"

"No, they didn't have shit for exercise. But there was a Y a few blocks away, and as long as I behaved myself, they'd give me a pass, so I could walk to the Y and swim every day." She propped her elbows on the counter and held her forehead in her hands. "That's what saved me," she said. "If I hadn't found that pool, I don't know how I would have survived."

I nodded. I relied on rowing and running to protect myself from the chaos of my own mind. Lara and I were alike that way.

"I'll tell you one thing," she said. "I'm never talking to another shrink in my life." She looked me in the eye. "Just stay clear of them, Helen."

Psychiatry had certainly fucked her up; that was obvious. I took this advice to heart, since I was well aware of the deep cracks in my own foundation. Of course, back then, neither Lara nor I could have imagined that one day she would *be* a psychiatrist.

———

I never told Lara or anyone else what had happened while I was with Emma in Berkeley a few months earlier during my winter break of 1976. I didn't understand it myself, and I wouldn't admit it for years.

The day I arrived, a classmate of Emma's, Hugh Mattling, a tall, loose-limbed lunk of a boy, took us out to dinner in San Francisco. I sat in the backseat of his tiny Datsun as he circled the block, looking for a place to park. He wanted to show off a great little German restaurant he had found, and he made a big deal of ordering us Weissbier with raspberry syrup. We sipped and talked. I didn't like the way he looked at Emma, the way his blue eyes lit up, the way he blushed and smiled with those winsome dimples, the way his long dark hair fell over his face when he leaned in to her. He barely looked at me, as if I were a knapsack on the chair next to her.

A waitress came by in a dirndl, which I thought was overdoing it a bit. Fake grapevines hung from the ceiling to suggest a biergarten, and the menu was written in Gothic script. Hugh advised us what to order; he said the spaetzle were quite good.

I had flown across the country to spend my winter break with my best friend. I did not want to share her with anyone, and certainly not this guy, with his long, smooth arms and strong shoulders. You could see the muscles rippling under his shirt. Emma was mine, not his. But as I sat across the table from Hugh, I was surprised at the intensity of my feelings. Why did he grate on my nerves so? His head lolled, as if he had weak neck muscles. *He's lazy*, I thought. *Too lazy to lift his lovely head of hair.*

But now he was telling Emma about seat-racing on the Cal rowing team last semester, about getting up before dawn to lift weights and do sprints before practice. And he was going to double major in biology and environmental science and hike the Pacific Crest Trail.

Okay, so he wasn't lazy; I still hated him. What was my problem? He was a perfectly nice guy. Who cared if he was hitting on her? She too was long-limbed and athletic, and with her sparkling blue eyes and easy laugh, her silky blond hair that fell below her shoulders, she looked good sitting next to him. She was beautiful in an unselfconscious, almost accidental way. I was lucky, I told myself; I would always be her best friend, her *friend* friend. Hugh and I weren't rivals. Why did I always have to be so competitive?

After dinner, Hugh drove us home and invited himself in to see Emma's apartment near the university. It was a small studio with two twin beds. Her roommate was out of town, so I had spread my sleeping bag on her roommate's bed. While I was brushing my teeth, Emma came up to me. "Helen," she whispered. "Um . . . he wants to sleep over!" She laughed nervously. "I mean, I don't know how to get him out of here!"

What a jerk, I thought. I was relieved that Emma seemed to think so too. I felt for her; we were both young and inexperienced, and neither of us wanted to appear . . . well, young and inexperienced.

"Are you okay with that?" she asked.

I shrugged, affecting nonchalance. "Sure," I said. "I don't care." To say anything else would have been unthinkably uncool.

After washing up, I got into bed. Emma laid a sleeping bag on the floor for Hugh, brushed her teeth, and climbed into bed while Hugh took his turn in the bathroom. He came out and flicked off the lights. Next I heard them whispering. "Hugh! You can't just—" Then the rustling of sheets. "Ow! What are you . . ." My ears pricked up, every nerve in my body on high alert. I held my breath, listening: Snuffled giggles. Sheets swishing. My heart was pounding so hard it seemed it would fly out of my chest. Momentary quiet, then more giggles. What should I do? It was up to her to throw him out, not me. I remained tense, listening. It was nearly dawn before I fell asleep.

The next day, after Hugh left, Emma apologized. "I didn't think he was going to *get into bed* with me!" she said. "Not that we did anything—but that's not what I had in mind!"

I waved it off, relieved that she too had been shocked, but hadn't known what to do. It seemed obvious that now she would tell him she wasn't interested. But she didn't. Hugh came over the next day, and the day after that. He walked Emma to their first day of classes, and since I had another few weeks before my semester started back east, I tagged along. Soon it was apparent that Hugh was not going away, and despite Emma's assurances to me that she didn't like him "that way," his persistence seemed to be working. He and Emma became more or less inseparable. Not knowing what to do with myself, I spent hours wandering up and down Telegraph Avenue in Berkeley. I was utterly unconscious of my attraction to Emma; my feelings of physical longing were buried deep beneath the ocean floor of my awareness. Instead, what I felt was an insatiable hunger for sweets.

While Emma went to her classes, I started going from one bakery to another, eating pastries, cookies, muffins, chocolate—and washing everything down with ice cream sundaes. With horror, I saw myself as a giant steam shovel, rolling down the sidewalk, taking out entire city blocks of pastry shops.

I didn't gain much weight because in the evenings I went for long runs up the fire trails in the Berkeley hills, sometimes with Emma, and sometimes alone, trying to understand what was wrong with me. *Starting tomorrow*, I would tell myself reasonably, as if I were someone I could trust, *no more sweets*. The next morning, I would feel strong and good, and I'd eat breakfast with Emma and walk her to classes, and then I'd wander the bookshops and cafés of Berkeley. And then it would happen. Like a sudden tidal shift, some overpowering force rose up within me and drove me into a bakery. It was as if I'd lost control over where my feet took me. I felt like a serial killer—no, a serial eater—someone criminal, dangerous.

"Um, could I have a chocolate chip cookie, please?" I asked the girl behind the counter. My voice sounded like someone else's—higher, more tightly strained than my own. *It's okay. One cookie can't hurt.*

The girl slipped the cookie into a paper bag.

"Um, maybe two," I said, feeling my face burn. *I'll save one for later. I'll give it to Emma tonight.*

I waited till I was outside before opening the bag and peeking inside. I inched my hand in and broke off a small piece. It was still warm, and the taste was exquisite. But then I felt a prick of panic. *What am I doing? I'll get fat! Where is my fucking self-control?*

To shut myself up, I shoved half a cookie into my mouth and ate it so quickly I could not object. Without even thinking, I tore into the second cookie. In seconds, both were gone. I crumpled the paper bag and looked for a trash can to get rid of the evidence. Suddenly I was starving. I couldn't go back into the same bakery, the girl behind the counter would think I was a pig. I crossed the street to another shop, and bought a dozen cookies and brownies and chocolates. I walked down the street and ate everything, one after the other, until I had completely filled myself with shame and self-loathing.

———————

Months later, Lara and I were sitting at the kitchen counter watching squirrels blitz Dad's bird feeder, and she told me about her experience in the Institute of Living. Of course it was the shrinks, I agreed. They had driven her crazy. Lara and I were in the same boat, facing the same pressures to succeed, to become superstars that our parents could be proud of. If Lara could go crazy, so could I.

"I quit premed," I told her, an offering of my own failure. "I decided to major in English." Maybe it wasn't as great a failure as losing a semester to the Institute, but it was an effort to bring us closer to-gether.

"Good for you," she said.

"So I'm thinking maybe law school or something. You know, it's only three years. And there are no prerequisites."

She nodded. "Yeah, that sounds a lot better."

We fell silent, exhausted from our tiny admissions, and commit-ted to our greater silences, allied in the daunting production of grow-ing up.

part two

nine

Lara and I grew closer over the next few years, hiking and biking and skiing together on our vacations as if we'd never had a disagreement in our lives. By the summer of 1978 we were in nearly perfect alignment. We had both graduated from college. Lara had just been accepted into medical school, and I had gotten into law school, and we had almost a month to relish our good fortune—until September, when the grim reality of actually going to medical school and law school would drastically reduce our exuberance.

We decided to spend our last two weeks of August together hiking in the White Mountains. We crammed our tent, stove, and sleeping bags into two expedition backpacks, drove north to New Hampshire, and parked at a trailhead in Franconia. We hoisted our gear onto our backs and tore across the Presidential Range. Then we continued through the Mahoosucs into Maine. When we ran out of high peaks, we dropped into the valley, hitched a ride back to our car, and drove farther north in Maine to find another week's worth of hiking. We were in ridiculously good shape, and we galloped over the terrain, bagging peaks at breakneck speed. We wouldn't slow our pace until we reached the tree line, when we allowed ourselves a glance back at the view that had sprung up at our feet—rock ledges that cut the world in two: sky above, boulders below. At the summits we shrugged off our frame packs and guzzled water. Within minutes we saddled up again and scrambled down the trail until our legs burned and our knees felt rubbery.

There was a certain joy to this mad dash through the wilderness, a euphoric blend of mountains, wind, and endorphins run amok. There was no room for rumination. We had become bodies, pure and simple, and our bodies gave us pleasure. They took us through moss-green woods, lush as a fairy tale, and over mist-covered peaks. At the end of the day, we quickly pitched tent, ate a cold snack, and dropped into our sleeping bags like felled timber. Lara woke us at first light, and we broke camp by the time the sun nosed above the horizon.

As long as we kept moving, we were content. We ate little, spoke less, and disappeared into the mountains. Our bodies provided camouflage for our minds; it was our minds that were dangerous. We did not imagine that we were running from ourselves, from the history we held within us. We were only vaguely aware of a looming fear of failure that propelled us faster and faster along the trail. The result was bliss. The mountains gave us everything we needed: a place to run wild.

Toward the end of two weeks, a few signs of problems: Lara's knee gave out; my ankle puffed up. We pushed on until we couldn't walk, and then we limped back to the valley for our final day. When we got back to our car, we were shocked by what we saw in the mirror: dirt-smudged, sunbaked faces with crazy hair, bruised elbows, salt-bleached T-shirts and sweat-stained shorts. We drove the back roads of Maine, looking for the thrill of a general store, a cold soda, a pint of ice cream. We spent a few dollars on gas, a few more on food and two bottles of cheap wine.

Our last night in the mountains, we hiked to a lean-to on a remote mountain lake. The air was soft, and we slipped out of our packs and sat at the edge of the water. In another week we would be in separate cities, starting separate schools. We opened the first bottle and passed it back and forth. It was sweet and sharp, but after a while the taste didn't bother us. The sun slipped through the trees and dropped into the lake. The air turned cool and the water lapped the shore. Loons called to one another. My sister and I were grinning and talking, taking sloppy slugs of wine, and feeling woozy.

"I love you," I told her.

She seemed pleased, almost to the point of tears. "Yeah," she said. "Me too."

"It's like Zosia told me," I said.

"What?"

"Well, it was weird," I said. "The day before we left on this hiking trip, Zosia pulled me aside and said, 'You know, Helen, what the most important thing in the world is? The most important thing of all is the love between two sisters.'"

Lara nodded.

"She said the bond between her and Mom was stronger than anything else in their lives. And she said it made her so happy that you and I are finally devoted to each other, the same way they are."

Lara smiled. I felt very close to her then, brimming over with warmth and love and confidence in our future together. I felt at that moment as if we would always be like this; I dismissed all of the fights in our past in a heartbeat.

"We'll team up," I said. "You and me. Someday we'll go into business together."

"Yeah." She raised the bottle. "I'll take care of you. I'll be your doctor."

I giggled. "And I'll handle all your malpractice claims."

She shoved me playfully and I rolled to the side and bounced back, like those children's weighted punching bags.

"We'll be a 'loctor-dawyer' team," I said.

"Here's to us!" She raised the bottle again and took a swig. "The loctor-dawyer sisters."

We sat at the edge of the lean-to with our arms around each other and stared at the dark lake. Every so often we could see ripples where fish had jumped. The air smelled of summer and freedom, and I felt lucky and sure of myself. I wanted what my mother and aunt had: a sisterhood powerful beyond words. It was enough to topple nations and bring continents to their knees. My sister and I would rule the world. Nothing would separate us.

———

Lara and I got home in time to wash the mountains out of our hair and clothes, spend a night between clean sheets, and pack for our first year of professional school. Our parents beamed with pride that we were going to become a doctor and a lawyer, while Lara and I grew quiet under the descending blade of reality. We nodded to each other as Lara got in her car and drove north to med school in Vermont; I headed east to law school at Boston University.

I'd rented an apartment with two other women on the first floor of a triple-decker in Allston. Our landlady, a squat woman shaped like a jar of gefilte fish, lived upstairs with her two sons in their forties. A few blocks from our apartment, Harvard Avenue crossed Commonwealth Avenue, with its liquor stores and bars with boarded windows. Spanish grocery stores mysteriously opened and closed at will. Our street boasted the highest number of rapes in Boston that year—no small feat, since the competition was fierce. At night we'd run the few blocks from the trolley stop to our apartment with our keys clenched between the fingers of our fists. It took a minute or two to open the two dead bolts and the police lock, and then we were safe. We chained ourselves in till morning.

I wanted to like law school, but the Darwinian atmosphere got to me. In the hallways my classmates argued about the fine points of cases we'd been assigned to read, radiant with the sound of their own voices. It began to dawn on me that I'd made a serious mistake. I was studying law because my mother believed a law degree would come in handy; Uncle had a law degree, and he had used it to save my mother's life in 1942. My classmates, on the other hand, seemed to be in law school because they actually wanted to be *lawyers*. We had nothing in common, I thought.

Heavyweight, 1979

The eating problem I'd acquired in Berkeley three years earlier sprouted up with a vengeance my first year of law school. I would starve myself for days, run great loops around the city, drink liters of diet soda and nibble on iceberg lettuce—all the tricks I'd learned as a lightweight rower in college. A week later, or sometimes only a few days later, I would stuff myself with pints of Häagen-Dazs, unable to control the hand that held the spoon to my mouth.

I came home from my first year of law school in May weighing twenty pounds more than I had at winter break. My mother was alarmed. "Are you eating right?" she asked. "Yeah," I said with a shrug, "I guess so." I was too ashamed to admit my bingeing to anyone. But I could see that Lara, an Eating Disorder Lifer, was eyeing me with a knowing satisfaction; she knew exactly what was up with me. We silently sized each other up now, calculating who was keeping her weight down, and who was losing the battle.

My father sent me to see an endocrinologist, to rule out some kind of hormone or blood chemistry problem. I played along, and was not surprised when everything turned out to be fine. The doctor was about my parents' age—sixtysomething—a tall, trim man in a starched white lab coat. He invited me into his office to tell me the results.

"Great," I said. "Thanks." I stood to leave, but he didn't, so I sat back down.

"Tell me," he said slowly, "are you happy?"

I nearly fell off my chair. This struck me as an inappropriate violation of my privacy. "Yes!" I said, shocked by the implication that I might not be. "I'm very happy." *Of course I'm happy! There's nothing psychologically wrong with me!* "Except about my weight," I added.

"You're sure?"

"Of course!"

He shrugged and stood, shook my hand, and wished me luck.

My parents were relieved that nothing was wrong with me, and that was the end of it. I dropped the weight after a few weeks of virtuous dieting and running. But soon I found myself once again eating on the sly. I ate for solace and for company and for fun. I ate out of rage and fear and shame. I focused all these feelings into everything I ate and turned them into a larger, more undeniable problem: Helen the Overweight. In the month of August alone, I had gone from a trim 135 pounds to a shameful 150. Weight had become a measure of my self-worth.

As September approached, I finally confessed to my mother that I had a problem with eating. She consulted my sister, and they both decided that what I probably needed was a carefully circumscribed intervention.

"*Behafe-your modifeecation,*" my mother said.

"Stay away from Freud," Lara said. "You don't want anyone messing around with your childhood and all that crap. Just tell them you want behavior modification."

"Right," Mom said. "No digging up the past. Just to control the appetite."

"I'd like behavior modification," I told the Mass Mental Health Center when I called, as if ordering a lunch special.

They gave me names. Before fall classes started, I drove out to Newton to meet a shrink named Martin Flak in his psychiatric empire called Learning Therapies, Inc. It was a huge Victorian on Walnut Street, filled with therapists. I wore a large green tent of a dress and embarrassed myself by leaking tears when I told Dr. Flak about my problem with food.

"It's a question of who's in control," he said.

This struck me as the most brilliant thing anyone had said to me in my life. I thought he was a genius. I nodded and blew my nose. Then he suggested I might be a good candidate for psychotherapy.

"Oh no," I said, alarmed. "I just need to lose a few pounds."

He gave me an appointment for another session a week later. I left his office and went home, changed into running shoes and shorts, and went for a run. A thread of hope slipped through me, and as the traffic thinned and the sun rose higher, I ran with relief in my newfound mental health. I was cured. It was a miracle.

I returned home, showered, and made myself a salad. The next day I was fine. I ran. I studied. I ate sensibly. I was happy.

A week later I returned to the shrink, and told him I was all set. He seemed surprised and pleased. He suggested I keep a daily log of my eating and exercise.

I met with him weekly all fall. I lost tons of weight. I increased my running to sixty-five miles a week. I chatted with Dr. Flak about my progress, and he chatted with me about his own running regimen, and together we spent a lot of Blue Cross Blue Shield's money, without ever having to look at what might be wrong.

———

Like my mother, I had always been able to arrange my denial in such a way as to enjoy the illusion that I was mostly just fine, at least compared to everyone else. Lara, on the other hand, was so painfully in touch with her feelings that she was incapable of self-deception. As long as I had Lara around to act like a maniac, it was easy for me to preserve my ignorance of the extent of my own problems. Perhaps the same was true for my mother. It would be years before I could see that our family drama served as a brilliant, albeit uncalculated, distraction from the past that Mom and her sister kept hidden from us. But all that would come later. Back in our twenties—the same age at which our parents had suffered through a *real* war—Lara and I found ourselves engaged in battles with ourselves that felt shameful, strange, and unjustifiable.

September 1979

Another thing happened that fall. Right before classes started, Emma—more or less out of the blue—came to Boston. We hadn't seen each other in four years. She and her new boyfriend, Travis, an Alaskan bush pilot, had rented a Cessna, flown from Berkeley to Boston, and landed at my doorstep. Emma was starting grad school at BU while Travis finished up college in California. "You and I can room together!" she said.

Seeing her again was like being blindsided by a Mack truck of joy. I felt as if I'd spent the past few years living in a tunnel underground. She'd flown east, and the sun came up.

We waved good-bye to Travis and set up house together. I was ecstatic. Every morning we bicycled to classes, and at the end of the day, after my run, we fixed dinner and talked. We spent our weekends together when we weren't studying. Gone were my eating problems, gone was my excess weight, life was good. At twenty-two, I still wasn't aware of wanting to hold her hand, or drape an arm over her shoulders, or touch her face, her neck, her arms. I was happy just being with her. The fact that she had a boyfriend in California was fine with me. Even law school was tolerable now, and I started thinking maybe I'd actually be a lawyer after all. I was doing an internship with Greater Boston Legal Services that year, so after classes I biked to the GBLS office, put on a suit, and picked up cases assigned by my supervisor. I liked my clients; they mattered to me in a way that my equity and evidence classes did not. When I won a case, I felt I'd actually helped someone; I felt important and grown-up, with just the hint of an underlying feeling that I didn't know what I was doing.

But a few weeks before Christmas, Emma came running into my room to tell me her good news. "Travis and I are getting married!" she said. "Next summer! Oh, H, I'm so excited!" She did a little dance of joy.

Oh, wow, I thought. My life was over. *Over.*

"It's a secret, okay? We're not going to tell my parents or anyone till Christmas. Promise me you won't say a word."

I nodded. I still didn't know why Emma's news was so devastating to me.

"Travis is flying out here to take me home." Her eyes lit up, and her blocky nose was strangely endearing. "We're going to drive back to California together. And I'm going to take next semester off and prepare for the wedding!"

I forced a smile, and in a fit of friendship, I stood and embraced the love of my life. I was stunned with grief.

"That's wonderful," I said. "I'm so happy for you."

I *was* happy for her. It was me I felt sorry for. "Let's have some champagne." I searched the refrigerator, although I knew we had nothing but a heel of white table wine.

"H, you have to come out next summer, okay? It'll be our last time together, just you and me, before the wedding in August."

"But I have to get a job," I said. "With a law firm or something."

"My dad knows tons of lawyers in Sacramento," she said.

This was encouraging. I could spend the summer with her, and maybe then I'd just move out to the West Coast myself. Maybe I'd get a job there after law school, and I could be near her all the time. My heart opened to the possibilities.

But the fact was, Emma was going to leave me. In three weeks she would be gone, and I'd be alone with my equity and evidence notes and Greater Boston Legal Services. I didn't really understand what I was losing, but I knew that the loss was almost too much to bear.

When Travis arrived a few weeks later, Emma seemed to burst into flower. She wore a goofy grin on her face all the time. She was unbearably happy. So was Travis. They were in love, they did not even see me, and that was probably a good thing. I helped them pack up the car with her backpack, clothes, books, hiking boots, running shoes, and tennis racket. I waved to them as they backed down the driveway.

Then I laced up my sneakers and went for a two-hour run. I studied for finals. I went to the legal aid office and helped poor people fight their landlords and the government and their lousy lot in life. I went to therapy and talked about moving to California.

———

Two weeks later I went home for the holidays. On Christmas Eve, my father and I were sitting around the fireplace reading. Lara flopped into the green sling-back chair next to me, one leg hooked over the chair arm. My father hated it when we didn't sit properly in a chair. He believed it was bad for the furniture. But Lara was twenty-five years old; he glanced at her swinging foot and said nothing. She'd come home the day before, absorbed in a corona of her own rage after squeaking through her fall semester of medical school on the slimmest margin of mental health.

"Helen!" She kicked the leg of my chair.

"What?"

"Helllenn. . . . Helllenn. . . . Helllenn. . . ." She punctuated each word with a kick.

"What do you want?"

"I want to go out and do something with you." Her voice was angry; it sounded like an offer to throw me off a cliff.

"I don't feel like going out," I said. "It's freezing outside."

Mom brought out a tray of cheese and crackers, set it on the coffee table, and sat down to join us. Lara leaned forward as if to take a cracker, but instead picked up a paper napkin. Very slowly, she tore it into small strips, and let the pieces float to the floor. When she reached for another napkin, my mother placed her hand on Lara's. "Darling," she said. "Talk to me. I know you're upset. Please tell me what's bothering you."

Lara yanked her hand away. "Leave me alone! Go cook your precious Christmas dinner!"

My mother's eyes welled. She stood and retreated to the kitchen. Soon we could hear her chopping vegetables and preparing the turkey. My father, sitting across from me, said nothing, but his hands tensed on the business section of the *Times*. I picked up my book and reread the same paragraph.

Lara started kicking my chair again, and I asked her to stop.

"Make me," she snickered.

I ignored her. The words on the page ran together and I couldn't concentrate on the sentences. I let my eyes ride the coattails of the words, hoping to pick up their meaning as I went along. Lara kicked my chair harder. I could feel the heat rise in my ears. I closed my book. Night had fallen, and our living room was reflected like a Rembrandt in the floor-to-ceiling windows behind the fireplace. I got up and went to my room, locked the door behind me, and flopped onto my bed. I opened my book and began again.

Within minutes, I heard a thump on my door. I sat up, and it came again. *Thunk.* It sounded like Lara was pounding the door with something—her fist? Her foot? I tried to keep reading. The noise grew louder, more rapid. *Thunk. Thunk. Thunk.* I closed my eyes and waited. How many years? My sister was a second-year med student, learning to save lives. Her classmates at school liked her; she was thoughtful and considerate, an ideal roommate in the house she shared with half a dozen other budding doctors. How did she pull it off? *Thunk.* Maybe the supreme effort of holding herself together in the world was so exhausting, she simply fell apart when she got home.

Thunk. I fought the urge to scream now, to blast from my room and bash her head against the brick wall. Instead I remained on my bed, book open, eyes closed. The pounding seemed to make a small explosion at the base of my skull every two seconds. I had nine more days of vacation before I was due back at school for the second semester. I wasn't sure how long I could hold out.

I finally opened the door and found Lara sitting on the floor in front of it, legs splayed, a tennis ball in her hand. So that's what she'd been doing—throwing a stupid tennis ball at my door, over and over. I stepped over her legs and returned to the living room, where my mother was picking up the shredded napkin from the rug. I sat in the chair across from my father. Lara followed me and collapsed into the chair next to mine, and started kicking my chair again.

"Lara," I said in a tired voice, "cut it out." It took all my concentration to keep my voice calm.

She took a balled-up Kleenex from her pocket and tossed bits of it at me, laughing.

"Come on, Lara, just leave me alone. I want to read."

"So read," she said.

I glanced at my father, who sat stone-still, holding his book in his lap, pretending to read. His newspaper had already gone up in flames in the fireplace. I returned to my book, resolute. Bits of Kleenex landed in my hair and on my shirt and in my lap. Finally I got up and went into the kitchen. "Can I borrow the car keys?" I asked my mother.

"Why?" she asked, alarmed.

"I want to go for a ride," I said. "I want to see if I can find something."

"What?"

"It's a surprise." In fact, I wanted to find a coffee shop where I could sit in peace and read my book. But I knew this would upset my mother.

"It's Christmas Eve," she said. "Stay here with us. Let's be together as a family."

"She's driving me crazy," I said.

A sad look came over my mother's face, and my heart ached for her. "Oh, Helen. She can't help it. She's not well."

A wave of guilt washed over me. If my parents had to deal with her, then so should I. After all my parents had been through—the war, the camps, the killings—I owed them my loyalty. The least I could do was be with them now.

"We all have to try," my mother said. "We have to do our best."

I took the car keys. I drove through the empty streets of town in a snow squall, and headed east toward the shopping mall. I pulled into the Tri-City Diner, open twenty-four hours a day. A glass tower of pies and cakes rotated at the entrance. I slid into a booth near the window and opened my book. And I began to cry.

———

Years later, during an interval when Lara and I were the best of friends, I sometimes broached the subject of those times when she had acted like this, when she'd soaked our house in her silent rage. The few times I tried to talk with her about it, her body sank as if I'd struck her: her head dropped, face drawn in pain, and she squirmed with such discomfort, I could not bring myself to pursue it further. It was too painful to talk about the damage we had all done to each other in the past. Like our parents, Lara and I left those storms alone, survived them as best we could, and tried to enjoy the moments of reprieve when we got along well.

———

Christmas morning the sun crashed through the woods outside our house. I could hear the coffeemaker gurgling in the kitchen. The news was on the radio: the Soviet Union had invaded Afghanistan. From the living room, I heard a violin sobbing on the hi-fi. I found my mother in the kitchen in her home-sewn bathrobe, her hair standing up in stiff peaks like whipped egg whites. "Oh," she said, "put on slippers!" Then she tilted her chin up, kissed me on the cheek, and said, "Good morning, how did you sleep?" Before I could answer, she pointed to my feet. "Slippers!"

The heat came through the floor and felt good on my bare feet. I went back to my room for slippers.

My father joined us in the kitchen. He'd been up since six, as usual. He'd shoveled the path around the house, filled the bird feeder, brought in another load of wood, and built a fire. Now he pulled out a stool and sat at the kitchen counter as my mother poured us coffee. We stared out the window at the squirrels stealing seeds from the bird feeder. This drove my father crazy. He jumped to his feet and reached for the kitchen door.

"It's Christmas," my mother said. "Let them eat."

————

At noon Mom went to check on my sister. I followed quietly. Lara's bedroom was dark, drapes drawn.

"Lara?" My mother's voice sounded tentative. She leaned over my sister. "Lara, darling? It's noon. Come to the living room. Come join us. It's Christmas."

"Mrrrrmph." Lara rolled over under the covers.

Mom waited another minute, then turned and stepped out of the room.

We didn't speak until we reached the kitchen. "Let's have a cup of tea," she said. Mom and I divided time into cups of tea. She placed the kettle on the stove and we began to fill the kitchen with chatter. We loved to talk, my mother and I. She could be so animated, so funny, so opinionated and lively. We would talk about books and movies and opera singers and people we knew and people we didn't. She and I were, as they say, *verbal*. We hid things with words.

The kettle sang. My mother took a used Lipton tea bag from the saucer by the sink. Its waist was cinched by its string, which had dried and turned rust-brown. We could afford a fresh tea bag, but it was a point of pride for my mother to extend the life of a tea bag from hours to days, so as not to waste even a single leaf. I loved this about her, and I followed the ritual in my own kitchen, much to the horror of my roommates over the years. My mother ceremoniously unfurled the string and let the tea bag drop first into one cup, then into the second. She coaxed a bit of color from the bag, then scooped it up, strangled it with its string, and set it on the saucer.

"Do you have a bird feeder?" she asked.

I nodded. Emma had bought us one, and filled it regularly. She cared about living things in a way that I didn't. Something was missing in me.

Behind us we heard the soft scuffing of my sister's bare feet. She rubbed her forehead with the heel of her hand and seemed to be emerging from the bottom of the ocean.

My mother jumped up. "Darling," she said. "Sit! Would you like some tea? Stollen?" She bustled to get the coffee cake from the serving tray. "Let me heat it up for you."

Lara staggered to the counter and collapsed on a stool. It was too soon to tell what would happen. Would she perk up and decide to open presents? Or would she tear her napkin to shreds? I pretended not to care. Everything depended on not caring in our house. You had to suspend all hope. You watched the signals carefully, and tried to assess her mood from moment to moment.

Lara let my mother cut her a slice of stollen. That was good. She let her serve her a cup of tea. That was good. She sipped her tea and blew her nose. All good.

Twenty minutes passed. My father tiptoed into the kitchen. "So are we opening presents?" he asked.

My mother shook her head and motioned him to leave.

Lara finished her tea, rose, and walked into the living room where the Christmas tree was drowning in a sea of gifts. She pushed the hair from her face and straightened her back. A light came into her eyes, and her face was suddenly transformed. She leaned over and picked up a gift. "Here, Helen," she said brightly. "Open this."

For the next few hours we opened presents. We burned the wrapping paper in the fire and put on another log and our faces glowed in the warmth. The floor was covered with our spoils: cross-country ski gloves and glacier goggles and lip gloss. My aunt had sent checks; my mother had bought sheets. My father flipped through the pages of the books we got him, and finally settled on the book about quarks and hadrons. The dog, exhausted, lay at his feet, jowls sunk over the arch of his shoe. A miracle had occurred and we had all pulled it off: we had gone from danger to delight. While it lasted, it seemed that our family had always been this way, that we could never be anything else.

———

Trouble didn't start until the next day. You could feel it when she walked into the kitchen. It was in her posture, the angle of her head, the scowl on her face. Lara dropped onto a kitchen stool, propped her elbows on the counter and scuttled her fingers through her hair. When I left the room, she followed me into the living room, and demanded that I do something with her. I declined and went to my bedroom, closed the door, and locked it.

I was a crucial member of this family, and I was expected to do my part. If I took her out hiking or skiing, at least it would give my parents a few hours' reprieve. But I couldn't rise to the occasion. I didn't *want* to rise to the occasion. I had been through my own semester with my own problems.

Thunk.

I sat up with a jolt.

Thunk.

The tennis ball again. "Helen," she called. *Thunk.*

I opened the door, stepped over her, and went to the telephone. I looked up Greyhound in the Yellow Pages and called for the schedule of buses. Then I told my parents I planned to take the bus to Boston the following morning.

My father looked up, alarmed.

"What?" my mother said.

"I want to go back to Boston."

"But you just got here!"

"I know," I said. "I'm sorry, but I can't take it anymore."

"You and Lara should do something together," my mother said. "Take her skiing."

I bit my lip. The realization that I could actually take a bus and leave home was both heady and disturbing. I couldn't bear to disappoint my parents, and I felt ashamed to leave them alone with Lara. I was shirking my duty as one-third of the family reserve to cope with her.

The next morning, my father drove me to the bus station. We said little. "Do you need money?" he asked. I shook my head. "She is not well," he said.

We hugged outside the bus. He slipped twenty dollars in my pocket.

———

Boston was bleak after Christmas. The students had disappeared overnight and the streets were empty. My apartment was dark; it accused me of family desertion. Emma was gone. I was alone.

A day later, the phone rang. It was my mother. "Helen," she said, "I wish you would come home. Please, darling. Take Lara skiing. Or hiking. It would do her so much good."

I listened to my mother with a growing sense of shame. It did seem like very little to ask of me. Why couldn't I just go home and help my parents out? Last March I'd sped across Massachusetts at midnight, rushing to my sister's side when she'd called in tears. I'd felt proud of my virtue—the heroic daughter, rushing to the rescue—and had taken a perverse satisfaction in my own sacrifice. The glow from mild martyrdom was not so different from the pride I took in not eating, in pushing myself to run farther and faster than ever before. It was mastery of the *self*, and it was precisely this self of mine that had always caused me so much difficulty in my family.

But now I found myself unwilling to sign up for another tour of duty at home. It was hard enough to sort out my own life. I didn't even begin to understand the depth charge of Emma's engagement and move to California. At twenty-two, I had about as much self-knowledge as a seedpod.

"Mom, I can't," I said, trying the words out to see if they would stick. "I'm really sorry."

"Why? What are you doing there?"

The fact was, I was trying to preserve my sanity. "I have some cases I'm working on," I lied.

"Please, Helen. Just take the bus. Let us know when you're coming, and Dad will pick you up. All right, darling? It would be so good for Lara if you could—"

"Mom, I just can't," I said. "I really need to be here right now."

There was a silence on the other end of the phone, and when my mother spoke again, her voice was cold. "All right," she said. "I'll tell you what happened!" I was stunned by her sudden anger. "I didn't want to tell you, but you've left me no choice! After you left, I walked into Lara's room, and do you know what I found? I walked in, and she was lying in the bed, and her arms were covered in blood! Yes! She had cut herself up, and she was bleeding!"

A chill came over me, and I squeezed my eyes tight. Without even thinking, I could feel my arms outstretched to catch my mother's perfectly thrown pass of guilt.

"Do you know what it's like," my mother said, "for a mother to walk in and see her daughter like that? Do you have any idea?"

I was crying now, and rocking myself on the floor. Lara had cut herself up. Because I'd left home. These two thoughts were connected. *Proximate cause. Damages.*

"Now, get on the bus," she commanded, "and you come home."

I pictured my sister in the darkness of her room at the far end of the house. Her arms on the sheets, blood oozing from her wrists, streaming over the covers. Had she passed out? Was she conscious? I couldn't ask.

"I'm sorry," I said weakly, squeezing each word out like dots of glue from a tube. "But I can't come home."

"What?"

"Mom, you can't ask that of me." I didn't dare open my eyes. I was already drowning in guilt, and my mother's pressure felt cruel.

"You have always been selfish," my mother said coldly. "You've always only thought about yourself."

It was true. I did not want to go home. I did not want to save Lara's life. Although I couldn't be sure at the moment, I didn't actually believe that I had caused Lara to cut herself up. Had I? It wasn't my fault, I thought. But part of me believed that it was. Part of me felt that I must now undo what I had done. I did not know whether I could resist the pull to go home and redeem myself. I didn't know if I would be able to live with myself if I didn't.

———

Looking back on those years, I'm struck by how Lara was the focus around which our family revolved. She was our Id du Jour, the gasket we blew when the pressure got too great. Yet Mom and Zosia had always been at the center of the production, pouring all their energy into sealing off the past. Together, we were all sucked into a performance of aggression and loss and fear and betrayal, but the stage on which it was set—suburban America in the late twentieth century—made no sense at all. In the context of our lives in 1980, Lara looked crazy.

It wasn't until a dozen years later, in 1992, that Lara and I would begin to research our family history and discover the secret that our parents and aunt had hidden from us all our lives—that we were Jewish, not Catholic, and we'd lost our entire family in the Holocaust. This revelation in our midthirties would radically change the way we understood our family. Maybe we weren't so crazy after all; maybe it was just our history that was crazy.

ten

It was already late at night when I put on my sweats and sneakers and ran down the empty streets to the river. The skin of the Charles was blistered with ice, and the path was rutted with frozen ski tracks and footprints from what seemed like prehistoric runners.

I was running from the image of my sister, blood pouring down her arms and over the sheets. From the image of my mother walking into Lara's room, the shock of that first impression. I ran past the frozen playing fields and boat slips and tennis courts, deserted and windblown at this time of night. I turned at the Museum of Science and ran back, listening to the river groaning under ice. An occasional car sprayed salt from Storrow Drive.

I spent the next two days running. I found that I could not bear to be still; I couldn't be alone with myself in my apartment. I could not read. As long as I was on the move, sweating, heart pounding, I could hold the feelings at bay. The minute I stopped, I was flooded with guilt and a terrible anxiety.

Emma seemed a world away, on the sunny West Coast of happiness, preparing for her wedding, joyfully in love. I'd lost her not once, but twice. I was in a permanent posture of losing her. Even now, five years after I'd lost her to Hugh in Berkeley, it still did not occur to me that I might be queer or that I was in love with her. I knew only that I was achingly lonely and that I was an impostor—a law student who did not want to be a lawyer, a woman who did not want to date men, a daughter who would not go home. The gap between Emma and me now seemed impossible to bridge. I didn't call her.

And I didn't even consider calling Flak, who was on a ski vacation somewhere. What could he do anyway? This was my problem, and in the grand scheme of things, it really wasn't such a big deal. After all, I wasn't living in a bombed-out building or freezing in a forced labor camp above the Arctic Circle. I needed to grow up and get a grip. It was time to prove to myself and to Flak that I had outgrown my weakness, my dependence on others. Last year I'd lost control and gained weight, but now I was fine. I had to be fine.

Except I was scared of the telephone. Nobody had answering machines in 1980; if the phone rang, you picked it up. I was afraid Mom would call again, and that I'd be sucked back into the vortex. So I took myself to matinees, sometimes one after another. I spent my days in coffee shops, reading novels that failed to distract me. I wrote in my journal. I went to the Greater Boston Legal Services office and pretended to work on my cases. There was nothing, really, that needed my attention.

I kept running: midnight, one, two in the morning. I had no reason to follow the sun. I slept long and hard and dreaded waking. Days flipped over on themselves. I began to nurse my anxiety with coffee cakes and ice cream. I was starting to lose my sense of self-control. I ran and ate and slept and fretted.

And I could not hide from the phone altogether. One evening it rang and rang and rang; I held my breath until it stopped. Then it rang and rang again. I finally unplugged it, but could not remain in its company. I drove aimlessly through the streets of Newton, Brighton, Allston. I wanted desperately to prove that I could survive without my family, that I could flourish, but it was an impossible test. I was sunk from the minute I'd left Schenectady. I was going to have to sabotage everything I did from now on. I did not deserve peace.

Reflections on Suicide

Despite her years of violent moods and crazy behavior, I still had trouble believing Lara had a bona fide mental illness. In public, among friends or acquaintances or even strangers, she was always charming. "She's sick," my mother would tell me in a low voice. "She can't help it."

I believed she was only selectively sick. If I were sick, I thought, I would not do it in such a pantywaist way. I would not limit it to my family or my home or my loved ones. And if I were suicidal, I vowed, I'd do it right. I wouldn't spend all that time threatening to do it, or making half-assed attempts that made everyone wring their hands and talk about "cries for help." Mental illness, I believed, came with moral imperatives. If you were going to kill yourself, you should stop dicking around and just do it.

A week after school started, I received a letter from my father. His sharp handwriting on the envelope seemed to cut my hands. I opened the letter, took a deep breath, and read.

Lara's condition had gotten worse, Dad wrote, and she would not be returning to medical school that semester. They used the old excuse that my father had had a heart attack, and Lara had to stay home to tend to him. The irony was almost too rich, but I recognized it as my family's quintessential solution to the truth.

Lara's psychiatrist had advised my parents to handle Lara with "kid gloves." *She is homicidal,* my father reported, *and suicidal.* Mom was calling Lara's doctor two, three, five times a day: Lara won't get out of bed. Lara won't eat. Lara has found where I hid the knives.

> *We are closely monitoring her medications, to make sure she doesn't hide them. Mom has taken over the role of full-time nurse, to prevent her from having to go into a hospital. Her condition is volatile. She could snap at any minute.*

It had been three years since Lara was institutionalized during college, and it had nearly torn my parents apart. Lara had never forgiven them. My mother would never let it happen again—and despite my father's overbearing presence, it was Mom who held the power in our family.

As I reread Dad's letter, my heart went out to him. What I loved most about it was that he did not suggest that I was the cause of Lara's breakdown, or that I should come home. He simply wanted me to know that their home life was hell. He asked how I was, how my studies were going. *Lara is very angry at you,* my father wrote. *She is fixated on you. Write me at the office.*

I folded the letter and replaced it in its envelope, grateful that my father had extended a hand from behind enemy lines. The suggestion of using his office address was a relief. My letters would be safe there;

Lara wouldn't even know about them. I wrote my father back, telling him that I was fine, that I was busy with classes and studies. I tried to make my life sound interesting and upbeat.

But soon my eating disorder was back in full swing, and I didn't want to admit it to Flak. It was too humiliating to tell him how many gallons of ice cream I was eating, or that I'd missed days and then weeks of running. I gained weight—a pound or two at first, and then a surge: ten, fifteen pounds. I missed Emma. I was listless and losing control, and although I would never say this to him, I was ashamed of letting Flak down. I was afraid that if I didn't perform well, Flak would give up on me.

"Does your father know?" Flak asked.

"Know what?"

"How you are."

I shrugged. "We write. My parents are having a horrible time with Lara."

"Maybe we could have a session with him," Flak said. "Do you think he would be willing to come out and have a session with us?"

The idea appealed to me. I knew my father would never go to a shrink for his own sake, but I was pretty sure he would do so for me. Now that my mother had turned against me, I needed Dad more than ever.

———————

My father and I sat next to each other in identical chairs facing Flak. Dad had driven to Boston that morning in his brand-new Ford Escort, a car that did not do him justice, but one that appealed to his sense of economy.

"Thank you for coming," Flak said. "How are you?"

"The situation at home is very bad," my father said, wasting no time on pleasantries. "We are keeping Lara under twenty-four-hour supervision." His voice was quiet, deep, and matter-of-fact. "My life is anguish."

"Oh, I'm sorry."

"The home is essentially a mental institution."

Flak nodded. He already knew this from the letters I'd been getting from my father. "How do you feel about that?" he said.

My father gazed at the ceiling for a moment. "What I wish for, quite simply, is to put an end to it all."

This sounded pretty normal to me. I too had often wished that we could simply remove Lara from our midst and put an end to our agony. I was only surprised that Dad would say this to a stranger, to Dr. Flak.

"Yes," Flak said, as if he'd been hoping for precisely this sort of confession. "When do you think of this?" He leaned forward and gazed at my father.

Dad's broad forehead was creased now.

"Do you think of this often?" Flak said.

My father shrugged. "Most of the time."

Flak was sitting so far forward in his chair, he was in danger of falling onto the carpet at my father's feet. "And have you thought about how you would go about it?"

Flak's question alarmed me in a way that my father's words had not. Flak, I suddenly realized, was talking about *suicide* here. It had never occurred to me that my coolheaded father was in danger of killing himself. My mother was the one who always wished she'd died with her parents. And it was Lara who was now recuperating from her recent adventure with razor blades. But Dad?

I stared in shock at the two men. Everything else in the room seemed to fall away, and all that was left was the line between their eyes. Neither of them looked in my direction. I had ceased to exist. I was the Soviet bug in the chandelier, the unseen, unacknowledged eavesdropper.

"I'm a physician," my father said. "I have all the means at my disposal."

I felt as if a vacuum cleaner had sucked out my insides. I couldn't listen to this.

Flak nodded. "How close have you come to doing anything?"

His eyes were riveted on my father. Dad was staring out the window now, and I followed his gaze. Suddenly I wanted to bolt from the room, get out of Newton, get out of my own skin.

"You've come pretty close, haven't you?" Flak said.

I looked from my father to Flak. I could barely breathe. Although it didn't occur to me at the time, my claim to pain had been preempted. Dad didn't appear any more depressed than usual, but his declaration of the wish to kill himself was new, and it scared me. He was in worse shape than I was.

My father tilted his head. White hair rose in a column from the top of his head and was combed straight back. "I'm a physician," he repeated. "I have all the means at my disposal."

I pictured Dad in the little lab of his office, concocting a potion that would remove him from his misery. He would calculate the dosage, titrate the chemicals, prepare the syringe, the pills, the *means*.

Flak nodded. Here we were, in the shrink's office, mano a mano with death. The deeper my father and Flak explored his suicide, the more I needed to remove myself from it. I transported myself in my mind to a palatial movie theater with stadium seating; I looked down with a critic's detachment, and considered the performances. The struggle was an ancient one: a father's wisdom and patience succumbing, in the end, to psychological torture. The able young psychiatrist using all of his Harvard training to contain the threat, to ascertain its dimensions, and then, very carefully, to disarm the overwrought hero.

"Have you thought about what it would be like?" Flak asked. It was so lovely, so intoxicating, the degree of attention Flak packed into those words. His entire body—his shoulders, his waist, the muscles in his legs—was poised.

"Yes. Yes. It would be an enormous relief," my father said. He did not sound terribly upset. You could see him going over the steps in his mind. Opening his office door, striding to his lab, flipping on the light switch . . .

"Do you ever think how it might affect Helen?" Flak asked.

My father glanced at me, then back at Flak. "Yes," he said. "That is why I haven't done it yet."

Holy shit, I thought. *I'm the only reason he's still alive.*

My sense of self-importance bloomed, but the pressure made my knees buckle.

———

After the session, my father and I drove in silence back to my apartment. The plan was that he'd return to Schenectady that afternoon. I wondered whether he might put himself out of his misery that night or that week or that month, but I was afraid to ask. I sat up straight, as if to demonstrate reliability and strength. I knew that my own problems— whatever they were—were nothing compared to my family's drama.

Now I needed to focus all my attention on helping my father not kill himself.

My father turned left off Comm Ave and wheeled onto Algonquin Road with élan, which is hard to do in a Ford Escort. Then he pulled into the driveway outside my apartment, but declined to come in. "I don't want to get caught in traffic," he said.

"You should call him, Dad. Call Flak."

My father shook his head. "What for?"

"Just to talk about stuff. He really wants you to. I think he wants to help."

"Well, are you feeling better?" he said.

Was he kidding? Was I supposed to feel *better* now? "Yeah," I said. It was the required answer. And relatively speaking, I was in no position to complain. I was the only one in my family, it seemed, who did not have the immediate urge to kill herself.

"That's what matters, then." He put the car in reverse. "Okay, well. Good-bye."

I went into the apartment and stared at my tax and commercial paper casebooks. I felt nothing, just numb. I considered changing clothes and going for a run. You didn't have to solve anything on a run. Just breathe in and out, put one foot in front of the other. It took up all the concentration in the world; it kept you safe from feeling.

Instead, I opened the freezer and found a quart of Brigham's ice cream. A package of Chips Ahoy! in the cupboard. A bag of Doritos. I was suddenly starving. I could always run later, I reasoned—after dark, when there was nothing left to eat.

eleven

Labor Day 1980

The following fall, before starting my last year of law school, I spent the Labor Day weekend with a friend on Martha's Vineyard. We walked for miles along the shore, swam in the ocean, and talked late into the evenings. Obeying my family's rule of secrecy, I didn't mention a word to her about my summer—I had been exiled from home by my parents, who were still caring for Lara around the clock. The last time I'd called home, Lara had grabbed the phone from my mother and screamed that she would kill me, and Mom too, if I ever called again.

The Labor Day traffic back to Boston was heavy. When I finally pulled up in front of my apartment, I froze. There in my parking space was my mother's Plymouth. *Lara's killed herself*, I thought. *She's finally done it*. I jumped out of the car and ran up the steps. *Breathe*. I fumbled with the keys, then burst into the apartment. My mother was lying on my bed reading the *New Yorker*, and rose to greet me.

"Hi, darling," she said pleasantly. "Your landlady let me in. She's very nice."

"What happened?"

"What do you mean?" My mother gave me a hug and took my knapsack from my shoulder, as if it were the most natural thing for her to be in my apartment on a Monday afternoon.

"What are you doing here?"

My mother shrugged. "I just thought I'd come for the weekend."

Mom had never shown up unannounced before. She sidestepped past me into the little kitchen. "I'll make tea," she said. "Are you hungry?" She flipped on the electric hot plate and filled the kettle with water.

"Why didn't you tell me you were coming?" I asked.

My mother shrugged. "I didn't even know till Saturday morning, and when I called, there was no answer."

"I'd just left for the Vineyard—"

"It's all right," Mom said. "I was fine here. I had a very nice time. I read and relaxed."

"Mom, what's going on? Is Lara okay?"

She narrowed her eyes and picked her words carefully. "Well . . . last week was very difficult. But everything is all right now. I think I'll be able to go home tomorrow."

I didn't know what to make of this. My mother didn't just drive three hours across Massachusetts and show up out of the blue for no reason. The last time I'd seen her was three months ago, when I'd driven home for the summer. Before I could even get out of the car, she and Dad had intercepted me in the driveway. "You can't stay here," Mom had said. "Lara is too unstable. She's very angry at you." Stunned, I'd driven back across the river, got a room at the Y, and started my summer clerkship in Troy the next day.

"Where's Dad?" I asked my mother now.

"He's fine. He's at home."

"And Lara?"

"She left for Burlington this afternoon. She's going back to medical school."

My mother set two cups on the table and poured the tea. "You see, darling," she said, "last week with Lara, it was very touch-and-go. You know how hard it's been for us."

I nodded and leaned toward her, a flower to the sun.

Mom cut two micro-slices of lemon and dropped them in our teacups. Lara had intended to return to medical school for the fall semester, Mom said, but last week she suddenly took a turn for the worse. So my parents and Lara's shrink came up with a plan: they decided that my mother would have to leave the house. "As long as I was there, we knew Lara wouldn't leave for school," Mom explained. "So we told her that I was going away."

"What do you mean? You told her you were coming to visit me?"

"Oh no!" Mom said. "She would have been furious! No, she must never know that I'm here!"

I rolled my eyes.

"You must promise never to tell her!"

"Okay, okay," I said.

It seemed so bizarre, so crazy, the lengths to which my parents went to keep Lara out of the hospital, and now en route to medical school.

"And the plan worked," my mother said proudly. "Dad called me this afternoon and said that she had just left. She's gone back to school."

"So Dad knew you were coming here?"

"Of course! But he couldn't tell Lara. Otherwise she wouldn't have gone back to school. She must never know."

This is nuts, I thought. My mother always insisted on secrecy, as if we would all die from the truth. "So where did she think you were going?"

"We wouldn't tell her. Just *away*."

My mother left the next morning, once she'd gotten the all-clear signal from my father. Lara had started her third year of medical school.

————

Dr. Flak asked me to join a new group he was starting that fall. On Tuesday and Thursday evenings, we sat in a circle on hard plastic chairs. The good thing about group therapy was that it was cheap. The bad thing was that it didn't work. Each of us went up in flames that fall. Terrence had a psychotic break and landed in a mental institution, Edgar wound up in the ICU after a near-fatal car crash on the Mass Pike, and Gwen wrestled with her husband and manic depression. I was fine, I decided, and I spent weeks listening to everyone's woes, believing that I would win Flak's love and respect by helping them with their problems.

But in the quiet of my apartment, I started having completely random bouts of shaking and hyperventilating that brought me to my knees. I didn't know what to make of them. In the beginning, they always struck when I was alone—usually at home, or sometimes outdoors at night. After the initial few minutes of slam-dunk terror, they felt strangely reassuring to me—at least they signaled to the tyrannical Helen sitting at the switchboard of my mind to back off; I was suffering enough already. In the aftermath of the attack, I didn't hate myself quite so much; I treated myself gently, with care. I was ready to be a little nicer to myself.

I kept meaning to bring this up in group, but I could never find the right moment. We spent our evenings talking about Gwen's husband who had grabbed her (we agreed it was good that she'd told him, "You're hurting me!"); we questioned Terrence about his plans to marry his girlfriend, and the pros and cons of paying for sex with men. We tried to help Edgar, whom we considered boring but not utterly undatable, and we offered strategies for meeting women.

None of these seemed like a natural segue to a confession like, "I collapsed on the floor and hyperventilated this afternoon." So I stayed quiet.

One night as I was driving home after group, the attack hit like a karate chop from God. I was suddenly doubled over at the wheel, shaking uncontrollably. I managed to pull over to the side of the road. When I finally calmed down, I turned the car around and gingerly drove back to Flak's office. His little VW Bug was still in its spot in the parking lot. Through the bay windows, I could see that he was running another group, and I decided to wait for him. It would probably go till eight-thirty or so.

I walked around the block and tried to figure out what was wrong with me. I could not make any sense of my distress. I decided to ask Flak for an individual appointment. I rehearsed what I would say: "Doctor Flak"—I was very respectful—"I'm sorry to disturb you so late, but I just wanted to ask if I could make an appointment with you sometime this week. A private session." I ran these lines over in my mind, and waited.

It was almost eight-thirty; I watched the door to Flak's office open.

His patients spilled out like supplicants after communion with heads lowered. One by one, they filed out, climbed into their cars, and drove off. But the parking lot was still pretty full. To my amazement, Flak's office door remained open, and another seven or eight patients from the waiting room piled into the room for the next group session. I looked at my watch. Flak wouldn't get out till ten. The guy was practically working around the clock, a real-life Energizer Bunny for mental illness.

I stood on the sidewalk, trying to make myself go home, but my agitation was too great. I was afraid that if I waited till tomorrow morning to call, I would lose my nerve. So I walked out to the empty soccer field, and practiced my lines. The more I walked, the more anxious I got. "Doctor Flak," I repeated over and over. "Doctor Flak . . ." My hopelessness finally knocked me down, and I found myself on my knees, heart racing, unable to catch my breath. The earth was soft, and I felt momentarily comforted by the fact that I was a complete wreck.

I finally walked back to Flak's office at ten and stood outside the building. I was too ashamed to go inside and wait in the waiting room. I did not want to be seen by the other patients. I checked my watch. Five after ten. Nothing happened. Ten-ten. Nothing. Was he going to keep them there overnight? What if he literally never stopped working?

Suddenly the door opened and people came out. They were a livelier group; they chatted with each other as they tramped down the three stairs to the parking lot. I waited for them to sing their good-byes before approaching the door.

My hands were sweating, and I had trouble turning the knob. Once in the foyer, I heard Flak straightening chairs and turning out lights. Before I reached the hallway, he was right in front of me, and we both jumped back, startled.

"I'm sorry to disturb you," I blurted, staring at my feet. "Um, I know it's late, I was just wondering if I could make an appointment for a private session with you."

Having recited my lines, I looked up. Flak was slowly shaking his head. "What's this about?" he said coolly.

His reproach threw me off; I didn't want to get into it now. I didn't even know what *it* was.

"I don't know," I said. "It's just that . . ."

"Well you need to bring this up in group. Talk about it on Thursday."

"But I can't," I said. "I can't talk in group. I mean, it's like everyone has worse problems than I do. Compared to them, you know, I don't feel like I have the right —"

"Whoa," he said, holding up his hands. "You're making this larger than life."

"I know! I know I am! It's just—" The words caught in my throat. I felt tears on my face, and I quickly wiped them away with my sleeve. It had never occurred to me that he could just say no like that. After all, I wasn't asking for free advice. I was asking for an *appointment*. During normal business hours. He couldn't even give me that?

And then, to my horror, I started shaking. The shame and frustration were a brushfire in my chest, rising, heating my face. My lips started quivering, and soon my legs and shoulders were shaking, and I couldn't stop. "Sorry!" I mumbled, and started to run out the door, but Flak grabbed my wrist.

"Wait a second," he said. His tone was completely changed. He sounded warm, caring. His hand on my wrist sent a shock wave through my arm. I looked up at him now with uncertainty. Tears were pouring down my face, and I wanted to wipe them away, but Flak was trying to hold my hand. Despite my humiliation, I was stunned by his sudden change, as if a light had switched on behind his eyes. He was smiling and looking at me with genuine concern. I stood shaking before him for some time, unable to speak, trying to catch my breath.

"You're feeling scared," he said quietly. "You're very frightened."

And I thought, *No, I'm not frightened, I'm frustrated.*

"You're having what's called a classic panic attack," he said.

The term was new to me. I was pretty sure I felt no panic, but now was not the time to quibble. His eyes gazed into mine, a calm, heroic beam. "It's all right." He adjusted his grip on my hand. He cared. He actually cared! I felt slightly dishonest, knowing I didn't feel the slightest bit of panic or fear—just shame at being so out of control.

But I let him talk on in his soothing voice, and he was so gentle and kind, and the touch of his hand was so warm, I was reassured, even if his words didn't exactly make sense.

"And I'm sorry," he said. "I didn't realize it was so bad. How long have you been having these?"

I rolled my eyes. "All along," I squeaked. It was true—not only did I have them at home, but I'd started having them at moments when I was about to get on the T, or sometimes in the hallway outside court. I was working as a student defender that semester, and I liked my clients who were charged with breaking into houses, beating up their girlfriends, or slashing tires on police cruisers. But I had problems with my heartbeat. Sometimes I would step into the hallway on the thirteenth floor of the Cambridge District Courthouse and stare out the window, at the wild expanse of the city spread like a series of dioramas below me—the Necco factory and the triple-deckers of East Cambridge, the river beyond, and the skyscrapers of Boston. And I thought about soaring over all of those chipped rooftops and rusted handrails, the poured concrete and the nailed porches, how pure the air would be and how soft the landing.

Then my case would get called and I would return to my life as a baby lawyer, a buttoned-down, briefcase-toting kid playing grown-up.

"And you're right," he continued. "We should set up an individual session. Let's meet tomorrow, okay?"

I nodded, unable to take my eyes off my sneakers.

"Tomorrow, two o'clock?"

I nodded, but still couldn't look at him.

"You going to be okay?"

I nodded again.

"Okay, then. I'll see you tomorrow at two."

I flew out the door. When I got around the corner, I fell to my knees by the side of the street, unable to breathe. My heart was pounding as if it would gallop out of my chest and down the street. I curled into a ball, clutched my head to my knees, and waited out the storm.

Suddenly I heard footsteps behind me. "Helen?" It was Dr. Flak.

I leaped up and tore down the road as fast as I could. When I reached my car, I fell again, shaking and sobbing, and waited a long time till I felt calm enough to stand. Then I opened the door and slowly drove home.

What had just happened? What a pathetic ruse to get attention! How wonderful Flak was! What a worthless fuckup I was! My neediness was an oozing wound, and because of my failure to control myself, I had snared the god's attention. What a manipulative bitch. What dreamy eyes he had! What was wrong with me? Jesus! But how lovely to feel his gaze on me, to feel him hold my hand.

I fell into bed, but couldn't sleep. I kept replaying those few moments over and over in my mind. It seemed important, a *breakthrough*, as they said in the movies. Everything would be all right, I thought. I would place myself in Flak's hands. He would take care of me. Everything would be fine.

Flak and I met the next day, and he persuaded me to tell everyone in group about my attacks. I even gave them a demonstration, since it took almost nothing to set me off. I think I scared the shit out of one of Flak's new recruits, a pretty young Harvard boy whom Flak seemed crazy about. But the whole thing felt fraudulent somehow—a little performance that Flak and I had staged for the others. I was so removed from my own experience I had trouble feeling anything but disgust at the entire charade of my suffering. Group, it seemed, was just another dysfunctional family in which I didn't know who I was or how I really felt.

twelve

The Confusion of Sex

Years earlier, when I was still in college and things had been good between Lara and me, we never talked about boys or romance or sex, perhaps because the topic was just plain taboo in our family. Besides, I didn't really know what to make of romance. When I was a junior in college, almost all the women on my rowing team were paired off with one another. Even our pixieish coach lived with another woman. Through the powerful magic of denial, I never realized that these relationships could be sexual in any way. It was as if gay sex were an insoluble solid suspended in the solution of my mind—it was right there in front of me, but I couldn't absorb it. Sure, my friends cuddled and hugged and wrestled with each other, but I never saw anyone kiss or act in an *explicitly* sexual way. So it never dawned on me that my friends might be lesbians.

I only knew that I felt terribly lonely my junior year. Harriet had graduated the summer before and moved back to Minnesota, and Emma was at Berkeley. All my other friends seemed to be involved in passionate friendships that made me feel left out. I had no words for this, just a vague sense of loss.

I decided to go on exchange to Dartmouth College in the spring of my junior year, and over the summer I met Philip, a tightly muscled, curly-haired guy in the Outward Bound program. We spent ten weeks learning to rock climb, to portage canoes across miles of muddy bogs, and to survive alone in the wilderness for days without food or shelter. Although I was much more drawn to my roommate, Claire, it was Philip who kissed me at the end of the summer.

A few months later, with grim determination, I decided it was time to lose my virginity. Philip and I succeeded at this task in workmanlike fashion, and we more or less stayed together for two years, portaging our relationship like the bulky canoe of good intentions that it was. I found sex a colossal disappointment. The entire human race—centuries of literature and art—had led me to believe that sex was this thrilling experience of galactic proportions. Instead, the best thing I could say about sex was that it was mercifully quick work. I managed to fake my way through it, which was how I got through much of my life in those days. I didn't talk about this with any of my friends. I simply decided that romantic love and sex were ridiculously overrated and unimportant to me. I liked Philip well enough; he was a Russian studies major, and he was fascinated by my father, with whom he conversed in Russian when I brought him home for Thanksgiving. I, in turn, was fascinated by Philip's tales of working on an offshore oil rig in the Gulf of Mexico, and his love of Texas, a place as remote as Siberia to me. Philip and I protected each other from loneliness. But over time we got on each other's nerves, and I refused to move in with him after college. He went to Germany for the summer and had a fling with a girl, which gave me a legitimate excuse to stop seeing him. I still didn't know I was queer; I just knew that I didn't care for Philip nearly as much as I did for my girlfriends.

I never brought any of this up in group, because the great landmass of my family seemed to block out whatever other problems I might have.

Fall Semester 1980

In the evenings that fall, after I'd prepared my cases as a student defender for the next day, I found myself getting into my Plymouth Duster and driving aimlessly through the dark residential streets of Newton and Chestnut Hill. Usually I would stop at a convenience store and pick up a package of chocolate chip cookies, which I would then eat methodically through the western suburbs, while trying to figure out what was wrong with me. I was too depressed to talk to my law school friends; I had to figure this out for myself. Eventually I would turn over in my mind the magic card that Flak had given me. It had his telephone number, and he had encouraged me to call him anytime I needed to.

Problem was, that word *need*. The daughter of Holocaust survivors, I was a strict constructionist of the word. As my father had always told us, all one really "needed" was:

a. food and water
b. shelter
c. clothing, a means to stay warm

I had yards of everything I could possibly need. I fairly reeked of privilege. So why, in the midst of my riches, did I still hold out my beggar's bowl for some unidentified "more"? After all, I thought, sizing up my circumstances, I already had a heated apartment, a closet of clothes, a refrigerator of food, a registered car, a right of free speech, a right to bear arms . . .

Don't think it didn't occur to me.

Inevitably, thoughts of what I needed led me to consider what I would do with a gun. Every morning in court, I watched the slow shuffle of prisoners in and out like cattle before the auctioneer in the black robe. Evidence: all the pretty guns, assault rifles, sawed-off shotguns, .45s. All the ways to bear arms and bear them poorly. If I had a gun, I would be efficient. I would not fall into that unseemly, bogus bucket of would-be suicides. I would distinguish myself from Lara. No half-assed cutting up my arms or swallowing a bottle of pills. *This is how you commit suicide, you dipshit*, I would say with my elegantly dead body, a single breathtaking bullet to the skull.

But I knew I would never get a gun.

All the guns in court were sealed in clear plastic evidence bags and fondled by cops; I was certainly not going to get my hands on a gun in court. And I would never ask a client for a gun. I had a hard enough time convincing them I was their lawyer. Besides, like most law students, I had an exaggerated sense of professional ethics.

Buying a gun legally was also out of the question—I had no patience for applying for a license and registration, the sheer bureaucracy of preparing for violence. I could not picture myself walking into a gun store, asking for advice from the sales clerk at the counter, discussing different models, making sure I would get the best quality for the lowest price. All of this was too mundane, too public, too time-consuming. But I also knew I'd be inept at getting a gun on the street—I would get one that malfunctioned; I would get arrested before I could use it; I would not know how to load it properly, or how to release the safety.

The whole point of suicide, I thought, was to succeed at it. My sister's completion rate was pathetic. She would never get into the Suicide Hall of Fame with her record of attempts and failures.

And so I finally decided that the way to kill myself would be in my Plymouth Duster. A midnight high-speed single-car crash into a rock wall. This had a number of advantages: it involved heart-thumping action, collision, blood, and a pretty quick resolution. It also seemed a likely success, and in any event, it would be colorful, and it would put Lara's paltry efforts to shame.

I cruised around the Chestnut Hill Reservoir in search of optimal conditions to carry out my plans. Too many intersections, not enough walls. I would have to go out of town, perhaps even out of state—to New Hampshire, where one was encouraged to live free or die. But thinking about New Hampshire always put me in a good mood. I'd take my snowshoes, go camping for the weekend, and feel better. I'd forget to kill myself till I got back to Boston Monday morning, and there, in court, would be all the pretty guns.

———

At last I called him. Not because I needed to. Not because I had really scared myself into thinking I would kill myself, but because I finally grew tired of myself. It was a Friday evening when I left a message for Flak to call me. This was an extraordinarily bold move, and my heart was racing at the sheer audacity of calling a doctor—an important man! A man with patients, employees, a wife, children, countless pressures I could only guess at. And here was I, Little Helen of the Perpetual Worries, adding one more complaint to his burden. And what was it, exactly, that I wanted from him?

I couldn't admit it, but what I wanted, quite simply, was a bit of his warmth and attention. Or maybe more than just a bit. I wanted him to say, "Helen, I love you. You are the most amazing person in the world." Or maybe he could just say something reassuring, and we would talk like coach to athlete: he would tell me I was brave and strong, and I would be fine. "Now, just go back out there and stay loose," he would say. "You'll do fine, I have every confidence in—"

The phone rang. I practically jumped out of my skin.

"Hello, Helen? This is Dr. Flak." He sounded brusque, all business.

I sat with the receiver pressed to my ear, paralyzed for a moment, before a stream of words rushed from my mouth. "Thanks for calling back," I said. "I'm sorry to bother you—I mean, it's really not a big deal, but, um . . ."

He was silent. A cold emptiness on the other end of the line. He was probably listening, I thought with rising alarm, in that shrinky way—with narrowed eyes and pursed lips, evaluating my sanity.

"I'm okay," I said quickly. "I mean, I guess . . . maybe it's getting worse."

"What's worse?"

"I don't know! I'm not sure what I expect you to—"

"Where are you?" he asked.

"At home." I was sitting on the mustard-colored shag carpeting, propped between my desk and my bed. "I don't know what I want," I said. "It's not like I—"

"Well, I expected this," he said flatly.

This was disappointing. He didn't sound the least bit loving.

"I think you need medication. I thought you needed this before, but I figured we'd see how it goes, and—"

My face went cold. Everything in my body lurched forward. "No!" I said.

"Listen to me," he said. "This is what I want you to do. I'm going to call in a prescription for imipramine to the CVS on Charles Street, near Mass General. It's open till midnight. Do you know where that is?"

I did. I often went to the movie theater a few blocks down the street. But I was horrified to think that I was being sent downtown to get psycho medication on a Friday night, like it was some kind of emergency.

"I don't want any drugs," I said in a thin voice.

"Well, I think you need them." He'd turned into Dr. Authority. No more Mr. Nice & Listen. I was mortified at what I had unleashed. If only I'd kept my big mouth shut! What had compelled me to call him? I was never satisfied, I thought. Always wanted more.

"Please," I sniveled. "Please, no drugs."

"Can I trust you to pick these up?" he said.

I held my breath. What could I say to start this conversation over again?

"Helen?"

"Yes," I said meekly.

"Can I trust—"

"Yes." I was the obedient, good girl after all. I would have no tantrums, no hysterics like Lara. I would gather whatever dignity was left me and drive downtown to the drugstore, where I would wait until they bagged my prescription and cashed me out.

Once home, with a sense of resignation, I read the label, swallowed a pill, and chased it with a glass of water as instructed. Then I allowed myself the unsatisfying indulgence of hopelessness. I would sink now, I thought. There was nothing left of me, a hollow shell. Flak was no different from my father, from anyone else. They were autocrats and they would treat me in the order in which I placed my call. Like anyone else who asked for help, I would be given the dosage recommended by the *Physician's Desk Reference*, and left to live somehow on my own.

Sleep hit at some point in the middle of the night, and knocked me to the side of the bed, where I stayed until late morning. Groggy, I stumbled to the bathroom, turned on the shower, and then felt the world tip on its side. I grabbed the edges of the spinning shower stall and gradually dropped to the floor. *Side effect: dizziness.* I was a mental patient. Just like Lara, I was now taking a mind-altering drug that would make me crazy.

———

A few weeks later Lara called and asked me to go hiking with her in Vermont. I hadn't spoken to her in half a year, and the sound of her voice—so friendly and gentle—made me cry. It was like hearing the voice of a long-lost love.

I didn't want her to hear me sniffle—it seemed weak and shameful. Neither of us said much. She asked me how I was. "Okay," I said. "And you?"

"Okay."

We were both lying, pretending that nothing had happened over the past six months: her suicide attempts and threats to kill me, my panic attacks and exile from home, my parents' insistence on secrecy—it was safer to say nothing. Instead we agreed to meet at the Appalachian Trail south of Bromley Mountain for a weekend in the woods.

I got up before dawn, threw my gear in the trunk, and drove to

Vermont. A nor'easter was thrashing New England, and the wind hurled sheets of rain onto the roads. Three hours later I was sitting in my rusting Plymouth at the trailhead off Route 8 in the pounding rain. In another five months I was supposed to graduate and become a lawyer—a ludicrous idea to me at the time. I was much too young and immature to be a lawyer. I couldn't even figure out how to be me.

————————

Headlights turned into the parking lot. Through the driving rain, I could barely make out the shape of my sister's drab-green Chevy Malibu with its dented fenders and broken defroster. She rolled up beside me and lowered her window an inch. I did the same. We eyed each other across the no-man's-land of angry rain. She did not look any different than she usually did, except her hair was combed, and although it billowed out behind her ears, it looked quiet. And she looked lonely and a little scared; her shoulders were hunched as if she were protecting herself from a blow. Under her mountaineering parka, I could see her stretched-out cotton turtleneck. She was a third-year medical student, but she didn't look any more like a doctor than I looked like a lawyer.

"Hi," she said.

"Hi."

"This sucks."

I nodded.

"Want to get a cup of coffee and see if it lets up?"

My face brightened. We wouldn't have to trudge out in this mess, slip on rocks, and crawl into soaked sleeping bags at the end of the day. We didn't have to hurt ourselves too badly. The competition was postponed due to good sense.

I followed Lara's taillights down the mountain, through the lashing rain. We parked at a coffee shop in Manchester, bought coffee and blueberry muffins at the counter, and slid into an empty booth. We were the only ones there. A long-haired boy drifted behind the counter, scruffy and sleepy-eyed. Somewhere in the back, the Stones were on, Jagger singing *I sit and watch the children play*. . . .

Lara looked thinner than when I'd last seen her in the spring, when she was so angry at me. She seemed gentle now, with a shy, sweet smile, and warm green eyes and a perky nose. I suddenly realized how terribly I'd missed her. I had felt part of myself sliced off, an arm, or perhaps both arms, and as I'd wandered through my days at law school and through the streets of Boston, I had felt stunned by my loss, unable to grasp anything, clumsy and mute with pain. And now she was here. She was whole—her round face and strong shoulders, the terribly ravaged fingers; my sister was here before me, sipping coffee from a tall paper cup.

"I don't know where to begin," I said. And then we began, patching together the intervening time.

"I wasn't allowed home last summer," I said. "As long as you were there, Mom and Dad said I couldn't set foot in the house. I guess they were afraid of what you'd do."

Lara looked bewildered.

"You were in really, really bad shape," I said. I stared at my coffee, unable to meet her eyes. I was burning to talk about the past summer, about meeting my father on the sly at the hospital coffee shop to get updates on Lara's condition. About Mom showing up in my apartment over Labor Day. But it seemed cruel now to remind Lara of how she'd acted, of how frightened we'd all been. I separated the wax paper from the muffin and broke off a piece. Lara tore into hers, spreading crumbs across the table. "Mom and Dad said you were . . . well, they said it was very, very dangerous," I said carefully. "They were afraid you'd kill yourself. You were furious at me." I took a sip of coffee and sneaked a glance at Lara to see how she was taking this.

Lara shook her head slowly. "That's nuts," she said. "That's completely wack. They told me you wouldn't have anything to do with us. That you refused to see us."

What? Did she really believe that? "I used to meet Dad," I said.

Lara's eyebrows went up.

"We'd have coffee at the hospital."

I used to get up before six on Sundays and drive through the sleepy streets of Troy and west to Schenectady, and I would park on the opposite side of the hospital parking lot, so as not to be seen. And I would go into the familiar halls of my father's hospital. He would be standing there in his gray suit, waiting inside the doctors' entrance next to his nameplate, on a wall panel of all the doctors' names. He would flick the little switch, lighting up his name to show that he was there, he was on the premises, and if anyone needed him, all they had to do was page him over the loudspeaker.

I always felt a surge of pride at seeing this, the simple flick of my father's index finger lighting up his presence in the world. It spoke to his importance, that he was actually ingrained in the walls of this hospital, that he was part of the edifice of healing. I followed him down the hall to the coffee shop, and people stopped and greeted him; everyone knew him, everyone admired him and joked with him and smiled at me and shook my hand when he introduced me as his daughter. And my head swelled to think that I was attached to this great man, and through no credit of my own, I had managed to gain this exalted position as my father's daughter. It wasn't just doctors who stopped to talk with him, but nurses and orderlies and cafeteria workers and janitors and patients and volunteers who worked the gift shop and the flower stand.

"We got together once a week," I told Lara.

She stared at me. I couldn't tell whether she was puzzled, or angry, or what. My father had told me he'd had to sneak out of the house unnoticed, to prevent Lara from finding out he was meeting with me.

"In the beginning, I called Mom," I said. "I wanted to see her. But she said you were too sick, and she couldn't leave you alone."

"Sick?"

I nodded. "And she said I couldn't come home because you were ready to kill me or something. And you'd flip out if you found out she was even *talking* to me. So she hung up."

"What?" My sister fidgeted. Her fingers found each other on the table and she began tugging at the skin over her cuticle.

How could Lara have forgotten how crazy she'd been? I glanced at her shaggy brown hair falling over her face. She looked like one of those lovable mutts in Hollywood movies that chew up the carpets and then win you over with their sheer scruffiness. *Oh, who cares?* I thought. *Let it go.* I was exhausted from years of trying to make sense of Lara and my family. All that mattered now was that my sister was here, sitting across the table from me, and that we were friends.

Lara got up to get more coffee, and when she sat down again, I realized that she and I were no longer in competition; we had both failed to make our parents happy. As I had done so many times before, I now rearranged what I knew about my sister to accommodate my loneliness, my need to be aligned with her. Perhaps, I now thought, it was our parents who were nuts, and it was Lara who was my real friend and ally.

"They had me drugged to the gills," Lara said, staring at her coffee. Her fingers picked at each other as if they were separate entities beyond her control. "I didn't even know what was going on."

There was something so plaintive in her voice, I felt the solidarity of a fellow sufferer. I could no longer pretend that I was the healthy one, the normal one, and she the crazy one. I had finally joined her ranks in the battle for mental health: I was a walking, talking psych patient, with a panic disorder and imipramine running through my veins. I had lowered my head and offered it to the profession, and I was now in their clutches, just as she was.

"That must have been awful," I found myself saying.

She shrugged. Her hair had begun its outward stretch, growing like a hydra as it absorbed the humidity in the air. "I missed you," she said.

I nodded, and smiled. "Well, you were also really pissed at me."

Her head snapped back as if struck, and her brow furrowed.

Alarms went off in my head. *Just like always*, I thought. *She's conveniently forgotten everything she did.* "At the end of May," I reminded her. "When I called home from the mountains—remember?"

Lara was shaking her head and slouching lower in her chair. She seemed to grow smaller before me, a snail curling into its shell. I couldn't bear to see it. I changed the subject. I told her about my panic attacks. It was an offering—to show her that I too was crazy.

"They come out of nowhere," I said. "I'll be standing on the subway platform, and all of a sudden, I'll get a tingly feeling. And then I can feel my lips trembling, and I know it's coming. It's like holding your breath underwater, right before it hits."

I could see that she wasn't listening to me, she was still lost in the words I'd left in the air before. I could see her working over the details of that phone call in May, when she'd screamed that she would kill me, and Mom too, if I ever tried calling again. So complete was her grip on me then, I'd been certain she would kill us. But now, sitting across the table from her, with her hunched shoulders and bleeding fingers, it seemed impossible that she could have ever struck such fear in me.

"Lara, you listening?"

She rolled her shoulders wearily and brought her eyes even with mine. "Yeah."

I didn't know where she'd gone, but I tried to get her back. "Listen, never mind about last summer. It's over. It doesn't matter. I'm glad you called me. I'm glad you took that chance."

And at this moment, sitting in a coffee shop in Manchester, Vermont, I was so grateful to have my sister with me, to have the warmth of her presence, the light in her soft green-brown eyes, her shy smile. I needed her, pure and simple. I did not understand my own unhappiness, but I knew this much: I loved my sister and had missed her terribly, and something of that wound was healing here at this table. I felt myself being repaired by her presence and by her friendship. I might not be able to solve the problem of my life, but I could bask in the glow of our friendship. We were together again.

thirteen

Rubin Vase

I first saw the image in my psych textbook in 1974 as a college freshman—a stark white goblet on a black background. The caption under the picture asked whether you could see the two faces in profile, facing each other.

All I saw was a white goblet. I read further, and it said to focus only on the black "background" of the picture and bring that image forward. It took me a few minutes before I could find the two identical faces in silhouette, their noses almost touching each other. Seeing these two faces was like an electric shock. How could I have studied the picture so closely, yet missed something so obvious? Once I found the two faces, the goblet simply disappeared.

The text went on to talk about human perception; about how the brain receives stimuli and matches patterns to make mental interpretations of what we see. When you look at the picture, you cannot simultaneously see both images at once. It was called a Rubin vase after the Danish psychologist who had developed the image and similar optical illusions.

The goblet with the two faces became an image for my relation-ship with my sister. When I was younger, I saw Lara as the goblet filled with some toxic fluid that would burn on contact. But then, for no ap-parent reason, my image of her would flip, and all of a sudden I would see my sister and me as two identical faces, joined together, aligned. The goblet was gone. It was just the two of us—Lara and me looking directly into each other's eyes with love and devotion. She and I were exactly the same.

These two images of our relationship kept flipping back and forth on me throughout our lives. There was never any transition—no warn-ing, no sense of in-between. It was always black or white. One moment we were best friends, two sisters seeing eye to eye. The next, mortal en-emies, the vase of poison.

———

1980

Lara and I spent hours on the phone that fall, finding companionship in suicidal thoughts. At twenty-three and twenty-six, the obligation to make up for our parents' unspoken losses was too great. We owed them our happiness and our lives, and suicide seemed like the fastest way to get out of debt.

Also, there was the terrible burden of make-believe—the pressure of pretense—that we could no longer sustain. Our family had always looked fine from the outside. Our surfaces sparkled. Our lawn was green, our grades were good, our expenses paid. A double suicide by the children would certainly give lie to all that. We were frauds—desperate to appear successful and well-adjusted on the outside, while harboring the rage and grief of a destroyed people. Suicide would be more honest. My sister and I felt a certain sense of entitlement to apocalypse.

My father had always dismissed our unhappiness as the ennui of privileged youth. We were bored and restless and unhappy, he explained, because we had too much of everything. And he seemed to be right: our lives had become too easy to bear, and therefore unbearable in light of all that had come before. Hardship would do wonders for us, Lara and I believed. But neither of us wanted to give up too much comfort for the sake of happiness. We would rather be miserable.

"I think a car crash," I said. I was sitting on the shag carpet of my one-room apartment across from Boston College. I cradled the phone receiver against my ear while doodling on my tax notebook. "What about you?" I asked.

Lara sighed. The world turned on its axis with that sigh, wind fluttered through the trees, stars died. "I think knives."

Lara, the doctor, scalpel in hand. She had taken anatomy twice—her first year in med school, and then the summer afterward, for good measure.

"Or drugs," she added.

"What drugs?"

"There's zillions of meds. I can get anything I want."

Medical school had its advantages, I could see that. I tried to imagine swallowing a bottle of pills and lying on the narrow bed against the wall of my room. It seemed too depressing. "I want more of an impact," I told Lara. "I want something noisier, faster, explosive. Drugs are so . . . passive. So quiet. It's like, why bother?"

She didn't answer.

"A car crash would be fast, it would be active. It wouldn't be like lying around, waiting to die." Listening to myself, I wondered how serious I was. Would I really kill myself? I didn't think so, but I thought Lara might.

"It doesn't matter how," she said. "It's all the same. Nothing matters."

"Okay, but I'm just saying—"

"It doesn't matter how you do it."

When my mother was my age, she'd been smuggling food to her parents in the ghetto by night; by day she worked for the occupying army in Lvov; and by October 1942, she'd escaped Poland altogether, posing as a young Italian infantryman. She had lost her fiancé to the Russians, her parents to the Germans, and her sister to the Italians, until finally she had lost herself as a person whom she could recognize at all.

And now, as a third-year law student, I did not know who I was or what I was doing. No one was trying to kill me, no one was shooting my friends or gassing my loved ones. What right did I have to be unhappy? My inner and outer worlds did not match. I was starting to break down, and I turned to my big sister as my model of decompensation.

"Let's just do it," Lara said. Her voice was so low I could barely hear her.

"Yeah?"

"Yeah," she said.

"Okay." The idea of killing ourselves together had growing appeal. It would be more like a mission, a bond we would share. Something that would draw us together. "When?"

"This weekend," Lara said.

I had nothing planned this weekend. It would be a perfect time to kill myself. "You serious?" I asked. My sister was the most unreliable person I knew. It would be so like her to set something up, and then back out at the last minute with some lame excuse.

"Yeah."

"Me too," I said. I wondered what my obligation was. If we agreed to do it, and I finked out, would I be responsible for her death? If I went through with it, she'd better kill herself too. Otherwise, what was the point?

What, exactly, was the point?

"All right," I said. "So what day? Saturday?"

"I don't know. Maybe. Or maybe Sunday."

Here we go, I thought. *She can't even commit to the day. She's never been able to make a decision in her life.* I felt my irritation rising. "Well, pick one," I said.

"I'm not sure yet."

"But you're sure you want to do it, right?"

"Oh yeah."

"Well, I don't want to talk you—"

"I said I want to do it."

The sun was out. In two hours the Patriots would host the New York Jets at Foxborough. It all sounded so crazy. Lara and I were being dramatic. She had tried to kill herself before, but my depression was sharp and fresh. I wanted to be serious enough to go through with the plan, but I was pretty sure I didn't have the guts. It all seemed so unreal. "Then we'll do it," I said.

"Together," she said.

"Well, you do it your way, I'll do it mine." I didn't think we should have to synchronize our acts. But I needed her support, and she needed mine, and together we might be able to pull it off.

"All right," she said. "This weekend."

We were quiet for a moment. "So what are you going to do now?" I asked.

"I don't know."

"Are your roommates around?"

"No. They're never here."

She lived with a group of med students who barely skimmed the surface of the planet. They studied all day and night; they partied and slept with each other between classes. My sister was isolated by a scrim of gloom that her roommates could not guess lay behind her convincing smile. I had spent my life distancing myself from her, and now I was closing the gap. We were not so different after all. We were both lost.

"You all right?" I began to worry that she might kill herself ahead of schedule.

"I'll be all right once we do it," she said.

We hung up, and I felt better. Maybe it was not the healthiest of relationships, but Lara and I bonded well over suicidal depression. It felt good, knowing that she was also depressed. I didn't feel so alone. And there was something we could do about it: we could kill ourselves. I felt an obligation to her. I would have to find a road on which I could really slam into a wall without killing anyone else. I had to do it responsibly. I would not be a menace to other drivers. When I did it, I would do it right.

———

The weekend came. My conversation with Lara seemed ages ago. I wasn't in the mood for suicide, and I was pretty sure she wasn't either, and anyway, neither of us called. I didn't even think about it until Sunday night, when I vaguely wondered whether maybe she'd gone ahead and done it. But I knew she hadn't.

It wasn't until a week or two later that Lara called. We talked for a while, both of us miserable, but neither of us mentioned our suicide pact. Apparently it had expired for lack of interest.

Looking back now, I think we needed our pact to get us through whatever blackness had descended. For that half hour or forty minutes, we'd gotten some relief, some acknowledgment that we weren't alone, that we were, in fact, "normal" sisters, since both of us were suicidally depressed. If we weren't both feeling exactly the same way at the same time (whether up or down), the vase of poison would come between us.

———

A dozen years later, in 1992, after we discovered that Mom and Dad were Jewish Holocaust survivors, Lara and I never discussed those times in our twenties when we had been so troubled. Just as our parents had avoided talking about their war, Lara and I avoided talking about ours. Instead, we searched for clues from our parents' past, and tried to find people who had known them before and after the war. We even tracked down Dr. Grokle, the shrink at the Hoffman Children and Family Center, who was now seventy-five, to see if she could shed light on our family.

"I remember your family quite well," she said, sitting in a wingback chair in her living room in Schenectady. Lara had contacted her twenty-five years after we'd seen her as children. "I have seen so many

patients and families over the years, you know, and I'm more or less retired now. . . ." She looked down at her hands. They were thin, spotted
with age, free of jewelry except for a gold band. "I've forgotten a great
deal, but you and your parents stuck in my mind."

She looked at Lara and smiled. "I'm afraid we didn't really do
much for your family," she said.

No shit, I thought.

"You see, family therapy was in its infancy in those days," she said.
"In the sixties, we really didn't know that much about family dynamics
or treatment techniques." She paused, perhaps remembering the low-
lit room of the Hoffman Center, where my family took our appointed
seats each week and waited to be cured. "I must confess that I was a bit
intimidated by your parents," Dr. Grokle said. "I mean, given what
they'd gone through in the war. I never tried to ask them about their
past. Frankly, I was relieved that they didn't talk about it. In those
days . . . well, none of us wanted to talk about the war. We were all too
happy to sweep it under the rug."

fourteen

December 1980

I was home for winter break during my last year of law school. The phone rang and I picked it up. The voice of my high school boyfriend, Kevin, surprised me; we hadn't spoken in years. I still had the leather belt and wallet he'd made for me. Our romance had been doomed for a number of reasons—first, my mother forbade me to date boys, and second, I'd lost interest in guys altogether when I went off to college. But over the past few years, Kevin sometimes came over when Lara was home and they'd run a five-mile loop together.

"Helen? I didn't know you were home."

His voice was sweet, and it made me think, suddenly, of Lake Tear of the Clouds in the Adirondacks. In January six years earlier, he and I had climbed to its frozen shore, just below the final pitch up Mount Marcy.

"How are you?"

"Good," I said automatically. Actually, considering I'd contemplated suicide with my sister a few weeks ago, I *was* pretty good. "How've you been?"

"Okay," he said. "I'm taking some classes at SUNY, you know, doing some work for Greg Crump, just hanging out." I remembered coming home for Thanksgiving three years earlier with my then-boyfriend Philip, and the awkwardness when Kevin joined Lara, me, and Philip for a run. Philip had felt the need to sprint past us all at the end. I was ashamed to think of it.

"Well, look," Kevin said. "I was going to invite Lara for dinner—I've been working on a couple quiche recipes I got out of the *Times*, and they're pretty good. You know, Craig Claiborne's column. You want to come too?"

"You're cooking quiche?"

"Yeah, I know, I'm a total Renaissance man."

My mother was a huge Craig Claiborne fan. She clipped his recipes and folded them into her little metal recipe box. It would blow her mind if she heard Kevin was making Craig Claiborne's quiche lorraine. She had always considered Kevin some sort of blue-collar rapist.

We made a date.

———

Lara seemed relieved that I was coming along for dinner at Kevin's. She and Kevin had been uneasy classmates in high school, and although she didn't mind him coming over for a run now and then, she still suspected him of being a jerk.

She and I put on clean jeans and sweaters and drove out to Kevin's. He lived in a little apartment above Crump's Garage, an old truck repair shop near Verdoy, with dead engines and parts out back and a retired 1960s gas station in front. In the winter of 1980, Kevin was the tow-truck driver in residence. He received free use of the premises and a regular paycheck in exchange for responding to calls for disabled tractor-trailers. In bad weather, he often spent entire nights in subzero temperatures, hauling out rigs that had skidded on ice and snow off the Northway a few miles away.

Kevin served us a knockout meal of quiche, salad, and hot rolls with a bottle of chianti. We ate by candlelight, killed the bottle, then opened another. Lara, as usual in the presence of others, was perfectly polite, drank half a glass, and watched Kevin and me get blotto.

To my delight, Kevin was exactly my size of silly. We entertained ourselves with a freewheeling sense of humor that swung dangerously between the sublime and the ridiculous, often crashing into delicate subjects, doing damage to friends, loved ones, and entire segments of the population.

"Worth it!" he said.

"Who needs friends?" I agreed.

By nine o'clock, Lara had had enough. She signaled toward the door with her eyes, and poked me with her elbow to get me to leave. But I didn't feel like going.

"I'll drive Helen home," Kevin offered. "Don't worry—I'll wait till I sober up."

Lara frowned. Her self-appointed responsibilities as big sister included preventing me from having too much fun, or, alternatively, from getting splattered across Route 7 in a drunken car crash.

"Go ahead," I said. "I'll catch a ride with Kevin later."

Lara clomped down the stairs and out the door. We heard the Chevy's engine struggle in the cold, then the wheels crunching on the snow as she turned onto Route 7. Kevin put the Stones on the turntable and opened another bottle of wine.

"This is just temporary," he said, meaning his life. "Crump pays me pretty good money, but I just don't know what I want to do yet—you know, like a *career*."

We put our feet up on the coffee table and talked about the future, which scared us with its sheer size.

"I can't really see being a lawyer," I said. "I don't know if I can survive wearing pantyhose for the rest of my life."

"At least you're close to finishing school." Kevin was taking the scenic route through college, a few courses here, a few there.

"Well, I've had some real problems this year." I told him about my odyssey through the land of psychiatry: the panic attacks, group therapy, medication. I told him Flak had now proposed I might be *uni*polar, which was like bipolar, but without the benefits of mania. I just had depression, with intermittent breathers of okay-ness.

You could say I put Kevin on notice.

But he did not seem shocked or uneasy with my revelation of crazy. On the contrary—he was interested and sympathetic. "That sounds really rough," he said. "I'm glad you're feeling better."

He was no stranger to unhappiness. I liked that about him.

We talked for hours. He told me about his former girlfriends, what he had hoped for, and why they hadn't worked out. We looked up, and it was already past midnight. By then we were kissing, and then we found ourselves on the bed, and one thing led to another, and by the time he drove me home at two-thirty in the morning, I couldn't wait to see him the next day.

And so, absurdly, over winter break, I fell in love.

———

When I got up the next morning and came into the kitchen, my mother's face turned to ice. She watched me pour my coffee in silence, then left the room. Zosia was staying with us over the holidays, and I could hear the staccato of their voices as my mother intercepted her in the hallway. I knew, without her saying a word, that she was furious at me for having stayed out late with Kevin. I had violated the solemn law of family loyalty.

"You left coffee for Zosia, didn't you?" Mom asked, staring daggers.

"There's a whole pot, Mom."

She brushed past me, too angry to speak.

"What's the matter?"

She said nothing.

"Mom?"

She took the coffeepot and a mug out to the dining table for Zosia. I left them alone.

Kevin called, and I drove downtown to meet him at the library. We both had classwork to do, so we studied for a few hours and grabbed lunch at the Lark Street Grill. I told him my mother and Zosia weren't talking to me.

"I do have that effect on your mother, don't I?" he said. "But what did I ever do to your aunt?"

"Package deal." I finally didn't care what my mother thought of me and Kevin, or at least that's what I told myself. Being with him these two days had felt like opening the curtains after a long hard winter. I think I was happy. I think that's what was going on here.

———

The problem with falling in love was that I was starting to separate from the family, and that was not okay with them. And it put a crimp in my sisterhood with Lara; our bond in the fall had been based on mutual depression and anguish, neither of which I was feeling at the moment. Now when she called in a blue mood, I listened and sympathized, but it was disconcerting for both of us that we didn't match. I think it fueled her resentment.

Despite her wild rampages, Lara's loyalty to our family had never been in doubt. She might try to blow us up, but she would never run away. I, on the other hand, was always trying to duck my family to be with my friends. "Escape artist," my mother always called me. "You're always trying to get away!"

Many years later it would occur to me that what my mother most resented about me was precisely what she saw in herself. Throughout her life, she was racked with guilt for having abandoned her own parents in order to survive the war. She had built the façade of a new life on top of the secret of her old one, and from the outside, it looked smooth. But within our family, her invisible past filled our rooms. She had nothing left but her children, and she watched in shock as we dismantled first the walls she had built, and then ourselves.

fifteen

Spring Semester 1981

Law school graduation was less than a month away. Between me and graduation lay three weeks of classes and four final exams—a mere hop, skip, and a jump before launching my career as a word-wielding lawyer.

But the closer graduation loomed, the more I dreaded the prospect of being a lawyer: the suits, the seriousness, the world of corporate finance and commercial real estate. I was not interested in money; I was interested in mountains. Perhaps it was just starting to dawn on me that law, for the most part, was practiced indoors, and this seemed to have been a terrible miscalculation on my part.

Although the conflict between me and my career path seems pretty obvious now, at the time I didn't know what my problem was. I was holding my entire life in the fist of my mind. Any effort to loosen my grip felt dangerous—as if the contents of my life would simply blow away, and there would be nothing left of me.

During this time, I was seeing Kevin on weekends, taking my meds, and attending individual and group therapy, the purpose of which eluded me. I was on autopilot, fulfilling my mandate to live up to my Potential. I needed to get my law degree and satisfy, if not exactly impress, my parents. I had a desperate, prenatal need for their approval.

But despite my love for Kevin, the panic attacks came back in March with a vengeance, and I found myself in a free-fall funk. There are no precise words for this feeling, and even less reason, but feelings often find rooms that reason cannot enter. I reported this to Flak, who, in those pre-Prozac days of psychiatry, prescribed another drug, Thorazine. I was a walking pharmaceutical experiment, a panic-attacked, unfocused twenty-three-year-old.

"Tell me about your schoolwork," Flak said one day in late March.

I examined his sharply creased gabardine trousers and pressed shirt. He had the most beautiful liquid-brown eyes. I wondered where I had gone wrong in my life. Lara was right. I *was* a fuckup.

"Are you keeping up with your classes?" he asked.

We'd never talked about my classes before, and I wondered why he wanted to know now. Flak was not a detail-oriented guy.

"I'm not sure," I said.

"When are exams?"

I looked at my watch as if exams might happen any minute. "A few . . . um, three weeks."

"Well, are you able to study?"

I shook my head.

"Have you thought about taking a leave of absence?"

I jerked to attention. "No, I would never do that."

"Why not? It might make sense. You know, rather than failing to complete the semester."

The thought of interrupting my education was shocking. How

would I ever explain it to my parents? Suicide was one thing, but in order to really get attention in our family, you had to drop out of school.

"Do you feel like you can complete your exams?"

I dropped my head and fought back tears.

"Helen?" Flak's voice seemed to come from very far away. He sounded kind. I started to cry.

"Look," he said, leaning forward. "Here's what I think you should do. Go see the dean, and explain that you've got some medical issues that prevent you from completing the semester. Just ask to take a leave of absence."

Outside the window, buds dotted the oak trees across the road. There was a baby-green newness to the world; it looked foreign, even psychedelic.

"I'll write a letter for you," Flak said. "I'll recommend a medical leave from your studies."

———

It all happened very quickly. I walked into the dean's office the next morning as if in a dream. I had put on a new pair of corduroys and a freshly washed shirt. I had even combed my hair. The dean was an energetic man in striped suspenders, with a warm smile and youthful exuberance that I envied. He seemed genuinely happy to see me, and he offered me a seat in a shellacked black chair with the university's seal embossed in gold.

"What can I do for you?"

I felt strangely old, like a soldier returning from a distant war. "I need to ask for a leave of absence," I heard myself say.

He smiled. "It's that time of year, isn't it?" he said cheerfully. "This is when the pressure gets to people, with exams looming." He crossed one leg over the other and clasped his knee with his hands. "I think you'll find that if you just take a deep breath and get through the next week or two, you'll do fine. It's always this time of year when people panic."

I looked at him, realizing he couldn't possibly comprehend what I had been going through. I had traveled a long distance from the bloody battlefield of my heart to ask for a furlough. He, on the other hand, was used to students who were simply afraid of exams.

"I don't think so," I said, looking down. My lower lip started to tremble, and I felt the beginnings of an attack rising. When I glanced up, I knew that he saw it too—a look of terror spread across his face.

"It's okay," he said quickly, unclasping his hands. "Please, it's okay."

I tried to speak, but my head was beginning to shake, and I had trouble getting the words out. "My psychiatrist advised me to do this," I said. My hands and shoulders were quivering. Soon, I knew, I would have trouble remaining in the chair.

"It's okay!" the dean said again. "Really, please, don't worry."

"He'll write you a letter."

"Okay, that's fine," he said, jumping to his feet. "I'm so sorry. You just take all the time you need, and feel better, okay? I'll see to this, and you just take care of yourself and feel better."

I hadn't meant to scare him, but I was relieved that I didn't have to explain further. Panic attacks had become my most eloquent form of speech.

I nodded gratefully and walked out of his office. It had taken nothing to drop out of law school. It seemed so strange and unreal and liberating. *Too easy*.

―――――

The hard part was getting up the nerve to tell my parents. They would be devastated. And I cringed at the thought of Lara finding out, her smug satisfaction that I had finally gone up in flames, after all those years I'd acted so superior to her. She and I were connected to each other as if we were on a seesaw. I was falling fast; Lara would get a nosebleed from her sudden ascension in my parents' eyes.

"This is because of Kevin!" my mother said when I called her. "He got you to do this, didn't he?"

"No, Mom, that's completely—"

"Kevin is a dropout," she said. "You're stooping to his level." She hung up.

The next day, my father called. "We need to meet with Flak," he said. "Schedule an appointment. Mom and I will drive out Saturday."

I was used to being told what to do by my parents. At this point, I even welcomed my father's directions—thinking had become difficult for me these days. It was easier just to follow orders. He also told me to get a consult with another psychiatrist. Flak and I had botched things on our end, and he and Mom were going to have to come straighten me out.

They arrived at my apartment Saturday morning, and we drove to Flak's office.

"You have failed in your treatment of my daughter," my father said as soon as we were seated. He enumerated the conditions of employment, the expectations of services, and the glaring disappointment in results. "She was better off at this time last year than after a year of treatment with you."

No one could disagree, so my father continued: "She has taken up with this Kevin, who has distinguished himself by reaching the age of twenty-seven without securing a college degree."

"He drives tow trucks," my mother added.

I knew better than to say anything. By quitting law school, I'd forfeited my right to speak on my behalf. Besides, I felt oddly proud of my parents' ruthlessness—they were certainly a force to contend with, and I didn't think Flak stood a chance. As usual in family therapy, I was once again a spectator, watching the adults duke it out.

Afterward, in the car, it was my turn to get the law laid down. "No more Kevin," my father said. "From now on, you will not see him or speak to him."

"You can't do that!" I was shocked by my father's ultimatum. "Kevin had nothing to do with this. Besides, it's my choice who I see!"

"Not anymore," he said.

My mother said nothing and stared straight ahead.

"First thing Monday morning," my father said, "you'll make sure the law school credits your tuition for the semester toward next fall, when you will repeat the semester and graduate. Then call and get a consult with another psychiatrist before the end of the week."

My parents dropped me off at my apartment and drove back to Schenectady, leaving me with a to-do list and instructions to report back to them.

———

Dr. Russell's office had a giant aquarium of neon-colored fish and a long wall of books behind it. I had gotten his name from a friend, and I liked him immediately. Paul Russell was the opposite of Flak: a little shy and very sweet. Although he was easily as tall as my father, with the same stork-like legs, he lacked my father's fierce athleticism. Smiling, he offered me a chair and sat across from me. I noticed he wore a pair of high-top suede Clarks Wallabees, the exact color as mine in high school.

"Tell me why you're here," he said.

And so I did. I told him about dropping out of law school weeks before graduation; I told him about the panic attacks, about all the medication Flak had prescribed for me, and how I didn't think it was working. I told him about my older sister's hospitalization and suicide attempts. I told him I entertained myself with thoughts of crashing my car. I told him about group therapy, which I believed was pointless; I told him about Kevin, whom my parents hated. I told him I'd skipped my senior year of high school to go straight to college, and that I'd gone immediately from college to law school. I told him my parents' story, how they'd been engaged to marry before the war. That they'd been separated by the war in which everyone was killed. I told him how my father miraculously found my mother in Rome and married her ten years to the day after they'd first met. I told him about the Hoffman Children and Family Center where we'd gone to family therapy when I was a kid, and how—

"I think we need to schedule another appointment," Paul said, opening the calendar on his desk. I'd been talking nonstop for nearly seventy minutes.

The following day, to my amazement and delight, Paul told me he didn't think I needed medication; he thought "there's enough other stuff going on." And if I didn't want group therapy, he said, I should just quit. He encouraged me to trust my instincts and figure out what I wanted.

This was a radical idea. I was fairly blown away by professional advice *to do what I wanted*.

When I got home, I tossed my meds in the garbage and called Flak to tell him I was quitting group. It was a heady feeling, just doing whatever I goddamned pleased. I called the dean, and he assured me he would credit my tuition for next fall. Then I packed my hiking boots, sleeping bag, and backpack into the trunk of my Plymouth and drove north to New Hampshire. All I wanted to do was get out of Boston and head for the hills.

My parents insisted that I find a new shrink to see over the summer, but I figured I'd deal with that after I found a job. I arrived at Dartmouth after dark, sneaked into a dorm, and crashed in the lounge. The next morning, I showered and walked into town to look for a job. I tried the bookstore on Main Street, the hardware store, the sporting goods store, a couple of restaurants, and a pizza joint. No one needed help. Finally I sat in a coffee shop with the local paper and checked the Help Wanted ads. There were ads for auto mechanics, secretaries, and nurse's aides. And this:

> Farmhand: dairy farm, Woodstock, Vt.
> $50/wk + rm/bd. (802) 555-6745

I knew exactly nothing about farming, had zero experience with livestock, agriculture, or manual labor, but the ad instantly appealed to me. Without thinking, I walked to the pay phone on the street corner, plugged in a dime, and dialed the number. A woman with a scratchy voice answered the phone.

"I'm calling about the ad in the paper," I said. "I'd like to apply for the farmhand job."

"Ya ever worked on a farm?"

"No, but I'm a hard worker," I said. "I'll work one week for free, and you can decide if you want to hire me after that."

She gave me directions. "Come tomorrow morning, around seven," she said. "We'll talk."

————

The farm lay four miles north of Woodstock, on a frozen dirt road rutted by tractor wheels. It was early April, twenty-eight degrees Fahrenheit, sugaring season. The old farmhouse lay in a crook in the snowy hillside, and I pulled into its gravel drive.

At my knock, a bulldozer-shaped woman who looked to be about 104 years old yanked open the front door. Her long gray hair was braided and pinned to her head, and she stood stoutly, eyeing me up and down. "Come in," she said gruffly, brandishing a wooden cane. Her arms, hefty as a butcher's, emerged from the short sleeves of her cotton housedress. A faint pattern of indeterminate color was barely visible on the threadbare fabric. I followed her across the room to a wooden table crowded with doilies.

"Where ya from?" she asked.

"Schenectady," I said. "But I just drove up from Boston—I went to school there."

"Ya ain't in college, are ya?" Her voice rose, and behind her thick plastic-framed glasses her eyes were fierce.

"No," I said. "I was in law school."

She seemed relieved. "That's good," she harrumphed. "We got no use for them college kids. All that fancy schoolin'. Think they know everything." She narrowed her gaze. "So you're a flatlander!" she said with a mischievous grin.

"What?"

"FLATLANDER," she bellowed, laughing now. "That's what we call folks ain't from around here."

I smiled. "Well, I lived in New Hampshire for a little while," I said, careful not to reveal that I'd gone to Dartmouth College as an exchange student.

"Well, you're a flatlander all the same. Ya ever worked on a farm?"

"No, but I'm pretty strong."

"Well, I can see that," she said, sizing me up with a critical eye, then grumbled, "Probably eat a lot too." After a moment, she added, "My name's Edwina. Randall's my son. You'll have to talk to him about it. I don't have no say in it, but I like ya okay."

With that, she stood up painfully, and I followed her into the kitchen. "That's my sister Darline," she shouted, waving her cane at a small woman scrubbing clothes on a washboard and wringing them through a hand-crank into a large metal bucket.

"Go out there to the barn," Edwina said, waving her cane in the direction I should walk. "Talk to Randall. You'll have to see what he says."

She threw open the kitchen door and sent me off across the yard.

Inside the barn, the thick odor of cow milk and manure swallowed me whole. It was warm and musty, an altered universe of low ceilings and worn floorboards. Once my eyes adjusted to the dark, I spotted a man at the far end of the barn. I walked past the long row of cows' hindquarters. He was leaning over a cow, and straightened to his full height when I approached. Randall was a lanky man in his fifties, with a chiseled and clean-shaved face, very short-cropped gray hair, and the same plastic-rimmed glasses his mother had. He was wearing a worn-out zippered jacket covered with the short hairs of his cows.

I introduced myself, and he looked me over carefully. "Ya know anything about cows?" He pronounced the word with two syllables; it sounded like "cayoos."

"No," I said. "But I like hard work."

He nodded slowly. "Ya Catholic?" he asked.

"Um, yes," I said, surprised, but I figured it couldn't hurt my chances.

"I don't trust Catholics," he said.

"Well, I'm not much of a Catholic," I said quickly. "I mean, I haven't been to church since I was, like, six. It really doesn't mean anything to me."

"Catholics are always tryin' to convert ya," he said, studying me closely.

I shook my head and laughed. "I don't even know enough about Catholicism to tell the difference."

He nodded. "Well, I believe ya," he said.

And so in March 1981, within ten days of dropping out of law school, I became my mother's worst nightmare: I became what she would have referred to as a *peasant*.

———

"I've got a job," I told my parents when I called to check in. I gave them Randall's phone number. "I'm helping out on a farm—it's really beautiful up here."

I heard my mother suck in her breath.

"You will finish law school," my father said from the other phone.

"Of course. My tuition for the fall semester is all set."

"Have you found a psychiatrist?" he asked.

I had forgotten about that. "Um . . . not yet. But, you know, I really don't think I'll have time. I mean . . . well, maybe I'll just take the summer off from shrinks."

I waited for a response, but there was none. I think my parents were worn out. Perhaps they were simply relieved that I would be returning to law school in the fall. And that they had effectively gotten rid of Kevin, whom none of us even mentioned.

We also said nothing about Lara, though I was pretty sure she would rise as Star Achiever, now that I had crashed and burned. I hadn't heard from her since spring break, when she'd blasted me for choosing to spend the week with Kevin instead of her. Lara and I wouldn't speak again until the following fall, and by then we'd both pretend that nothing at all had come between us.

———

I slept in the spare bedroom of Randall's ranch house perched on the steep hillside above his mother's farmhouse and the cow barn, with a view across the valley to the blue waves of mountains beyond.

At three-fifteen each morning, Randall and I slipped through his house in stocking feet so as not to wake his wife, who worked as a bank teller in town. We pulled on our boots in the basement, refilled the woodstove that heated the house, and trudged down to the barn by moonlight. The nights were well below freezing, and my fingers and toes were always numb. When we stepped into the barn, the damp heat of the cows hit us like a soft wall of warmth. Randall went for the milk cans, while I hooked up the crapper barrel, hefted the shovel, and started lifting a few metric tons of shit.

Mucking out and milking the cows—our three hours of "chores"— were the bookends of our days. In between was the work. In April Randall and I spent the daylight hours climbing up and down miles of his wooded hills, flushing out maple sugaring lines, bundling them, tagging them, and carrying them back to the sugarhouse for storage until the following spring. The snow was still knee-deep on the northern slopes, and by the time we returned to the barn for evening chores, I could barely walk. Three hours later, at seven, after the last can of milk was poured into the enormous holding tank, we staggered back up the hill under the stars to Randall's house, where his wife was preparing dinner.

My body felt as if every muscle had been beaten with a rolling pin. It's hard to say which I loved more—dinner or sleep—and although I showered in seconds and we ate quickly, I often had trouble keeping my eyes open through dessert. Falling into bed was like diving directly into a dream. Minutes later, it seemed, my alarm clock jarred me awake at 3:15 a.m.

———

I was so fully occupied, and so completely exhausted, I couldn't even think about Kevin or law school or my parents or anyone. After that meeting with my parents and Flak, I had called Kevin to tell him my parents had ended our affair. "I don't know what's going to happen next," I said. He seemed to take the news as if he'd seen it coming. We hadn't spoken since then. My life before the farm slid out of my mind into some slag heap that I had no energy to visit right now.

My schedule was simple: I worked sixteen hours a day, from three in the morning till seven at night. Every two weeks I got a Sunday off. Never before had I relished the Lord's wisdom in commanding rest on the seventh day—or in my case, on the fourteenth. I used those Sundays to sleep and do laundry. The rest of the time, I worked alongside Randall, a brilliant self-taught engineer, mechanic, and farmer.

And I fell in love with the cows: thirty-five big-boned hulks standing in their stanchions, butts out, tails swishing. I loved their clammy breath from giant nostrils, and the steam rising from their slops. I would lean my head and shoulders against their warm, massive flanks, and they leaned gently against me out of friendliness, while I washed their udders with a soapy cloth. Then I'd slip the suction cups onto their teats, and set up the next cow. My favorite was a giant Holstein with a head like a boulder and a whiskered pink muzzle. Hey You was her name. And Gert, the big beautiful Guernsey, with her strawberry-blond eyelashes.

We poured the cans of milk into the giant stainless steel tank, then took apart the milkers, washed everything with soap and a chlorine rinse, and hung them up to dry in time for the next milking, which started nine hours later.

———

By May, the snow was gone, the days were longer, and we let the cows out each day to graze on the hills. During the hours that I was working the distant fields, I had time to reflect on the wisdom of my chosen profession—law—compared with the joy of my current employment— shoveling cow shit, posting fences, and harrowing hillsides. I began to think that maybe I wasn't crazy after all; maybe I just didn't want to be a lawyer. Over the past month I had grown attached to Randall, who cracked me up with his taciturn one-liners. And I loved the hard work and fresh air, the rhythm of the days, and the warmth of the animals.

————

One day in May, when evening chores were over, I stopped at the farmhouse for a glass of water. "Ya boyfriend's here," Edwina said with a grin. "Seems like a pretty nice fella." I rushed up the hill and saw Kevin coming out of the basement door of Randall's house. He smiled and wrapped me in his arms. I was relieved he wasn't angry at me for having disappeared.

"How did you find me?" I asked.

"Well, it wasn't easy!"

He'd called Flak, who told him I was working on a farm near Woodstock. So he drove up and started going from farmhouse to farmhouse. "I had no idea there were so many farms out here!" he said.

Randall let him camp out in the field below the house for a few days, and Kevin helped with the farmwork before returning to Crump's Garage outside Schenectady. This became my destination every two weeks for my twenty-four hours off. As soon as the last cow was milked every other Saturday night, I'd run up to Randall's house to shower and change, jump into my Plymouth, and speed down the dirt road toward Schenectady.

Kevin would be sitting up waiting for me, nursing a Rolling Rock and listening to the Who, reading the *Times*, or studying *Foxfire* for ways to build an eco-friendly underground dwelling. We would collapse into bed together, thrilled to have outwitted the forces of nature (my parents) by managing to be together after all.

Best of all was sleeping in the next morning. For the first time in two weeks, I was not awakened by my alarm clock at 3:15 a.m. We slept till the sun spread itself across the room, till hunger finally forced us out into the world in search of breakfast. We'd go to a small diner in Cohoes and read the *Times* over pancakes and eggs. Eventually we'd go back to Kevin's place, usually to bed, until about four in the afternoon, when I had to get back on the road and return to the farm.

I don't remember how the topic came up, but as the summer wore on, Kevin suggested we get married. The idea began to grow on me; it made the prospect of becoming a lawyer more tolerable—I figured I could balance doing something dull and dreary (law) with something fun and comforting (Kevin).

"Are you going to tell your parents?" he asked one Sunday afternoon as we lay in bed, dreading the moment I would have to drive back to Vermont.

Just thinking about my parents made me break out in a sweat. "Sooner or later, I'll have to."

"How do you want to do it? Do you want me to be there?"

"No way," I said.

Kevin looked relieved.

Two weeks later, on my next day off, Kevin and I went to his parents' house to announce our engagement. His father jumped up and gave me a big bear hug. Mrs. Flanagan pecked me on the cheek, and I blushed, wondering if I could really pull off something as surreal as marriage. I liked the Flanagans, and they liked me, and in any event, they did not consider it any of their business whom Kevin married.

I drove straight from the Flanagans' to our house to tell my mother. I knew my father would be at work, and it was always easier to talk with Mom than Dad. She could break the news to him later.

But when I came up the stairs from the driveway, her face was stony with anger before I'd even opened my mouth. She didn't even offer me tea—instead, we sat in the living room at a chilly distance from each other.

"Mom," I said. "Kevin and I have decided to get married."

She stared at me.

"I know you don't approve, but I wanted you to know."

I could see her face shut down, as if a steel grate had just been lowered.

"Why are you doing this to us?" she said in an ominous voice.

"What am I doing to you?"

"Oh, you know perfectly well!" Her eyes narrowed. "Look at yourself."

I glanced down at my T-shirt and jeans. This was how I always looked. "What do you mean?"

My mother scowled. "As if you didn't know."

"Because I want to marry Kevin? That's why you're so angry at me?"

"Well, isn't that what you wanted?" My mother's lips came together in a tight pinch. "Ach," she said. A Prussian spitting champion. "Do whatever you want, I don't care. Go ahead. Throw your life away." She stood and walked out of the room.

Shaken, I drove back to Kevin's above Crump's Garage. He was happily inebriated after spending the afternoon at his cousins', celebrating his betrothal. He welcomed me with a goofy grin. I burst into tears.

"What?" he said.

I shook my head. We were miles apart, I thought. What had made me think this could work? I sank into the couch, put my head in my hands, and sobbed.

Kevin stumbled into the kitchen and cracked open a beer. "Wanna brewski?" he said.

What an idiot, I thought.

Kevin's good mood could not be undone. He told me how happy the rest of his family was when he announced our decision to get married. His cousins had gotten a keg of beer, and all the aunts and uncles and kids had come over and sat around the yard in lawn chairs, talking and drinking the afternoon away.

"I'm really sorry," he said when I told him how it had gone with my mother. "At least you got it over with."

He was right. But long after he went to bed, I stayed up, milking my loneliness, realizing that what I'd *actually* gotten over was the desire to get married in the first place.

It would be months before I could admit this to Kevin. I've always tried to avoid acknowledging my mistakes. By the time I brought it up, Kevin was neck-deep in a ROTC program, slogging through the swamps of Ranger School, and seemingly unsurprised by my latest reversal. I couldn't explain my sudden change of heart, and I was ashamed of it. It would take me several more years to grapple with the fact that I was gay. But being queer was only part of the problem; at the age of twenty-four, I still didn't know much of *anything* about myself. That summer I'd latched on to the idea that maybe I could stow myself away in marriage, but almost immediately I realized it wouldn't work. I still didn't really know what I wanted, much less who I was.

part three

sixteen

1982

Lesbian coming-out stories tend to be similar in at least one regard: most women figure out they're lesbians when they fall in love with a woman. Usually the body knows what the mind denies, and the body manages to wake up the mind to its needs and desires. In my case, however, there was a complete disconnect between my body and my mind, a sort of Iron Curtain between the Wild West of my heart and the Stalinist regime of my brain. That dividing line was my mother. Or rather, it was my mother in me.

Like my mother, I had the uncanny ability—well, disability, really—to believe what I wanted to believe about myself, and then to act the part, to direct myself in such a convincing performance that I lost track of who I really was. I was able to fool myself, resulting in the charade that was my life.

During the winter of 1982 I was studying for the New Hampshire bar exam in Concord. I still hadn't found a new shrink, so out of laziness, I returned to Dr. Flak for a few months. Once a week I would drive the hour and a half from New Hampshire to Boston to his office, and it was there, suspended in the middle of nowhere in my personal life, that I came upon the realization of my sexual orientation, as one might come upon a large outcrop of rock in the middle of the woods that had been sitting there all along, but had gone unnoticed because it was covered with leaves. I don't remember how that session started, but I found myself talking about my college days, about the intensity of my feelings for Emma Dunlap, and then, and then . . . As I talked, my mind unspooled, and a light flickered on, and then another, and another—a little string of lights snapping to attention as I listened to what I was saying. Like a surprise party in my head.

I didn't want to admit it to Flak, but as I talked about the women I'd been crazy about, I realized that I'd always been a boy at heart; I'd always played war and football and hated the onslaught of breasts and hips, and I realized I had never liked sex—not with Philip, not with . . . well—but I did love Kevin. Okay, I really did love Kevin, and sex was even nice sometimes, but setting Kevin aside for the moment, I realized it was tomboys I'd always loved, just like Lara—she and I had been rough-and-tumble kids who loved sports and tests of strength, and it wasn't just our attraction to starvation and grueling workouts and punishing hikes in subzero temperatures; it was our love of *guy* things and our disgust for *girl* things; we didn't care about makeup or dresses or fingernails or jewelry or any of the stuff girls were supposed to like.

And setting Lara aside, I kept coming back to the overpowering passion I felt for Emma my freshman year. And then for Harriet as a sophomore. And then, junior year, for Claire! And long before college—in a line going all the way back to first grade—I'd always had a best friend, a girlfriend with whom I'd wrestled and played catch and stayed up late at night talking and laughing and planning daring escapades.

So my coming out was a process of elimination—I sorted through all my experiences with boys, and realized they didn't amount to much.

But. Yet. There was Kevin. My lone straw in the other juice box. He was proof that I was not quite 100 percent lesbian. He was my holdout for bisexuality.

I drove back to New Hampshire from that session with Dr. Flak giddy with excitement. Of course! All the evidence came rushing in, flooding the "queer" side of the scales. *I'm queer! I love women! What a relief! I'm a dyke!* My elation was through the roof. It explained so much! After so many years of not understanding what was wrong with me, I finally made sense to myself.

Not that I knew what it meant to be queer. I just knew that I was, sort of. I tried to attach a feeling of attraction retroactively to Emma. It was a process of reconstruction in my mind. As I said, it was a head game; my body was barely implicated.

But now I started looking around me, and there they were, everywhere! The girl at the register at the grocery store—we exchanged a knowing smile. The woman at the post office. The woman who sat three seats away in the bar review class. Everywhere I looked I saw lesbians.

———

I told my sister about my revelation that winter, and she nodded and smiled with what I took to be recognition and something like relief. A few years earlier, she had told me about a brief flirtation she'd had with another woman in med school, but Lara was crushed when the woman decided to remain faithful to her girlfriend back home. Being gay—or

bisexual, or whatever I was—was something Lara and I had in common, something that brought us closer together, something we shared
as sisters. Neither of us had ever dated a woman, but we both knew this
about ourselves, and that knowledge was huge.

Of course, we didn't breathe a word about any of this to our parents, or at least not until many years later. It was hard enough figuring
out who we were and what we wanted while our parents were still
calling the shots in our lives.

———

As soon as I decided I didn't have to be a lawyer, my panic attacks simply melted away. In retrospect, I think I had to go a little crazy my third
year of law school in order to give myself permission to disappoint my
parents on a grander scale. Maybe that's what Lara had been doing all
her life—acting psycho to earn the right to catch a break and figure out
her own path. Not that any of this was conscious, but looking back, I
think our family relied on mental illness as a sort of free pass from our
responsibilities as members of our Family Cult of Success.

Years later, after we learned that our parents were Holocaust survivors, Lara and I immersed ourselves in the psychiatric literature about
children of survivors. *Often in families of survivors,* we read, *"separation"
becomes associated with death. A child who does manage to separate may
be seen as betraying or abandoning the family.* It was oddly reassuring to
realize that Lara and I fit a pattern carved by a history of genocide. But
that still didn't explain the secrets that Mom and her sister continued
to hide from us throughout their lives.

seventeen

Fall 1982

After passing the bar, I applied for the Peace Corps. I told my interviewer I wanted to go to Nepal or anywhere in the mountains, and he laughed and assured me that no one was actually sent to a country he or she requested. In September, I received my assignment: I would teach science and English in Lesotho.

I had never heard of it, and looked it up: a small black mountainous kingdom in the Drakensberg Range, completely surrounded by the Republic of South Africa. This was back in the days of apartheid, when Nelson Mandela was still in prison. A few days after I arrived in the country, special forces of the white South African regime invaded Lesotho and assassinated several members of the African National Congress. Later I would live in the midst of the bloody infighting between the African National Congress and the more radical Pan Africanist Congress.

My parents considered my decision to serve as a Peace Corps volunteer in Africa a giant fuck-you to them. Of course I'd known they would disapprove; but what I didn't expect was that they would cut me off altogether. Not once while I was in Africa did I hear from either my parents or my sister.

To complicate matters, I had injured my knee playing basketball shortly before leaving for Africa and was on crutches for two weeks. The orthopedist in Schenectady, a friend of my dad's, grudgingly cleared me for the Peace Corps. I'd had sports injuries all my life, and I wasn't about to let this hold me back.

My last day at home was Thanksgiving. As usual, my mother roasted a huge Butterball for the four of us, complete with enough side dishes and desserts to feed . . . well, a small African nation. After we ate, I stuffed my backpack with everything I thought I'd need for the next two years. A nervous energy ran through me, as if I had just launched myself from a very high diving board, and now hovered in midair—that delicious but nerve-racking moment of suspense before falling headlong into the water below. Something about my decision felt desperate—I was more afraid to stay on firm ground in America, where I would have to figure out what to do with my life, than I was to catapult myself into the unknown, halfway around the world. The Peace Corps, I thought, would give me a chance to grow up, something I couldn't seem to do here in America. My attraction to deprivation was at once punishing and hopeful—I assumed it would toughen me, I later realized, as Siberia had toughened my father.

Lara had arrived home the day before. She was working as a general practitioner in a rural county upstate, not far from Evans Mills, where my father had first put out his shingle in 1953. She described her practice as primarily tending to fishing accidents—sewing up every imaginable part of the body where a fishhook could get stuck. But she was growing tired of the drudgery, and she had finally decided to accept a residency in psychiatry to begin the following summer.

It was in the evening—the night before I was scheduled to leave—that my parents and sister summoned me into the living room. "Sit down," my mother said. All three of them stared at me as if I were being arraigned on criminal charges.

"What?"

"Don't go to the Peace Corps," Mom said. "We are asking you to reconsider."

"What do you mean? My flight leaves *tomorrow*."

"You're only doing this to hurt us," my mother said. "You have no right!"

I shook my head, amazed that after months of explaining myself, she acted as if I'd just sprung this on her a minute ago. "Mom," I said. "We've been talking about this since August! This is what I really want to do. I have so much to learn and—"

"What, a law degree and a Wellesley education, that's not enough? You're throwing it away to go to the jungle?"

"I'm not throwing anything away, Mom. And it's not a—"

"You will get sick," my father said. "You will get sick in the middle of nowhere. What will you do then?"

"Peace Corps will take care of it. They have a nurse—"

"And your knee is not healed. You should not go in this condition," he added.

I was worried about my knee, but I didn't want to admit it.

"I don't understand why you're doing this," Lara said. She shook her head. "I just don't get it."

I was surprised by Lara's response. She had never said anything one way or another about the Peace Corps, and I had assumed she'd be on board. Unlike my parents, surely Lara would get the lure of adventure, the tantalizing hardship and challenge of it.

Then again, I thought, looking at her in her tidy white turtleneck, Lara was anything but an adventurer. She played things safe; she stayed close to home. Yes, she was an outdoors woman and more or less indestructible when it came to feats of physical strength and endurance, but at the end of the day she liked to come home to a shower, family, and friends.

"After all the sacrifices we've made," my mother said. "After all we've gone through . . . this is how you repay us?"

We argued for hours. I was foolish, I was selfish, I was trying to destroy them. Nothing I could say would change that, and eventually I gave up trying. By the end of the evening, I couldn't wait to leave.

The next morning, we drove in silence to the airport. Like robots, we hugged good-bye at the curb, and I promised to write regularly. Then, with my crutches as carry-on baggage and a sinking feeling in my heart, I flew halfway across the world to southern Africa.

Twenty years later, when I was disowned by my family, I realized that they had done something similar to me, back when I had gone into the Peace Corps. My crime in both instances was the same: I had chosen to do something so perfidious, so beyond the pale, that in their eyes, it was I who had effectively severed our relationship. Later, with the codicil to my father's will, my parents and sister would simply make the break final.

After six weeks of in-country training, the other trainees and I were asked our preferences for permanent assignments. I wanted *adventure*, so I asked to be placed in the most remote part of the country, far from any other volunteers. A week later I found myself sitting in the passenger seat of a jeep on an eighteen-hour, teeth-jarring journey across mountain passes and deep gorges to a tiny village in Mokhotlong. Two men with machine guns hung off the back of our vehicle as protection, in case of ambush by rebels. In the higher elevations, the wheels of the jeep barely clung to the edges of precipices, and when you looked straight down, you could see the twisted metal carcasses of other jeeps that had not negotiated the track as well. At last we arrived at my site: a hut perched high on the escarpment, overlooking endless miles of mountains. Massive and rocky, their sides plunged like green velvet drapes to a narrow sliver of a creekbed, invisible from my hut. I felt I'd arrived in heaven. The weather was sunny and cool; every afternoon, a brief hail- or rainstorm blew through, leaving brilliant, glistening rainbows behind.

In the morning I woke to the acrid smell of breakfast fires of burning dung, shrouding the village in a bluish fog. I was one of the only white people within half a day's travel, and people wondered at my skin, my hair, and touched me gingerly, as if I might disintegrate or explode upon contact. During the day I taught science and English at the local mountain school and grew inexpressibly fond of my students, especially the older ones, who had outgrown the wide-eyed shyness of their youth, and who laughed uproariously at my fledgling Sesotho, a language so tricked out with grammatical twists and noun declensions that it made my head spin. And my pronunciation of words containing the impossible letter *x*—a sort of clucking sound made by snapping your tongue on the roof of the mouth, while somehow uttering the word with the rest of your mouth—made them literally roll on the floor laughing.

But as time went by, I grew lonely. Occasionally I made the half-day hike across the mountains to the regional camp where four other volunteers lived. They invited me to stay the night, and the following morning, I bought supplies—a candle and matches, a head of cabbage, tins of sardines—and hiked back to my village. I was troubled to discover how much I missed the company of Westerners. As much as I loved my students and the villagers and other teachers, I felt more alone than ever before in my life.

I wrote upbeat letters to my parents several times a week, hoping to appease them, to reassure them of my safety and well-being. I also wrote to Lara, describing my isolation and the beauty of the mountains, the double rainbows that sprang up in the midst of afternoon showers. I wanted to be blameless, even though I knew that they blamed me for deserting them. The silence of their rage felt natural and familiar to me. This was simply how my parents were, and it didn't occur to me that their reaction was particularly unusual. Although I sometimes hoped they would send me something—even a postcard, some token symbol of connection—I was not really surprised that they didn't. What did strike me as odd was that every other volunteer in my training group received regular letters and packages from their families.

And I was surprised and hurt that Lara didn't write. Perhaps it pissed her off that I could so neatly remove myself from her for two years. I don't know; we never talked about it. Perhaps Lara simply needed to align herself with my parents out of loyalty. If my parents refused to recognize my existence, then Lara needed to follow suit.

I had trouble imagining what Lara's life was like in those days, working as a small-town doctor. I tried to picture her in a white lab coat, seeing one patient after another, writing notes in their charts. But what I saw, instead, was an image of my sister and my parents turning their backs, closing ranks against me. After all, what right did I have to complain about their silence? Wasn't I the one who had left them?

The emptiness of the mountains, beautiful as they were, crept into me and left me hungry, ravenous. I longed for the voice of a friend. I wrote hundreds of pages in my journal and exchanged long letters with Kevin and other friends in the States, and with fellow volunteers scattered across the country. Mail was sporadic, depending on the weather, the availability of petrol, and the chance that a Land Rover could manage the arduous day's journey from Maseru. It was in one of those letters that I learned of the death of my college roommate, Janet. She and I had bonded as freshmen over our shared homesickness and fear of inadequacy at Wellesley. The cancer had announced itself and killed her in less time than it had taken the letter to arrive, and by the time I received the news, she had already been dead for months. Like me, she was twenty-five. I sat on the floor of my hut, lit by a single candle, and cried in shock and disbelief. I moved through the next few days in a haze, standing in front of my students in science class and teaching them about gravity, velocity, the forces that act upon us without our even noticing.

eighteen

Over the next few months in Africa, instead of healing, my knee got worse. Without warning, it would suddenly buckle and I'd find myself on the ground—sometimes on the trail outside the village, sometimes in the classroom. I hobbled around like that for another half year, and (as I would later learn) succeeded in tearing three of the four ligaments in my knee, completely severing the anterior cruciate. In a letter to the Peace Corps nurse, I finally admitted that I was having trouble with my knee, but I certainly didn't want to make a big deal about it. In my experience—perhaps having learned from my parents' dismissal of Lara's attacks on me as a child—complaining was shameful, and certainly didn't help your case. In any event, my self-image did not allow for weakness; my body was expendable in the interest of my self-esteem.

Despite my effort to downplay my condition, the wheels of the U.S. government had been set in motion. One evening I was writing in my journal by candlelight when the school director appeared at my door. "Hurry," she said. "You must get to Mokhotlong by morning.

A plane is coming for you." The Peace Corps had lined up surgery for me in Washington, DC, so I could recover in time to return to Lesotho for the start of the next school year six weeks later. The news reached me by pure chance; someone in a nearby village had overheard it on a shortwave radio and ran to tell my director.

I barely had time to throw some clothes into my backpack before starting down the path from my village in the dark. The trail was studded with loose rocks that skidded off into darkness with each step. Although I had a headlamp, I turned it off because it was easier to see by moonlight. This was the sort of harebrained adventure that Lara would have dragged me into during one of our hiking trips, but now it was pure Peace Corps. To meet the bush pilot at dawn, I'd have to hike four hours in the dark on a busted knee.

At last I arrived at the airfield and was weighed on a giant scale together with my backpack and a couple boxes of cargo. The bush pilot flew me and a few other government types to Maseru, the capital of Lesotho. From there, it was another flight to Johannesburg, then twenty hours to Liberia, and finally another twenty-hour flight to Washington. When my plane touched down in DC, I was sent to the Peace Corps office, where they had already typed up termination papers for me to sign.

I burst into tears. "No," I said. "My director told me Peace Corps was arranging surgery here and would send me back in a few weeks."

The Peace Corps administrator, an impossibly white woman with gold earrings and a bright-green dress, scanned the papers. "I'm sorry," she said flatly. "I have instructions to terminate you."

"But—"

"Sign here, please."

"What about surgery?"

"You'll have to look into that yourself. Contact OWCP to have your medical bills covered by FECA."

I was in shock. The fluorescent lights of the office were too bright. The street traffic outside was freakishly loud. I had come from silent long-distance landscapes to this cacophony of earsplitting noise, blinding lights, too many white people, and everyone moving and talking at an incomprehensible speed.

"Where do you want to go?" the woman asked me, signing the papers below my signature. Her words came out as quick and sharp as the clicking of a typewriter. It took me a moment to understand her.

"Can I . . . I really want to go back to my site. I'm supposed to be there in time for the school year."

Without looking up, she shook her head. "You're terminated."

I couldn't make sense of this. I didn't move.

She finally glanced up at me. "You can stay at our residence hall for tonight only," she said. "Tomorrow we will fly you home, or wherever you want to be sent in the United States. Where do you want to go?"

I stared at her.

"I need to issue you a plane ticket. I don't have all day. You're flying out tomorrow. If you don't give me a destination, you will need to make your own arrangements."

Tears poured down my face. "I don't know," I said. The last place I wanted to go was home; I couldn't bear the thought of facing my parents. Boston had good surgeons, I thought, but I hadn't lined up anywhere to stay. I didn't even have enough clothes in my backpack to live for more than a few days. "Schenectady," I whispered.

"New York?"

I nodded.

"Your parents have been notified of your return to the States," she said, stapling copies of forms and filing them in a drawer. "If you want, you can call them on the WATS line in the other room." She pointed to an adjacent room with a desk and telephone.

I picked up the black receiver, such a foreign object in my hands. This was all so surreal. I dialed my parents' number, and my mother answered the phone.

"Hi, Mom. It's Helen."

"Oh, Helen. Where are you?" She sounded relieved, and I nearly burst into tears. I did not want to be here, I did not want to be calling my mother, I did not want to be sent home, but I tried to keep my voice steady.

"In Washington."

"When are you arriving?"

"Tomorrow morning at ten-fifteen."

We hung up.

———

I stumbled out of the Peace Corps office into the stifling heat of Washington, DC. The streets were a blur of noise and light—cars and buses flashing in the sun, engines roaring, brakes squealing—I had to lean against the building to get my bearings. It was as if the world had cracked open, people rushing up and down the sidewalks, running for their lives. Yet no one looked frightened; they all looked purposeful— going to work, to shop, to meet, to eat. They rushed past me as I walked to the residence hall where Peace Corps had directed me to go. My leg felt fine, and I could almost believe there was nothing wrong with it.

I climbed the stairs to my room. It was mercifully dark and quiet—so quiet, in fact, that I didn't realize at first that I had a roommate—a very pale-skinned blonde around my age who was lying on the other bed, staring at the ceiling.

I introduced myself and told her I'd been a teacher in Lesotho.

She looked at me blankly.

"Are you okay?" I asked.

She told me that she'd been psycho-vac'ed from her village in East Africa because her school had been overrun by marauders. The men had raped and killed many of the local students and teachers, and Peace Corps was letting her hang out for a day or two before sending her home to the Midwest. I wondered whether she too had been raped, but I didn't ask any questions. She seemed grateful for the silence.

The next morning, I took the Metro to the airport and flew home, where my mother was waiting for me at the arrivals gate. She was wearing her no-nonsense brown slacks and a button-down shirt. "Do you have luggage?" she asked. I shook my head.

"Lara is starting her residency in a few weeks," she said.

I resented the pleasure in her voice, the pride she took in Lara's success.

"She got into a very good program!"

I didn't want to talk about Lara, and apparently Mom didn't want to talk about me. We drove home in silence, but the air around us crackled with tension. I'd refused to heed my parents' warnings, yet here I was, crawling back to them, dragging my ruined leg behind me.

"Are you hungry?" my mother asked when we got home.

I nodded. We sat side by side at the counter, eating babka and sipping tea, but could not find a way to talk to each other. She and I had always had a talent for chatter, for covering over everything with words, but now it was as if weights were tied to each word we uttered. They dropped at our feet like dumbbells, and we could not pick up the strand of a conversation.

My father returned home from work that evening and eyed me carefully before speaking. "How is the knee?" he asked.

I shrugged. "I'll look for an orthopedist in Boston," I said. I couldn't bear to be at home another moment.

The next morning, I drove to Boston and started shopping for surgeons. I crashed on the couch of friends in Cambridge; they were working and studying and we barely saw each other.

After a few consults, I realized my prospects were grim. All the surgeons said I'd be lucky if I could walk again without a limp, but none of them could get me into an OR for months. I was devastated. And I was overwhelmed by the sheer noise, speed, and shiny surfaces of America, which after Lesotho felt as foreign to me as the inside of a combustion engine. Michael Jackson's "Thriller" was blasting from the speakers in every store; people spoke so quickly I had trouble understanding them.

After a few days, I returned home to Schenectady in defeat. I was angry at the Peace Corps for dropping me like a piece of sheep dung; angry at myself for getting into this mess; angry at my knee for betraying me. And I was angry at my parents, who rose before me, a formidable force of reason and experience that I could not get around. Whenever I mentioned anything about Africa, my mother's mouth drew a sharp line that shut me up. "What are your plans *now*?" she wanted to know, eliminating the past tense from my vocabulary.

I didn't know. There was no way I would make it till October, the first available surgery in Boston.

Miraculously, Lara, like some enchanted Goddess of the North, came to my rescue. "Come stay with me," she offered. "We've got one of the best sports medicine departments in the country." Her voice on the phone felt like the warmth of the sun after a hard winter. In a flash, all of my memories of Lara's genuine goodness flooded me. She was once again my dream-come-true big sister, the sister I had caught glimpses of throughout my childhood and adolescence. She had always had this guileless quality of caring for the downtrodden, the broken, the forgotten. I basked in her sudden shower of love and concern, and, like so many times before, I simply dismissed the parts of my sister and our past that did not fit this glowing vision.

"I'll talk to the head of the department," she said. "He does all the knees for the UVM ski team. He'll have you back on the slopes in no time." Within a few days, she'd arranged for him to do reconstructive surgery on my knee. She drove down to Schenectady to pick me up.

My parents greeted her like a hero, and I too saw Lara as my savior, amazed at how gentle and generous she was with me. At the time I didn't realize how our family had always depended on this role-playing between us: one daughter in crisis, the other coming to the rescue. For her first twenty years, Lara had been our crisis, and I had been suited up by my parents to help her, to take her hiking or skiing at her bidding. I had always bristled under these expectations, and when I refused the role of rescuer, I was considered deplorably selfish. Now Lara and I had switched roles: I was the calamity that needed saving, and Lara was our knight in shining armor. Perhaps she also felt this was a setup, a trap, but she seemed to assume the role with genuine good nature, as if she were born to it, as indeed she was.

"Thanks for doing this," I said as we zoomed north on I-87 in her Toyota Tercel. "I was going nuts at home!"

She laughed. We were on common ground, and no one understood me better than Lara. When it came to our parents, to their regimented eyes-on-the-prize attitude and their commandeering ownership of us, Lara and I were the only two people on the planet who knew—really *knew*—what it was like to be their daughter. Our bond had been forged ever since I was a toddler in Italy, running after Lara while our parents and Aunt Zosia disappeared into their strange languages, holding their mysterious history close to their chests.

Lara listened good-naturedly as I talked about Lesotho. Before I knew it, two hours had flown by and we were pulling into the gravel driveway of her house a dozen miles outside Burlington. It was set on a hillside, surrounded by woods, with a deck overlooking green rolling hills.

"Wow," I said. "This is nice. But far out."

"Yeah, my roommates and I missed the country," she said. "Working inside all the time, we wanted to be able to get away from town at the end of the day."

She helped me carry in my backpack and sleeping bag, and showed me around. None of her housemates were in. We made a salad and sat down to eat. I told her I didn't know where I would be without her.

And this truth has never changed, throughout the many years and swings in our relationship. Where I am and who I am has always been directly tied to my sister.

That evening, I laid out my sleeping bag on the soft carpet in her dining room, and she introduced me to her roommates—all medical students or residents—who barely lived there, and didn't seem to mind.

The day before I had to report to the hospital for surgery, Lara took me for a walk on a trail in the woods near her house. The trail was gentle, through stands of tall pines and spruce, and the air smelled like freedom, our footsteps silent on the soft floor of pine needles. "You'll be fine," she assured me. "They'll fix your knee, and you'll be as good as new." I hung on her every word. She was the leg I stood on.

nineteen

One morning, at the age of eighty-eight, Uncle walked down the street in Rome as he did every day in his tailored three-piece suit, tie, and matching handkerchief, to get fresh milk and the morning paper at the corner store. On his way back, he was hit by a car that sped off down the narrow street. Uncle was rushed to the hospital and lay in a coma for the next several months. Although Zosia and my mother kept up their daily correspondence, it would be months before Zosia finally let my mother know that Uncle had been in an accident. Zosia had also forbidden Renzo to tell my mother. "I didn't want you to worry," Zosia explained when she finally wrote Mom the news. My mother got on the next flight to Rome. She stayed with Zosia for more than a month, until Uncle died. Then she helped Zosia clean out Uncle's room.

It would be many years before I learned that in cleaning out Uncle's room, Mom and Zosia threw out all the letters and documents and photos of my family's past. Uncle had kept everything, my mother later told me—family mementos that Zosia had brought from their parents' home in Poland; letters from German and Italian officials during the war, when Uncle managed to save first Zosia, and then my mother. Documents from the Vatican, when my uncle obtained papal dispensation for my parents to marry in Rome in 1946 as Catholics. And hundreds of letters from family and friends in Europe, America, and Israel. Mom and Zosia got rid of all the remaining evidence of our past.

After Mom returned to the States that summer, Zosia suffered a breakdown. For the first time in their lives, Zosia became so angry with Mom that she refused to speak or write to her. When Zosia finally did respond to Mom's repeated pleas for contact, she accused my mother of having betrayed her. "I have no idea why," Mom told me at the time. "I don't know what happened or how to reassure her. Something just broke in her when Uncle died." It would take a year before the two sisters resumed their daily correspondence. Neither mentioned the break again, Mom said, and they continued as if nothing had happened between them.

Lara and I always covered up our rifts the same way—relieved to be back together, we avoided talking about whatever had separated us.

———

When I woke up, Lara was leaning over me in a goofy shower cap. "You okay?" she said, jiggling my arm. "Hey, Helen, you okay?" I was gulping air and shaking uncontrollably. My right leg, cocooned in a white cast from groin to ankle, felt as if it were being roasted on a spit. "You're in the recovery room," she said. "The surgery went fine."

The betrayal was what hit me first: no one had told me it was going to *hurt* so much. I groaned.

My sister got right on it. "More morphine over here," she said to a nurse. "Her pain threshold is very high."

I was too miserable to argue with Lara about my pain threshold, which was in fact not high in the least. I knew I was a big crybaby, that I would never make it in Auschwitz or Mauthausen or Siberia. Still, it was nice that my sister was looking out for me. The needle went into my thigh, and I passed out.

———

My mother came to Burlington to supervise my recovery. She swept into my hospital room like a gust of wind, threw open the blinds, and sat on the vinyl chair next to my bed. I was barely conscious when she touched my arm.

"Helen," she said. "What have you eaten today? Have you exercised the leg?"

I lay in a cloud of morphine. "Hurts," I said.

"You can't lie around all day. It isn't good for you."

I closed my eyes.

"I'm going to run out and get a few things for dinner."

She was staying with my sister and came to visit me every day at the hospital. When I was released a week later, she brought me back to Lara's house and began to work on my future. Lara had started her ER rotation and stumbled home every couple of days, stunned by sleeplessness and haunted by visions of catheters falling out of body openings. All three of us were deeply unhappy, in the way that mothers and daughters can be when they want to believe they are helping one another.

"Would you like me to type your résumé?" my mother asked. "You'll need cover letters too."

I closed my eyes and drifted off to the mountains of Lesotho.

"I could do a template for you, and you could fill in the names and addresses of the firms you apply to."

The idea of a legal job depressed me. I was a failure. Only a year earlier, I had made the exhilarating and career-defying decision to work in Africa. I had wanted a life of danger and adventure, but I'd underestimated my need for conversation. And not just conversation, but companionship and love and intimacy and so many other things that I pretended I didn't need.

Now, as I lay in bed, it was starting to dawn on me that my ability to walk—never mind to run or climb mountains—was in question. I would have to rejoin civilization behind an office desk. Trips to the ladies' room and the watercooler would be my only response to the call of the wild. My self-pity knew no bounds.

After two weeks, the surgeon cut my cast open, exposing an emaciated yellow celery stalk of a leg. Angry seams ran up and down either side of my knee, tied off with black, blood-crusted knots. It was breathtakingly repulsive. "In another few weeks you can start PT," he said cheerfully, strapping on a full-length, metal-ribbed leg brace. It had a giant knob and hinge at the knee: Frankenstein in blue Velcro. Gingerly, I swung out of his office, careful not to hook the knob on my crutches.

My mother returned to Schenectady and I lay around my sister's house reading magazines and eating Tylenol laced with codeine. The leg was tender, and voyages to the refrigerator or bathroom required careful planning and mental toughness. Every day or two, my mother called.

"How are you doing with the résumés?"

"Um, I'm working up to it," I said.

"I put a new ribbon in the typewriter before I left."

"Yeah. Thanks."

"Are you eating?"

"Uh-huh."

"What are you eating?"

"Um, chicken. Salads. You know." In fact, I was following my usual diet of Doritos, M&M's, and ice cream.

"Did you get the check?"

"Oh. Yeah, thanks." My mother was sending me money to cover my household expenses. My active-duty Peace Corps salary had been paid in Lesotho maloti, which did not enjoy a favorable exchange rate with the U.S. dollar. By the end of my service, I had amassed $230 in my savings account. This was another source of shame—I was twenty-five years old, and once again my parents were supporting me. It complicated my anger toward them.

"How's Lara?" Mom asked.

"Okay." Lara and I had exchanged half a dozen words in the last week. She came home exhausted, opened the refrigerator, ate something out of a plastic container, took a shower, and fell asleep until she was due back at the hospital.

———

Weeks crawled by. My sister was getting the hang of being a doctor, and I was getting the hang of being a wreck. We started swimming together at an outdoor pool when Lara got off work. A standout swimmer in college, she moved through the water like a windup shark. Warily, I removed my Frankenstein brace at the edge of the pool and slipped into the lane beside her. As she powered up and down the pool, I pushed off gingerly and swam next to her, dragging my dead leg behind me.

Every twenty seconds I'd choke on the tidal wave of Lara's wake as she crashed past me. We kept this up for an hour or so. It was our quality time together.

By July I had established my rehab routine, paid for by Uncle Sam (I was on workers' comp as a federal employee). Every other day I went to physical therapy, where I cranked out hundreds of reps on the Cybex machine to the soothing voice of a sports medicine man. Then I proceeded to psychotherapy with a psychiatrist in Lara's department. (As a new intern in psychiatry, Lara had offered me a little free professional advice: "Helen, you should really see a shrink.") So at Lara's recommendation, I started seeing a colleague of hers, a funky, frequently distracted young woman who wore long hippie skirts and great earrings.

On alternating days, I started working as a volunteer at the local legal aid office, researching an appeal on a murder case. Despite my resistance to gainful employment, I was attracted to criminal law. Our client had killed his girlfriend after they'd gotten into a drunken argument over whose turn it was to go out for cigarettes. When she refused to budge, he called her a worthless bitch. "Well, why don't you just shoot me?" she'd said. "Not a bad idea," he agreed. He got up, went into the other room for his rifle, and shot her in the head. He immediately called the police in tears. "She's the only woman I ever loved," he kept saying.

I was trying to challenge the admissibility of his confession. We called it the "Not a Bad Idea" Murder Case, and although we had a decent argument, I had the feeling it was not going to be a winner.

One Friday afternoon, Lara came home from work restless. Her weeks of sleepless nights, dealing with psychotic patients and unpredictable emergencies, were wearing her down. She now had the week-end off, and while wolfing down a container of leftover grilled vegetables, she tried to entice me to go home to Schenectady with her. "We can be there in three hours," she said, stabbing a chunk of black-ened zucchini.

I would sooner have walked across a desert in high heels than go home to my parents. "No thanks," I said. "You go ahead. I'll hang out here."

"C'mon, Helen, it'll be good. I really need a break."

A feeling of unease slid over me. Lara didn't like to go anywhere alone. She *needed* me to join her.

"You should go, then," I said carefully. "That's a good idea." Even as I said this, I sensed that she couldn't manage to go home without me. Perhaps she didn't want to acknowledge how much she needed Mom to take care of her. Perhaps, like me, she was ashamed of how depen-dent we were on our parents for comfort and support, even in our midtwenties, when our friends had left home long ago. Her house-mates spent their days off with their boyfriends, throwing parties, in-viting friends over. How would it look if she went home for the weekend and left me to hop around the house on my own? I didn't know; I only knew that something more was going on here, and it made me nervous.

"We can hit Record Town," she offered. She knew I'd been eyeing the new Eurythmics album. "And we can stop at Ziggy's and get ba-gels."

I shook my head. "I just can't handle a weekend with Mom and Dad right now. They'll drive me crazy."

Lara's face clouded over. I recognized that look. The hairs on the back of my neck stood up, and I could feel the familiar panic seep through me.

"I'm really not up for it," I said as gently as I could. "You go ahead."

Something flashed in her eyes, and in an instant, I knew I was in trouble. She flung the food container across the room. "You're coming to Schenectady!" she said.

I was up on my crutches in an instant. She lunged at me, fists clenched. "You're coming with me!"

I ducked and spun away from her. My mind raced. I had to grab whatever I could of my belongings and get out of the house. I'd sleep in the woods if I had to. Frantically, I crutched into the dining room where my sleeping bag was stuffed into its sack in the corner. I scooped it up with one hand, managed to grab my wallet and shove it into the pocket of my shorts. In my haste, I slammed my leg into the dining room table. The pain took my breath away, but I kept going.

Lara was bearing down on me. "We're going to Schenectady!" She grabbed my shoulder and slammed me against the wall. I tried to keep my balance and protect my leg, holding the crutches in front of me to keep her at bay.

"I don't want to! Leave me alone!"

She grabbed the sleeping bag and used it to bat my crutches aside, shoving me into the wall. She was breathing hard now, her face red with fury. She was the Lara of my childhood, and we were once again alone with her rage, in a house in the middle of nowhere. I tried to protect my face with the crutches, but she kicked my leg instead. I let out a shriek, twisted free, and hopped across the room to the foyer. Her fingers clawed at my back. I reached the front door, threw it open, and hopped out to the landing. The sleeping bag flew out after me, hitting me in the back of the head. "Fuck you!" she yelled, and slammed the door.

My arms were shaking as I leaned over and picked up the sleeping bag. It was nearly six in the evening, and the sky was steel gray. I side-stepped puddles from earlier showers, and made my way down the driveway onto the country road. The highway was visible in the distance. I began crutching the half mile or so toward it. I had just cashed a check that week, and I had eighty dollars in my wallet. It began to sprinkle lightly, and I realized I was crying. Tears streamed down my face, and the rain felt good. My arms were getting tired, but I didn't dare slow down. I had to hitch a ride into Burlington. Once there, I could find a place to stay for the night. Tomorrow I'd go to the university and look for a cheap room. My clothes and belongings were in Lara's house, but I had my down bag and my wallet, and that was enough.

By the time I neared the entrance ramp to the highway, my armpits were burning. A solid drizzle pasted my hair to my forehead. I stood on the shoulder of the two-lane road propped on my crutches, holding my thumb out. My leg brace absorbed the rain like a sponge—it felt as if a baby whale had attached itself to my thigh. I knew I looked deranged. There was almost no traffic, but the few cars that passed me swung out in a cautious loop, and I could see the drivers and passengers peering out at me as if I were an axe murderer on crutches.

Nearly an hour went by. I was soaked and chilled. I considered hopping up the ramp and onto the highway itself but I didn't want to get stopped by a trooper. So I stayed on the road near the ramp and waited. Surely someone would be heading to a grocery store in town. Finally a car appeared in the distance, coming slowly toward me. It was taking its sweet time, and I thought my chances might be good— maybe a local farmer or his wife. When it was a few hundred feet away, I realized it was Lara's dark-blue Tercel. I began crutching down the road like a maniac. Within seconds, she was upon me. I cut across the road, reversed direction, and hopped wildly, hoping another car would come by. Now I had to get to that ramp, get up to the highway, where I would be able to head against traffic so she couldn't reach me. I no longer cared about state troopers. I was running for my life.

Lara had turned the car around and rolled up beside me, the passenger window down. "Come on, Helen," she said in a tired voice. "Get in the car." I wheeled around and darted back across the road.

"I brought our swimsuits and goggles," she said. "Let's go for a swim." Her voice was empty of emotion. She turned the car again and the engine purred as she crawled up beside me.

"Leave me alone!" I shouted.

She pulled the car over and got out. I started shrieking as if I were being torn apart by hyenas. "DON'T TOUCH ME!" I started leaping through the crutches, taking a running hop between swings. My knee was on fire. I heard her get back in the car and slam the door. She crawled up beside me again.

"I'm not going to hurt you," she said quietly. "Just get in the car, and let's go for a swim."

I was exhausted now, and my arms were worn out. I stopped and stood on the side of the road, leaning over my crutches, shaking with sobs. I knew how crazy I looked, how hysterical, compared to Lara, who had calmed down. And this sudden flip of my reality, from having been attacked by her to being rescued by her, made me even more unhinged. I felt the repetition of my entire history with Lara, my impotent rage when she suddenly reverted to being the calm, rational older sister, as if nothing had happened at all.

She waited behind the steering wheel for me to calm down. Then she leaned across the front seat and flipped the door open. A minute or two went by, while I tried to come to terms with my anger and defeat.

"I'm moving out," I said. "I am not going home with you."

She took a deep breath. "We can talk about that later. You need a swim. A swim will do you good."

"I can't live with you," I said. "I mean it."

"You're upset now," she said patiently. "You'll feel better after a swim." She held up the gym bag with our towels, suits, and goggles. "We'll just go to Sand Hill, go swimming, and then you can do anything you want."

Humiliated, I inched toward the passenger door, took baby hops to ease myself into the car, and sank into the front seat next to her. I dragged my crutches and sleeping bag in after me and yanked the door closed. My leg was throbbing, a monster with its own beating heart. Lara drove up the ramp onto the highway. Sitting as far from her as I could, I stared out my window, crying.

At the pool I changed into my suit, removed my leg brace, and examined the damage. My armpits were raw; they burned when I eased myself into the water. The rain was coming down hard now, in thick sheets, so we had the entire fifty-meter pool to ourselves. I swam with the fury and frustration of the past year, of the past twenty years, of my miserable future as a cripple. My goggles filled with tears, and I kept swimming. An hour went by, maybe more. I lost count of my laps, I lost track of Lara, and just swam without stopping, wishing I could swim all the way back to Africa.

Someone was shouting. "Hey! HEY!" It was the lifeguard. He was leaning over my lane at the shallow end, screaming at me. "We're CLOSED. Get out of the water."

I went to the showers. My teeth chattered and my lips were blue, and I toweled dry, replaced my brace and wet clothes. I let Lara drive me back to her place. "I'm moving out tomorrow," I told her, and crawled into my sleeping bag.

———

The next morning, I packed my backpack with shirts, jeans, a toothbrush, and my sleeping bag, and waited by the car for her to drive me into the city.

She came out to the front stoop. "Helen, you don't need to do this," she said, annoyed at my stubbornness. "You can stay here."

I stared at the ground and moved a stone with the tip of my crutch. "I'm not living with you anymore."

"Oh, come on, Helen. You're being ridiculous."

I shook my head. "Just give me a ride to town, and I'll find my own place."

She let out a sigh and rolled her eyes. We drove in silence into the city, and she dropped me off at the medical center. I felt nothing but relief when she drove off.

I studied the bulletin board at a nearby coffee shop, and a notice caught my eye: a battered women's shelter on Stanford Road offered safe rooms, a common kitchen, and group therapy for $26.50 a week. I didn't think of myself as a battered woman, but I did need a cheap, short-term place to stay, and this seemed perfect. I made a phone call and took the city bus across town. I completed the intake interview with the program director, an MSW more or less my age. I was her first lawyer. She accepted me into the program, and although I was assigned my weekly chores (cleaning the kitchen, vacuuming and dusting the lounge and rec room), she said I didn't have to participate in group therapy, since I was already getting physical therapy and psychotherapy at the medical center. Her name was Adrianna, but everyone called her Andi. We became friends. We almost became more, but she was married, and her days with women were over, she said. And mine had not yet begun.

That evening I called my parents from the pay phone at the shelter to let them know how to reach me, and to tell them everything was fine.

"Lara told us you moved out," my mother said. I could hear the exasperation in her voice. "What has gotten into you?"

I knew better than to try to explain myself. Mom never considered Lara's behavior a reason for me to leave. "I just can't live with Lara," I said. "And I found a great place! It's super cheap, a county-funded housing program."

The next day, my mother left a message for me to call her. In the meantime, she and Lara had talked, and Lara had recognized the name of my housing program. She and my parents were horrified that I'd chosen to go to a *battered women's shelter*. What was I thinking? Why didn't I just go home to Lara? She was my sister! Just because we had a fight, my mother said, I didn't need to make such a big deal out of it.

I was a little ashamed myself. The other women at the shelter looked truly needy—empty-eyed, beaten down by life. Most were African American, and many had children who tugged at them as they did load after load of laundry in the coin-operated machines. I felt so much luckier than these women; I worried that I might be taking advantage of the system. Yet there were plenty of beds available, and I needed the housing. And although I didn't want to admit it, I actually had a lot in common with my housemates. I was disabled and unemployed; I had been assaulted by a family member, and didn't feel safe at home. So I was legit—a bona fide battered woman, by the county's own definition. I told myself I was giving back by volunteering at the legal aid center downtown.

————————

"She's my closest friend," I told my shrink in Burlington. "I just can't live with her." I was always talking about Lara—Lara my hero, Lara my tormentor—always swinging from one extreme to the other within the blink of an eye. Once I moved out of her house, I felt much safer. Of course, I still had to live with myself, someone I didn't know very well, someone who careened into eating binges and pockets of depression without warning. Even so, I genuinely liked living on my own, getting around on the city buses, doing my own shopping and laundry.

My shrink nodded thoughtfully. The phone rang, and she held up a finger. "I'm sorry," she said. "I have to take this." I waited while she gave instructions to admit someone to the hospital. Here was a real emergency, I thought. It made me feel marginally better. I was not *that* wretched. There were people who had it a lot worse.

"I'm really sorry," she said, gathering her purse. "I'm the only one covering." She glanced at her watch, a thick-banded contraption with multicolored beads. "We'll talk next time, okay? I have to go."

I wanted to impress her with my composure and maturity. "No

problem." I collected my crutches and hopped out the door. It occurred to me then that perhaps she didn't believe my story that Lara had actually attacked me. I must sound like a hysteric. After all, Lara and my shrink were colleagues in the same department. For all I knew, it could have been Lara on the other end of the phone, alerting my shrink to an emergency they had on their hands. My therapist probably felt for Lara, for having to put up with such a wack-job sister as me.

Lara and I never spoke about that summer, and now I wonder what her version would be. Memory is unreliable, a beam of light with which we bend the past to suit our needs. In the end, I finally learned, all I can do is lay claim to my own memories.

twenty

1983

My first job as a lawyer was at the Office of Bar Counsel in Boston, steps from the courthouse in Pemberton Square. To my surprise, I actually liked the work. My office of ten attorneys was responsible for overseeing the professional conduct of every lawyer in the state, funded entirely by bar dues (including our own). It was an efficient way to make attorneys pay for the brooms and detergents necessary to clean up their own messes. We were sort of the janitors of the profession.

We prosecuted complaints of attorneys stealing their clients' money; attorneys sleeping with their clients' wives; attorneys snorting coke; attorneys who didn't answer their phones or their mail—in short, attorneys who were pretty much just like everyone else in the world. I started at $18,000 with full benefits, and the first thing I did was go shopping for a shrink. Paul Russell, the psychiatrist who had freed me from group therapy, medication, and law school two years earlier, now referred me to a former student of his in her own private practice.

Her name was Lisa. I sent her a letter before meeting her. *My sister,* I wrote, *is borderline, and also my closest friend.* Years later, when Lisa showed me the letter, I was shocked to see that I'd used that term—*borderline*. Had I really already known this back then? I realized that Lara herself had told me this; she had come up with the diagnosis, and discussed it with her own shrink. For years, I would refuse to believe it; I would pretend it wasn't true, I'd pretend it didn't matter. Each time I landed on this word as an explanation for my relationship with Lara, I would evade or minimize it.

So she had a borderline personality disorder, I would think—but hey, who didn't?

So did I, so did you, so did everyone I knew. Borderline or not, Lara was the only person in the world who understood me, who shared my history, who knew in her bones the strange warp and woof of the war my parents had survived and carried to America with them to wrap around our shoulders.

1984

Like most medical residents, Lara was saving lives on little sleep, while I spent my days chasing lawyers whose clients' funds somehow wound up in their own bank accounts. She called me a few times in the spring, moody and depressed. "Helen, this sucks," she said. "I mean, I like psychiatry and all, but . . . I don't know."

"Can you get out to the mountains for a break?" I was still on crutches from a second knee operation in January. The surgery in Burlington eight months earlier hadn't worked.

"Helen, I get, like, six hours between crazy-long shifts."

As usual, we never mentioned our last crisis—the time she'd attacked me when I was on crutches the previous summer. It was uncomfortable to acknowledge these violent rifts in our relationship, and so, by unspoken agreement, we pretended they had never happened.

We commiserated over our limitations, and compared shrinks. "Lisa is all I think about when I'm not working," I said. "She's amazing."

Lara too had finally found a therapist she liked a lot, but her shrink was young and pregnant and about to take a maternity leave, which made Lara anxious. We talked about how inconvenient it was to be in love with your shrink. How crazy it seemed to have to respect all those rules and roadblocks—the fifty-minute session; the lopsided conversation focused on you, you, you; the supposed blank slate of the shrink, when she was sitting right there, with her legs and arms and breasts and lips and . . .

"I know," Lara said. "I understand the need for boundaries, but . . ." She sighed. "It can get ridiculous sometimes. You know?"

"Yeah. It's not like I'd want Lisa to go on a date with me," I said. "I mean, that would completely freak me out. But at the same time, I think I would just like to marry her. You know? We could just live together."

Lara laughed. It felt good to know she felt the same about her shrink as I did about mine.

Within moments of having met Lisa, I was smitten. I was in love with her soft lilting voice, I was in love with her asymmetrical smile, I was even in love with her nose, which was perhaps a bit longer than absolutely necessary. She moved with a feline grace, tantalizing and mysterious, but it was the quality of her attention that tipped me off balance and removed my free will. She gazed at me with warmth and interest and intelligence, drawing me into her confidence as easily as a wave pulling me onto the beach.

I could never keep straight what color her eyes were—blue? gray-blue?—they were somewhere in there, a mountain stream. She was quiet but fierce, and I had the feeling she could fight with surprising verbal strength if she had to. I felt sure she'd had to—but then again, I didn't really know anything about her.

I once called her in the evening, because she'd urged me to call if I felt depressed. When she answered, I heard classical music in the background, and I became so overwhelmed by her voice in my ear and the violins in the background that I had trouble remembering what I said or what she said, or why I had called in the first place. It was her presence, her voice, her *self* that held me transfixed; and although I tried very hard to hold on to the actual words she spoke, the substance of our talk fell away, leaving me adhered to her sublime Lisa-ness.

She didn't look the least bit dykey—I was pretty sure she wasn't queer, and that was fine for a while. I told her that I thought I probably was, though I hadn't dated any women yet.

Unlike Dr. Flak, Lisa was highly professional, which posed a number of problems for me. The hour started right on time (this was good), but it ended promptly fifty minutes later, which was difficult to accept. Fifty minutes was a pathetic little serving of love. It seemed absurd for me to be expected to walk out of her office twice a week and resume my life, which was clearly not all that it could be.

I started bringing her carefully selected gifts to make her love me more: a small beaded witch-doctor doll from Lesotho; a smooth stone I found at the beach; a book of photographs by André Kertész, whom I worshipped; a mix tape I compiled of my favorite garage rock, opera, and jazz tunes. We had to analyze all of these gifts, why I liked them, why I wanted her to have them, why, why, why. It was an exercise in delay of gratification. I don't think I ever said precisely that I wanted her to love me more than anyone else in the world, and that each gift was calculated to make her do so. Overall, they did not accomplish the intended objective. But it was obvious that some were better than others. Poems were good. I brought her poems from various books I was reading, until a couple of those backfired. To a poem by Ai about the moon and knives and severed heads, Lisa remarked drily, "All this drama." I defended the poem as art; Lisa dismissed it as sensationalism. She tried to get me to talk about me.

"I *am* telling you about me," I said. "This poem is about me."

She looked skeptical, an eyebrow up. "The moon as a severed head. That's you?"

"Never mind. Forget it."

"Why don't you tell me what you're feeling right now?"

I looked behind her shoulder at a small statue on her bookcase. I wondered what she'd done with the rock from the beach I'd given her. What was I even doing here? I was sick of myself, irritated with my inability to snap out of it, to stop being such a loser. It was my habit of self-loathing that got me down. I found myself boring and hopeless and, well, angry.

"Are you angry?"

The clock above my head ticked quietly. *What a waste of time*, I thought. At least this was covered by health insurance. I didn't have to pay a penny out of pocket in those days.

"I'm depressed," I said eventually. *Would it kill you to be a little nicer?* I thought.

We argued about why I was depressed, but I held my ground about not being angry. I don't know why this was such a point of pride for me, but obviously a patient must put her foot down somewhere. Over the next few weeks, I admitted to being "frustrated," "upset," and "annoyed," but never angry.

Lara was the angry one in our family. Not me.

Of course I wanted to get fixed—I was suffering from mind-reeling bouts of depression and occasional periods of bingeing, and obviously, whether I could admit it or not, plain old-fashioned rage. But it seemed that my first order of business was making Lisa fall in love with me. I wanted to seem worldly and intelligent, a person of substance. I was an elitist, just like my parents, and I had a great deal of disdain for popular culture, which caused problems for me because I was completely and utterly a creature of popular culture, right down to my passion for football and punk rock and popcorn. I wanted to be the sort of person who played classical music and sipped Courvoisier, but instead I played "Sympathy for the Devil" and guzzled Diet Coke.

I don't know what she really thought of me. She listened as if everything I said was of enormous import, as if my feelings mattered, which I had trouble believing myself. I fell in love with her just by listening to myself talk to her. It would take a long time—years—before I realized that she was teaching me something I didn't even know I needed: to look at myself with the same openness and curiosity that she offered, to trust my own truth.

———————

The call came in early April. I was alone in the apartment—my roommates were all out for the evening—and I was standing on crutches in the kitchen trying to solve dinner. The phone rang, and I hopped over to answer it. It was my mother, calling to let me know that Lara was in the hospital. I could hear the strain in her voice as she fought to compose herself.

"It's all right, she's going to be okay." My mother took a deep breath, and I realized I had been holding mine. "She tried to kill herself."

My stomach lurched. I felt like one of those cartoon characters that get knocked down and have stars and squiggly marks around their heads. "What . . . I mean, how—"

"It's my fault!" my mother cried. "I gave her permission— remember when she broke down during medical school?"

She was talking about the summer three years earlier, when I was working as a law clerk in Troy and my parents told me I couldn't call home because Lara was so angry at me.

"Mom, it's not your fault."

"I gave her permission that summer," my mother said. "I told her that she could. She begged me and I—"

My face was wet with tears. I was sitting on the floor now, crutches by my side, staring at the scratches and scuff marks on the pale-yellow kitchen cabinets. I'd never noticed them before. Time seemed to collapse and expand. Four years ago my mother had called to tell me that Lara had cut herself up with a razor. But now, instead of demanding that I come home, Mom was blaming herself for Lara's self-destruction.

"She was so desperately unhappy." Mom was saying. "And she begged me."

"Mom, there's nothing you—"

My mother talked over me. "And I realized then that I couldn't help her out of her pain. I couldn't do anything anymore. I told her it was all right. That she had my permission."

My face felt hot. Now I'd managed to crawl under the kitchen table and held my good knee to my chest and rocked.

"Mom, that was years ago. That doesn't have—"

"She's in the ICU now. We're very lucky. Tanya found her and got her to the hospital."

Tanya was Lara's closest friend, a surgical resident.

"She's going to be all right," Mom said. Her words sounded hollow. "She just needs to rest. They'll keep her there for a while."

After Mom hung up, I stayed under the table, crying. I was scared. My sister had nearly done it. She was really sick. I needed to wake up.

———

Lara was transferred to the psych ward of a community hospital outside town so she wouldn't be treated in the same hospital with her patients. After a few weeks, she called and invited me to visit her for Easter. I could take her out to a restaurant. I was so eager to see her, I splurged on a plane ticket and rented a car at the airport. I was no longer on crutches, but my knee was still swollen, and it ached as I drove out to pick her up at the psych ward. Lara looked surprisingly good—thinner than when I'd seen her at Christmas, but her face was pink and fresh and she was in good spirits. We hugged, and I nearly burst into tears with relief to see her.

"I took a bunch of pills," she said over brunch. "I was just in a really bad mood. Really pissed off."

I was grinning idiotically, just happy that she was alive. She looked positively radiant. Although she was telling me about one of the worst days of her life, she spoke easily, almost with wonder, like an adventurer to the North Pole who had survived a terrible storm.

"And I guess I . . . um, I had a bottle of vodka, and I drank some of that. . . ."

It was so good to have my sister alive and sitting across the table from me. I didn't think about how this had affected me or my parents yet. All that mattered was that she was here.

"So I got pretty fucked-up, you know. And I guess . . . I must have called Tanya at some point." She paused and looked at her hands. They were remarkably smooth, free of the usual dried skin and torn cuticles. "I don't really remember." Her voice drifted off. Around us, families were helping themselves to seconds at the buffet, and the smell of scrambled eggs and roasted chicken filled the room. "Tanya told me about it later," Lara said. "She was working a shift at the hospital, and I guess she got really worried. So she managed to get off duty and drove out to the house. But there was some huge traffic jam, and she got tied up."

I tried to picture Tanya in her little VW, stuck in a snarl of traffic. They had been friends since their first year of medical school, and Tanya must have been freaking out. I sympathized with Tanya in a way that I couldn't yet feel for my parents or myself.

"She said by the time she found me, I had no pulse," Lara said. "I'd stopped breathing." Lara seemed amazed and a little impressed by this fact. As if she were talking about someone else entirely.

"Jesus, Lara." My scalp prickled.

"She did CPR, and called nine-one-one, and they brought me to the ER. I don't remember that part."

I took a gulp of my wine spritzer and nearly choked on the bubbles. Tanya had saved her life. If she'd arrived a minute later . . . If she weren't a surgical resident, if she hadn't known CPR . . .

"I didn't mean to kill myself," Lara said, rolling her eyes, as if this should have been obvious to anyone. "I just didn't realize I'd taken that much." She shook her head with disgust. "They didn't have to make such a big deal out of it."

"Well, it is a big deal," I said, suddenly annoyed. I clamped my mouth shut so I wouldn't say something I'd regret. What a nightmare for Tanya. Lara's cavalier attitude was maddening. She'd scared the shit out of everyone.

"But you know what pisses me off?" Lara said. "At the ER, they cut up my beautiful blue ski sweater—you know, the one Zosia gave me?"

I knew exactly which one she meant. Zosia had given me one too, but I had outgrown mine years ago.

"I'm still really mad about that." She shook her head. "I mean, they didn't need to cut my clothes off me! Jesus! That was a good sweater!"

I looked down at my plate, unable to meet Lara's eyes. I didn't want her to see how angry I was. It was inconvenient, this anger of mine; it didn't seem to belong here, at this nice meal we were having, this joyous reunion after a terrible scare. I was so happy she was alive. But it pissed me off that she seemed more concerned about her sweater than anything else. Didn't she get it, that she'd nearly died? She didn't seem to realize that she'd put her best friend in the position of having to save her life. What if Tanya hadn't gotten there in time? What if Lara had died despite her efforts?

All I managed to say was, "Lara, this is serious. You nearly died."

She shrugged. "So how are you? How's the knee?"

———————

By the time she was released from the hospital after a month, Lara had fallen in love. Maybe that explained her good mood when I'd visited over Easter. Jess was a psych nurse in the hospital, and it was complicated. But eventually Jess managed to disentangle herself from a bad marriage, and moved in with Lara.

I visited them over the summer, and I liked Jess immediately. She was sweet, she was smart, and she loved my sister. Lara seemed to glow in her presence.

And something else happened. Now that Lara was living with Jess, Lara and I magically got along better than ever before. Jess's presence in Lara's life seemed to smooth out all the waves in our relationship— as if Jess served as a buffer for Lara's rages, for her demands on me and her anger at me for failing her. These seemed to melt away. Lara listened to Jess. She wanted to keep Jess. And she would, for the next twenty-five years or so.

Eventually Lara returned and completed her psych residency, passed her boards, and became a psychiatrist at the same hospital where she had trained. She seemed pretty happy. She began to live her life. Our sisterhood blossomed. I came to rely on her for advice, for solace, for friendship. We were a team.

———————

It's strange to think about that time now, thirty years later, after I've been disowned by my parents—after they've unequivocally declared Lara their only child. Because back in 1984, I came pretty close to being my parents' only child. It's as if there was only room for one daughter, and Lara and I played Russian roulette with each other all our lives. As if one of us could actually win at the game.

Despite the fact that death—murder, suicide—was such a big topic of discussion among us, none of us ever succeeded in actually killing ourselves or each other in person; I got killed off on paper. Being disowned is violent and shocking, and although you can still move your arms and legs, it's a permanent display of murderous rage, and it gets you thinking. How do you go from being the most treasured creature in the universe, the embodiment of your mother's and father's hopes and dreams, to being wiped out by them? What had I done?

twenty-one

The years after Lara's near-suicide and hospitalization in 1984—before we found out we were Jewish, long before the publication of my book about our discovery—were a sort of golden age for my relationship with Lara. We emulated the perfect sisterhood of our mother and Zosia, who had taught us that the bond between sisters was sacrosanct. Husbands were nonessential family members, compared to sisters. You tended a husband more or less like a shrub: he needed to be fed and trimmed, but then you left him out in the rain. Sisters came inside with you.

But like many of my mother's lessons, what had enabled her to survive the war did not always translate well into living in America in the late twentieth century.

One evening in the fall of 1991, Lara called me in tears. I was in my living room in Cambridge, watching a football game when the phone rang. "There's something I have to tell you," she said. Her voice teetered, as if the words were strung across a high wire. "Oh God, what am I going to do?"

I muted the television. "What happened?"

"I . . . I'm starting to remember things. About Dad. When I was really little."

Something recoiled inside me. On TV, a running back plowed into a wall of bodies in breathtaking silence.

"It's . . . This is really going to freak you out." Lara choked back tears. The men disentangled themselves and trudged back to their huddle. "Look, I'm sorry to tell you like this, but . . ."

"What? Just say it."

She drew in her breath. "I'm having recovered memories. I remember Dad raping me as a baby."

A silence opened up in me, like a dark lake under a ceiling of stars. I stood and walked in a small semicircle, twisting the phone cord around me.

"I know it sounds crazy, Helen. Just listen. I've been having these memories, and they're hard to make out. I've been working on it in therapy. It's been completely overwhelming, and—"

I felt a little queasy and placed the palm of my hand on my forehead. Lara had always had a gift for the dramatic, but I didn't know what to do with this revelation. In my bones I knew it wasn't true, but I wanted to be supportive. "It's okay," I said, though I was pretty sure that nothing was okay, and nothing had ever been okay in our family.

"The images that come back to me are just horrible," Lara said. "It's been really, really hard. And—it also involves you, Helen. I remember him doing the same thing to you."

"*What?*"

"Dad raped you too, Helen."

I froze.

"When we were infants. Toddlers. Before we could even speak."

On TV, Jerry Rice leapt five feet in the air and caught a pass one-handed over the heads of two defenders. I stared at him, as if he could help me make sense of what my sister was saying.

"Helen, you there?"

"Yeah. But I don't think—"

"I've been reading the literature, and it's terrifying. I guess this is pretty common with trauma victims. Especially when it happens when you're so young, as we were. The only way to survive the trauma is to repress it, split it off. . . ."

Her voice galloped on, but I had trouble following her. Was she confusing her patients' memories with her own? My fingers hurt, and I realized I'd been gripping the phone so hard my hand was white. *My sister's crazy*. I tossed sibling loyalty out the window.

"Are you there, Helen?"

"Yeah, sorry."

"Look, I'm sorry to dump all this on you, but I think you need to know. I mean, it's bound to come up for you too. And I just want to warn you, it's really hard going. You might find that—"

Her words swept past me now like a strong current. The more confused I felt, the more self-assured she sounded.

"You've got to believe me, Helen. Do you believe me?"

"I guess . . . I don't know. I mean, I gotta think about it."

"I always knew something was wrong with Dad," she continued. "He's really, really sadistic. You know? He's very disturbed. He's a monster."

I closed my eyes.

"With my therapist," she said, "I've come to see so much. Dad's a paranoid schizophrenic. When you start looking at our past, it's really obvious. Everything is starting to fall into place."

Everything was falling apart. Nothing made sense. Allegiance had always been so confusing in our family. Either you supported each other, heart and soul, or you were archenemies. My sister and I had been pitted against each other throughout our childhood, and I couldn't afford to lose her now. But I wasn't prepared to give up my father for her. Sex abuse? It was ludicrous, it couldn't be true. Our father could barely bring himself to touch us; how could he have had sex with us?

"I don't know, Lara." I tried to remain calm.

"I need you, Helen."

The trouble was, I couldn't find what she needed anywhere in my house or in my mind or in my experience. A dark line fell between us, like a crack in the earth, and it grew deeper and more impossible to cross. I wanted her to go out for a run and come back to her senses and realize it was all a mirage, a strange, scary mix of memory and imagination that had created a bogeyman out of nothing.

"Maybe you should talk more with your therapist," I suggested.

I could hear her crying softly. The gap between us opened wider, and I couldn't find the words to close it. I held on to the receiver as if holding her hand. The silence grew uncomfortable.

"Helen, don't you remember it?" Her voice was soft, clear, chilling.

I bit my tongue. "I don't know," I finally said. "I just—I don't think so."

"You should think about it," Lara said. "You should try to face it. But go slowly. It's really, really hard. It's the hardest thing I've ever had to do. The urge to repress it is huge. It's classic PTSD." She had regained her confidence now, and was explaining it from her expertise as a shrink.

I pictured my father, the hard line of his jaw, the pale blue of his eyes. I'd just been home a few weeks ago, and as usual, he had sat in the living room, reading a medical journal, listening to Dvorak on the hi-fi. He was mildly interested in hearing about my work as a public "offender" as he liked to call it, but we didn't say much; we were happy simply hanging out together. It seemed impossible to think of him as raping anyone, much less me and Lara as little kids.

"It explains so much," Lara said. "I mean, look at us—we're both lesbians. We're so much alike. I think that stuff is deep-rooted. It goes back to what Dad did to us."

The following day I reported the news to my shrink, who cast a fishy eye and found it just a little alarming how much recovered memory of child rape and incest was going around these days. She reminded me that my sister was doing a fellowship in child psychiatry, and had been treating youngsters who had been sexually abused. Perhaps the power of suggestion had led her to make similar associations in her own life?

I called Lara back that evening, but she was adamant. "I know what happened to us," she said. "And at some point, Helen, you'll re-member too."

Over the next few days, Lara's words followed me wherever I went: to the swimming pool for my early morning laps; on the T downtown to work; back home where I vacuumed and did the laundry. The more

I thought about it, the more impossible it seemed. Dad had been our family doctor since before we were born. He had brusquely steered us through mumps, chicken pox, scraped knees, sprained ankles, fevers, the flu. "Say 'ahhhh,'" was one of his more endearing remarks. His examinations were quick and precise. "Okay," he'd say, with a perfunctory pat on the head. "You'll live." He had always seemed about as interested in my body as in a banana peel.

It was curvy blondes he found attractive, women with large breasts, narrow waists, and swishing hips. Like his first love before the war, a blond Polish girl who'd accompanied him on the piano when he played violin.

I also knew something about sex offenders from my work. A few years earlier, as a trial lawyer, I had defended men charged with rape. Child rapists tend to be unable to stop preying on children until someone *forces* them to stop. (Lara claimed our father abused us when we were babies, but never afterward.) I had once cross-examined a six-year-old child who believed he had been raped at a day-care center by one of my clients. I'd called an expert psychiatrist who testified to the lack of credibility of such recovered memories. "A child's mind is highly susceptible to suggestion," he'd said. "A kaleidoscope of factors can influence the reconstruction of false memories." Like all criminal defense attorneys, I worshipped the god of reasonable doubt; I believed in the possibility of mistake.

But what if Lara was right, and I was repressing everything? After all, I was hardly the picture of mental health myself. So I tried to remember. All night I lay awake in bed, picturing my father coming into my room when I was a child. It's true, he did have a creepy way of suddenly materializing in a room without warning. He used to slink around the house, appearing now in the kitchen, now in the hallway, his size-twelve shoes soundless on the shag carpet. I tried to conjure images of my father leaning over me at night, and I managed to freak myself out. I have a wonderful imagination. But it was hard to ascribe these shadowy images of my father to memory. They were inventions, suggestions. In my clear moments, I saw that they were born of a desire to be like Lara, to have no barriers between us. Sexual abuse at the hands of our father would bind us together like nothing else. Her hand was extended across this terrifying new land; I just needed to remember what my father had done to me.

But I couldn't. And because my memory was different from hers, our alignment as sisters was threatened.

"I got ahold of Dad's journals," Lara told me later that fall. She was calling regularly to see if I had finally recovered my own memories. "Last weekend, you know, when I went home. After Mom and Dad were asleep, I searched the basement. They were sealed shut in cardboard boxes labeled with your name on them. Among boxes of your childhood stuff."

"You went through my stuff?" The old rage welled up in me, calling up the times Lara had broken into my room and read my diaries. I used to go wild—it was as if she'd broken into my mind.

"They're *his* diaries. I didn't take any of your stuff."

"He was going to give them to me! He told me so!"

"Helen, listen, you won't believe what he's written in here. I took them to Kinko's for photocopies—there's a million pages."

"How could you—?"

"Don't worry. I put the originals back—no one will know. Besides, it's not like he confessed to anything in writing."

I'd known about my father's journals for years—he'd shown them to me one night in his office the summer after my first year of college. We were holed up there while my sister was rampaging through our house on one of her marathon tantrums. We'd spent many hours like that, my father and I, joined in our helplessness and anger. His office was quiet and free of my sister, and we'd feel like temporary deserters from a long and dirty war.

It was on one such evening that my father had taken out several big loose-leaf binders from a locked cabinet. He opened them for me and paged through them. They were impressive for the sheer quantity of words, miles of ink running across the pages. "One day these will be yours," he said. "I am writing them for you." I felt honored by my father's confidence. He was tight-lipped and did not divulge much. But he had poured himself onto these pages, and he had written them for me.

"You had no right!" I told Lara.

"What do you mean? After what he did to us? He's the one who violated *us*! We were *babies*!"

"I don't care," I said. "It doesn't give you the right to go through his private journals."

"Jesus, Helen, how can you defend him? Why are you protecting him?"

"Look, he's my father too! I mean, I'm trying to be open-minded, Lara, but I don't know. You're asking me to believe that he raped us when we were babies, and—"

"I'm not asking you anything! I'm *telling* you. It happened. He did it. I remember it. I was there, and so were you. You don't have to like it, but you can't deny it forever." She hung up.

————

How do you choose between members of your family? Lara and I had swung from one extreme to another, and in our family, you always had to pick sides. The stakes were too high, the feelings too intense, the accusations too violent. You couldn't just float above the crisis. One way or another, you were going to be dragged into battle—as if opposition was the only way we could show our love for one another.

twenty-two

My loyalty to Lara was instantly restored a few months later. Apparently in the midst of her crisis over her recovered memories, Lara had been sending inquiries to various international organizations, hoping to learn more about our family. Now in March 1992, she received a bombshell: a packet of documents from a rabbi at Yad Vashem in Israel proving that we were Jewish and that we had dozens of family members who had been killed in fields, ghettos, and camps in Eastern Europe. This discovery knocked the wheels out from under us, and Lara's allegations of child abuse now took a backseat to the Holocaust. Although her recovered memories would haunt her for decades, she stopped trying to convince me that I had shared her experience.

Instead, for the next year Lara and I spent hours on the phone, trying to understand the enormity of the secret that our parents and aunt had kept from us all our lives. In August, we traveled to our parents' hometowns in Eastern Europe and found witnesses who led us to the sites of mass shootings in the woods outside their villages; we went to Israel to meet with the rabbi who had sent us the pages of testimony.

The story that emerged was overwhelming, and I wanted to write a book about it.

But given my parents' and aunt's insistence on silence, writing about my family was complicated. I spent the next few years agonizing over whether I even had the right to tell their story. By 1996, four years into the project, I was finally on a roll, which meant that I could string together two or three sentences before having to stop, play a dozen games of solitaire on the computer, and worry about my mother's likely reaction to what I'd just written. I figured my father would be okay with it (I'd shown him sections, and he said he didn't care whether people knew he was Jewish), but I was pretty sure that my mother would flip out. It was Zosia who insisted on keeping the secret, and my mother was terrified of doing anything against her sister's will. Just as I was now terrified of doing anything against my mother's will.

I had been living with my partner, Donna, for two years by then, and she was supportive of the project. But it was my sister who really championed my writing of the book. "You can't worry about what Mom and Dad think," Lara said. "They've lied to us our whole lives. You're thirty-eight years old! You have a right to your own voice—your own truth."

In what was shaping up to be a battle between the old generation and the new, I felt lucky to have Lara, the star psychiatrist, on my side. She was even more zealous than I. Not only did I have the *right* to write my memoir, she insisted, I also had the *historical obligation* to do so. "Your book will be a testament to the lives of our grandparents and aunts and uncles and cousins!" she said. "It's kind of ironic, don't you think, that by denying their own past, Mom and Dad are actually participating in covering up the Holocaust?"

I enjoyed this brief tour of grandiosity provided by my sister—it was a welcome respite from my usual state of drowning in guilt over my project. I needed Lara. I'd even given her a copy of my very rough manuscript for safekeeping. Now, instead of blaming each other for our little-shop-of-horrors history, Lara and I could finally join together in blaming Hitler for our shattered parents' lies.

———

That spring, I was invited to give a short reading with friends at a fund-raiser in Boston for a small press. I was nervous—still afraid of my mother's wrath if she were to find out I was writing about our Jewish identity.

"Don't worry, you'll be great," Lara said over the phone. "What section of the manuscript are you going to read?"

"I don't know, Lara. It's just a mess of rough draft pages, and I'm scared. I don't want to read anything about Mom and Dad or being Jewish. I don't think I'm ready to put that out there."

"Then just read the few pages about us as kids," she said. "You know, the part about how crazy we were, and our fights, and going to family therapy and all."

So I polished up the section and read it at the fund-raiser, and I thought, *Well, that wasn't so bad*. I told Lara all about it the next morning, during our debriefing.

"Way to go!" she said. We high-fived over the phone. She asked me to send her a copy, so I popped the seven pages in the mail.

A few days later she called me up excitedly. "Helen, this is fantastic! You have to publish it!" I was thrilled, of course, that she liked my writing. But I still didn't feel ready to publish anything. I was having enough trouble just writing the damn thing.

Lara, however, had already thought it through. She'd even found a publisher for me—a professor at her university was putting together an anthology of essays by adult children of Holocaust survivors. "Your piece is perfect, Helen—don't change a word, just stick it in an envelope and send it to him."

It took me another week to work up the nerve to send my seven-page essay to the professor. The day after I dropped it in the mail, Lara called. I could tell from her voice that something bad had happened, and I knew immediately it was about my writing.

"Listen, Helen, um . . . I've been thinking. You know that piece you wrote about us when we were kids? Well, you gotta change some things in it. I mean . . . I'm a psychiatrist here, and . . . I have a reputation and all—"

Oh shit, I thought. *Here we go.* It was as if some part of me had been expecting it. All these years that I'd been relying on Lara's support of my writing, I seemed to have forgotten this—her tendency to flip. I kept doing that, forgetting the parts of my sister that she and I both needed to forget, in order to fuse our relationship. It's what my family had always done—just sweep the bad parts under the rug, and *poof!* return to Happy Family. Rinse and repeat.

"Helen, you've got to take out that part about me hearing voices as a little kid. I mean, that's psychotic, and that would really hurt my career."

"Okay," I said carefully, "I could take that out."

"And you also have to take out the part about me being anorexic. That's really loaded; that could ruin my reputation. And also about my nighttime checking—the whole OCD thing."

I tried to sound calm, but I could hear my heart banging in my ears. "Lara, you *told* me to send it out without changing a word!"

"I know," she said, "but I've had a chance to think about it some more. And you have to take that stuff out."

"But all that happened ages ago! We were just little kids!"

"It doesn't matter, Helen. This is my career!"

How could this hurt her career any more than her near-fatal suicide attempt seven years ago? She'd been a resident at the same hospital where she now worked as a psychiatrist; she'd overdosed on
Tranxene and vodka and landed in the ER. Certainly *that* could have
put a crimp in her career, yet her teaching hospital had welcomed her
back with open arms. She'd risen through the ranks as a beloved and
respected colleague ever since.

"Lara, the whole point is that our family was a disaster!" I said. "The
Holocaust didn't just affect Mom and Dad; it affected all of us. I mean, if
we were a perfectly happy family, we wouldn't have wound up in family
therapy in the first place. It wouldn't make any sense! I have to show that
this family has serious problems, to get us into that room with the shrink."

"Well, you could make me bulimic," she said. "But not anorexic."

Seriously? I thought. *Bulimia is okay, but anorexia isn't?* I said nothing. *Okay*, I thought, *I can work with bulimia.*

"Well, how about this," Lara said. "Why don't *you* be the sick one?
Why not just write yourself as the one with all the childhood problems?"

I actually considered it. After all, who really cared? I wanted to
please Lara. "I guess I could do that," I said.

But then I realized it would pose narrative problems. "I can't have
Character A grow up to be Character B," I said. "I don't think that's
going to work." Besides, I explained, it would blow the whole purpose
of memoir—if I made stuff up, then it would no longer be memoir, but
fiction. I'd lived my whole life in my parents' fiction, governed by lies
and secrets and half-truths. I needed to write something that was my
own truth.

"Well," Lara said, "I'm just telling you that you can't put that stuff in about me."

————

Less than a week later, I received a letter from my father. *We heard from Lara about your intention to go ahead and publish our life story very soon. . . .* He went on to accuse me of destroying my family for my own personal glory. Exposing my parents as Jews would undo them. My mother would flee to Rome, he wrote, and since he hated Italy, he would have to relocate to another state. In effect, I would be forcing my parents to separate and leave their home, their state, and their country. What I was doing was immoral, he said; my conscience would never forgive me.

And then, in his final sentence, he suggested that perhaps if I changed their names, all might be well.

I sank to the sofa. I had feared that my writing would somehow kill my mother—irrational as that seemed—but here it was, irrationality confirmed. I was condemned by the two people I worshipped most, and I hadn't even published anything yet.

And then my rage rumbled in—not at my parents, but at Lara, who had called them into the fray. I burst into tears and showed the letter to Donna. She looked shell-shocked as she read it. "What did Lara tell them?" she said, sitting next to me on the sofa.

"Who the fuck knows?"

Donna held me and said everything would be okay. She was firmly on my side, and I needed her. Once I calmed down, I immediately wrote my parents back, reassuring them that of course I would change their names and protect their privacy, and in any event, the manuscript was nowhere near completion; the possibility of publication was even more remote. This was true: the book would take another three years to complete. And since I'd never published a book before in my life, the chances of getting the thing published were about as likely as my mother marching in the Gay Pride Parade.

I also immediately wrote the professor and withdrew my submission, explaining that my family was having a meltdown over it. He called and asked me to reconsider, but I was so shaken, I couldn't imagine letting him publish the piece. I wasn't yet strong enough to defy my parents. Even though I was almost forty years old, I still saw things through their eyes, and had trouble relying on my own.

And then there was the timing of all this.

In two weeks, Donna and I were getting married. It wasn't legal in those days, and we'd invited a total of ten guests, including Lara and her partner, Jess. I'd told my parents about our plans in an awkward phone conversation months earlier, and they'd met the news with dead silence. They liked Donna, but they could barely bring themselves to pronounce the word *homosexual*, much less congratulate me or ask for details. To spare us all the discomfort, I didn't invite them, and they never said a word about it.

Now Donna and I were running around, cleaning the house, planning the meal—so many last-minute details to attend to—when Lara called again. "By the way," she said darkly, "I'm *not* coming to your wedding." She slammed down the receiver.

"Thank God," Donna said.

I called Lara back and got her answering machine. "I think you're right," I said. "I think it's *not* a good idea for you to come."

But over the next few days, Lara called and left half a dozen messages begging to attend our wedding: *"I really want to be there, Helen.*

Why are you being so mean to me?" She followed with a postcard, a letter. *Please, please, please. Why won't you let me come?* It amazed me that she could not acknowledge what she'd just done.

Perhaps even more surprising was that I had trusted her in the first place. How many times had she and I repeated this pattern? How old was I?

She had not changed, I realized; *I* had. After all, Lara had always been like this—one moment my closest ally, the next my worst enemy. In her mind, she'd done nothing wrong; I was overreacting.

She continued calling, so I stopped answering the phone. This gave me a sense of safety, a bit of breathing room, although I still had nightmares of Lara showing up at our door, or breaking into our apartment and stealing my writing and journals. I did not return her telephone messages. I did not respond to her cards either. I was afraid of the slightest contact with her, lest I be sucked back into the vortex, like an alcoholic's first mesmerizing sip of whiskey after a long separation. In that sublime unity with Lara, I would forget the other side of her, the parts that we both preferred to ignore as if they'd never existed.

So what was different this time?

For one thing, there was no time. I was getting married in two weeks. Donna was my beloved, the one in whom I placed my troth and trust and faith. Maybe this was precisely part of the problem for Lara: she was losing me.

And then, of course, there was the problem of my book. I was trying, however ineptly, to feed it, to protect it, to nurture it into existence. This fledgling manuscript, scruffy and malnourished, was the voice within me that would not compromise. I could finally stick up for it. And I had Donna to help me.

Wedding, May 1996

Our spontaneity surprised us. Months earlier, on an evening in January 1996, when gay marriage was still completely illegal in all fifty states of America, Donna was cooking Country Chicken—a double-barreled cholesterol bonanza with bacon, cream, and black pepper—and I was sitting on the stool in our kitchen, yakking about nothing in particular. She held out the wooden spoon for me to taste. It was so amazingly good, I asked her to marry me. She tilted her head, a sly smile forming. "Okay," she said.

"Really?" I jumped off the stool.

"Yeah." She threw her arms around my neck, spoon still in hand.

———

Donna's foster brother, Frank, was a heretic Presbyterian minister in Kentucky, and she called him first. "That's wonderful!" he said, and agreed to be our minister. He gave us some dates he could be in Boston, and we picked Cinco de Mayo.

Neither of us wanted anything big. We figured we'd just invite some close friends, and have a sit-down wedding at home. If we emptied the living room of furniture and stacked it all in the bedroom and on the little deck, we could stretch out the dining table and fit everyone in. Donna planned the meal: she'd make four thousand hors d'oeuvres to start things off. Champagne, and sparkling cider for the folks in recovery. Next she found a recipe for an appetizer of boiled cabbage and lox, in honor of my shtetl roots. Main course: beef tenderloin (everyone we knew ate red meat back then) and potatoes au gratin with haricots verts, in honor of Donna's French grandmother. I was responsible for the words—writing vows for us to say over the main course, and choosing various friends' poetry and prose to recite at other points during the meal. Donna would make my mother's mocha torte (a recipe she'd gotten from an Auschwitz survivor friend), and I'd bake a flourless boule that registered eleven on the chocolate Richter scale.

Donna was in charge of dress selection, which she accomplished in less than a week: we both wore white linen, though mine was a little tunic-thing you might find on a schoolgirl in the British colonies, while Donna's was longer, graceful and flowing. We had our rings custom-made by a metalsmith with Paul Bunyan fingers, whose shop was in the belfry tower of a church overlooking Copley Square. Donna wore flip-flops for the wedding, or maybe she went barefoot—I forget.

It was easy to come up with a guest list: at the top were my sister and Jess; Donna's brother, the minister; Victor, our opera singer friend who had set us up two years ago; my young Italian cousin Nina— Renzo's daughter—who had just come out as lesbian; and a handful of close friends in the area. As it turned out, a few guests canceled: Donna's colleague from work backed out because she couldn't hack the whole gay thing. And my sister and Jess were last-minute casualties of Lara's mood swing over my writing.

Considering everything else that was going on that spring, our wedding went really well. The food was out of this world; our friends made us feel special; our vows actually meant a lot to us (including our promises to be patient, to seek help when we needed it, and to take the dog out even when we didn't feel like it). Lara's absence was palpable, but not devastating. I was beginning to see that I could survive without her.

twenty-three

I didn't speak to Lara again for two and a half years. It was my mother who begged me to reconcile with Lara, and I finally agreed to go home for the weekend after Christmas in 1998. By then, my book had been sold and was scheduled to be published in February.

Lara and Jess were already at my parents' house when Donna and I arrived the day after Christmas. The house was mercifully filled with golden retrievers—my parents' dogs, my sister's, and now ours—and their wriggling, happy bodies relieved much of the tension. After a mandatory cup of tea and piece of linzer torte, Lara and I decided to take the dogs for a romp on the golf course, leaving Jess and Donna to themselves.

We took two cars so we could fit all the dogs in, and I followed Lara's Toyota hatchback down Natchaug Road, the same route we used to run twenty years ago when we were both home from college. New houses had popped up where small farms and woods used to be. There was a new traffic light at the corner of Cromwell, where I had once hitched a ride with Suzanne Murphy in the seventh grade, certain that we would be raped and murdered, but in fact we'd been safely dropped off at her house half a mile away. I turned right at the light and followed Lara's Toyota up the hill. It was comforting to see Lara's car ahead of me, as if I were behind her on skis, following her tracks without having to think. We parked at the golf course, and as we opened the car doors, the dogs hurled themselves out into the icy air, overjoyed to be galloping across the snowfields. My sister and I both smiled—the automatic pleasure in seeing our dogs running with wild abandon. My dog had pulled a tree branch from the nearby woods and was now proudly prancing around with it, chest out, head high, tail wagging like a flag. Lara and I started walking side by side along the perimeter of the course.

"You look good," I told her.

"You too."

The dogs raced back and forth across the fields, circling back every so often to make sure we were okay. We threw sticks for them to fetch. As usual after a period of absence from Lara, she was friendly and fun to be with, and I felt foolish for having been so afraid to talk with her for the past two years. And also as usual, we did not say a word about what had caused our rift in the first place. Instead, we talked easily about our day-to-day lives, work, friends, activities. To my surprise, Lara already knew that my memoir was due to come out six weeks later. A friend of hers ran an independent bookstore, and kept Lara posted.

"When are you going to tell Mom and Dad?" she asked as we walked back to our cars.

"Once I get the advance copy in my hands," I said. "It doesn't seem real yet."

She pumped me for more details, but I told her I'd rather not talk about it, and she let it go. When we returned home, we found Donna and Jess talking in the TV room. Years earlier, when I'd left Donna and Jess together, Jess had told her the story about Dad sexually abusing Lara. "I wouldn't leave your *dog* alone with him," Jess had warned her.

"Your family is scary," Donna had told me afterward. I'd smiled, as if this were a point of pride; if you were going to have a crazy family, you might as well go for broke.

Of course, you would never have known it, to see Lara and Dad together that evening as we sat around the fireplace. She and my father talked about medicine, music, science, you name it. The strange thing about our family was that we didn't just love each other; we genuinely *liked* each other. We liked being together. If you'd looked at the four of us—Dad, Mom, Lara, and me—that holiday weekend, you'd have thought, *What a happy, loving family.*

After my book came out in February, I did not hear from my mother or sister again for nearly three years.

———

My dad was the only one who seemed to be okay with my having revealed that our family was Jewish, and that our parents had survived the Holocaust. I'd sent my parents an advance copy of *After Long Silence* as soon as I received it from my publisher after Christmas. I'd attached a note to my parents saying that I loved them, that the book was written out of love, and without any intention of hurting them. I told them that they need not read it, but that I simply wanted them to know that it would be published soon and I did not want them to feel hurt.

A week later, I received a letter from my father. *I do hurt*, he wrote, and chastised me for writing about private matters that were *not intended for public consumption*. His next paragraph began, *So much for ethical squabbling*. He went on to praise the book and my writing. He pointed out some misspellings of Polish words. He told me it was a good book, and that he was proud of me and loved me.

My mother did not respond. I imagine it was then, in early 1999, that my mother's world must have crashed around her, when she must have decided I was dead to her. It would be another few years before she made it official with the help of an inexpensive lawyer, but it was when the book was first published, I think, that she killed me off in her head.

All I knew at the time was that she returned the Mother's Day gift and card I sent her that spring. I knew she had to be out of her mind with rage, because she didn't simply refuse delivery of my package; she made a special trip to the post office and paid the postage to send it back to me unopened. And to do that—to get in the car and drive to the post office; to write out a new label in her own handwriting with my name and address on it; to bring it to the postal clerk and not care that the clerk would see that a package addressed from Helen Fremont to "Mom" for Mother's Day was being returned to the daughter unopened—my mother must have been so angry, she would have been unrecognizable even to herself. Mom had always been very big on appearances, on what other people thought. And my book—however filled with my admiration and love for her—had ripped open her façade. At this point, Mom didn't care what anyone thought about her relationship with her daughter Helen. She even spent the $5.95 for Priority postage to make sure that the package I sent her—a nightgown and letter, all unopened—would be returned to my door.

I understood, of course, the humiliation of having one's secrets exposed. I understood the sense of betrayal. But I hadn't grasped the degree of her distress, or what was at stake for her. By the time I'd finished writing *After Long Silence*, Mom had already had seven years to come to terms with our discovery of our Jewish identity. During that time, she knew I was writing the book. She knew that I'd agreed to change their names to protect their privacy. She also knew that, with Lara's encouragement, I had already revealed our discovery to Zosia and Renzo.

So why, seven years later, in 1999, when my mother was eighty and Lara and I were already in our forties, did Mom have such a violent reaction to the long-delayed publication of my book? What was still so important to her that she killed me off in her mind, after we were all adults? Who *cared* whether we were Jewish or Catholic?

That's when I began to wonder whether there might be more to my mother's and Zosia's story that I hadn't yet grasped. I don't think my father knew the whole story either. Uncle Giulio, I suspected, had played a bigger role than I'd thought. After his death in a hit-and-run accident in 1988, my mother and aunt had destroyed all of his personal belongings, documents, and photos, but now I tried to reconstruct what I remembered about him.

The Count

I had always adored Uncle; he was gentle and charming, and whenever I visited Zosia in Italy, he seemed to live with us like a very sweet, very polite housemate, his movements small and delicate, quiet as a well-dressed mouse. Zosia ignored him, for the most part, or dismissed him with an irritated flick of her wrist if he got too close to her. He cooked his own meals, ate at his own hours, took a siesta by himself, and spent his days poring over the mountains of legal and heraldic documents in his bedroom that doubled as his office.

While Zosia spent her summers with my mother, either in the States or in Europe, Giulio spent every August at his favorite spa in Tuscany with his friends. My aunt scoffed at his careful attention to his diet, his digestion, and his grooming. We joked that Uncle was the only true lady in our family, attending to his toilette with greater attention than any woman we knew. Dad dismissed him as a weakling and "unmanly." Mom treasured him and always said he was born in the wrong century. He was a romantic, she said, and although he was born in 1900, he was better suited to the Renaissance. He was proud of his heritage as a count from a long line of nobility, but Uncle Giulio had been estranged from his aristocratic family for reasons that no one ever spoke of.

One winter while I was staying with Zosia in Rome, I asked her whether she and Giulio had ever wanted to have more children after Renzo. She looked startled. "Oh yes," she said. "Yes, of course."

"So why didn't you?"

"There wasn't enough room," she said, gesturing to indicate the penthouse apartment in which we were seated, where she had lived with Giulio since the war. The apartment was enormous, extending across half of the apartment building, with two roof-deck terraces, three bedrooms, an enormous living and dining room area, and a separate room for a live-in maid. I said nothing, and she quickly changed the subject.

———

It never occurred to me in those days that Uncle might be queer. One didn't talk about sexuality in our family. Many years later, after Uncle had died and I was in my thirties, I finally came out to my aunt as gay. She smiled thoughtfully and said, "You know, Giulio was like that; he would have understood."

twenty-four

November 2001

My sister called to let me know my father had died. She and I hadn't spoken since that Christmas of 1998 when we'd gotten together in Schenectady, six weeks before the publication of my book. "There's going to be a funeral service in Schenectady," she said. Her voice was cold, a hint of frost. "Are you going to want to be there?"

I was standing in the living room of our apartment in Boston. My hand on the telephone felt strangely foreign to me. "I don't know," I said slowly. "I may have to process this in my own way."

"Well, I'll let you know when I find out more details."

"You don't have to," I said. What did it matter? My father was gone.

"I'll let you know," she said in a kinder voice.

We hung up, and I waited to feel something. My father was eighty-six. When I'd last seen him three years earlier, he was already quite wasted from Parkinson's; he'd had trouble speaking and moving. We'd cut his food for him, but it was hard for him to get it to his mouth. And he had shrunk to a fraction of his size, the Olympic decathlete decreased to a hunched figure of skin and bones.

Over the years since that Christmas, my father and I had continued to correspond, his handwriting becoming more jittery and illegible with each letter. My mother was caring for him at home, and I was not welcome to visit since the publication of my book. Despite my repeated efforts to reach out to her, the last time I'd heard from Mom was in May 1999, when she'd returned my Mother's Day card and gift. Other cards and letters I sent her went unanswered. I clung to my connection with my father, yet it was my mother whose love I craved, my mother whose anger I couldn't bear to face. I kept hoping that at some point she would relent, respond to me, invite me back in. But as the months and years went by, I resigned myself to the fact that as long as he depended on Mom for his care, it was unlikely I would ever see my father alive again.

Why didn't I just drive to Schenectady and show up at their door? I could have forced my way in, demanded to see my father, whether Mom liked it or not. But in truth, I didn't have the stomach to stage such a confrontation. It was hard enough to take my mother's rage from a distance. I didn't think I could bear to have her slam the door in my face.

So it could be said that in this way I collaborated in receiving my family's rejection by legal instrument, delivered via the cool remove of the U.S. Postal Service six weeks after my father's death. It was I who had chosen to avoid a face-to-face confrontation in our home. Clashing swords was Lara's style; that's what she had done all our lives. I was different. I was a writer. I gave and took my blows on the page.

And in some way, I accepted estrangement from my mother as punishment for having published a book I knew she would object to. Of course, I had waited for her to come around, but over the six years it had taken me to write *After Long Silence*, I had finally reached the decision to put my book out in the world and just hope for the best. I was, in effect, throwing down the gauntlet, standing up on my hind legs and saying, *I can't remain silent any longer. The secrets are crippling me. Choose me over the secrets.*

It was a risky gamble, and I miscalculated. I lost my mother. And in the package deal, I lost my father too.

But was it really a miscalculation? I had, in fact, considered the possibility of losing my mother forever. I had hoped that she would rise to my challenge, but I was determined to speak my truth even if she couldn't join me. Perhaps, painful as my excommunication from my parents was, it was the only way to be free. I was no longer an appendage of my parents, no longer an apparatchik of the family enterprise. Terrifying as it was, I was finally my own person.

———

So when Lara called to tell me that my father had died, I was not surprised. I was not filled with grief or sadness or rage or relief or remorse or any of the things I should be feeling. All I felt was nothing.

Donna tried to reassure me. "It's so complicated," she said. "It's like your father has been held hostage by your mother for years. You don't get to have a simple reaction to his death."

I went to work the next day and didn't tell anyone my father had died, because I was ashamed of my lack of feeling. Here it was, I thought, incontrovertible proof of my psychopathology. All day I observed myself at work. I went to meetings, laughed with colleagues, drafted memos, investigated complaints. I had to remind myself, *My father died*—to see if anything had changed in me. I called a friend. "It's okay," she said. "Give it time. At some point, we should do some kind of ceremony or something—just a gathering of friends here in Boston, something to help you process it."

I had trouble imagining a ceremony. Wouldn't that be awkward? We'd sit around and talk. About what? How could I begin to describe my father, to explain how trapped he was in our family? How trapped I was?

Six months earlier, Donna and I had flown to Atlanta for her mother's funeral; Lucy had died suddenly of a heart attack. At the time, Donna was also quite sick—she had endured six months of chemotherapy after a recurrence of cancer, and it had seemed that death was everywhere. Thinking back on Lucy's death, I was grateful that Donna's family accepted me as one of their own. But it was disturbing to realize that I had been more welcome at Lucy's funeral than I would be at my own father's.

I returned from work the following evening and found a phone message from my mother on the answering machine. Hearing her voice for the first time in nearly three years knocked the wind out of me. Her accent was thicker than I'd remembered, but it was Mom, and her tone was warm and wistful, and I could hear the tears in her voice. "Helen, it's Mom. We are having a service for Dad on Monday." Then her voice cracked: "I know that Dad would have loved for you to be there." She paused, and I could hear her collecting herself. "And so would I."

And so would I. I'd been waiting to hear words like this from my mother for what seemed like forever. Now, finally, with the death of my father, Mom wanted me. She wanted to see me, she wanted me there. I burst into tears.

I called her back, and she picked up on the first ring.

"Mom! It's Helen." The words came easily to me, as if I knew what to say to my mother after such a long time. "I just got your message . . . about Dad's funeral. And I want to—"

"Who is this?" my mother asked.

"Helen," I said louder. "Mom, it's me, HELEN."

"Who?"

"I'm Helen," I said. A chill crept down my spine. "Your *daughter*. Mom, it's *Helen*."

Silence.

"Mom, you called me about Dad's service, and—"

I heard my mother break into a sob. "Helen? Can it be . . . Helen? Is it you?"

"Yes, Mom, I just got your message." She had called me only an hour or two earlier.

"Oh, I'm so glad you called!" she said. "Dad's service is on Monday. I hope you can attend." Suddenly she was all business.

She gave me the address of the funeral home, I promised to be there, and we hung up.

I couldn't know it at the time, but four years later, my mother would be diagnosed with dementia. In retrospect, it is likely that she was already suffering from the beginning stages of the disease in 2001. Her inability to recognize my voice on the phone alarmed me, but in other respects, her brusque response to my call was not so different from how she had always been.

———

It wasn't a funeral. It wasn't a memorial service. It was at some random funeral home in downtown Schenectady. Lara and my mother had arranged it, but my father wasn't even there. He was in a box of ashes in the basement at home. The funeral home provided a large room where people could show up, express their condolences, and either hang out or leave. My father had always said he didn't want any kind of service or ceremony—no hoopla, nothing that would draw attention or cost money. Just burn him and be done with him. But this place seemed about as far as one could get from my parents' taste. It was like a mobster's idea of swank. The wall-to-wall carpet was busy with burgundy and white doohickeys reminiscent of fleurs-de-lis; the wallpaper was striped with garish hints of silver and gold. A few love seats in an aggressive shade of pink or green sat back-to-back, and an end table offered a small glass bowl of peppermint pinwheel candies. It took me a while to notice two cloth-covered consoles along the wall. My father's old leather medical bag and stethoscope were displayed on one table, next to two issues of the *Harvard Review* in which his personal essays about the Gulag had been published. They'd also laid out his violin in its velvet-lined case—a sort of miniature open casket with his bow leaning against it. On another table rested an intricately carved rectangular wooden box that he had made for my mother in Rome as a surprise for her twenty-eighth birthday in 1947. It was large enough to fit documents and letters, photos and knickknacks. The lid had warped with age, and the delicate trim he'd carved out of ebony had started to break off. The broken pieces were loose inside the empty box that would no longer close.

———

Donna and I had driven the Mass Pike from Boston earlier that afternoon, and arrived at the funeral home at dusk. My anxiety was through the roof—I was afraid to see my mother after such a long and painful silence. She was the one person whose love I still longed for. Would she be gracious or cold? Would she pretend nothing had happened, or would she pretend not to recognize me at all?

The prospect of seeing Lara also made me nervous. Ever since her flip in 1996 over my writing, I had ceased to trust her—or rather, I'd ceased to trust myself around her; I was afraid I'd be lulled back in by her charm. I missed her terribly, and my longing for her scared me.

When Donna and I entered the funeral home, a clutch of people I didn't know were milling about on that hideous carpet. My eyes landed on a beautiful woman in an elegant black wool dress that made her look like she belonged on Fifth Avenue. Cultivated, sophisticated, a commanding woman of good taste: my mother. Her hair was swept up in a wild burst of silver and white with some darker notes, like a very rich, very lush black-and-white photograph.

Mom walked briskly toward me, saying, "Oh, here she is," as if I had just stepped out for a cup of coffee. Before I could say a word, she linked my arm in hers, and off we went. My sister, I realized, was on her other arm; I could feel Lara's eyes assessing me. We said nothing. Mom was steering us around the room as if we were the prow of a ship, the three of us, aligned and intertwined, moving as one.

Donna had simply disappeared. I don't know how it happened. One minute I was walking into the funeral home with her at my side, and the next minute my mother—how radiant she looked!—collected me as if I were a package she had been expecting. She didn't even pause to greet or thank the delivery person—Donna, my wife. And I was too caught up in the world that is my mother to notice that my wife had fallen by the wayside. I was pulled into the world I knew by heart, that I knew in my bones: Planet Mom.

My mother was introducing Lara and me now to Mr. So-and-So, who had been a patient of Dad's, and to his wife, whose parents and even *grandparents* had also been his patients.

I smiled and nodded, and on the opposite side of my mother, Lara did the same. Off we went to greet someone else. I let myself be paraded. It was surreal, my hopes through the roof. Just like that, I seemed to be welcomed back into the fold as if nothing had happened. A wonderful relief, a giddy sense of possibility, and also that unreal quality that I recognized so well: the whiplash of going from three years of estrangement to instant intimacy, without passing Go, without a moment's pause. Like an alternate universe we had all just stepped into, over an invisible threshold.

Hours later, when the room emptied, Donna materialized, together with our Italian cousin Nina—Renzo's daughter—who now worked on Wall Street. Nina's girlfriend, Claudia, and Lara's partner, Jess, had both stayed back at Mom's house with Jess's kids, aged five and two. My mother turned to me. "Are you coming home?" she asked. "We'll have dinner—there's plenty for everyone."

Donna and I agreed, and we drove back to the house. I hadn't been there in years. It was strange to enter now—the dark brick floors of my childhood, the majestic Oriental rugs, the immense fire in the fireplace. Nothing had changed. Everything had changed. *I* had changed.

By the time Donna and I arrived, the house was already full of lesbians. We were everywhere—cooking a giant pot of pasta in the kitchen, setting the table, finding extra chairs, playing with Lara and Jess's kids. For the first time, I met Claudia, and marveled at how young and sharp she and Nina looked together. Earlier at the funeral home, Mom had made sure that none of our partners were present or came near us. She'd introduced only Lara and me to the guests; occasionally she might introduce our cousin Nina. I was used to playing it straight around my mother. But now in the privacy of our home, Mom seemed perfectly happy to be the matriarch of a family of six lesbians and two little girls conceived with the help of an anonymous donor. Dad's death had left the family completely free of testosterone.

Dinner was boisterous and good-humored. Wine helped. I started to relax a little, enjoy myself. We laughed and told stories—some involving Dad's battles with squirrels and snow and peanut shells; others about our own foibles. Although Lara couldn't meet my gaze, I felt relieved to be welcome at home. We seemed to draw closer with each story, each peal of laughter. As if we were a family again.

"How long are you staying?" my mother asked at the end of the evening.

"Just overnight," I said. "We're staying at a motel on State Street."

"So come for breakfast!" she said.

Donna and I exchanged glances. I was quietly elated that my mother had invited us, but I also wondered whether perhaps we should quit while we were ahead. I tried to assess how Donna was holding up, whether she could take any more of this. She was doing the same with me. Optimism won out, and we exchanged an *oh, what the hell* shrug.

———

By the time we got to the house at nine the next morning, everyone but Mom and Lara had already left. Jess had driven the two kids back to Burlington; Nina and her girlfriend had taken the train to New York. Mom made us a fresh pot of coffee. Her homemade babka, sprinkled with powdered sugar, rose proudly from a platter of crumbs, half of it already ravaged.

"Sit, sit!" my mother commanded, and rushed around, pouring coffee, cutting giant slabs of babka onto plates. Lara hesitated before sitting across from me. She seemed uneasy in my presence and shifted sideways in the chair, facing Donna, who sat next to me.

Donna smiled at her. "So, how are you doing?" she asked Lara. Donna had always liked my sister, but had been jolted by Lara's outburst five years earlier, when she had called in a rage, backed out of our wedding, and slammed down the phone. It was the first time Donna had seen that side of Lara for herself.

Lara shook her head. "It's really rough," she said. "But you know, it's also sort of bittersweet. Dad was so debilitated—this past year, it's been really touch-and-go. So in a way, it's almost a relief. But still . . . I don't know . . . have you ever lost someone close?"

Donna nodded. "My mother died in March."

Lara's eyes went wide, and she looked as if she'd been sucker-punched. I was pleased. It didn't seem to have occurred to her that our lives might not have gone swimmingly this past year either.

"Oh, wow," Lara said. "I'm sorry. Um . . . how did . . . ?"

"It was very sudden," Donna said. "She had a heart attack."

"Oh," Lara said. "So you've been through all this. . . ." She looked uncomfortable.

My mother said nothing.

Lara slouched lower in her chair. She had avoided eye contact with me ever since I'd arrived yesterday, and now that we were sitting directly across from each other, her discomfort was even more evident. I studied her closely, interested in how she would handle my presence, and surprised by her obvious difficulty in playing the part of friendly sister set for us by our mother. Instead, Lara stared at her hands, picked at her cuticles, and turned to face Donna. "So how are you doing now?" Lara asked.

Donna shrugged. "Well, I just finished chemo. I had a recurrence of cancer, and surgery last year. So I was still on chemo when my mother died. I had to interrupt treatment for a week to go to Atlanta." Donna didn't mention that after surgery, six out of the eight lymph nodes had tested positive for cancer.

I enjoyed seeing Lara's reaction. It seemed to take the wind out of her sails. I dared Lara to look at me, but she kept her head down. She even had trouble looking at Donna now.

My mother remained silent, but I could see that she had been following the conversation closely. Her face was attentive, but she said nothing.

"Oh," Lara mumbled. "I'm sorry."

Donna changed the subject. "The babka is delicious!" she said.

My mother beamed. "Would you like another piece? Another cup of coffee? Helen?"

We shook our heads.

I realized that I was hoping for something like sympathy from my mother. At least some acknowledgment that Donna and I had been through our own nightmare during the past year. But Mom seemed utterly unaffected by our news.

"I was afraid I would lose her," I said to my mother. "It's a very aggressive cancer."

My mother's eyes flashed. "This was my *husband*!" she said.

I felt as if I'd been slapped. I kept quiet.

Lara abruptly pushed away from the table. "I'm going to do some work outside," she said. She had been fidgety all morning, and she was already halfway across the room before my mother called her back.

"Wait, Lara! Wait, before you go—bring me one of your cards, would you? You know, your new business card."

Lara rolled her eyes. "Mom—"

"It won't take a moment—just bring the card. Please, darling?"

Lara sighed and left the room.

"Wait till you see it!" my mother said excitedly. "I am so proud of her! You know, she was just wonderful to Dad over these past years. . . . I don't know where I would be without her. She helped with everything—the doctors, the medication, the paperwork. . . . It's her thoughtfulness, you know—she is so generous, so loving and devoted."

I found my throat tightening with hatred for my sister and irritation with my mother. *She's just lost her husband*, I reminded myself. *I have no right to expect anything from her. I'm lucky she's even invited me into the house.* Still, it grated on my nerves, her going on and on about what a fucking hero Lara was.

My mother smiled. "You know, whenever Dad asked, Lara would drive home to be with him. He wanted her all to himself, so she would come alone, without Jess, without the kids. I think this was a very important time for them—they repaired their relationship, you know."

I said nothing, but thought acidly, *Wow, it must have taken quite a while to repair Lara's memories of Dad repeatedly raping her as an infant.*

"Oh! Here it is!" My mother jumped up when Lara came back with her wallet. "Look at this!" Mom said, holding Lara's business card out to me. "Just look at this!" My hackles went up, the old jealousy. At forty-four, I was still angered by my mother's rapture over my older sister.

Lara dropped her head, apparently uncomfortable herself under the circumstances. I almost felt sorry for her. She tried to slip out of the room, but Mom called her back.

"She's a professor! Do you see?" Mom said. "Here, look—take it, read it! You see? She's a professor, chair of the department at the medical school!"

I pretended to look at the card—I noted the university's seal in red and black ink—okay, so she'd rated a card with color. Big deal. I used to have a business card with two colors too, till Massachusetts suffered budget cuts and everything went back to black and white. Mom motioned for me to pass the card to Donna. "Imagine! Chair of the department! A professor!"

Lara managed to escape out the back door and started attacking the yard with what looked like some kind of giant machete. My mother sat down, still beaming, staring at the card. "You see," she said in a more solemn tone. "It was all worth it." She nodded thoughtfully. "All those years . . . We had some hard times. . . . But it was all worth it."

I was too stunned to say anything. On the one hand, I was relieved that Mom acknowledged those "hard times." That was not like Mom. Usually she swept anything unpleasant out of memory, and certainly out of mention. She edited the story of her life over and over, as one might crop a photograph in a darkroom, so that she could bear to see the image of herself reflected back at her. I hung on to this tendril of validation from my mother, and choked back my rage. Lara's career achievement made it "all worth it"? Thank God Donna was here, I thought. I needed a witness. I needed someone to tell me that I hadn't made all this up.

My mother poured herself more coffee and began talking animatedly about the last year with my father, how crippled he was from Parkinson's, how she'd insisted on taking him outside on forced marches to keep him moving, holding on to him with a thick leather belt she tied around his waist so he wouldn't fall over.

I could picture her doing this, my eighty-two-year-old mother marching Dad up and down the long driveway, feeding him when he could no longer hold a spoon, cleaning him, nursing him with her matter-of-fact love. She told us about the times he passed out at breakfast, the times his heart stopped and she had to call an ambulance, the times she'd followed in her car, and then taken him home once they'd brought him back to life. She had been through such a hard year, I thought. Yet she was not complaining; on the contrary, she spoke about these ordeals as if they had been a series of challenges and accomplishments. She even joked about how she had felt like Dad's personal trainer, proudly dragging him around when he could barely move. She was nothing if not a survivor. The two of them, tough, stubborn fighters.

Outside the window now, I could see my sister hacking up giant tree branches, hauling them across the yard, and raking up the smaller branches as if she might rip the tree's roots right out of the earth.

My mother kept talking vivaciously, filling us in on every detail of the past few years. Donna listened quietly, while I jumped in now and then with a comment or a question or a laugh. It felt so good to be talking and catching up like this, to feel the warmth in Mom's voice, the evident pleasure we took in each other. She said nothing at all about my book, nor the cause of our break in communication for three years. But she did mention the "deal" she had made with my father.

"What we agreed on, Dad and I, is that he would have a separate relationship with you. Of course, his Parkinson's was very bad, you know, he could barely hold a pen. But I agreed that as long as he could still address the envelopes to you, I was willing to attach the stamp and put his letters in the mailbox." She leaned toward me, smiling warmly. "But I was so relieved," she said, with a confidential nod, "when he finally forgot your birthday this year, so I wouldn't have to post the card to you."

Strangely, the content of Mom's words slid right past me and Donna; we were both enchanted by the tone of her voice, the sweetness in her face. It wasn't until we were driving back to Boston that afternoon that we began to make sense of what Mom had actually said, the meaning of the words she had spoken.

"Did she really say that?" I asked.

Donna nodded.

"Wow. That's pretty wild." And yet, it was so like Mom. She had always seemed so comfortable with contradictory feelings. Had I challenged her, I'm sure she would have thought nothing of it. Of course she loved me, she would have said blithely, but surely I could share her relief when Dad forgot my birthday?

We stopped on the way home for Donna to call her father from a phone booth. She had been calling him regularly since Lucy's death; today was her parents' anniversary. "I think Helen and her mother are finally reconciling," she told her father. Afterward she told me that he was genuinely relieved. I smiled, my grief at having lost my dad now mixed with gratitude for the reawakening of my relationship with my mother.

———————

Later during our drive, Donna told me what Lara had said to her as we were getting into our car to leave. I was hugging my mother good-bye, while Donna was talking with Lara. "You've certainly been a saint through all this," Donna told her.

Lara looked at the ground. "You wouldn't say that," she said, "if you knew what I've done."

Six weeks later we would learn what she was talking about.

———————

If madness reflects an inability to cope with reality, then in the context of my family, I had always been the "normal" daughter as a child, and it was Lara who had been crazy. But years later, Lara emerged as the true-blue, stable, and devoted daughter of our parents, and it was I who had gone off the rails; I was the one who no longer fit the family norm.

Did Lara have a real mental illness? She wasn't schizophrenic or bipolar or diagnosed with multiple personality disorder. The only word ever mentioned consistently was *borderline*. But I think it's more accurate to say that she is imbued with the madness that comes with being the loyal daughter in a family of secrets and trauma.

———————

The envelope arrived Christmas Eve. It was bulky, so I assumed my mother had sent me an article from a magazine that she thought I'd find interesting. But when I opened the envelope my mother's short note fell out—*It is a sad and difficult time for all of us.* The cover letter addressed to her from her attorney unsettled me, but I felt relieved when I skimmed through the ten pages of my father's will dividing everything equally between me and my sister. And then I reached the last page, the codicil. A list of numbered paragraphs, each starting with the words *Delete HELEN FREMONT* and ending with the word *prede-*

ceased. The blow felt visceral, and I collapsed to the couch, unable to breathe. The papers fell to the floor at my feet.

Donna was in the kitchen, finishing up her rice casserole which we were going to bring to our friends in Sudbury, as we did every Christmas Eve. I had already made the dessert, a flourless chocolate torte with raspberry coulis. "What is it?" Donna said, stepping out of the kitchen.

I looked at her, but no words came. She rushed over to me. "What happened?"

"I'm . . . dead," I finally said.

"What?"

"My mother sent my father's will."

Donna picked up the pieces of paper at my feet, trying to understand what had happened.

And then a sound escaped me, a long-drawn-out howl of rage that sounded utterly foreign, a sound so loud and strange, it seemed to have issued from somewhere else altogether. It didn't sound human. It alarmed me, and it must have scared Donna too, because she started crying. She was sitting next to me now, and had thrown her arms around me, and we started rocking back and forth, and I was crying, hot tears that streamed down my face. I tried to speak, but no words would emerge, just that terrible scream, that gut-wrenching wail.

I don't know how long we stayed like that, holding each other and crying. I finally calmed down enough to speak. "He signed a codicil and killed me off."

Donna shook her head. "Oh, Helen," she said.

———

The following weeks were a blur. I did not contact my mother or sister, and I did not hear from them. I managed to stumble through my days at work, but kept my head down and my door closed and avoided conversation. My shrink wrote me a scrip for an anxiolytic that helped me get some sleep, but I still found myself awake in the middle of the night, shaking with rage. I wrote in my journal and tried to pass the time until the gym opened at five, when I could work out for a couple of hours.

Later that winter, I hired a lawyer and drove to Schenectady to meet with him. He helped me find out more about the codicil: my mother had driven my father to the small-time lawyer who preyed on the elderly—*Don't let Uncle Sam take your hard-earned money!*—and Dad had signed the codicil removing me from the family four months before he died. My mother signed an identical codicil to her own will that day, though I wouldn't find out until I received hers in the mail after she died twelve years later, at the age of ninety-four.

Contesting a will is rarely successful, my lawyer told me. But when he saw the name of the attorney my family had chosen, he blanched. Apparently their attorney was not known for his scruples. If you were going to contest a will, my lawyer said, you had a chance of finding something wrong with a will written by the attorney my parents had hired. I suppose I had a slight case, if I wanted to fight. My father had been suffering from Parkinson's for fifteen years by the time he signed the codicil. Although he had been a ferociously willful man in his prime, it's fair to say that he was under my mother's and sister's influence at the end.

"Just be aware," my lawyer advised, "if you contest the will, it will mean war."

That seemed fitting. Fifty-six years after my parents had survived one war, I could start a new one in a court of law.

I drove home and mulled it over for the next few days. The days turned to weeks, and then the weeks became months. I tried to imagine what it would be like to take my mother and sister to court. I tried to picture Lara and Mom driving to their attorney's office and spending money to defend themselves from me. It seemed like a colossal waste of time and money, and besides, what good would it do? Even though my parents had squirreled away hefty savings, I didn't really care about their money. I cared about their killing me off.

My new status as "predeceased" occupied my life now. I became a sort of Dead Helen Walking, defined by that piece of paper, and compelled to tell everyone about it. Being disowned seemed to fit naturally into even the most casual conversations with colleagues and friends. For a dead person, I certainly inhabited the role with great gusto.

But despite my rage, I couldn't generate the desire to fight my mother and sister. Contesting the will would only keep me more closely bound to them: we would be engaged, literally, in a battle of wills, and we would become even more entrenched in our outrage at each other. So I decided not to contest the will, and not to sign it either. I had spent four decades wrapped tightly around the open wound of my family's past, and now I'd been sliced free. It was a violent separation, to be sure, but there were no bloody limbs, and I had Scotch-taped together a new family for myself: I had Donna; I had the dog and a cat and two fish and an apartment in Boston and a job and a small but solid group of friends.

And I had a lot to think about.

twenty-five

Over the following years, I continued to try to make sense of what had happened to my family. It's instinctive to search for meaning, to arrange and rearrange the pieces of the puzzle in such a way that they fit, that there is a satisfying snap of recognition, a sense of truth, of something resonating deeply.

As I discovered in 1999, soon after the publication of *After Long Silence*, my family's Jewish identity wasn't such a big secret after all. Although my parents had hidden it from Lara and me, and from their postwar friends and colleagues, it turned out that dozens of *other family members* (of whom Lara and I had been unaware) knew all about us. My mother had sworn them to secrecy.

It was only after my book came out that these cousins of my mother's—living in the States, in Canada, in Europe—contacted me and invited me into their homes, where they showed me decades' worth of correspondence from my mother, dating back even to before the war, when Mom had still been in high school. The cousins explained that in 1961, when I turned four, my mother told them never to contact me or Lara again; Mom was afraid we would re-member them and realize we were family.

For the next forty years, unbeknownst to Lara and me, Mom and Dad had continued to get together with these relatives for bar mitz-vahs and weddings and other celebrations. Here was a photo of my fa-ther in a yarmulke, standing in a synagogue in New York at my American cousin's bar mitzvah. There was a picture of my mother smiling with the bar mitzvah boy, her own cousin's son. My mother continued to send her cousins photos of Lara and me in grade school, junior high, and high school each year, together with news of our lives. There I was, in a red jumper in the first grade with my front tooth missing; here was Lara in her blouse buttoned up to the collar. My mother's handwriting on the pictures identified our grades and ages.

Ultimately whatever secrets Zosia and my mother were keeping played a hand in defining my relationship with my own sister. Our family was built on a construction of lies that rattled our very foundation and held us in a state of madness. But even in writing *After Long Silence*, I didn't understand the extent of the secrets. It would take another decade be-fore I could see more clearly what had eluded me for most of my life.

The first lie was simple and obvious: like thousands of other Jews during the war, my mother and aunt denied their Jewish identity and pretended to be Catholic in order to survive. In 1945, after the war was over, most survivors let go of this pretense and reclaimed their heritage. But my mother and aunt couldn't do that. They both owed their lives to Uncle Giulio, the only real Catholic in our family. By marrying Zosia during the war, Giulio not only provided her with a Catholic identity, but he also elevated her to the status of countess. She was safely above suspicion during the wartime roundups of Jews in Rome. Their marriage was convenient for my uncle as well, I think, since it provided Giulio—who I believe was gay—legitimate cover as a family man.

Giulio also used his influence as a prominent lawyer and government official to rescue my mother when she was arrested at the Italian border in 1942 after escaping from Poland. As the (presumably) Catholic sister of Giulio's wife, Mom was later spared the Nazi deportation of Jews in Italy.

In short, neither my mother nor my aunt could expose their benefactor. To reveal that he had married a Jew—even after the war was over—would have destroyed Giulio, both financially and socially.

And then there was Renzo.

"I wouldn't be surprised," Renzo told Lara and me years ago, "if, in fact, I'm your mother's son." Lara nodded; she'd already done the math. Nine months after Mom escaped from Poland with Luigi, the Italian officer who saved her life, Renzo was born. Mom's arrival at Zosia and Uncle's apartment in Rome in 1943 coincides with Renzo's birth.

At the time Renzo suggested this, I have to admit I was skeptical. This was 1993, fifty years after Mom's escape and Renzo's birth, and I was still struggling to understand the implications of our sudden discovery that Mom, Dad, and Zosia were all Jewish Holocaust survivors. By comparison, the question of whether my cousin was really my half brother seemed less pressing.

It's only now, after so much else has unraveled in our family, that I find myself returning to this conjecture, turning it over in my mind, examining it from every angle. The stories that my mother told me of her escape and imprisonment came in small snippets over decades. Now, piecing them together, the narrative emerges more clearly.

Mom told Lara and me that Luigi, the Italian officer stationed in her hometown of Lvov, had risked his life to help her escape Nazi-occupied Poland in October 1942 by providing her with false papers and an Italian soldier's uniform. At the age of twenty-three, she posed as a soldier under his command, and Luigi brought her with him on furlough to Italy. But the two were arrested at the Italian border, and Mom, presumed to be a spy, was held for execution by a firing squad. Uncle Giulio sent a lawyer to the border who explained to the Italian officials that Mom was not a spy, but the Italian officer's *girlfriend*. Luigi had a wife and children in Bologna; he needed to keep the story of his Polish girlfriend a secret. The Italian officials had a soft spot for romance, and with the help of Uncle's bribe, they released my mother.

From there, Mom said she was transported to an Italian concentration camp in the south of Italy, where she and the other inmates (all women) were treated surprisingly well, and allowed to spend their days knitting and reading.

"Really?" I asked her when I was in college. "They let you knit and read in a *concentration camp*?"

My mother had smiled. "Yes," she said, adding in a whisper, "Many of them were *prostitutes*."

"But prostitution was legal in Italy," I said. "Why were they in a concentration camp?"

My mother shrugged. "It was the war," she said.

I kept quiet.

"We had it easy," she continued. "We were fed reasonably well and didn't have to work." She smiled mischievously, admitting that in the concentration camp, she had more food than most people in Italy had during the war.

So why was she released nine months later in June 1943, when the war was still raging?

"Oh, the warden let me go," Mom said, waving her hand as if this were a silly question. "Zosia came to visit and buttered him up with her baked goods."

So according to Mom, she was released from the concentration camp on the whim of the warden, who became good friends with Zosia. Mom arrived in Rome that summer and lived with her sister and my uncle Giulio, and the newborn Renzo. "I was *fat* then," Mom told me years later. She said she'd destroyed all the photos taken of her during that time because she hated how "chubby" she looked when she first got to Rome.

I never questioned Mom about it, but now I wonder. She'd always told us how hungry everyone in Italy was during the war; there was never enough food to go around. She and Zosia and Giulio had had to sell their clothes and belongings for food; Mom often skipped meals, so that Zosia and Giulio would have something to eat.

In retrospect, it seems less likely that Mom could have gotten fat as a prisoner in an Italian concentration camp during those nine months of the war, than that she had grown large with child at a home for unwed mothers in southern Italy.

I'm guessing that when Mom and her newborn infant came to live with Zosia and Giulio in Rome, all three pretended that Renzo was my aunt and uncle's son. They baptized Renzo and raised him as a Roman Catholic count, the legitimate heir to his father, Giulio, and mother, Zosia. He was exempt from the Nazi roundups of Jews in Rome a few months later. In the privacy of their home, I imagine that my mother nursed Renzo and raised him as her own. Renzo was three years old when my father—Mom's long-lost fiancé from before the war—miraculously escaped from the Gulag and turned up at my mother's doorstep in Rome.

My father's survival was inconceivable. "No one came back from Siberia!" Mom told me. Since learning of his deportation by the Soviets in 1940, she'd heard nothing further. People simply disappeared in Siberia. Until he showed up in November 1946, my mother and aunt and uncle had pretty much solved the problems of genocide and homophobia and illegitimacy. They had outwitted Hitler and Mussolini and proper society. The sisters had come under Uncle's skirts; he had taken them in and covered them all with his Catholic nobility. He sired a son—it was a perfect story. It worked. They had forged a family of four, just like that. It was brilliant.

My father's appearance a year and a half after the war ended threatened to blow the lid off that story. They had to scramble to incorporate him into it, but this is where the lies became corrosive. This is where the secrets began to do real psychic harm, I think. My father had made it out of the Gulag, and into the arms of a plot so twisted that he was trapped and frustrated by it for the rest of his life.

Within days of my father's arrival in Rome, Zosia and Uncle had arranged for Dad and Mom to be married during my mother's lunch break from work. Dad agreed to pretend to be Catholic; he couldn't have married her otherwise. After six years in Siberia, he told me, he no longer cared what religion he was. Time was short; he wanted a family.

What was more difficult for him to accept, he told me, was the "unnaturally close" attachment between three-year-old Renzo and Mom—my father's new wife. Renzo had always slept in Mom's room, and now the child threw a fit at the prospect of being moved into Zosia's room when my father showed up. "We were newlyweds!" my father told me. "But Mom wouldn't part from the boy, so the child slept in the same room with us. I was very hurt by that." My father would resent Renzo for the rest of his life. Years later when he told me about Mom's overriding attachment to the child, he was still angry. Why wasn't she happy to be reunited with him, her long-lost fiancé? Why did she only care about her *sister's* child?

It wasn't until five years later—when Renzo was eight years old—that my mother finally left Renzo behind with Zosia and Uncle, and emigrated to the States with my father. The parting at the Rome train station was so traumatic, my mother told me, that she couldn't bear to leave the boy. "Renzo was in hysterics," she said, her eyes tearing up forty years after the fact. "It was devastating." Heartbroken, she traveled with Dad north to Hamburg, the port from which their ship would take them to America. But my mother was so distraught by the separation, she left my father the next day and returned to Rome, in order to spend one last day with the child. The following day, she rejoined my father just in time to board the ship for America.

As Mom tells the story, my father was also hurt that she had refused to have children right away. "I put him off," my mother told me. "I wasn't like the other women who survived the war. They couldn't *wait* to have babies! The DP camps were filled with screaming infants, and Dad was desperate to start a family. But I didn't want to have a child until I was settled down."

My mother managed to postpone for three more years, until Dad finally put out his shingle in Evans Mills, and Mom ran out of excuses. In 1954, Lara was born. This is when my mother collapsed in an all-consuming depression that lasted years.

If my conjecture is true—if Renzo is actually my mother's son, fathered by Luigi, the Italian officer who saved her life— then the baby embodied all that my mother had lost and left behind: her parents who were murdered soon after her escape; her friends and other family members who were gassed, shot, and starved; her hometown and community that were destroyed. She escaped with nothing but the seed of this child growing inside her. Years later, to be ripped apart from Renzo must have been cataclysmic for her.

How does someone survive what she went through? How could Mom endure the weight of her secrets and losses? At least she and my father could share the secret of their Jewish identity with each other and with a handful of her other surviving relatives in the U.S. But I imagine Mom was utterly alone with the anguish of her separation from Renzo. Only Zosia and Uncle knew the truth. No wonder she depended so desperately on her sister. Their bond was built on a lie so difficult and painful and protective, Mom would have lost her mind without Zosia. As for Lara and me—we were the malleable offspring, living receptacles of a contorted reality of which we were unaware.

That's madness. Maybe that's why we had no diagnosis when we went to family therapy in the 1960s. Our madness was an ill-fitting story that chafed against the reality of who we were and whom we loved and why. We weren't in the *Diagnostic and Statistical Manual*. We were just what people look like who are suffering a mistaken identity, people who are forced to live in a plot they don't understand and cannot make sense of.

———

In 1992, after Lara and I discovered we were Jewish and learned of our parents' experiences during the Holocaust, I asked my mother why she had hidden this from us. After all, many of their Jewish friends had posed as Catholic during the war, but dropped the façade afterward. "But I couldn't do that," my mother said. "Don't you see?"

"Why not?"

"Because—" She stopped abruptly, and a look of despair crossed her face. "I would lose Zosia."

"What do you mean?"

Mom shook her head. "Zosia wouldn't have allowed me to continue to be her sister," she said. "And Renzo—" She choked up. "I could have visited only as a friend, but never as family." Then she looked away, and I couldn't bear to press her further. She changed the subject, and I let it go.

My father survived the war on his own wits, with luck and minimal outside help. But my mother and her sister—their story would have ended in the war. Without Uncle, they would be statistics, folded into the six million. I would not be here to figure this out and write about it.

There's irony for you—so I am predeceased, after all. By exposing the truth, I have revealed the fact that I shouldn't even be here in the first place, that I'm alive only thanks to the lies that Uncle, Zosia, and Mom made up in order to survive the war in Fascist Italy in the 1940s. If not for my father's arrival in 1946, I have no doubt that my mother,

Zosia, and Giulio would have raised Renzo together and lived in Rome for the rest of their lives. Mom always told me that by the time she got to Rome, she had no interest in men or marriage, and she flatly refused all the men who asked her out. But my father's miraculous survival messed up the arrangement. He wanted a family—his own children— and my mother's attachment to her son nearly broke her in two.

It was this broken mother, stripped of her own son, who became my father's wife, and my sister's mother and my mother, on a new continent, across the sea from her firstborn. My mother raised me and Lara in a state of loss that she could not admit even to her own husband.

The Jewish thing—that was just the loose thread hanging out. That's the piece that had been dangling in our faces all our lives, but Lara and I didn't realize it till we were in our thirties. That's the string we pulled, and look what fell out!

It must have thrown Mom into a panic. You pull on that string, and it's only a matter of time before the entire delicate weave of stories unravels. Mom and Zosia made it to the finish line. They protected my father from finding out, but only by cutting me off and away. They could not risk losing their story in order to keep me. That's the bargain I made them choose: me or the story. They chose the story they had made, the fictions they had spun, the others who depended on those lies for their lives.

And Lara? Like me, she is collateral damage of the war. She too suffered the loss of sense and the loss of her sister in the fallout of our family. Lara and I tried to make up for our parents' losses, but more often than not, we reenacted them. Our bond is strong; we are tied together in our estrangement.

epilogue

My sister and I are now in our sixties. She's a good person. Following my mother's death at the age of ninety-four (twelve years after my father's death), Lara offered to share what was left of my parents' finances, and I accepted. It was all arranged through lawyers and bankers. She has never acknowledged her role in disowning me, and despite her efforts to reconnect, I feel safer keeping my distance. It's not clear whom I trust less with our relationship—my sister or myself. I have learned to be more realistic about the limitations of repair.

For decades I tried to figure out what was wrong with our family, whether Lara was actually mentally ill or whether her behavior—and mine—was simply the result of living in the contorted reality of a history that was hidden from us. I can't put a name to what was wrong with my sister, or what was wrong with me. She and I are survivors of a family of secrets, and perhaps that's the most accurate diagnosis of our condition. We represent two sisters' different expressions of a similar past.

I've also wondered whether scientific evidence could prove that Renzo is my mother's biological son, rather than Zosia and Uncle's child. But having been disowned and declared dead by my family, I'm in no position to obtain DNA samples from them. As a lawyer, I'd like that kind of proof. But as a writer, I need something more important—to understand who my mother was and how she managed to survive with the lifelong debt she felt to her sister, the love she felt for Renzo, and the obligation she felt to us. And I need to understand how my father managed to carry on, feeling that he had married a "deranged" woman, but unable (and perhaps unwilling) to know the details of the six years during the war in which they had been separated. And finally, of course, I need to understand my own relationship with my sister, to have compassion for the children we were and the adults we became, and to come to peace with how we managed to live under the burden of so many secrets and lies.

Even with scientific proof, I would still need this narrative to help me make sense of my family, to understand the crazy logic in the decisions we made and learned to live with. After the war, Zosia forced Mom to make a choice: either be true to her own identity, and lose her sister and Renzo; or choose to live a lie, but remain sisters with Zosia. Fifty years later, I faced a similar dilemma—I could either continue to live a lie, and remain in my family; or I could lose my sister and family, but speak my own truth. Unlike my mother, I chose my truth, and in so doing, I lost Lara and my family.

Families are proof that love and loss go hand in hand. My family is gone; my family is everywhere. They live inside me, and we're finally learning to get along with one another. Or at least to accept what is, and love what can be loved. After all, there is an awful lot of love in our stories. It would be a mistake to think otherwise.

acknowledgments

I am ridiculously lucky to have had so many people help me with this book. My *bashert* editor, Jackie Cantor, and agent, Gail Hochman, form the greatest dynamic duo of superheroes in the galaxy. Jackie, your smarts, enthusiasm, zany sense of humor, and friendship mean the world to me, not to mention the freakish amount of time and hard work you've put in on my behalf. And Gail, you are at once fairy god-mother and magician, having managed to tease a manuscript out of the 400 pounds of alphabet soup I kept sending you. Thank you for your tireless encouragement, savvy, and pizazz.

I'm bowled over by the extraordinary talent and dedication of the whole team at Gallery Books and Simon & Schuster. Special shout outs to John Paul Jones, Joal Hetherington, and Lisa Rivlin for making this book so much better than it was before it reached your nimble minds. I am equally indebted to Jennifer Bergstrom, Sally Marvin, Lisa Litwack, and Sara Quaranta for your support and expertise—dreamboats all.

Elise and Arnold Goodman, thank you for your unwavering support and energetic work for over two decades. I don't know where I'd be without you. I'm also grateful to Sam Gelfman and Kirsten Wolf, whose thoughtfulness and advice were invaluable. Deanne Urmy, a bouquet of thanks for your generosity and for offering me a way forward.

Helen Epstein was the instigator and overseer of this project for nearly twenty years, providing meticulous editorial and writerly advice, psychological counseling, excellent meals, and friendship. Helen, I would probably still be frozen before a blank screen if not for you.

Heartfelt thanks to Lisa Rubinstein for listening to me for the past thirty-six years, for nevertheless believing in me, and for patiently teaching me to believe in myself.

I have subjected a number of dear friends to countless awful drafts of this book, and their patience, insight, and friendship made it possible for me to continue. Special Gladiator gratitude to Mari Coates, Susan Sterling, Tracy Winn, and Stan Yarbro. Additional shipping containers of thanks to Jim Ayers, Joanne Barker, Charlie Baxter, Michael Collins, Nancy Gist, Cynthia Gunadi, Trish Hampl, Ehud Havazelet, Richard Hoffman, Marjorie Hudson, Madeline Klyne, Geoff Kronik, Maria Lane, Guillaume Leahy, Sumita Mukherji, Bob Oldshue, Lisa McElaney, Kevin McIlvoy, Peg Alford Pursell, Mary Elsie Robertson, and Robin Romm for providing help and support along the way. For those of you not listed here (you know who you are), thank you.

I am grateful for the generosity and support of Henry Ferrini and the Gloucester Writer's Center and to the Warren Wilson MFA Program for Writers and its merry band of alumni who have sustained me all these years.

Finally, thanks to Donna, my first and most faithful reader, accomplice, and soul mate. This is not the only line she's fixed in this book.

MARGARET
UXORI DILECTISSIMAE

Preface

In 1980 when I published a book on Alexander I wrote that my aim was 'to state most of the evidence and bring the reader into the task of evaluation'. Thus, to take as an example the Battle of the Granicus, I reported the incompatible versions of the ancient writers (Diodorus, Plutarch and Arrian in particular), added some topographical details, and put forward my reconstruction, which rested on my own evaluation of the worth of the rival accounts. The reader was thereby equipped to make his own assessment of what actually happened, and he was enabled to carry his study further by consulting the works of other scholars to which reference was provided. Thus it was a book designed to provoke inquiry into and estimation of Alexander's achievements.

Since 1980 I have carried my researches very much further. In particular I have published two books (*Three Historians of Alexander* and *Sources for Alexander*) on the central problem which faces any Alexander-historian. It may be summarised as follows. The narratives which survive were written between three and five centuries after Alexander's career, and their portrayals of Alexander vary widely not only in what might be regarded as matters of fact but also in interpretations of Alexander's personality. The latter range from intellectual brilliance and statesmanlike vision to unbridled lust for conquest and drunken debauchery. The temptation for the modern writer is to pick and choose from these narratives what suits his own conception of Alexander's personality and to bring the portrayal of Alexander into line with a modern scale of values. This temptation is extremely strong in our modern age which is marked, to cite the words of Thomas Carlyle, 'by a disbelief in great men' because our age has so signally failed to produce statesmen and leaders of such stature. To take an example, it may be more attractive to attribute the burning of the palace at Persepolis to an act of drunken vandalism by an Athenian prostitute and an inebriated king than to a deliberate decision of policy.

In my own work since 1980 I have tried to resist that temptation and to concentrate my attention on a detailed analysis of the surviving narratives, in order to ascertain their historical worth at each stage. Arrian, for instance, tells us that he derived his facts from the narratives of Ptolemy and Aristobulus, who 'campaigned with Alexander' and 'were more trustworthy'. Plutarch on the other hand relied largely on the account of Cleitarchus, a contemporary but not a campaigner, and we are told by Quintilian that Cleitarchus' work was 'brilliantly ingenious and notoriously untrustworthy'. Thus, when we find different versions of an event in Arrian and in Plutarch, we have to ask which previous author each was using and only then judge what actually or at least probably happened.

Retirement has given me the opportunity to undertake and complete thorough studies of these and similar problems, studies of which many have been republished in my *Collected Studies* II and III. It is to be hoped that they will open a new era of Alexander-scholarship in the future. At present it seems appropriate to put my conclusions together and to write an account of Alexander which may claim to be close to the actual facts of his career and the nature of his personality. Because the picture which emerges is of a man who did more than any other individual to change the history of civilization, I have entitled my book *The Genius of Alexander the Great*.

The narrative is designed primarily for the general reader, for it has no footnotes. Sometimes a passage is in inverted commas, which indicates that it is a translation from an ancient text or inscription. An Appendix is provided for those who wish to know the basis of my views. For ease of reference the Appendix is arranged chapter by chapter and topic by topic, and the reader is directed to those of my studies which are relevant. In them he will find discussion of other scholars' views. The Bibliography is limited to relatively few books in English, because extensive bibliographies are available for instance in *The Cambridge Ancient History* 6 (Cambridge, 1994). The chronology is as in my earlier book on Alexander, pp. 312-16, except that I now date his accession to October 336. I am most grateful to Sonia Argyle for help with the Index, and to Deborah Blake for guiding the book through the Press.

I owe a debt of gratitude to David Cox of Cox Cartographic Ltd., who drew the originals of the maps and the plans, and for constant encouragement and shrewd criticism to Margaret, to whom this book is dedicated.

Clare College, Cambridge   N.G.L.H.

Illustrations

Figures

Figs 1(b) to 6 and 16 were drawn by the author and Figs 7 to 15 and 17-19 by A. Cox of Cox Cartographic Ltd, Waterstock, Oxon. Acknowledgement is made to Oxford University Press for permission to reproduce Figs 1(a), 2 and 19, and to Sidgwick and Jackson for Fig. 1(b).

Plates
(between pages 114 and 115)

1. (a) Gold medallions of Philip and Olympias (source, Ad. de Longperier in *Rev. Num.* 1868)
   (b) Ivory heads of Olympias and Alexander (source, M. Andronicos)
2. Fresco of a Royal Hunt (source, M. Andronicos)
3. (a) Phalanx of pikemen (source, P. Connolly)
   (b) Alexander in action (source, Mansell Collection)
4. (a) Silver oenochoe with the head of a Silenus (source, M. Andronicos)
   (b) Head of a young Heracles on a silver amphora (source, M. Andronicos)
5. (a) Gold larnax (source, M. Andronicos)
   (b) Gold wreath (source, M. Andronicos)
6. (a) Mosaic of a Lion Hunt (source, Ph. Petsas)
   (b) Mosaic of Dionysus riding on a Panther (source, Ph. Petsas)
7. The righthand half of the Boscoreale fresco (source, C.M. Robertson)
8. (a) Satellite photograph of the Pelium area (source, NASA)
   (b) The plain beside Pelium (source, A. Harding)
9. Alexander in action (source, Hirmer Fotoarchiv)
10. Satellite photograph of Cilicia (source, NASA)
11. The family of Darius before Alexander (source, The National Gallery)
12. The Alexander Mosaic (after Hammond *AG* Fig. 33)
13. The Porus medallion and the Indian archer (source, The Trustees of the British Museum)
14. The Derveni crater (source, The Archaeological Museum, Thessaloniki)
15. A young Alexander riding Bucephalus (source, M. Andronicos)
16. A mature Alexander somewhat idealised (source, The Pella Museum)

Acknowledgement is made to the following: the late M. Andronicos for 1(b), 2, 4, 5 and 15; P. Connolly for 3(a); The Mansell Collection for 3(b); Ph. Petsas for 6; C.M. Robertson for 7; NASA for 8(a) and 10; A. Harding for 8(b); Hirmer Fotoarchiv for 9; The National Gallery for 11; The Trustees of the British Museum for 13; The Archaeological Museum for 14; The Pella Museum for 16.

Bibliography

A short list of books in English only:

Andronicos, M., *Vergina: the Royal Tombs and the Ancient City* (Athens, 1984)

Bosworth, A.B., *Conquest and Empire: the Reign of Alexander the Great* (Cambridge, 1988)

Bosworth, A.B., *From Arrian to Alexander* (Oxford, 1988)

Brunt, P.A., *Arrian with an English translation* I (London, 1976) II (1983)

Cook, J.M., *The Persian Empire* (London, 1983)

Engels, D.W., *Alexander the Great and the Logistics of the Macedonian Army* (Berkeley, 1978)

Fraser, P.M., *Ptolemaic Alexandria* (Oxford, 1972)

Green, P., *Alexander of Macedon* (London, 1974)

Griffith, G.T., *The Mercenaries of the Hellenistic World* (Cambridge, 1935)

Hamilton. J.R., *Alexander the Great* (London, 1973)

Hammond, N.G.L., *Alexander the Great: King, Commander and Statesman* (1st edn. New Jersey, 1980 and London, 1981; 2nd edn. Bristol, 1989; 3rd edn. Bristol, 1994)

Hammond, N.G.L., *The Macedonian State* (Oxford, 1989)

Heisserer, A.J., *Alexander the Great and the Greeks of Asia Minor* (Oklahoma, 1980)

Lane Fox, R., *Alexander the Great* (London, 1973)

Marsden, E.W., *Greek and Roman Artillery* (Oxford, 1969)

Milns, R.D., *Alexander the Great* (London, 1968)

Pickard-Cambridge, A.W., *Demosthenes* (London, 1914)

Price, M.J., *Coins of the Macedonians* (British Museum, 1974)

Sekunda, N., *The Army of Alexander the Great* (London, 1984)

Stein, A., *On Alexander's Track to the Indus* (London, 1929)

Tarn, W.W., *Alexander the Great* I (Cambridge, 1948), II (1948 and 1979)

Wilcken, U., *Alexander the Great* (London, 1932 and New York, 1967).

CHAPTER I

The boyhood of Alexander

Philonicus the Thessalian brought to Philip a stallion 'Bucephalus' at an asking price of thirteen talents. So down they went into the plain to put him to the test. The verdict was that he was savage and quite unmanageable. He would let no one mount him, disregarded the voice of any of Philip's company, and reared up to strike at one and all. Thereupon Philip was angry. He ordered the removal of the animal as utterly wild and undisciplined. Alexander was present. 'What a horse they are losing,' he said. 'They cannot handle him because they lack understanding and courage.' Philip at first was silent. But when Alexander persisted time and again and grew impassioned, Philip said, 'Criticise your elders, do you, on the ground that you yourself have a bit more understanding or are better able to manage a horse?' 'This horse at any rate,' Alexander replied, 'I'd manage better than anyone else would.' 'And if you do not manage him, what price will you pay for your rashness?' 'By Heaven,' he said, 'I shall pay you the price of the horse.' There was an outburst of laughter. Then, as soon as the terms of the bet between them were settled in monetary terms, Alexander ran to the horse, took the bridle-rein, and turned him round to face the sun – realising, so it seems, that the horse was completely upset by the sight of his own shadow dancing about in front of him.

For a while Alexander ran alongside the horse and stroked him. Then on seeing that he was full of zest and spirit, he quietly cast aside his cloak, made a flying jump, and was securely astride him. For a time he held him back, using a touch of the reins to check the bit, but without pulling or tearing his mouth, and when he saw the horse had rid himself of the fear and was eager for the race, he let him go and actually urged him on with a bolder cry and with the pressure of his leg. At first those who were with Philip were agonised and silent. But when he turned the horse in the correct manner and rode back proud and jubilant, all the others cheered, but his father, it is said, wept a little for joy, kissed him when he dismounted, and said. 'My boy, seek a kingdom to match yourself. Macedonia is not large enough to hold you.'

On my interpretation we owe this vivid account to an eyewitness, one Marsyas Macedon, who was an exact contemporary of Alexander and many years later wrote a book called *The upbringing of Alexander*. In accordance with the etiquette of the court, King Philip and his chosen Companions were attended daily by some of the Royal Pages; and on this occasion Alexander and Marsyas, both probably in their fifteenth year, were in attendance. Bucephalus, meaning 'Oxhead', so named from the brand-mark on his haunch, was a stallion some four years old. He was 'of large size and noble spirit', as indeed we see him portrayed in the Alexander Mosaic commemorating the Battle of Issus (Plate 12). He had already been broken by his trainer Philonicus. Now he was bridled and available for bareback riding (stirrups and saddle were not to be invented until our Middle Ages) by anyone who wanted to try his paces. His wild and dangerous behaviour daunted everyone except young Alexander.

In his handling of the situation Alexander showed an independence of judgement, an understanding of the horse, and a degree of courage remarkable in a boy of his age. It is no wonder that the spectators were in an agony of apprehension, for Alexander was risking his life. It is a measure of that apprehension that Philip is said to have wept for joy when his son returned in triumph. To those who lived to see Alexander in Asia, this event foreshadowed many occasions on which his independence, intelligence and courage brought triumph after triumph. At the time the wager was won by Alexander, and we may assume that Philip paid the price of the horse, which became Alexander's personal possession, was trained as a warhorse and would not accept any other rider. The words attributed to Philip as 'a saying' were probably not historical; for when father and son were dead, men liked to draw comparisons between them. But there is this much truth in the account: Alexander was striving to compete with his father and he was willing to risk his life to that end.

The following incidents and sayings were probably also taken by Plutarch from the work of Marsyas. Whenever news came that Philip had captured a famous city or won a remarkable victory, Alexander used to say to his contemporaries: 'My father, boys, will be the first to win everything; and for me he will leave no great and brilliant action to carry out together with you.' What he wanted as a young boy was not the enjoyment of pleasure or the spending of his wealth but the winning of 'excellence and glory', that is to excel and be recognised as excelling, and to win glory and be acclaimed as glorious. He had no doubt that one day he would be king. Indeed he felt he had to act already in a manner worthy of a king. That is the point of the story that, when the boys in his company asked him whether he would compete in the foot-race in the Olympic Games (for 'he was swift of foot'), he said, 'Yes, if I am to have kings as fellow-competitors.' To some of his companions he may have seemed precocious; for as Plutarch observed, probably citing Marsyas, 'his ambition kept him serious in mind and lofty in spirit'. But he had also a great gift for friendship of the finest kind. For instance, he was very deeply attached to Hephaestion, and he was loyal almost beyond reason to Harpalus, as we shall see. He carried his friends with him in his ambitions; that is why he spoke of winning renown 'together with you'.

In stature Alexander was below the average height for a man of his time. His voice was loud and assertive. He was of a strong and untiring physique. On the march he would practise mounting and dismounting from a running chariot; and it was this strength and his athleticism which enabled him to jump onto the back of Bucephalus. Whereas his father had rugged features and a strongly masculine aspect, Alexander as a youth was remarkable for the softness of his features, the slight protuberance and the melting glance of his eyes, a fair skin and a ruddy complexion. He probably inherited his looks less from his father than from his mother, Olympias (see Plates 1(a) and 15). Until the age of fourteen he was educated at home where life was simple; for there were no slaves and the womenfolk of the royal family cooked the meals and made the clothes. He must have been much influenced by his paternal grandmother Eurydice, who as Queen Mother was held in the highest esteem. She dedicated altars in the city-centre of the old capital Aegeae to 'Eukleia', 'Fair Fame', which was the guiding star of young Alexander, and she composed a delightful epigram which accompanied a dedication to the Muses:

> Eurydice, daughter of Sirras, dedicated this (statue probably of Hermes) to her city's Muses, because she had in her soul a longing for knowledge. The happy mother of sons growing up, she laboured to learn letters, the recorders of the spoken word.

Alexander too was devoted to the Muses. The *Iliad* of Homer was his favourite, he delighted in the works of Pindar, the great tragedians and the dithyrambic poets, and he had a natural love of learning and of reading.

When Eurydice died, Alexander was about fourteen years of age. There was a separate area at Aegeae where women of the royal family were buried, and it was there that Professor Andronicos excavated the earliest and largest vaulted tomb yet known. He dated it late in the 340s and identified it as 'The Tomb of Eurydice'. Alexander will have been at the ceremony of cremation and at the placing of Eurydice's ashes in the main chamber of the Tomb. He must have admired the *trompe l'oeil* fresco of a façade on its back wall, which created the illusion of a room beyond.

Alexander's strongest emotional attachment was to his mother, Olympias. We have to remember that not only in Macedonia but also in the city-states, the giving of a girl in marriage was arranged by the man who was 'responsible' for her. Commoners used such marriages to strengthen family ties and connections. Kings normally made marriages with, and arranged a daughter's marriage with a member of another royal house for political purposes (or as a cynical writer, Satyrus, put it, 'for purposes of war'). Thus Eurydice, a princess of the royal house of Lyncus, had been given in marriage to Amyntas and lived thereafter in Macedonia. Nor was she the only queen. For the kings and sometimes other males of the royal house practised polygamy in order to ensure a supply of heirs in the direct line and to extend their political connections. Amyntas, for instance, had at least two wives and from them six sons. In the two years 358 and 357 Philip, now in his mid-twenties, took four wives, of whom at least three bore him children. One of the four was Olympias, a princess of the royal house of Molossia, who was given in marriage to Philip by her uncle, Arybbas, the Molossian king. Later writers invented a love-match, which stemmed from a meeting of the young pair at the shrine of the Cabiri on Samothrace; but that is ruled out by consideration of their respective ages. The four wives were treated as equals in queenly prestige.

Olympias had good looks and a fiery temperament. She was intensely religious, sacrificing to the Olympian gods of the Macedonian state and observing the rites of the mystery cults into which she had been initiated. One was the cult of the Cabiri, which was concerned with the fertility of men and animals and with survival after death in the underworld. Offerings were made to the Cabiri as 'The Great Gods' in a circular pit in Samothrace and just outside the city-wall of Pella. Another cult was that of Orpheus, which laid down rules of conduct and promised a happy afterlife to the faithful. The rape of Persephone by Pluto in accordance with Orphic belief was the subject of frescoes in the Tomb of Amyntas and of a painting in the Tomb of Eurydice. A related cult was that of Dionysus, made famous by the *Bacchae* which Euripides composed and produced in Macedonia. It was remarkable for the orgiastic rites of the women who were possessed by the spirit of the god, and it was said that Olympias was 'inspired and possessed more than any others' and handled huge tame snakes in honour of the god. When Alexander was in Asia, she recommended to him a priestly server who was an expert – like herself – in the Bacchic and Argeadic rites, the latter being those of the Macedonian royal tribe.

Her influence on young Alexander was very great. He grew up profoundly religious with a readiness to believe in the manifestation of the gods in many cults and in many places, and with many names; but as far as we know he did not follow her into the mystery cults of Orpheus and the Cabiri. The bond of affection between them was exceptionally strong. As he was to say later, one tear of his mother cancelled innumerable accusations which had been made in letters by Antipater, his senior marshal. And when a rift developed between his father and his mother, he took her side and together with her left the court. However, strong personality though she certainly was, Alexander was not dominated by her; after he became king he gave her many presents but depended entirely on his own judgement in public affairs.

On attaining the age of fourteen in 342 Alexander entered the School of Royal Pages. Its origin was in the distant past, but such detailed knowledge as we have dates from the reigns of Philip and Alexander. He was one of probably fifty boys, the selected sons of leading Macedonians, who at the age of puberty started on a four-year course and graduated on their eighteenth birthday. During these years they lived at or near the court as boarders, and they received instruction in military matters, especially in horsemanship, and in the liberal arts, of which grammar, rhetoric, dialectic, geometry, arithmetic, astronomy and music were the basic subjects. During the last year they served as the king's Bodyguards in battle and as huntsmen on foot, supporting members of the royal family who were required by law to hunt on horseback. See the fresco of the Royal Hunt in Plate 2 and note the statutory uniform of the Royal Page on the extreme right. Physical fitness was essential, and the boys engaged in athletics, gymnastics and wrestling.

The king acted as headmaster, and he alone administered corporal punishment to offenders. For instance, Philip flogged one boy 'unenviably' for falling out of a paramilitary exercise to visit a public house; and in the last year on military service discipline was very strict, even to the extent that a Page was killed by Philip for disobeying orders and laying aside his armour. Philip employed as trainers and teachers capable freemen (not slaves as was often the case in private education at Athens). One of them, Leonidas, a relation of Olympias, was 'a man of stern character' who was described as Alexander's second father and personal professor. He used to examine Alexander's boxes in case Olympias had packed some delicacy for him, and he reprimanded the boy for being extravagant in throwing too much incense on an altar-fire. Alexander evidently regarded him as a Mr Chips, for he later sent him sixteen tons of incense from Egypt.

In 342 Philip hired Aristotle at a handsome salary to teach 'philosophy', which embraced both practical and theoretical knowledge. Lessons and seminars were held usually in the open air in the sanctuary of the Nymphs near Mieza, a beautiful place with natural grottos in the limestone, which was visited by sightseers in Plutarch's day and still is so visited. The influence of Aristotle on Alexander was profound. Alexander accepted as correct Aristotle's views on cosmology, geography, botany, zoology and medicine and therefore took scientists with his army to Asia, and he was fascinated by Aristotle's lectures on logic, metaphysics, the nature of poetry, and the essence of politics. Above all he learnt from Aristotle to put faith in the intellect. In their personal relationship the boy's admiration developed into a deep affection, and they shared a special interest in establishing the text of the *Iliad*. No doubt Aristotle hoped to guide the future king in the performance of his duties, even as his own teacher, Plato, had tried to guide the younger Dionysius as the ruler of Syracuse. To that end he wrote for Alexander a treatise *On Kingship*, which unfortunately has not survived. Whether it had any effect when Alexander came to the throne may be doubted. But in 336, having been elected to command the joint forces of the Greeks and the Macedonians for the war against Persia, Alexander showed his regard for 'philosophy' during a visit to the ascetic philosopher Diogenes by remarking, 'If I were not Alexander, I would indeed be Diogenes.'

To be the son of the headmaster of the School of Pages cannot have been easy for a young boy who had a strongly competitive spirit. That Philip loved his son and admired his courage is clear from the account of the taming of Bucephalus. Alexander probably reciprocated that love; for his father had strong affections, a charismatic personality and cultured interests. That Alexander admired him exceedingly for his achievements goes without saying, for in 342 Philip was the leading statesman in the Greek world and had made his country the leading military power in Europe. From 342 onwards father and son were in close contact. As headmaster Philip guided and observed Alexander's progress, and he developed complete confidence in his son's abilities.

It was probably late in 342 that Persian envoys came to the court in the absence of Philip and were entertained by Alexander. They were impressed by his geniality and the perceptive nature of his enquiries about their country and its ruler. In 340, when Philip was undertaking a major campaign in Thrace, he appointed Alexander to act as his deputy, thereby indicating that he intended Alexander to be his successor if he himself should be killed during the campaign. We are told that Philip had had several sons by his wives, but that some died a natural death and others died in war, presumably as Pages. It may be that Alexander's only male sibling surviving in 340 was Arrhidaeus, who was much the same age but was intellectually retarded. The advancement of Alexander brought special prestige to Olympias, who was marked out as the prospective Queen Mother.

As deputy for his father Alexander was entrusted with the royal seal. He therefore carried out the routine duties of the king and with the seal validated documents of state. In particular he carried out the daily sacrifices. He had probably participated in these from the age of fourteen, and now he was qualified to conduct them on behalf of the state and on behalf of the royal family which had its own worship of Heracles Patroüs, that is of Heracles as the ancestor of the Temenidae. During 340 there was a rising by the Maedi in the Strymon valley, which Alexander defeated as commander of Macedonian forces. He captured their capital city, expelled the natives, and refounded the city as 'Alexandropolis' with a mixed population of Macedonians, Greeks and Thracians. Therein he followed the example of his father, who had introduced Macedonian settlers into the Greek city 'Crenides' and renamed it 'Philippi'. Alexander did so no doubt with the approval of his father, who was founding similar mixed settlements in central Thrace in the latter part of 341, one being named 'Philippopolis'. Father and son were evidently in complete accord.

In summer 338 Alexander and the contemporaries of his year graduated. They came of age on their eighteenth birthdays, and they knew what their careers were to be. The School of Pages, like Eton and Winchester in Victorian England, was famous as 'a training-ground of great governors and generals'. Physically fit graduates entered the Companion Cavalry as troopers. Those, like Harpalus, whose physique was impaired, entered the service of the king in an administrative capacity. Alexander emerged from the School with flying colours. He had won distinction as a cavalryman mounted on his warhorse Bucephalus, as a fearless huntsman, and as a deputy of the king. His future was assured, and he had every expectation that one day in the future he would be elected by the Assembly of Macedonians to be their king.

The strand in his personality which needs to be emphasised is his religious faith. Since childhood he had worshipped Heracles Patroüs, the son of Zeus and a mortal woman, and through his mother he was descended from Achilles, son of the goddess Thetis and a mortal, Peleus. In his mother's veins there was also the blood of a son and a daughter of Priam, King of Troy. To Alexander, Heracles and Achilles were not fantasies of poetic imagination but real people, who expected their descendants to excel as warriors and as benefactors of mankind. He hoped to rival or even to surpass them. Everything in his upbringing had conspired to instil in him a profound belief in the Olympian gods: daily sacrifice in the company of his father, participation in religious festivals, proximity to the throne of Zeus on Mount Olympus, and the religiosity of the Macedonian people. His father's coins proclaimed a devotion to Zeus, Apollo and Heracles; and as Alexander grew up, he saw his father triumph as the champion of Apollo in a 'Sacred War'. He too hoped that the gods would inspire him to excel in their service.

CHAPTER II

The world of Philip as king and Alexander as prince

1. The setting of Alexander's birth and boyhood

In 356, the year of Alexander's birth, a political pamphleteer called Isocrates wrote of the Greek-speaking world, 'Every part of Greece is filled and obsessed with war and revolutions and massacres and innumerable evils.' This terrible situation was the result of a century of internecine wars between city-state and city-state and of internal revolutions in most city-states, which had bred fierce hatreds and led to atrocities on a scale only too familiar in modern times. Many wars arose from local frontier-disputes, for instance between Athens and Thebes over the possession of Oropus, and were apt to recur with any change in the strength of the contestants. Major wars were initiated by states which wished to exercise leadership over other states, and then competed with one another. Thus in 460 Athens, already in control of many maritime states, started a fifteen-year war against Sparta, the leader of a group of land-powers; and in 431 she embarked on a second such war, which ended disastrously for her in 404. Undaunted, she made two further attempts, one starting in 394 and the other in 377. Her last venture ended with defeat at the hands of some of her subject-states in 356. Sparta fought two successful wars against Athens, but in the fourth century her despotic conduct as an imperial power led to revolts and to defeat by a new rival, Thebes, in 371.

Thereafter Sparta and Athens combined in war against Thebes and her associates. In 362 an indecisive battle was fought at Mantinea in the Peloponnese, in which most city-states of the mainland took part. In 356, when Athens was at war with her subject-states, Thebes tried to discipline her neighbour Phocis, which was a reluctant 'ally', but the result was that the leader of a Phocian political party seized the temple of Apollo at Delphi. That was the beginning of what became 'The Sacred War' in which at first all prisoners were executed. It was destined to last ten years, during which most states of the mainland were involved.

These general wars were in some ways less damaging than internal revolutions in city-states, which were initiated by party-leaders and often led to intervention by an outside power. A terrifying example at

Corcyra in 427 was described by Thucydides. The 'democrats' there had
the support of an Athenian fleet, and some four hundred 'oligarchs'
sought sanctuary in the temple of Hera. The democrats persuaded fifty
to come out and stand trial, and then condemned them all to death.

> The mass of the suppliants slew each other there in the consecrated
> ground; while some hanged themselves upon the trees, and others de-
> stroyed themselves as they were severally able. During seven days the
> Corcyraeans were engaged in butchering those of their fellow-citizens
> whom they regarded as their enemies .... Death thus raged in every
> shape; and as usually happens at such times, there was no length to
> which violence did not go; sons were killed by their fathers, and suppli-
> ants dragged from the altar or slain upon it; while some were walled up
> in the temple of Dionysus and died there. So bloody was the march of
> revolution (*stasis*) .... Later on, one may say, the whole Hellenic world
> was convulsed .... The sufferings which revolution entailed upon the
> cities were many and terrible, such as have occurred and always will
> occur, as long as the nature of mankind remains the same. (trs. R.
> Crawley).

Any civil war of this kind bequeathed a legacy of hatred and a desire
for revenge, which frequently led to a further civil war. In 353 Plato,
having visited the city-states in Sicily where revolution and counter-
revolution were endemic, wrote thus of *stasis*.

> To this there is never any end. What seems to be an end always links on
> to a new beginning, so that this circle of strife is likely to destroy utterly
> both factions, those of dictatorship and those of democracy alike. The
> Greek tongue will almost die out in Sicily as it becomes a province of
> Carthage and Italy.

How was the decline to be arrested? In 360-350 Plato was composing
his last dialogue, *Laws*, in which he described his ideal city-state. He
believed that his system of state-education would so inspire the citizens
under specified economic and social conditions that they would obey
their rulers, namely the laws. This was an intellectual's long-term
solution. Other thinkers wanted a quicker reform. In 355 Xenophon,
having written his *History of Greek Affairs* from 411 to 362, saw the
need to set up in Greece 'Guardians of the Peace' (*eirenophylakes*), and
he thought that if Athens abandoned her interventionist policy she
might be able to become the mediator of such a peace. As a first step he
urged Athens to persuade the Phocians to leave Delphi. Isocrates too
advised Athens to abandon her imperial ambitions and to concentrate
on a policy of peace, but he did not think her capable of leading the other
states towards reconciliation. Instead, in 356-355, he wrote an open
Letter to Archidamus, the King of Sparta, in which he proposed that
Archidamus as reconciler should wean the city-states from 'their mad-

ness and contentiousness' and lead them in a crusade against Persia. These proposals went unheeded, and the ensuing Sacred War plunged the states into further confusion and slaughter.

There were two parts of the Greek-speaking world at this time which did not suffer from revolution and did not seek to impose rule over the city-states. In Epirus there were three clusters of tribal states, called Molossia, Thesprotia and Chaonia, and although a tribal state might move from one cluster to another cluster, each state remained a tight-knit community (a *koinon* as it was called). The strongest cluster in 356 was the Molossian state. Its monarchy had exceptional prestige because the royal family, it was believed, was descended from Neoptolemus, son of Achilles. These states held the frontier against the Illyrians, whose institutions were fairly similar. In the fourth century down to 360 they were outfought by a cluster of Illyrian states which formed around the Dardanians (in Kosovo and Metohija), whose king Bardylis developed a strong economy. In 385 the Molossians lost 15,000 men in battle and were saved from subjection only by a Spartan army. They suffered losses again in 360.

The other part of the Greek-speaking world extended from Pelagonia in the north to Macedonia in the south. It was occupied by several tribal states, which were constantly at war against Illyrians, Paeonians and Thracians. Each state had its own monarchy. Special prestige attached to the Lyncestae whose royal family, the Bacchiadae, claimed descent from Heracles, and to the Macedonians, whose royal family had a similar ancestry. Although these tribal states occasionally fought one another, each was close-knit and free from revolution (*stasis*). They suffered most from the Dardanians who raided far and wide, even reaching the Thermaic Gulf where they imposed a puppet-king on the Macedonians from 393 to 391. Thereafter Pelagonia and Lyncus were frequently overrun, and in 359 the Macedonian king Perdiccas and 4,000 Macedonians were killed in battle against the Dardanians.

In the opinion of the city-states these tribal states were backward and unworthy of the Greek name, although they spoke dialects of the Greek language. According to Aristotle, monarchy was the mark of people too stupid to govern themselves. The city-states, on the other hand, with the exception of Sparta, had rid themselves of monarchy centuries ago. They governed themselves democratically or oligarchically, and their citizens were highly individualistic. There were other great differences. The northern states lived largely by transhumant pastoralism, used barter more than currency, and had no basis of slaves, whereas the city-state populations lived largely in cities, had capitalist economies and employed very large numbers of slaves, even in agriculture. Northerners herded their flocks, worked the land, and served as soldiers in person, whereas in the fourth century the most sophisticated southerners, the Athenians, preferred to leave labour to slaves and foreigners, and hired mercenaries for wars overseas.

The Balkan tribes beyond the Greek-speaking world were continually at war. For as Herodotus said of the Thracians, 'to live by war and rapine is the most honourable way of life, and the agricultural worker is the least esteemed'. The well-armed aristocrats of the Thracian tribes engaged in wide-ranging raids, such as that led by Sitalces, the king of the Thracian Odrysae, into Macedonia in 429. The Paeonians (in southeast Yugoslavia) and the Illyrians (in Albania) were equally warlike, and they too engaged in rapine. In the raids they carried off men, women and children as well as goods and livestock. One Illyrian tribal group, the Ardiaei, boasted at this time that it had acquired 300,000 serfs.

2. The Macedonian State

Wars not for conquest but for survival were the lot of the Macedonians. The institutions of the country were therefore designed for military efficiency. The population lived mainly in towns which they called 'cities' (*poleis*), because each had its own citizenship (e.g. *Pellaios*) and its system of government with magistrates, council and assembly. Each city trained its own militia for defence, and the training in the time of Philip was educational as well as military. The cities were subject to the rule of the central government, which consisted of two elements – the king and the King's Men under arms. When a king died, his successor was elected by the King's Men meeting under arms in assembly. If he obtained their confidence, his powers were very extensive. He sacrificed to the gods on behalf of the state, conducted the religious festivals, commanded the forces in person, and initiated diplomatic relations. He owned all mineral deposits, stands of fine timber, large areas of land and hunting grounds. He controlled recruitment into the forces of the King's Men from the city militia, directed promotion and enforced discipline. He brought matters of policy before the assembly of the King's Men, and he had to persuade them that he was conducting their affairs properly. In particular he could go to war only if he was assured of their support. When there was suspicion of treason, the king prosecuted and the defendant spoke before the assembly of the King's Men, which delivered the verdict and put it into effect. Thus the powers of the assembly were sovereign, but they were exercised only rarely. In the critical moments when raiders burst into Macedonia the King's Men went into action at his order.

Citizenship as 'Macedones', and with it membership of the assembly, was held only by the King's Men, who had the honour of being the king's 'Companions'. From them he selected his commanders and administrators, whom he called his 'Friends' and in a special sense his 'Compan-

ions'. On occasion and at his own discretion he consulted a group of
them, but he was not bound to accept their advice and they had no
constitutional standing. Many of them had graduated from the School
of Pages. Outstanding service was rewarded by the king, who granted
the revenues of an estate or other property to the recipient for life. The
Friends could rise no higher, for the Macedones would recognise as king
only a member of the royal family. The King's Men were divided into
two categories. In the reign of Philip the cavalrymen wore a metal
cuirass and a metal helmet, wielded a lance with a blade at either end,
and rode bareback into action. They had a long tradition of excellence
as 'heavy-armed cavalry', which required much training in horsemanship (see Fig. 1 (a)). The infantrymen had been organised as 'heavy-
armed' troops only in 369. Ten years later Philip re-equipped them with
his new weapon, the sixteen-foot pike, a small shield suspended from
the neck, helmet and greaves. They fought, like the 'hoplites' of the
city-states, in a solid phalanx of men, shoulder to shoulder, eight to ten
men deep. The pike outreached the seven-foot spear which the hoplite
wielded with one arm, so much so that a phalanx presented four
pike-heads to a hoplite's single spearhead (see Fig. 1 (b)). Whereas the
'Cavalry Companions' provided their own mounts and equipment, the
king supplied the 'Infantry Companions' (*pezhetairoi*) with pikes and
equipment from his own resources. To wield the pike and to maintain
the formation of the phalanx required intensive training and physical
fitness.

1. (a) A Companion Cavalryman

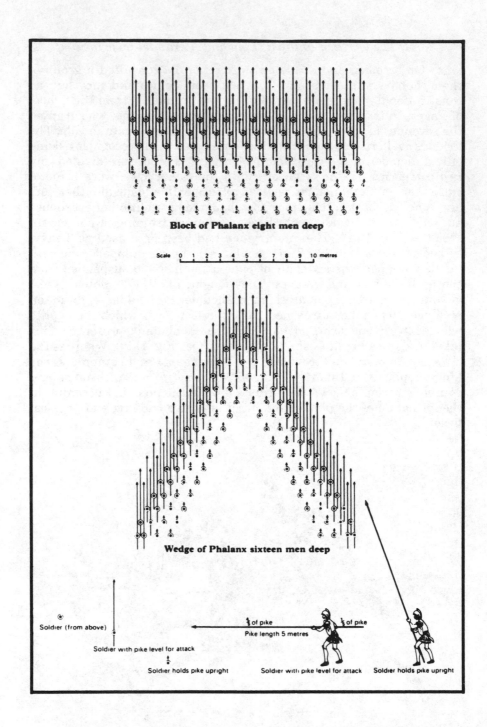

Block of Phalanx eight men deep

Scale 0 1 2 3 4 5 6 7 8 9 10 metres

Wedge of Phalanx sixteen men deep

Soldier (from above)

Soldier with pike level for attack

Soldier holds pike upright

⅗ of pike   ⅖ of pike

Pike length 5 metres

Soldier with pike level for attack

Soldier holds pike upright

1 (b) The pikeman-phalanx

CHAPTER III

The influence of Philip

1. From weakness to strength in 346

Philip took control in 359 not as king but as guardian of his nephew, Amyntas IV, a young boy. His country was on the verge of collapse, having lost 4,000 men in battle, while the victorious forces of Bardylis were in occupation of towns in Pelagonia and Lyncus and threatened to invade Macedonia itself in 358. Philip put heart into his army by holding assembly after assembly, rearming and training his infantry, and inspiring them with his own indomitable spirit. In spring 358 he convinced the assembly of the King's Men that they should take the offensive. In a decisive battle with almost equal numbers he inflicted a crippling defeat on Bardylis, established the east bank of Lake Lychnitis (Ochrid) as his frontier, and confirmed a treaty of peace with Bardylis by marrying his daughter, Audata. His victory freed Pelagonia, Lyncus and the other tribal states of West Macedonia, then called 'Upper Macedonia', from raiding and occupation by the Dardanians. He now invited the peoples of these states to abolish their monarchies and to enter the Macedonian kingdom with equal rights to those of the Macedonians. The invitation was accepted, and Philip showed his respect for his new subjects by marrying Phila, a member of the Elimeote royal family.

By this act, which Philip must have taken with the agreement of the Macedonian assembly, he doubled the resources and the manpower of the kingdom. It was important to raise the standard of life in Upper Macedonia to that of Lower Macedonia, and for that purpose he founded new towns there in which young men received educational and military training. As they graduated he recruited the best of them to enter the king's army and become members of the assembly as 'Macedones'. His innovations were so successful that the number of his Companion Cavalrymen rose from 600 in 358 to 2,800 in 336, and that of the Companion Infantrymen from 10,000 in 358 to 27,000 in 336. Alexander was to inherit the most formidable army in Europe.

By a combination of diplomatic skill and military opportunism Philip defeated Illyrian tribes beyond his western frontier, forced the Paeonians to become his subjects, gained posession of Greek colonies on his coast, defended Amphipolis against the Athenians and Crenides –

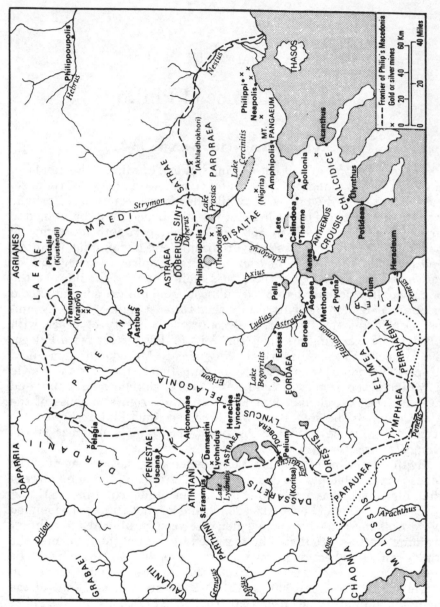

2. Alexander's Kingdom of Macedonia

GRABAEI

DARDANII ?DAPARRIA

Drilon

TAULANTII

Genusus

PENESTAE
Uscana ×

ATINTANI
S.Erasmus ×
Damastini
Lychnidus
Lake
Lychnitis (Koritsa)

PARTHINI

Apsus

CHAONIA

MOLOSSIS

Arachthus

PARAUAEA

ORESTIS

DASSARETIS
Pelium ·

Eordaicus

DOBERA
Heraclea Lyncestis
·ASTRAEA

Alcomenae ×
Pelagia ×

PELAGONIA

Erigon

LYNCUS

Lake
Begorritis

EORDAEA

Edessa ·

Berøea ·

TYMPHAEA

PERRHAEBIA

ELIMEA

Peneus

Peneus

D i u m

Dium ·
Heraclaeum

Haliacmon

Methone
Pydna ◃

Aegae

Astraeus

Ludias

Pella ·

Axius

PAEONES

Astibus

Tranupara
(Kratovo) × × ×

PAEONIA

Pautalia
(Kjustendil) ·

LAEAEI

AGRIANES

MAEDI

Strymon

ASTRAEA

DOBERUS ·
Doberus

SINT SATRAE

Philippoupolis ?
(Theodoraki)

Lake
Prasias

BISALTAE
(Nigrita) ·

PARORAEA

(Akhladhokhori)
×

Lake
Cercinitis

Nevtus

Hebrus

Philippoupolis ·

Amphipolis ·
Apollonia ·

MT.
PANGAEUM

Philippi ×
Neapolis ×

THASOS

Acanthus ·

CHALCIDICE

Olynthus ·

Potidaea ·

Heraclaeum ·

Echedorus

Aenea

CROUSIS
ANTHEMUS

Therme ·
Callindoea ·

Lete ·

Frontier of Philip's Macedonia
× Gold or silver mines

0   20   40   60 Km
0   20   40 Miles

renamed Philippi – against the Thracians, and advanced his eastern frontier to the river Nestus (Mesta), all by late 354. He was fortunate in that Athens was distracted by the war against her subject-states (357-355) and Thebes by the war against Phocis, which became the Sacred War (355-346); and he managed to make a treaty of alliance with his powerful neighbour, the Chalcidian League of city-states, on condition that neither party would enter into separate negotiations with Athens. During these eventful years he confirmed an alliance with the ruling house of Larissa in Thessaly by marrying a lady of that house, Philinna, and an alliance with the Molossian royal house by marrying Olympias in 357, as we have seen (above, p. 4). In that year, 357, he was elected king in place of Amyntas IV.

The Sacred War was declared by a majority of the members of the Amphictyonic League, of which the Council laid down rules of conduct in religious and other matters and in particular administered the temple of Apollo at Delphi. That majority was formed by the peoples of Thessaly, Central Greece and Boeotia; but the minority included Athens, Sparta, Achaea, and later Pherae in Thessaly, which all entered into alliance with Phocis. Other states showed sympathy with one side or the other. The Phocian occupiers of Delphi survived by looting the treasures and hiring mercenary soldiers, and in 353 an able leader, Onomarchus, launched an offensive against Thebes and sent 7,000 mercenaries to support Pherae against the other Thessalians. This was Philip's opportunity; for the Thessalians asked him for help and he enabled them to win a victory. But Onomarchus came north and inflicted two defeats on Philip. He withdrew, as he said, 'like a ram, to butt the harder'. In 352 Philip and his Thessalian allies won a decisive victory over Onomarchus' army of 500 cavalry and 20,000 infantry, to the amazement of the city-states. Philip paraded his championship of Apollo. For his soldiers went into battle wearing the laurel wreath associated with the god, and on his orders 3,000 prisoners were drowned as guilty of sacrilege. He also championed the cause of liberty and federalism against the dictators of Pherae, whom he now expelled together with their mercenaries. His reward was election as President of the Thessalian League, which placed its forces and its revenues at his disposal. At this time he married Nicesipolis, a member of the leading family in Pherae.

His chief fear was a coalition of Athens and the Chalcidian League; for the Athenian fleet could then blockade his coast and the armies of the two states could invade the coastal plain of Macedonia. In 349, when the Chalcidian League violated its treaty and entered into alliance with Athens, Philip invaded Chalcidice and despite the efforts of Athens captured Olynthus, the capital of the League, in 348. He held the Olynthians responsible for breaking the religious oaths which had bound them under the treaty. He razed the city and sold the population into slavery. He destroyed two other city-states (Apollonia and Stagira) and incorporated the peoples of the Chalcidic peninsula – both Chalcidians and Bottiaeans – into the Macedonian kingdom.

Meanwhile the Phocians were running short of funds and so of mercenary soldiers, and the Thebans had been hammered into a condition of weakness. Who would administer the *coup de grâce*? Envoys from most of the city-states hastened to Pella, hoping to enlist Philip on their side in 346. At that time Alexander, as a boy of ten, will have watched with interest as his father found gracious words for all of them and committed himself to none. When the envoys were on their way home to their respective states, the Macedonian army reached Thermopylae, where the Phocian leader and his 8,000 mercenaries accepted the terms offered by Philip: to surrender their weapons and horses, and to go wherever they wished. The Phocian people were now defenceless. They 'placed themselves in the hands of Philip ... and he sat in council with representatives of the Boeotians and the Thessalians'. He had already made peace and alliance with Athens, and he had invited Athens to send representatives to this council. The invitation was refused on the advice of Hegesippus and Demosthenes.

Philip had acted as the champion of Apollo. It was for him a matter of religious conviction. He therefore entrusted the settlement to the Council of the Amphictyonic League, on which his allies in Thessaly and Central Greece had a majority of the votes, and they no doubt listened to his advice. The terms for the Phocians were mild by Greek standards (one Greek state proposed the execution of all the men): disarmament, division into village-settlements, payment of an indemnity to Apollo and expulsion from the Amphictyony. In their place the Macedonians were elected members. The two votes of Phocis on the Council were transferred to the Macedonian state. On the advice of Philip the Council 'published regulations for the custody of the oracle and for everything else appertaining to religious practice, to common peace and to concord among the Greeks'. Within Boeotia Thebes had a free hand: she destroyed three cities which had been forced to submit to the Phocians and sold their populations into slavery. She would have preferred to treat Phocis similarly.

2. Philip's policy towards the city-states

Philip's aim was to bring the city-states into concord and set up a Treaty of Common Peace, of which Macedonia and they would be members. This was in the spirit of the proposals made by Xenophon and Isocrates in 356-355, and it coincided with the tenor of a political pamphlet, entitled *Philip*, which Isocrates published in 346 just before the capitulation of Phocis. He advised Philip as the ruler of the strongest state in Europe to bring the city-states into concord, lead them against Persia, liberate the Greeks in Asia, and found there new cities to absorb the surplus population of the Greek mainland. The price of concord was acceptance of the *status quo* and the abnegation of any interventionist policy. Despite Philip's offers to set up a Common Peace, Athens, Sparta and Thebes went their own way in the name of 'freedom', and Philip realised in 341 that he might have to use force rather than persuasion if he wanted to exercise control.

Athens depended for her food-supply on imports of grain from South Russia, which had to pass through the Bosporus and the Hellespont. On the European side Byzantium was able to exact 'benevolences' from shipping at the Bosporus, and Athens through her colonies on the Chersonese (the Gallipoli peninsula) could do likewise in the Hellespont. The Asian side was held by Persia, which had put down a series of revolts on the coast of the Mediterranean and could now muster a huge fleet. Philip approached this sensitive area through a conquest of the tribes of eastern Thrace. It was during the Thracian campaign in 340 that he appointed Alexander at the age of sixteen to act as his deputy in Macedonia (above, p. 6). From then on Alexander was fully aware of Philip's plans.

Events moved rapidly. Philip laid siege to Perinthus and Byzantium, whereupon Athens declared war. He was thwarted by Persia and Athens acting in collusion. He summoned Alexander to join him, invaded the Dobruja, defeated a Scythian king there, and extended his control of eastern Thrace to the Danube. During his return to Macedonia in summer 339 he had to fight his way through the land of the Triballi, a powerful tribe which captured some of his booty. In Greece another Sacred War had started, and the command of the Amphictyonic forces was offered to and accepted by Philip in the autumn. The sacrilegious state which he had to discipline was Amphissa. He took his Macedonian army and troops from some Amphictyonic states not towards Amphissa but through Phocis to the border of Boeotia, in order to threaten Thebes, which though his 'friend and ally' had been behaving in a hostile manner, and to act against Athens, with which he was still at war. The envoys which he sent to Thebes were outbid by the envoys of Athens. In violation of her treaty Thebes joined Athens and sided with Amphissa. Philip tried more than once to negotiate terms of peace, but in vain. The decisive battle was fought at Chaeronea in Boeotia in August 338. The troops of Boeotia, Athens, Megara, Corinth and Achaea numbered some 35,000; those of Macedonia and her allies somewhat less.

Alexander, in command of the Companion Cavalry, pitched his tent by the river Cephissus. When his father's tactics created a breach in the opposing phalanx Alexander charged through the gap, and it was he who led the attack on the Sacred Band of 300 Thebans. The Macedonian victory was total. Thebes was treated harshly as the violator of its oaths. Athens was treated generously. Alexander led a guard of honour which brought the ashes of the Athenian dead to Athens – a unique tribute to a defeated enemy – and the 2,000 Athenian prisoners were liberated without ransom. As Philip advanced into the Peloponnese, his enemies submitted and his allies rejoiced. Sparta alone was defiant. He ravaged her territory and he gave some frontier regions to his allies; but he did not attack the city. During his return northwards he left garrisons at Acrocorinth, Thebes and Ambracia. Meanwhile the Council of the Amphictyonic League reduced the restrictions on the Phocians, made the Amphissaeans live in villages and approved the acts of Philip.

The future of the city-states was in Philip's hands. He decided to create the 'Greek Community' (*to koinon ton Hellenon*), in which the states would swear to keep the peace among themselves, maintain existing constitutions, permit changes only by constitutional methods, and combine in action against any violator of the 'Common Peace', whether internal or external. His proposal, made in autumn 338, was accepted by the states in spring 337, and a 'Common Council' was established, of which the members represented one or more states in proportion to their military and naval strengths. The Council was a sovereign body: its decisions were sent to the states for implementation, not for discussion. The military forces and the naval forces at the disposal of the Common Council were defined: the former amounted to 15,000 cavalry and 200,000 infantry, and the number of warships, which is not stated in our sources, was later to be 160 triremes, manned by crews totalling some 30,000 men. Thus the Greek Community far outdid the Macedonian State in the size of the forces it could deploy. The Council had disciplinary, judicial and financial powers which were binding on the member-states. If we look for a modern analogy, we should look rather to the United States of America than to the European Community.

The next step was the creation of an offensive and defensive alliance between the Greek Community and the Macedonian State for all time. Because Macedonia was already at war with Persia, the Council declared war on Persia late in 337 and voted that the commander of the joint forces should be Philip. Within the Community his title was 'Hegemon', and the powers of his office were carefully defined. In the spring of 336 the vanguard of the joint forces crossed to Asia under the command of three Macedonian generals whom Philip appointed, and arrangements were made for the stipulated forces of the coalition to follow in the autumn with Philip as overall commander.

The brilliance of Philip's political initiative, power of persuasion and effective leadership is obvious. He brought into being the combination of a newly created Greek State, self-standing and self-governing, and a Macedonian State which was unrivalled in military power. If that combination should succeed in liberating the Greek cities in Asia and in acquiring extensive territory, it would provide a cure for many of the troubles of the Greek world. Theopompus, critical of Philip in many ways, entitled his history *Philippica* 'because Europe had never produced such a man altogether as Philip, son of Amyntas'.

3. Relations between Philip and his grown-up son

Alexander, who had come of age just before his command at the Battle of Chaeronea, was fully aware of Philip's plans and of the opposition to them; for he was in his father's confidence as his intended successor. The aim of Philip in Asia was revealed when he asked the Pythian priestess at Delphi whether he would 'conquer the king of the Persians'. Whereas the Greek Community intended to liberate the Greeks in Asia and punish Persia for past wrongs, Philip intended to carry his war to the logical conclusion, the defeat of Persia. Within Macedonia there was no doubt some dissent, due not only to the strain of war after war but also to the fear of defeat overseas and of risings in Europe. For it was no secret that many politicians in the city-states were opposed to the very concept of a Greek Community which was in their eyes a violation of city-state independence, and that they regarded the Amphictyonic Council and the Common Council as organs of Macedonian domination in Greece. The Balkan situation was far from secure, with the Odrysians and the Scythians only recently defeated and with the Triballi still defiant. Yet Philip was confident of success in the interest of the Greek-speaking world and of Macedonia in particular.

In battle the king fought as the leading man of his Cavalry Guard or his Infantry Guard. Philip was wounded seven times in action, and he owed his survival as much to the courage of his Bodyguards and his Pages as to his physical strength and his defensive armour. The projected campaign in Asia would put at risk both his life and Alexander's, and the only other surviving son, Arrhidaeus, was not capable of rule. Philip was not alone in wishing that a son of his should succeed him; for the Macedonians believed that the divine favour went from father to son in the royal house. In 341 he married Meda, the daughter of a king of the Getae. By then the four wives of the early years, 358-356, were passing or past the child-bearing age, and he hoped no doubt that Meda would bear him a son. In 339 he may have married a Scythian princess, whose hand had been offered to him by the king in the Dobruja, Atheas. It was probably early in 337 that Philip took in marriage not a member of his own royal house nor a princess of another royal house, but a young Macedonian commoner, Cleopatra. She was the ward of Attalus, a Bodyguard of the king; and this Attalus had been selected to command the Macedonian infantry which was about to invade Asia. Such a marriage was not in the Macedonian tradition, for it introduced a commoner family into the royal circle. It was said by a later writer,

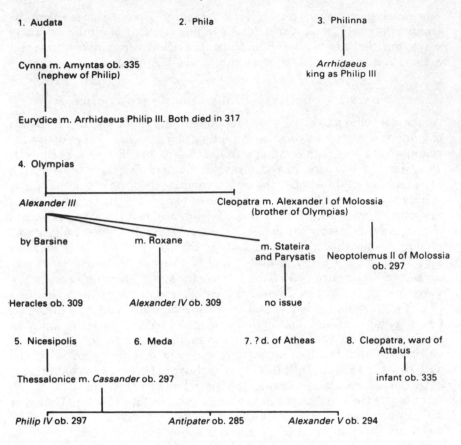

1. Audata

Cynna m. Amyntas ob. 335
(nephew of Philip)

Eurydice m. Arrhidaeus Philip III. Both died in 317

2. Phila

3. Philinna

Arrhidaeus
king as Philip III

4. Olympias

Alexander III

Cleopatra m. Alexander I of Molossia
(brother of Olympias)

by Barsine   m. Roxane

m. Stateira
and Parysatis   Neoptolemus II of Molossia
ob. 297

Heracles ob. 309   *Alexander IV* ob. 309   no issue

5. Nicesipolis   6. Meda   7. ? d. of Atheas   8. Cleopatra, ward of
Attalus

Thessalonice m. *Cassander* ob. 297   infant ob. 335

Philip IV ob. 297   *Antipater* ob. 285   *Alexander V* ob. 294

Note   Those who became king of Macedonia are in italics.

3. Philip's wives and descendants

Satyrus, that Philip, now in his mid-forties, had fallen passionately in love with the young girl and so made what was to prove a disastrous marriage.

Whatever Philip's motives, the marriage caused a rift between him and Olympias, and further between him and Alexander. The affairs of royalty were then, as now, of the greatest interest to journalistic writers, for whom scandal-mongering was more important than truthful reporting. Such a writer was Satyrus, who wrote a *Life of Philip* in the middle of the third century. According to his account, of which only a summary survives in secondary sources, the wedding banquet was the scene of the following fracas.

As Attalus toasted the bride, he proclaimed to the assembled guests: 'From now on those born to be our kings will be legitimate sons and not bastards.' Thereupon Alexander threw his tankard at Attalus, and Attalus hit Alexander with his cup. Philip drew his sword to kill his son; but he tripped, fell and collapsed in a drunken stupor. Alexander, turning to the company, said, 'See, you fellows, here is the man who plans to cross from Europe to Asia. Why, he has fallen flat on his face in crossing from one couch to another.' Olympias, already outraged because Philip was bringing one girl after another into her marriage-bed, let fly at Philip for trying to kill her son. Philip responded by divorcing her on a charge of adultery. Alexander sided with his mother. He went with her to Molossia, where she persuaded the young king to mount an invasion of Macedonia. But Philip was too clever. He gave to the Molossian king the hand of his own daughter in marriage. Alexander stayed away until an urbane Corinthian, called Demaratus, brought Philip to see reason and recall his son. Olympias, however, stayed in Molossia.

The setting of the story is Athenian, not Macedonian. Polygamy did not exist at Athens; thus for Philip to marry Cleopatra was to treat Olympias as a cast-off and her son as a bastard, and all other 'wives' of Philip were his mistresses or simply prostitutes. The idea that the Molossians would or even could invade Macedonia in 337 was absurd. The colourful story may confidently be dismissed as a fiction. But the fact remains that the marriage did cause a serious rift. We know this from a digression in the history of Arrian, whose source at this point was Ptolemy or/and Aristobulus, both being contemporaries of Alexander. The passage runs thus:

> When Philip was still king, Harpalus was exiled because he was loyal to Alexander. So too Ptolemy, son of Lagus, Nearchus, son of Androtimus, Erigyius, son of Larichus, and Laomedon his brother on the same charge, because suspicion existed between Philip and Alexander when Philip married Eurydice and dishonoured Alexander's mother, Olympias. On the death of Philip they were restored from the exile they had incurred on his account.

Of what honour had Olympias been deprived? The answer may be provided by Philip's renaming of Cleopatra as 'Eurydice', evidently at the time of the marriage. As we have seen, Eurydice was the name of Philip's mother, who had been held in the highest honour and had been buried in a magnificent tomb in about 340 (above, p. 3). These tributes had been paid to her as Queen Mother, presiding over the women's quarters in the Palace. On her death Olympias evidently succeeded to her position as Queen-Mother-to-be of the son whom Philip was promoting to the position of deputy and so of being his chosen successor in the event of his own death. But to call his new wife 'Eurydice' was surely to

demote Olympias and put Cleopatra in her place. In itself that might
have been a matter affecting only the women's quarters. But there was
the added implication that 'Eurydice' would become Queen-Mother-to-
be if she should bear a son to Philip, and that son would displace
Alexander as Philip's choice of successor. It is true that such a son
would probably be a minor, unless Philip lived on into old age, but
Alexander knew that the Macedonians had elected minors in the recent
past as their kings – Orestes, Perdiccas and Amyntas. So too the close
friends and contemporaries of Alexander realised that he might be
superseded and that their chances of promotion in his service would be
impaired. Alexander and those friends must have committed some
public act of defiance for Alexander to have fallen from favour, and for
them to have been exiled, and to have been kept in exile even after
Philip and Alexander were reconciled.

4. The invasion of Asia and the death of Philip

A different story about the rift between father and son was given by
Plutarch. It also ended with the exiling of Alexander's friends, but this
time in connection not with the dishonouring of Olympias as in Arrian's
account but with a proposed marriage between Arrhidaeus and the
daughter of an Asian satrap. The connection is obviously false; for the
statement by Arrian, being derived from Ptolemy and/or Aristobulus, is
to be accepted as true. The rest of the story too is false. It is that
Pixodarus, the satrap of Caria in the Persian Empire, wanted to marry
his daughter to Arrhidaeus, the half-wit son of Philip; that Alexander's
friends and Olympias told Alexander he was thereby about to be
displaced from the succession; and that Alexander sent a message to
Pixodarus that Arrhidaeus was 'a bastard' and Alexander himself was
a better match. When Philip heard of this, he upbraided Alexander.
Hence the rift and the exiling. When we remember that Pixodarus was
a Persian subject, we can see that he would have acted only in complete
secrecy, and that a marriage alliance had no value for Philip's purpose
while the Persian Empire was intact in Asia.

Whatever ideas Philip may have had about an eventual successor, he
had need of Alexander in the immediate future, either as commander
of the Companion Cavalry on the Asiatic campaign or as deputy in
Macedonia during his own absence on that campaign. In 337 Alexander
spent some time 'among Illyrians', i.e. at the courts of Illyrian client
kings. That was only possible with the approval of Philip and with a
military escort. Alexander may have been negotiating with them as a
preliminary to the campaign in autumn 337 which Philip undertook
against Pleurias, an Illyrian king (probably of the Autariatae in Bosnia). In any case we may date some form of reconciliation between
Philip and Alexander, which included Olympias in some way, to within

the year 337, because at that time Philip commissioned chryselephan-
tine (gold and ivory) statues of his parents, himself, Olympias and
Alexander for public display in the so-called Philippeum at Olympia.

In 336 the centre of attention was the war in Asia. The advance forces
of Macedonia and the Greek Community won striking successes under
the command of Parmenio, Attalus and Amyntas. For with a supporting
fleet they liberated the Greek cities of the west coast as far south as
Ephesus, where a statue of Philip was set up in the temple of Artemis.
Persia was slow to react. The defence of Asia Minor was entrusted to
Memnon, a Rhodian commander of Greek mercenaries, but there was
no Persian fleet in the Aegean to support him. Persian agents may have
reached the Greek mainland to subsidise anti-Macedonian politicians
such as Demosthenes at Athens; but the politicians would not act unless
the Persian fleet was in control of the Aegean. The main forces with
Philip in command were to land in the autumn, and it was anticipated
that during a winter campaign Philip would become master of western
Asia Minor.

While the forces of the Greek Community were gathering, Philip
chose to make the October festival at Aegeae an international occasion
by inviting as his guests envoys of the city-states and leaders of his
Balkan subjects. It was at this festival that weddings were celebrated
in Macedonia. The ceremonies began with sacrifices to the gods, weddings which included that of Cleopatra, the daughter of Philip and
Olympias, to Alexander, the Molossian king, and lavish state banquets.
The guests for their part presented gold wreaths to Philip, some as
individuals and others as official delegates of Greek city-states, Athens
being one of them. The second day was to begin with a religious
procession and with musical and dramatic performances in the theatre
just below the palace. So just before dawn the theatre was packed with
the leading Macedonians and the official guests of the Macedonian
State.

The procession was a dazzling display of wealth. It was headed by
richly adorned statues of the twelve Olympian gods and an equally
magnificent statue of Philip 'worthy of a god, as the king was showing
himself enthroned with the twelve gods'. In Macedonian belief the kings
were descended from Zeus, the most distinguished of them were worshipped after their death, and it seems from later instances that 'divine
honours' were in outstanding cases conferred on a reigning king by the
Macedonians. The best explanation of Philip's statue on this occasion is
that 'divine honours' had been so conferred, and that he chose to show
his elevation to divinity.

When the procession was over, some of Philip's Friends, headed by
Alexander as his chosen successor and by the other Alexander, king of
Molossia, entered through the *parodos* and took their designated seats
in the front row. Then came the Infantry Guardsmen, who posted

themselves at the edge of the *orchestra*. Philip entered alone, wearing a white cloak, and stood in the centre of the *orchestra*, acknowledging the cheers of the spectators. The seven Bodyguards, who had entered behind him, fanned out at some distance. Suddenly one of them, Pausanias, sprang forward, stabbed the king and fled down the *parodos*. Three Bodyguards ran to the king's side. Three others – named as Leonnatus, Perdiccas and Attalus – rushed after Pausanias, who tripped and fell. They killed him with their spears. In the *orchestra* the king lay dead.

CHAPTER IV

Alexander establishes his position in Macedonia, Greece and the Balkans

1. The succession and the trial of conspirators

The sight of his father being killed by a Bodyguard must have haunted Alexander for the rest of his life. The memory made him aware of the constant danger of assassination, and of the fact that in the last resort a king could not trust even a chosen Bodyguard. At the moment the first priority was the election of a successor. As many of the King's Men as could be summoned from the neighbourhood met as an assembly under arms in the theatre, where the corpse of Philip was laid out to witness proceedings. Antipater, Philip's senior Friend, presided. The election was not a foregone conclusion, because there was known to be some support for the claims of Amyntas, who had been king as a minor in 359-357, and some for the sons of Aëropus, king in 397-394. The Friends generally gathered round Alexander. One of them, Alexander Lyncestes, a son of Aëropus, was the first to shout 'Alexander, son of Philip', and the assembly elected Alexander with a resounding acclamation. The Friends put on their cuirasses, the King's Men clashed their spears against their shields, and the new king led a procession to the Palace.

Alexander was a fine orator. When the King's Men took the oath of loyalty, he harangued them and assured them that he would pursue the policies of his father, and he asked the envoys of the Greek Community to show towards himself the goodwill which they had shown towards Philip. His first duty was to conduct an inquiry into the circumstances of the assassination. The personal motive of Pausanias was soon established. It began with a homosexual affair between him and a Royal Page. Such affairs were as acceptable as heterosexual relations (indeed often concurrent with them), and formed part of a military tradition which at this time, for instance, commended the Thebans of the Sacred Band as 'pairs of lovers'. When the affair broke down, Pausanias taunted the boy, who took Attalus into his confidence and revealed his intention to commit suicide, which he did in the battle against Pleurias in summer 337. Attalus avenged the boy by inviting Pausanias to dinner, making him drunk and having him sexually abused by a gang of men. Pausanias complained to Philip, who gave him presents and promotion but took no steps against Attalus. In revenge Pausanias murdered Philip. Although the details may be open to question, the substance is correct, because Aristotle who was then at the court wrote that 'Pausanias attacked Philip because Philip let it pass that Pausanias had been sexually abused by those with Attalus'. But the personal motive of Pausanias did not preclude a conspiracy, of which he would be only a part.

Assassination was a hazard for any Macedonian king. For that reason his person was guarded daily by the seven Bodyguards, who were chosen by him from his leading officers, and by day and night by Royal Pages in relays. In addition the royal quarters were protected by men of the Infantry Guard of Macedonians, and in the latter part of Philip's reign by the Royal Hypaspists in their nearby barracks. But these precautions sometimes failed. Archelaus, for instance, was killed during a Royal Hunt in 399, Amyntas II was murdered by a Royal Page in 394, and Alexander II was assassinated during a festival, probably the *Xandica* of spring 367. The trial of any suspects was conducted before the assembly of Macedonians. In 399 three persons were arraigned, two being Royal Pages and the third an ex-Page, and it seems that the verdict was 'not proven', although Aristotle later held them all guilty. For the murder of Amyntas II we have only the name of the Royal Page, Derdas, and he may have acted alone. Alexander II was killed by more than one person, and one of the killers, a married man with children, was executed. Rumours, of course, proliferated. Marsyas Macedon said that the death of Archelaus was accidental, and that the death of Alexander II was due to 'the party of Ptolemy', who in fact was made guardian of Perdiccas and Philip and was therefore trusted at the time. Later reports even made Ptolemy the killer.

Polygamy bred complications. Any newly elected king was likely to have not only half-brothers but also cousins of varying degrees within the royal house. He tried to win their cooperation, for instance by giving a daughter in marriage, as Archelaus did to a son of the Amyntas who became Amyntas II. On the other hand, if they stood out as pretenders to the throne, he tried to have them condemned as traitors. If a man was found guilty of treason by the assembly of Macedonians, the law was that his relatives be put to death. Plato, for instance, wrote that Archelaus killed an uncle and that uncle's son, as well as a half-brother. When Amyntas III died, he had at least two wives, and each of them had borne him three sons. Thus the sons of Eurydice had three half-brothers. All three survived until the reign of Philip, who arranged the death of one; he captured the other two in Olynthus, and no doubt had them tried for treason and executed. Of Philip's cousins two were supported by foreign powers as pretenders, the death of one was obtained by bribery, and the other was surrendered after a battle.

When Philip was assassinated, there was suspicion of a conspiracy. For in trying to escape Pausanias ran not to one horse but to 'the horses at the gateway which had been provided for the flight'. These horses must have been for more than one killer to use. It seemed then that Pausanias had acted alone on impulse, and that another killer or killers had been thwarted. Who was the other intended victim, or victims? Alexander would surely have been one. For if Philip and Alexander, sitting next to one another, had been killed, the kingdom would have been thrown into utter confusion. The circumstantial evidence pointed towards a conspiracy with such a programme.

The trial of the suspects who were identified by Alexander and his assistants was held before an assembly of the Macedonians. A fragmentary description of it has survived from a Hellenistic history. It may be translated thus.

> Those with him in the theatre and those in attendance they [i.e. the Macedonians] acquitted and those round the throne. X [probably the dead man] he delivered to the Macedonians to punish, and they crucified him. The body of Philip he delivered to courtiers to bury.

'He' was Alexander. The corpses of Pausanias and of Philip were there during the trial. In the preceding part of the text other verdicts were no doubt reported, for we know from other sources that two sons of Aëropus were executed 'at the tumulus' where Philip was buried. A third son of Aëropus, called Alexander Lyncestes, of whom we shall hear later, was acquitted on the intercession of Alexander. The three sons of Pausanias were executed in accordance with Macedonian custom.

2. The funeral of Philip and the march to Corinth

The funeral ceremony after the trial was a military occasion. The King's Men paraded under arms, and the corpse of the king was accompanied by his weapons and his armour. A large pyre of wood had been prepared. Alongside it the horses towards which Pausanias had run and the two sons of Aëropus were killed. Some of the harness and the swords of the two men, together with the weapon used in the assassination, were placed on the pyre alongside the corpse of Philip and the corpse of one of his wives. After the cremation the bones of the king and queen were placed in separate gold coffers. The large tomb was still under construction, but the main chamber was almost complete. The coffer of the king, his weapons and armour, and many other paraphernalia were placed in the main chamber, which was then closed. The objects I have mentioned as being on the pyre were later collected and placed on the vaulted roof of the chamber. The antechamber, in which the coffer of the queen was placed, and the façade were completed at leisure. The corpse of Pausanias, crucified on a plank, was set up on top of the façade as a warning to others, and a beautiful fresco was painted below the cornice. When all was complete, the corpse of Pausanias was burnt and the place where he had hung was purified by fire. A wide tumulus of red soil, brought from elsewhere, was raised over the tomb, so that one end of the tumulus covered the Tomb of Amyntas and the other end was available for later burials. The two corpses of the sons of Aëropus were put into the soil. Sacrifice to the dead kings, Amyntas and Philip, was made at the shrine which lay just outside the tumulus.

The king's chamber was closed prematurely because Alexander had to hasten southwards with all speed. His father's death had occurred in the early stages of three great enterprises: the extension of a Balkan Empire from the lower Adriatic to the west coast of the Black Sea, the leadership of the newly formed Greek Community, and the opening campaign in Asia against the Persian Empire. It was expected that Macedonia would reel under the shock, that the succession might be disputed, and that even if Alexander did succeed he was by Greek standards 'a mere youth' at the age of twenty and would not be able to cope with three enterprises. It seemed to be the moment for the enemies of Macedonia to act. Some Thessalians occupied the Tempe Pass, the people of Ambracia expelled the Macedonian garrison and put the democratic party in power, the Aetolians voted to intervene in Acarnania on behalf of some exiled Acarnanians, the Thebans voted to expel the Macedonian garrison, the opposition in Athens became vociferous, and there were stirrings in the Peloponnese. It seemed that the Greek Community was a dead letter; for the Council had taken no action itself, and it was without a *Hegemon*.

Alexander marched south at the head of the Macedonian army. He outflanked the Thessalians by climbing the cliffs of Mount Ossa and occupied Larissa, where the leading clan, the Aleuadae, was pro-Macedonian. He convened the Council of the Thessalian League and was duly appointed President of the League with the same powers as his father. Advancing to Thermopylae, where he had arranged a meeting of the Council of the Amphictyonic League, he was assured of the League's support in Greece. The democracy at Ambracia was approved by Alexander. Thebes was pardoned. The Athenians voted to bring their property from the countryside into the city, in order to withstand a siege, but they also sent envoys to meet Alexander and apologise. He accepted the apology with all politeness, bypassed Attica and halted at Corinth, to which he had summoned the Councillors of the Greek Community.

He knew already that he could count on the support of the Councillors of the northern and central Greek tribes and city-states, and the presence of the Macedonian army was not unnoticed by the other Councillors. Alexander made a charming speech to the Council, and in response it appointed him *Hegemon* with full powers, which were duly specified in writing, and promised him full cooperation in the war against Persia. At Corinth he met Diogenes (above, p. 6). His remark 'if I were not Alexander, I would indeed be Diogenes' carried the meaning 'if I were not already king of Macedonia, President of Thessaly, the favourite of the Amphictyonic League and *Hegemon* of the Greek Community'. His successes had been meteoric, but he knew that they were not assured.

3. Arrangements in the kingdom

Returning to Macedonia for the winter Alexander appointed his own Bodyguards, Friends and Commanding Officers, and 'he busied his soldiers with constant training in the use of their weapons and with tactical exercises'. Some evidence was found that Amyntas was involved in a conspiracy. He had been loyal to Philip, who had given him his daughter Cynna in marriage and had sent him as an envoy to Thebes; and he was both older than Alexander and the son of a king senior to Philip. Whatever the evidence, Amyntas was executed for treason. Reports came from friends in Athens that Demosthenes was receiving subsidies from Persia and was in correspondence with Attalus, the commander of the Macedonian infantry in Asia, with whom he was very popular. Alexander was apprehensive, and it may be that Attalus admitted that he had been in touch with Demosthenes and expressed repentance. In any event Alexander decided to put him on trial for treason. He sent an officer to arrest Attalus, and if he should resist arrest to kill him, as indeed happened. The corpse was probably brought back for trial and condemned. The relatives of Attalus were executed, among them his ward Cleopatra, renamed Eurydice, and her child by Philip.

Within the kingdom Alexander made arrangements which would last during his intended absence first in the Balkans and then in Asia. Inscriptions have been published recently revealing actions which are probably to be dated not to this winter but to that of 335/4. One reads: 'King Alexander gave to Macedonians Calindoea and the places around Calindoea – Thamiscia, Camacaea and Tripoatis' (these three being the territories of three towns). Alexander was continuing the policy of Philip, who had created a number of 'cities of Macedonians' (we know of such at Oesyme renamed 'Emathia', Apollonia in Mygdonia and Pythion in Perrhaebia). It was a gift because the king owned spear-won land and disposed of it and its inhabitants as he thought fit. The Calindoeans – a Bottiaean people – were planted as a community elsewhere in the kingdom. The Macedonian assembly decided which Macedonian population was to be transplanted *en bloc* to Calindoea, where they took over the city installations and received the revenues levied upon the three territories, which were worked by the townsmen who continued to live in their towns. The Macedonians of Calindoea were engaged not in farming but in military duties and in administration; and in particular they guarded the arterial road which ran along the south side of Lake Bolbe in Mygdonia.

Philippi was treated in diplomacy as an independent ally. The actuality was that it had to follow the policy of the king and accept his final arrangements. A dialogue was conducted by envoys from Philippi who put their case to Alexander about his disposal of reclaimed land in the vicinity. Here also the land and its Thracian inhabitants were spear-won. Alexander gave some land to Philippi 'to possess' and some to rent, and he confirmed the right of the Thracians to cultivate some land, a right which Philip had granted. Two Macedonian officers were to redraw the boundaries. We see here that Alexander dealt personally and directly with the spear-won land and its people, whereas at Calindoea he invoked the Macedonian assembly to arrange the transplantation of a Macedonian community; and that he listened to the requests which Philippi made through its envoys.

The entire area of land between the Axius and the Nestus, except for Amphaxitis, was spear-won land. By redistributing the Macedonian communities and planting some in that area Philip and Alexander were tightening their grip on communications, placing King's Men at strategic points and spreading the use of Greek language and Macedonian ideas. The spear-won peoples provided the economic substructure and paid tribute on the land they cultivated. The Paeonians in the north and the Illyrians in the northwest of the kingdom fulfilled the same function. Small forces of light-armed cavalry, archers and slingers were recruited from these peoples and trained as specialists. We hear also of Companion Cavalry squadrons from Apollonia, i.e. from the 'Macedonian city' in Mygdonia, and from Amphipolis, where Philip had introduced some settlers of his choice and given substantial estates to deserving Companions.

4. The campaign in Thrace and the organisation of the empire

In 335, 'as soon as it was spring Alexander set off for Thrace against the Triballi and the Illyrians, who, he had learnt, intended to revolt'. He had already in person made provision for the manning of the northwestern frontier of the kingdom. He did not take Philip's most experienced general, Antipater, an expert on Illyrian affairs, but left him to act as his deputy in Macedonia. Alexander alone was to exercise command.

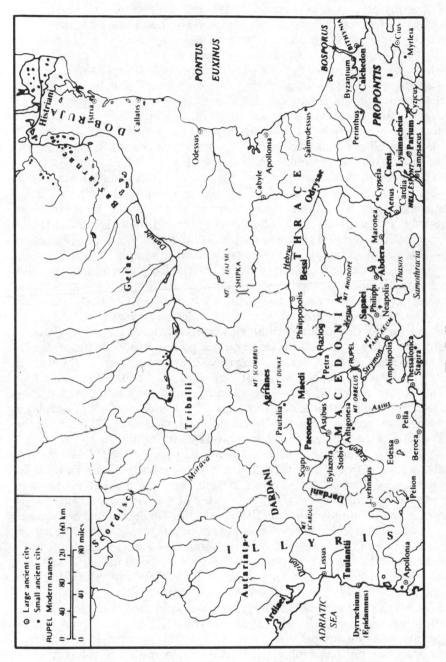

4. The Balkan area

The army consisted perhaps of 25,000 men, 5,000 horses, and a bag-gage-train which included siege-engines. He met no serious opposition until he reached the pass over Mount Haemus, which was defended by local tribesmen and Thracian troops, who had fled before his advance. Above the steepest part of the pass the enemy had placed a number of wagons, which, as Alexander surmised, they intended to launch against the infantry phalanx and smash its formation, so that they could defeat the phalangites in hand-to-hand fighting, in which the long pike was a disadvantage. It was a good plan, but Alexander had a better one. He instructed his phalangites to open ranks where there was room, and to lie down with their shields over their heads where they were restricted to close order. The wagons were let loose, and Alexander's orders were obeyed. Not a man was killed. The phalanx, aided by the enfilading fire of the archers, routed the enemy infantrymen, who were by comparison lightly armoured and had inferior weapons. Of them 1,500 fell. Their women, children and gear were captured and sent via the Aegean coast to Macedonia, where they were drafted into city populations.

A few days later Alexander surprised a force of Triballians, who were camping inside a wooded glen. He sent his archers and slingers ahead to fire at the enemy, who, as Alexander had anticipated, attacked and pursued onto open ground where his main force was awaiting them. Squadrons of Companion Cavalry charged into the exposed flanks, and a screen of light-armed cavalry and the phalanx in close order, led by Alexander, drove the enemy centre back and put them to flight. The enemy losses were estimated at 3,000, while 'Alexander is said by Ptolemy to have lost eleven cavalrymen and forty infantrymen'. De-scending to the Danube, he found a small Macedonian fleet of warships, which had come through the Bosporus and up the river. The king of the Triballians had taken the tribe's women and children to an island, which was already a refuge for some Thracian troops. Alexander's attempts to force a landing failed. On the far bank of the Danube he could see a force of Getae, estimated at some 4,000 cavalry and more than 10,000 infantry, and it was obvious that they would be able to reinforce and supply the Triballians and the Thracians on the island.

Alexander decided to cross the river at night. It was a bold but logical plan. Some of those nearest to him thought that he acted also from 'a desire' (*pothos*) to set foot on the far side of the Danube, something which his father had not done. Adding to his warships many dug-outs and rafts supported by leather tent-covers filled with straw, he trans-ported 1,500 cavalry and 4,000 infantry and landed them in a field of standing corn, which helped to conceal them. At dawn they set off, the infantry leading and parting the corn with their pikes at an angle. Once on open ground the cavalry, led by Alexander, moved to the right, and the phalanx formed a hollow rectangle in close order and advanced with pikes at the ready. The enemy, amazed at this bold crossing of the river and terrified by the bristling pikes of the phalanx, broke before the violent charge of the cavalry squadrons, each in wedge formation. Alexander pursued at speed, his infantry close to the river bank in order to protect that flank and his cavalry in extended line, until he turned towards the city of the Getae, some six kilometres inland. The Getae fled into the steppe country, taking some women and children on their horses' cruppers. Alexander razed the city and sacrificed to Zeus the Saviour and to Heracles and to Ister for permitting the crossing. On this same day he returned with his men all safe to the south bank. The booty was sent under the command of two officers towards the Aegean coast.

Syrmus and the Thracians on the island sent envoys and gifts to Alexander and asked for friendship. This was granted with mutual pledges. Other tribes along the south bank did likewise. The most westerly of these tribes were Celts near the head of the Adriatic Sea. According to Ptolemy, Alexander asked their envoys what they feared most, in the hope that they would say 'Alexander', but they replied 'the falling of the sky upon us'. He concluded a pact of friendship and alliance with the Celts, remarking to his Friends 'What boasters Celts are!' For four months Alexander was engaged in consolidating the work of his father, who had reduced the Thracian tribes to acceptance of Macedonian rule by many campaigns in summer and in winter. The key to Philip's success was the demonstration of military superiority, the pursuit and decimation of the Thracian aristocratic cavalry, and the enforcement of the peace. Alexander's campaign now set the seal on that success.

The Empire of the Macedonians in the Balkans was unlike that of Athens, for instance, in the Aegean area. The subjected tribes were left to govern themselves, maintain their own laws and customs, and arm their own militia. There was no imposition of a party system of rule, such as 'democracy' or 'oligarchy' which would lead to bitter party-strife (*stasis*), and no occupation in the form of a garrison. Rather, each tribal state kept its own traditions, character and self-respect. The Macedonians required the payment of a fixed tribute (probably a tenth of production), the provision of troops and labour on demand, and the acceptance of Macedonian foreign policy. The centuries-old system of inter-tribal wars and 'living by rapine' (above, p. 12) was to be replaced by an era of peace and prosperity, in which the agricultural workers would play an important part. To that end Philip had founded 'important towns in appropriate places and put an end to the unruly ways of the Thracians'. The population of the new towns, of which Philippoupolis (Plovdiv) was the largest, was 'mixed', in that it consisted of Macedonians, Greeks and the leading local people, and their purpose was to promote agriculture and trade and the spread of Greek as the official language of administration. The mixture of ideas and culture was the beginning of what modern scholars have called 'Hellenisation'. Other beneficiaries of peaceful conditions were the Greek city-states of the Thracian coasts, which 'entered most eagerly into the alliance of Philip' and now of Alexander.

The change in the fortunes of the Greek city-states was very great. Alexander now controlled both sides of the Hellespont, the Sea of Marmara and the Bosporus. The fleets of Macedonia and the Greek Community had complete thalassocracy in these waters and in the Black Sea, and they could sail up the Danube. They were able to put down piracy and to offer protection to city-states there against the native peoples. The result was a rapid expansion of commercial exchange and maritime trade. Philip and Alexander confiscated the rich mineral resources of Thrace as conquered territory, and they issued a fine coinage which became current in central Europe. The city-states of the Greek Community benefited greatly from the increase in trade and from the security of the corn-route from the Black Sea, on which Athens and many other states depended.

5. The campaign in Illyria

In late summer Alexander led his army southwards towards the land of the Agrianians (round Sofia) and the Paeonians (round Skopje). 'There messengers arrived reporting that Cleitus, son of Bardylis (in Kosovo-Metohija), was in revolt and that Glaucias, king of the Taulantii (round Tirana) had joined him; and also that the Autariatae (in Bosnia) would attack him on the march.' Such a combination was extremely formidable. The king of the Agrianians, who was a personal friend of Alexander and had led an embassy to him, undertook to attack the Autariatae; and when Alexander gave the order, he did so successfully. Meanwhile Alexander led his army through Pelagonia, Lyncus and Orestis, in order to protect the kingdom, and then swung north to reach the river Eordaicus, where he encamped close to an Illyrian fortified city, Pelium, which Cleitus had garrisoned. He had moved so fast that Cleitus was still waiting for Glaucias, in order to make a combined onslaught on the Macedonian kingdom. Next day he advanced to the walls of Pelium. The troops of Cleitus on the hills nearby made a sacrifice of three boys, three girls and three black rams, and then came down to attack the Macedonians. They were defeated so roundly that they abandoned their original positions and left the sacrificial victims there on the ground.

Alexander was now able to lay siege to Pelium. But next day the large army of Glaucias arrived and Alexander withdrew into his fortified camp. The pressing problem for Alexander was supply for his 25,000 men and 5,000 horses, because he had already drawn on his own territory to the south. He therefore sent Philotas, the son of Parmenio, with the horse-drawn wagons and an escorting force of Companion

Cavalry northwards into the fertile plain of Koritsa, where harvested grain and pasture were abundant. On the way they went through the Tsangon Pass, which is commanded by hills on either side. These hills were occupied by Glaucias, in order to intercept Philotas on his return. Alexander in person led a force of 400 cavalry, together with the Hypaspists, Archers and Agrianians, at speed to the Tsangon Pass, which he cleared of the enemy in time for the loaded wagons of Philotas' party to return. The relief was only temporary. Alexander's army had to move or starve, and movement seemed very difficult, because the route of retreat southwards would bring his army through country already stripped of supplies and eventually onto broken, hilly ground, where his phalanx could be shot down by the greatly superior numbers of the enemy's light-armed forces. 'Those with Cleitus and Glaucias seemed still to have caught Alexander on difficult ground', a comment which Arrian derived probably from Ptolemy. See Plate 8(a) and (b).

Alexander paraded his army with its siege-train but not its baggage on the level ground beside his camp. His orders were to keep absolute silence and obey each command smartly. The phalanx in close formation with a depth of 120 men went through a series of manoeuvres: with pikes upright, then pikes at the ready, advancing and retiring, wheeling this way and that, and finally forming into a wedge and charging at the enemy on the foothills. Squadrons of cavalry, each 200 strong, moved in concert to protect the flanks of the phalanx. The Dardanians fled to higher ground. The phalanx then turned about, raised the battle-cry and clashed their pikes against their shields as the preliminary to a charge against the Taulantians, who had come down from Pelium but now fled to the protection of the city's walls. Alexander had now cleared both flanks for his line of advance, which was into the very narrow pass which lay beween the Dardanian forces and the Taulantian forces.

The enemy positions are shown in Fig. 5. By advancing into the Wolf's Pass Alexander would keep those forces divided, but within the Pass he had to capture the steep-sided hill K2, before his phalanx arrived and came under fire. To this end he ordered his seven Bodyguards and his personal Companions to take their shields, mount their horses and charge towards the hill. On reaching it they were to fight, half on foot and half mounted, against the enemy. In fact the enemy fled at the sight of Alexander charging at the head of his élite cavalry, and Alexander strengthened his hold by bringing up 2,000 Agrianians and Archers. He ordered the Hypaspists and the phalanx brigades to ford the river and form into line in close order along the far bank. When this was done, Alexander's force was isolated on the hill K2, and the Taulantians came down the mountain side to attack it as it withdrew. But Alexander led his men in a counter-attack, the phalangites raised their battle-cry, and the enemy withdrew. Thereupon Alexander led his men at the double towards the river, was himself the first to cross, and

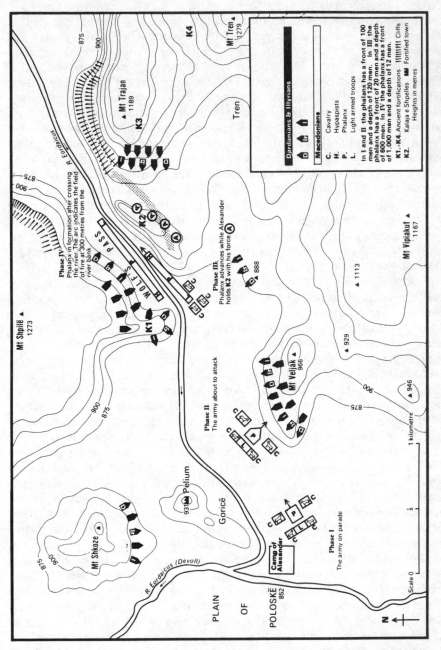

Dardanians & Illyrians ◣ ◤

Macedonians
◤ ◣ ◤

C.	Cavalry
H.	Hypaspists
P.	Phalanx
L.	Light armed troops

In I and II the phalanx has a front of 100 men and a depth of 120 men. In III the phalanx has a front of 20 men and a depth of 600 men. In IV the phalanx has a front of 1,000 men and a depth of 12 men.

K1.-K4. Ancient fortifications ‖‖‖‖‖ Cliffs
K2. Kalaja e Shpellës ■ Fortified town
▲ Heights in metres

Phase IV
Phalanx in formation after crossing the river. The arc indicates the field of fire at 300 metres from the river bank

Phase III
Phalanx advances while Alexander holds K2 with his force Ⓐ

Phase II
The army about to attack

Phase I
The army on parade

Mt Shpillë ▲ 1273

R. Eordaicus

R. Eordaicus (Devoll)

Mt Trajan ▲ 1189

K3

K4

Mt Tren ▲ 1279

Tren

Mt Veljak ▲ 966

Mt Vipiakuf ▲ 1167

▲ 1113

▲ 929

▲ 946

▲ 888

WOLF'S PASS

K1

K2

PLAIN OF POLOSKË

Pelium
Goricë
931

Mt Shkoze ▲
852

Camp of Alexander

N

Scale 0   ½   1 kilometre

5. The manoeuvres by Pelium

ordered the catapultists on the bank and the Archers in mid-river to lay down a barrage of fire which covered the escape of the rearguard. 'The Macedonians crossed the river safely, so much so that not a single man was killed in the withdrawal.'

Pasture was now available on the swampy shores of Lake Little Prespa, and supplies were obtained from the Macedonian villages near the head of the Lake. Alexander waited out of sight of the enemy for three days, but his scouts noted the disposition of the enemy, the undefended camp and the lack of sentries. On the next night Alexander gave orders for an attack which he led in person with the Hypaspists, the Agrianians, the Archers and two brigades of phalangites as the vanguard. The surprise was complete. Alexander and his men in deep formation broke through one wing of the enemy position and set the rest in flight. Alexander now led the pursuit by his cavalry across the plains 'right up to the mountains of the Taulantians', a distance of about 100 kilometres. 'As many as did escape (i.e. of the enemy cavalry) did so by throwing away their arms.' Cleitus took refuge in Pelium. When the pursuit was over, Alexander led his army south to deal with a rising at Thebes.

The genius of Alexander as a commander is indisputable. To break his way through the Haemus Pass, to cross the Danube and rout the Getae, and to withdraw his army through the Wolf's Pass without the loss of a single man in all three operations is unparalleled. Nor were his opponents weak; for the Thracians were greatly feared by the Greek city-states, and the Dardanians had inflicted very heavy losses on the Molossians and the Macedonians in the period 390-360. The Macedonian army excelled now in its professional expertise. The squadrons of heavy cavalry, each in wedge formation and armed with the long lance, and the phalanx in close order with pikes at the ready were as deadly in action as they were terrifying to behold. Provided they were on level ground and were coordinated in action, they were almost unstoppable. The supporting troops were equally professional: the catapultists, the archers and the slingers, the Agrianians armed with a long spear and a long sword and carrying a small shield, and the light-armed cavalrymen, some armed with the long lance and others with javelins. The 3,000 Hypaspists were particularly versatile; for they fought with the pike in phalanx formation, being stationed next to the phalangites proper, and they were trained to use hoplite equipment (large shield and seven-foot spear) and other weapons. Whereas the phalangites wore a metal cuirass or half-cuirass, only the officers of the Hypaspists were so equipped.

Alexander led the way into every action. He intended to outdo his seven Bodyguards in fighting, for he had a strongly competitive spirit. He encouraged competition throughout the army of the king's men. There was an order of precedence among the Bodyguards and the

Friends, and a similar order in the swearing to confirm diplomatic agreements. The élite units were the Royal Squadron of Companion Cavalry, the Royal Guard of Macedones (earlier called Pezhetairoi), the Royal Brigade of the Hypaspists, and the Royal Pages in their last year. There was the usual ladder of rank for officers and for those below officer level. Every one of the King's Men took an oath of loyalty to the king and depended on his favour for promotion. He was the centre of their world. He intended to act in accordance with his favourite line in the *Iliad* (3.179): to be 'both a good king and a mighty warrior'.

CHAPTER V

Sources of information, a rising in Greece and preparations for Persia

1. The sources of information for the Balkan campaign

We owe our knowledge mainly to four ancient writers, whose works were composed three and more centuries after the career of Alexander: Diodorus Siculus, author of a Universal History; Pompeius Trogus, whose work has survived in an epitome by Justin; Plutarch, the biographer and moraliser; and Arrian, the historian of *Alexander's Expedition*. It is obvious that these writers drew on the works of earlier authors who either had been contemporaries of the events or had composed standard works early in the Hellenistic period (which began after Alexander's death). When we assess the value of statements made by these four authors, we need to ascertain which of those earlier accounts was used by each author. For instance, we began this book with the handling of Bucephalus as described by Plutarch in his *Life of Alexander*. We inferred that Plutarch drew on the account of a contemporary eyewitness, namely Marsyas Macedon, who wrote for contemporaries, and that Plutarch's version was therefore soundly based. On the other hand, the accounts of a drunken scene at the wedding of Philip and Cleopatra which were provided by Plutarch and Justin have all the marks of scandalmongering. We inferred that the accounts were drawn from a common source, namely a *Life of Alexander* by Satyrus, a sensationalist and untrustworthy writer, who wrote in the mid-third century when anti-Macedonian feeling ran high and no contemporaries of the events survived. We therefore suspect that the accounts are not dependable in any respect.

It so happens that Arrian alone gave a detailed account of the Balkan campaign. Our other three authors merely alluded to it, because their interest and that of the authors upon whom they drew were in Greek affairs and in the crossing to Asia. Arrian and the author or authors upon whom Arrian drew realised the importance of the Balkan campaign in relation to the invasion of Asia: 'Alexander thought that, when he was going on an expedition far from the homeland, he ought not to leave his neighbours planning revolt unless they had been completely humbled.' As we have seen, Arrian's account was remarkably detailed, specific and consistent throughout, presumably because it all came from the same author or authors. Fortunately, and almost uniquely among ancient writers, Arrian told his readers that he was drawing on the accounts of Ptolemy and Aristobulus, that he recorded as 'completely true' whatever they said in agreement, and that where they differed he gave the version which he judged to be 'more credible and more worth reporting'. His words are certainly true; for his own contemporaries were familiar with the full accounts of Ptolemy and of Aristobulus and could have seen at once if he was not doing what he said he was doing.

It is thus certain that for the Balkan campaign Arrian gave an unadulterated version of the accounts of Ptolemy and Aristobulus, unadulterated because he believed those accounts to have been 'completely true' and because 'they had campaigned with Alexander'. The only occasion on which he noted a difference between them was that Ptolemy reported exact numbers of the Macedonian casualties in cavalry and in infantry (Arr. 1.2.7). From this we infer two things, that Aristobulus either did not report the casualties or gave less 'credible' figures, and that thereafter when exact numbers are stated by Arrian they will have been taken from Ptolemy's account. The question at once arises: how did Ptolemy know 'more credibly' than Aristobulus the numbers of the dead and also, as we shall see later, the numbers of the wounded in the actions of many years? Similar questions arise with regard to the citations of orders given by Alexander of which some were not enacted (e.g. two in the Balkan campaign at Arr. 1.6.5 and 1.6.10), the naming of officers, the specification of units in action, and the intervals of time in terms of days. When we realise that within books 1 to 6 Arrian reported 147 orders, 78 intervals by days, and some hundreds of officers' names, these questions become imperative. For one man to recall all these by memory alone is inconceivable. Ptolemy must have had access to a written record, which Arrian knew to be itself 'credible' in these respects.

That record can only have been the *Journal of Alexander*. It survived in Alexandria; a lengthy commentary on it was written by Strattis in the middle of the third century (a fragment of a commentary, presumably that of Strattis, survives for events of 335), paraphrases of passages from it were given by Plutarch and Arrian, and reference was made to it by Philinus, Aelian and Athenaeus. The nature of the *Journal* is known from these writings and from descriptions of contents in later Royal Journals. It was a record, made at the time, day by day, of the activities and statements of the king, and attached to it were some relevant documents, e.g. in matters of diplomacy and in official correspondence. The *Journal* was secret during the lifetime of a king and for the limited time thereafter during which his orders were relevant, and then it was deposited with the other possessions of the king at the place of his burial – in Alexander's case at Alexandria. There Ptolemy, the ruler of Egypt, had access to it. Aristobulus, however, did not, since he wrote his work in Macedonia. Thus Arrian was justified in giving the casualties of the Macedonians against the Triballi as 'eleven cavalrymen and about forty infantrymen, as Ptolemy says'. For he knew that Ptolemy's history was based on the bedrock of historical facts which had been recorded in the *Journal* at the time of their happening without bias or revision.

Arrian considered the question whether Ptolemy himself distorted the record. He noted that Ptolemy, writing after the death of Alexander, was not compelled, nor tempted by hope of gain, 'to set down anything otherwise than as it happened'; and that being in a public position as a king he would incur more disgrace if he was found to be lying. Arrian was here concerned with the facts as they happened. There is no doubt that Ptolemy selected and presented those facts in his own way, that is in a way which was generally but not always favourable to Alexander as his friend and patron; for Ptolemy rose to the highest rank, that of Bodyguard to Alexander. In addition to making use of the *Journal* Ptolemy drew on his own memory for many of the vivid details which were repeated by Arrian, gave his own interpretation of Alexander's aims and generalship, and was not averse to blowing his own trumpet. Like most ancient writers he saw himself as a literary artist. Accordingly he did not cite factual documents like the *Journal verbatim* or even in paraphrase, but he composed his own fine account. We see an example of this in Arrian's treatment of Alexander's last illness. He himself delivered his own paraphrase of the account in the *Journal*, and he added that Aristobulus and Ptolemy had written accounts which were 'not far from' that paraphrase. Here it is evident that Ptolemy had not paraphrased the *Journal* but had written his own independent account – not surprisingly when we remember that as a Bodyguard he will have watched over the king in his illness.

The next question is how far did Arrian misunderstand or change what he read in the accounts of Ptolemy and Aristobulus. He was far better placed than any historian of Alexander then and now to understand the conditions in which Alexander carried out his conquests and organised his kingdom of Asia; for he wrote treatises on tactics and hunting, conducted a successful campaign against the Alani of Georgia and Azerbaijan, and held the consulship and the governorship of Cappadocia in the heyday of the Roman Empire. That he did not make changes is apparent from his own assurance that he reported as 'completely true' what was stated in agreement by Ptolemy and Aristobulus, and he announced the principle on which he preferred one or other account where they differed. We know less about Aristobulus, a citizen of Phocis, who enjoyed the confidence of Alexander and was entrusted with the repair of the Tomb of Cyrus at Pasargadae. As his interests were scientific and geographical rather than military, he provided in his history of Alexander much less material than Ptolemy did, but he seems to have taken a greater interest in Alexander's personality. It is probable that Arrian derived from Aristobulus the idea that Alexander's actions were sometimes prompted by a strong desire or yearning (*pothos* in Greek and *cupido* in Latin).

'Some statements by other authors I have also recorded, because they seemed to me to be worth mentioning and to be not entirely incredible, but only as stories (*legomena*) about Alexander.' Some of these were different interpretations of events described by his main authors, and others conveyed additional matter, particularly about affairs in Greece and the Aegean area where Alexander was not personally present. That Arrian was critical of these other writers is clear from his comments, notably in variant versions of Alexander's end (Arr. 7.27). We shall discuss some of these *legomena* as they arise.

2. The revolt and capture of Thebes, and the sources of information

The fullest surviving account is that of Arrian, based on the longer accounts of Ptolemy and Aristobulus. We shall take it first.

Alexander had just returned from his pursuit of the Illyrians, when reports reached him of a revolutionary movement at Thebes. These were to the effect that exiles, returning to the city on the invitation of their partisans, had killed two unsuspecting Macedonians of the garrison; that they had reported Alexander as dead in Illyria; and they had persuaded the Thebans to rise in the cause of liberty and autonomy. Alexander realised the danger that the revolt would spread; for he had long been suspicious of Athens, Aetolia, Sparta and some other Peloponnesian states. Accordingly he marched his army at top speed over the high country of Mount Grammus, Mount Pindus and Mount Cambunia, where there was abundant pasture and where cheese, meat and transport animals could be requisitioned from the transhumant shepherds. Arriving unannounced at Pelinna in northern Thessaly after marching for six days at some 33 kilometres a day, he rested the army for a day. From there he reached Onchestus in Boeotia on the sixth day, having covered some 200 kilometres at an average of 40 kilometres a day. His march was so swift that the Thebans did not know of his approach. He had come unopposed through the Pass of Thermopylae and he could now draw supplies and troops from supporters in northern Boeotia and from Phocis.

The speed of Alexander's march enabled him to pin down Thebes on the next day and to deter any would-be helpers from Athens and other states. He waited in the hope that the Thebans would repent and send an embassy to him, but they made an attack on his camp and killed a few Macedonians. Even so Alexander waited. There was a division of opinion inside Thebes, but the ringleaders and especially the generals of the Boeotian League who had broken their oath of loyalty to the Greek Community persuaded the majority to fight. Alexander was now encamped close to the citadel of Thebes (the Cadmea) in which the Macedonian garrison was surrounded and likely to be overwhelmed. Even so Alexander was not intending to attack, but 'Ptolemy states' that Perdiccas, commanding the brigade on guard, did not await an order from the king but himself led an attack on the Theban field defences, which consisted of two palisades, one behind the other and both in front of the massive city-wall. When he broke through the first palisade, he was joined by another brigade. As they advanced to attack the second palisade, they were likely to be overwhelmed by Theban reinforcements. Alexander had no option but to move his army into action stations.

We learn from another account that the Thebans had received plenty of arms and equipment from Athens. They were famous for their field defences, their walls were almost impregnable by the standards of Greek warfare, and their hoplites had a high reputation. Since Alexander had come without his siege-train, everything seemed to be in favour of the defence. But the initiative of Perdiccas created a situation of which Alexander could take advantage. He ordered the Archers and the Agrianians to enter the space between the two palisades. There Perdiccas fell, seriously wounded. He was carried back to the camp. Alexander waited outside in command of the Infantry Guard of Macedonians and the Royal Hypaspist Brigade in phalanx formation, and behind the phalanx stood the two other brigades of Hypaspists. As Alexander foresaw, the attacking Macedonians were routed by a counter-attack, fled with the loss of seventy archers, and were hotly pursued through the gap in the first palisade by the Theban hoplites, who were no longer in phalanx formation but had scattered. The charge by Alexander's pikemen in formation was decisive, and the Macedonians in close pursuit followed the fugitives through the city-gates. One group liberated the garrison on the Cadmea, and another manned the walls and let the main army enter. Organised resistance soon broke down. The cavalry fled into the countryside. In the street-fighting which followed Alexander appeared now here, now there, but 'it was not so much the Macedonians as Phocians and Plataeans and the other Boeotians' who went on killing Thebans, even suppliants at the altars and women and children.

Arrian's narrative is a summary of the Macedonian view of the action as related by Ptolemy and Aristobulus. Other authors had reported a very different view, seen from the Greek side. According to Diodorus,

Alexander went from Thrace into Macedonia, mustered the full army of more than 3,000 cavalry and 30,000 infantry, and reached Thebes to find the garrison on the Cadmea hemmed in by field defences, such as palisades and trenches. Equipment had already been received from Athens thanks to Demosthenes, and the Assembly there had voted to help Thebes but then procrastinated. Arcadia, Argos and Elis responded to an appeal by despatching troops, but they stopped at the Isthmus on learning of Alexander's arrival. However, inspired by their leaders, the Thebans all decided to fight to the end in the cause of autonomy. They disregarded the divine warnings which the gods sent in the form of fantastic phenomena and oracular utterances. Alexander spent three days preparing for the attack. During those days he would have forgiven Thebes. For instance, he announced through a herald that any Theban might come over to him and enjoy the Common Peace of the Greeks. The Thebans countered by announcing that anyone should join them who wanted to take the side of the Great King of Persia and of Thebes, overthrow the dictator of Greece and liberate the Greeks. At these words Alexander flew into a towering rage, and in bestiality of spirit decided to destroy the city utterly.

An epic account was then given of the fighting which began with an exchange of missiles and went on to sword-play. The outnumbered Thebans, superior in physique, training and morale, outfought the Macedonians so that Alexander had to commit all his reserves to the battle. Even then the Thebans proved unshakable. They had high hopes of victory, but the king spotted an undefended postern-gate and sent Perdiccas with a large force into the city. The Thebans then retreated into the city in disorder, cavalry killing infantry under the feet of their horses, and there they fought heroically to the end. The Macedonians were merciless, and Thespians, Plataeans, Orchomenians and others joined in the massacre, which resulted in the death of more than 6,000 and the capture of 30,000. This account has much in common with later accounts of fighting by Diodorus. From a military point of view they are worthless; for they are fictions on the Homeric model in the style and mode of battle. The account is also blatantly pro-Theban.

There is no doubt that Diodorus derived this and later accounts from Cleitarchus, who was a citizen probably of Colophon in Asia Minor and ended up in Alexandria in Egypt. He did not serve in Asia, and as a young man he studied philosophy. Between 315 and 290 approximately he published a long, sensational account of Alexander's expedition which was widely read well into Roman times. In the judgement of Quintilian he was a talented writer, but as a historian he was 'notoriously untrustworthy'; in that of Cicero he was a rhetorical writer of rather puerile mentality, and as a historian he took the liberty 'to lie outright' in order to achieve a brilliant effect. Longinus scorned him as 'a superficial windbag'. The description of the fighting at Thebes and of the bestial rage of Alexander is itself an illustration of the qualities which were summarised by Cicero, Quintilian and Longinus. These capable critics knew the work of Cleitarchus in full. We have only paltry fragments, which afford no basis for modifying their judgements in any way. Cleitarchus' account was used also by Trogus (as epitomised by Justin) and by Plutarch, whose versions have much in common with that of Diodorus. One chapter in Plutarch's *Life* which described Alexander's chivalrous pardon of a Theban woman, Timoclea, was taken from the history of Aristobulus and reflects something of his fine style.

3. The judgement passed on Thebes by the Council of the Greeks

That Alexander treated the revolt of Thebes as a breach not of her treaty with Macedonia but of the charter of the Greek Community is clear from the accounts of Arrian, Diodorus and Plutarch. Thebes had indeed broken all the rules of the charter in recalling exiles, killing Macedonians of the garrison, denouncing the Greek Community as tyranny, and espousing the side of Persia against the Greek Community. It also suited Alexander as *Hegemon* of the Community to call up the troops of loyal members such as the Phocians and some of the Boeotian states, and on arrival outside Thebes to offer generous terms if Thebes would rejoin the Community. Had Perdiccas not acted, Alexander might have succeeded by diplomatic means; but as it was he had to save his own troops from destruction. Once Thebes was captured, he had to take into account the fact that Athens, Aetolia, Arcadia, Argos and Elis had been prepared to join in the revolt from the Greek Community.

How then should he handle the final verdict on the captured city? To take the decision himself would be to act as king of Macedonia and to disregard the very existence of the Greek Community. He could then be seen to be acting as a dictator in relation to the city-states. On the other hand, if he wished the Greek Community to continue and have any authority, he had no option but to refer the decision to the Council of that body. That was in fact what he chose to do. It was in line with his actions and proclamations at Thebes.

The clearest account is given by Diodorus, who was drawing on Cleitarchus. 'Convening the Councillors of the Greeks Alexander entrusted to the Common Council the question what should be done with the city of the Thebans.' Some light is shed on this meeting of the Council in the various accounts. 'The allies who took part in the action' – named as Phocians, Plataeans, Thespiaeans and Orchomenians – swayed the meeting by the violence of their hatred of the city which had massacred their citizens on more than one occasion. They and no doubt others who had reason to hate Thebes accused her of treason in joining Persia against the Greeks now as in the past. The majority of the Councillors present (we do not know how many were there) decided the fate of Thebes: 'to raze the city, sell the captives, outlaw any Theban escapees, forbid any of the Greeks to shelter a Theban, and rebuild and fortify Orchomenus and Plataea.' Then 'in compliance with the verdict of the Council the king [as *Hegemon* under the charter] razed the city and thereby instilled great fear in those who were revolting from the Greeks', i.e. in the leaders at Athens and in other states. It had a much wider deterrent effect thereafter, as Polybius, writing two centuries later, was to note.

That Alexander showed moderation in implementing the verdict was stated in more than one account. Those who had voted against the revolt, the descendants of Pindar, those who had diplomatic ties with Philip, Alexander and the Macedonians, the priests and priestesses, and Timoclea and her family were exempted and went free; and when he was in Asia, he treated Theban envoys and mercenaries in Persian service with generosity. He did not need to take the initiative against the states which had agreed to support Thebes. The Arcadians condemned to death those who had advocated that support. The Eleans reinstated those whom they had exiled as pro-Macedonian. The Aetolians, tribe by tribe, sent envoys to ask for forgiveness. The Athenians, after a debate in their Assembly, sent envoys to convey their decree in which they congratulated Alexander on his safe return from the Balkan campaign and on his punishment of Thebes. Alexander is said to have thrown it away in disgust. However, in reply he sent a *Letter* (a copy was no doubt kept with the *Journal*) in which he asked for the surrender of nine named Athenians whom he held to be as guilty as the Theban ringleaders for the revolt of Thebes and also responsible for the policy which had led to the Battle of Chaeronea, and for the offences at the time of Philip's death. They were to be tried 'in the Council of the Greeks'. Athens appealed against this demand and promised to try the men in her own court. The appeal was granted by Alexander with the exception of one man, the general Charidemus, who escaped to serve Persia. Thus Athens was treated very leniently.

Arrian's comment on the leniency of Alexander towards Athens is interesting: 'It may have been due to his respect for Athens, or it may have been due to his eagerness to embark on the expedition into Asia, he being unwilling to leave behind in the minds of the Greeks any suspicion of himself.' Philip and Alexander had always treated Athens with exceptional generosity for reasons which varied with the exigencies of the situation. But from the hour of victory at Chaeronea onwards they were anxious to form a genuine alliance and cooperation with Athens or at least to obtain her neutrality. Respect for her cultural leadership may have been an ingredient, but there is no doubt about the practical need to win over or at least place in baulk the Athenian fleet; for a combination of that fleet and the Persian fleet would dominate the Aegean Sea, the Hellespont, the Bosporus and the Black Sea, and it would put an end to Macedonian expansion.

Athens was only part of a wider problem for Alexander. The Greek Community was a form of political organisation which had three practical values for him: it kept the city-states at peace within Greece, it linked them to Macedonia in close alliance, and it committed itself to fight alongside Macedonia against Persia. Everyone knew that its existence and its policies were due to Macedonia's military power. Demosthenes and like-minded politicians saw it as the mask of dictatorship, the negation of city-state independence, and they urged their citizens to repudiate the Greek Community and to combine with Persia against Macedonia. To other politicians the Greek Community provided the best *modus vivendi* with Macedonia and the prospect of an actual Common Peace; moreover, a successful campaign in Asia would liberate the Greeks there and provide an outlet for the floating population of the mainland. In such a mixed climate of political opinion Alexander had to keep his military power in the public eye. His capture of Thebes in a matter of hours did so in an unforgettable manner. He had to maintain the authority and the principles of the Greek Community not only by entrusting to it the punishment of Thebes but also by finding peaceful means of bringing other malcontents to heel. Thus he showed respect for Athens as an independent state, outwitted Demosthenes' policy of collaboration with Persia, and in the crossing to Asia was accompanied by an Athenian squadron as part of the Greek Community's forces.

Alexander was eager to reach agreement quickly, not because his lion-like rage was exhausted by the savage destruction of Thebes, as Cleitarchus maintained, but because the vanguard of Macedonian and Greek forces in Asia was suffering reverses in the latter part of 335, and he had to go to its relief with all speed. It was also essential that the main force should be in Asia and in control of the harbours near the Hellespont, before the Persian fleet could enter the Aegean in the early summer of 334. He foresaw, no doubt, that once in the Aegean the Persians would try to promote risings by mainland states and thus break up the Greek Community. He could try to counter that attempt now only by convincing the city-states of his sincerity in respecting their political independence within the framework of the Greek Community. Hence in his settlement in autumn 335 'he was unwilling to leave behind in the minds of the Greeks any suspicion of himself'. For that reason he and his army did not enter the Peloponnese.

4. Alexander prepares for the campaign
against Persia

After these dealings [with Athens] Alexander returned to Macedonia. He
conducted the sacrifice to Zeus of Olympus at Dium in the form which
Archelaus had initiated, and he celebrated the games in honour of Zeus
of Olympus at Aegeae. Some say that he held a contest also in honour of
the Muses.

The national festival was that which Philip had celebrated at Aegeae
in 336. The sacrifice was a thanksgiving by the Macedonian State to
Zeus the Saviour and Protector. Alexander had good reason to give
thanks. In all warfare the time factor is important, sometimes all-
important. In 335 Alexander had been able to crush the Illyrians a
fortnight before he isolated Thebes. If the rising of Thebes had preceded
the massing of the Illyrian forces at Pelium, the Macedonian army
would have been in Boeotia and Macedonia would have been completely
overrun by the Illyrians. We may say that the time factor was fortui-
tous; but Alexander and his Macedonians saw the hand of Zeus in the
sequence of events. He had saved them from disaster. In Asia too the
time factor had been important. Troubles arising from the succession
at the Persian court and other distractions caused Darius III Codoman-
nus not to deploy the Persian fleet or mount a major counter-attack on
land during the time when Alexander was campaigning in the Balkans,
capturing Thebes and reaffirming the authority of the Greek Community. For that blessing also Alexander had reason to thank Zeus of
Olympus.

It had been a year of astonishing successes against Thracians, Getae,
Triballians, Illyrians and Thebans, with minimal loss of Macedonian
lives except at Thebes, where the figure of 500 Macedonian dead may
be exaggerated, since it comes ultimately from Cleitarchus. Alexander
had pardoned revolutionary moves by some city-states in 336, and he
had taken military action in 335 only against Thebes, where his hand
had been forced by the behaviour of Perdiccas. He would probably have
preferred a less severe sentence for the Thebans; but their fate had been
in the hands of the Greek Council and the recent history of Greece was
full of conquered populations being sold into slavery. Indeed by Greek
standards the Thebans had not suffered the worst; for the Thebans
themselves had massacred the adult males and sold all others into
slavery at Orchomenus in 363, and the Athenians had done the same
at Sestus in 353. If the charter of the Greek Community was obeyed in
the future, there would be no more cases of such destruction. In the
Balkans too Alexander made arrangements which he hoped would
promote peace and prosperity. When Glaucias acknowledged his defeat

and made submission, Alexander left him on his throne as a client king; and Cleitus was probably treated in the same manner.

After his absence of eight months the festival at Aegeae gave Alexander the opportunity to organise a lavish entertainment, which lasted for the nine days consecrated to the nine Muses.

> Constructing a marquee with one hundred couches, he invited to the banquet the Friends and the Commanders and in addition the envoys from the cities [of Macedonians] ... and by distributing animals for sacrifice and everything appropriate for feasting to the entire force of the King's Men he raised the spirits of the army.

Alexander had to make decisions on matters in Macedonia which had lain outside the scope of his deputy's powers. For instance, it was probably now that he heard an embassy from Philippi about the distribution of reclaimed land, and he initiated the setting up of a 'city of Macedonians' at Calindoea (above, p. 31). He convened a meeting of the Commanders and the leading Friends to discuss his plans for the crossing to Asia. According to Diyllus, a competent Hellenistic historian on whom Diodorus drew for this information, Antipater and Parmenio advised Alexander to beget an heir first and to cross to Asia later, but he replied that it would be disgraceful for the leader of the Greek and Macedonian forces to sit down and await the birth of children. With hindsight we see that they were right and that he made a serious misjudgement (for a wife could have accompanied him overseas). But his rejection of their advice is understandable. His father had married first at the age of twenty-four. Alexander was only twenty-one, and like most young men of that age he did not think of death as being near at hand.

The plans which Alexander put before his Commanders and Friends were extremely bold when we bear the situation in Europe in mind. He was to take to Asia one half of the remaining Macedonian phalangites (some were aleady active in the vanguard), some two-thirds of the Companion Cavalry and the light-armed cavalry, and a small number of light-armed infantry. If there should be a general rising of the Balkan tribes and/or of the city-states, Macedonia would be in a desperate situation; for her army would consist only of 1,000 Companion Cavalry, 500 light-armed cavalry, 12,000 phalangites, and some light-armed infantry reinforced by the militia of the cities. He planned also to take to Asia 22 triremes and 38 smaller warships, which was probably the full strength of the Macedonian fleet. Their crews, totalling some 6,000 men, were recruited mainly from Chalcidice. Arrangements had already been made for the Greek Community to contribute the following forces (in addition to those serving in the vanguard): 2,400 cavalry, 7,000 infantry, and 160 triremes with crews totalling 32,000. Some of

Alexander's officers may have argued that the Greek fleet was not to be trusted, and that it could easily turn on the small Macedonian fleet or desert *en bloc* to the Persian fleet. But Alexander persisted in the plan. The Balkan tribes were to provide 500 Agrianians and 7,000 other infantrymen from tribes which he had defeated in 335. Some officers may have doubted whether they would be dependable. We do not know what plans were made for the provision of auxiliary services in terms of merchant-ships, siege-train, baggage-train, wagons, draught-animals, engineers, grooms, cooks and so on.

A fragmentary inscription found on the Acropolis of Athens announced the regulations for payments in currency and in corn which were to be made to soldiers serving in the security forces at home. It seems that Macedonians served alongside men of the city-states, for a drachma a day was to be paid to a 'hypaspist'. Alexander was mentioned in his capacity presumably as the overall commander, and a copy of the regulations was to be set up in Macedonia, in the temple of Athena at Pydna. The officers responsible for publishing the regulations in this way were 'those in charge of the common defence', sometimes called 'guardians of the peace' (*eirenophylakes*, a term coined by Xenophon: above, p. 10). Their duties were 'to prevent massacre, banishment, confiscation of property, redistribution of land and cancellation of debts which were contrary to the existing laws of the member-states' of the Greek Community, and also 'to prevent the liberation of slaves for revolutionary purposes'. Thus Alexander and the Greek Council hoped to check any movement towards the party-strife (*stasis*) which would undermine the Common Peace and might invite intervention by Persia.

The financial strain on the Macedonian kingdom during recent years and now in prospect was very great. For the personnel of the army and the navy were well paid when on active service, not least because the loot from a successful campaign went not to the men but to the state. In addition Alexander planned to take to Asia 5,000 Greek mercenaries (over and above those already employed in the vanguard). Moreover, he had to pay his part in advance for the provisions which were needed to feed the entire force, until such time as it could overrun new territories. Aristobulus stated that Alexander had only 70 talents in hand for the final provisioning; Onesicritus – another contemporary but less dependable – said that he owed 200 talents; and a later writer claimed that he had taken supplies for 30 days only. Whatever truth there is in these statements, the personal credit of Alexander as king was almost inexhaustible, because he owned all mineral deposits in the kingdom and in the Balkan Empire, all stands of fine timber in the kingdom, and a large number of royal lands. Thus he was able on the eve of crossing to Asia to reward some of his Companions for outstanding service with the revenues of an estate, a village, a harbour or a hamlet (*synoikia*). Some refused to accept the rewards. One such was Perdiccas, who was so far from being punished for his initiative at Thebes that he continued to command a brigade and was soon promoted to be a Bodyguard of Alexander.

When Plutarch wrote of the distribution of rewards, he had Perdiccas ask Alexander what he had left for himself, and Alexander reply, 'My hopes.' This may come from Cleitarchus, but it has the ring of truth. Those hopes were confident hopes, partly because Alexander had calculated the risks which his country would run in Europe, but mainly because he believed that the gods were on his side. He sacrificed daily to them on behalf of the state; he believed that like his predecessors he was descended from Zeus and Heracles; and he was encouraged in his faith by omens and oracles. One such omen was reported by Plutarch and Arrian, who followed a common source, probably Aristobulus. A statue of Orpheus, made of cypress and revered at Leibethra in Pieria, was seen to be sweating profusely when Alexander was about to leave. Diviners gave various interpretations. Alexander accepted that of his favourite diviner, Aristander of Telmessus in Lycia, who prophesied that Alexander's deeds in Asia 'would cost poets and musicians much toil and sweat to celebrate'. To us this may seem childish. It was not so to Alexander. For he took Aristander to Asia, consulted him at critical moments, and accepted his prophecies except on one occasion, when Alexander was proved wrong and Aristander was proved right (Arr. 4.4.3 and 9). To say that Alexander believed in second sight is misleading. For it was an article of faith that the gods may reveal the future through physical phenomena and through the words of inspired individuals, men or women of whatever race.

5. Coinage and culture in 336-335

'Philip raised the Macedonian kingdom to a high pitch of greatness because he had an abundance of money.' All mineral deposits within the kingdom and the Balkan Empire were the personal possession of the king, and early in Philip's reign the techniques of mining were greatly improved. The gold and the silver of his coins were of a pure quality, which was important since coins were valued as bullion. Philip's most famous coins were his gold *Philippeioi* with the head of Apollo on one side and a two-horse chariot at the gallop on the reverse side. Being on the Attic standard of weight, they were intended primarily for large-scale transactions in the Mediterranean area. Hoards of *Philippeioi* have been found throughout Greece and the Greek West (especially in Sicily), Asia Minor, Syria, Cyprus and Egypt, and also in the Balkans and in South Russia. The largest silver coins were tetradrachms showing the head of Zeus wreathed with laurel and on the reverse side a racehorse ridden by a jockey. All the silver coins were on the Thracian standard, which favoured transactions in and beyond the Balkans.

Hoards of tetradrachms have been found there and in Greece and Sicily. The wide circulation of the *Philippeioi* and the tetradrachms gives us some idea of Macedonia's orbit of trade and transactions. Small denominations in silver and very large issues of bronze coins were used for internal exchange within the kingdom. Thus the economy of Macedonia became fully monetary, and Alexander inherited the strongest currency in Europe.

Philip was also a lavish spender, especially in financing the wars of 340-338 and in mounting the invasion of Asia in 336. In a speech which Arrian summarised, following Ptolemy's version, Alexander claimed that Philip left at the time of his death 'a few gold and silver drinking-vessels, a treasury of less than 60 talents and debts of some 500 talents'. The facts are no doubt true, but the picture is somewhat misleading, in that the king was not on the verge of bankruptcy but had enormous capital resources. Indeed it was those resources which enabled him to raise loans of such magnitude. Alexander spent money on an even grander scale in his opening years. No expense was spared in the funeral of Philip. Then within the span of twelve months he marched his army in full strength to Corinth, conducted campaigns in Thrace, Illyria and Central Greece, maintained his part of the forces in Asia, and celebrated his successes in a most extravagant manner during the nine-day festival at Aegeae. It was probably during these months, when Alexander surpassed his father in his commitments, that Alexander capped his father's debts by raising loans of 800 talents. In the winter of 335-334 he faced very great expenditure in the organisation of security forces at home, the payment of Greek mercenaries and Balkan troops, and the financing of the Macedonian forces and their infrastructure for the large-scale invasion of Asia.

During this period of financial stress and for some years thereafter Alexander issued his father's gold *Philippeioi* and silver tetradrachms with the lettering 'Philippou'. He used these for large transactions abroad, such as the hiring of companies of Greek mercenaries. It was wise to do so, because these coins were as acceptable everywhere as Victoria's gold sovereigns proved to be. In 335 he began to issue in his own name a silver coinage mainly in small denominations from a drachm downwards. Whereas his father's posthumous silver tetradrachms continued to be on the Thracian standard, Alexander's coinage now was on the Attic standard, probably for use by Alexander in his capacity as *Hegemon*, for instance for the payment of security forces. He made the change to the Attic standard for these and later silver coins because the interests of Macedonia were to be primarily in the Mediterranean area. It was also convenient to have his gold and silver coinages on the same standard, so that the ratio between the two precious metals could be fixed or modified more easily.

The first silver coinage in Alexander's name showed the head of a young Heracles and on the reverse an eagle standing on a thunderbolt, both being emblems of Zeus. He issued a large amount of bronze coinage in three denominations for exchange within the kingdom and the Balkan Empire. This had the head of a young Heracles and on the reverse the quiver and the club associated with Heracles. It is clear that Alexander wished his subjects to regard their new king as a young Heracles who enjoyed the favour of Zeus.

Coinage and culture are to some extent inter-related. The wealth of Athens in the Periclean period and to a lesser extent in the fourth century attracted men of all kinds of ability, many of whom became resident aliens and contributed to her prosperity. The wealth of Macedonia had the same effect. Among those who visited the court in the fifth century were Pindar, whose epithet for Alexander I, 'bold-scheming' (*thrasymedes*), might be taken as the motto for the kings of the Temenid dynasty; Euripides, who produced two plays in Macedonia and was made a Companion; Choerilus, an epic poet, who also settled and died in Macedonia; the leading historians Herodotus, Hellanicus and probably Thucydides; and the founder of scientific medicine, Hippocrates of Cos. The palace of Archelaus was decorated by the leading painter of fresco, Zeuxis, who came from Heraclea in Italy. Philip continued in the same tradition; for he attended the lectures of his philosopher-in-residence Euphraeus (he was to succeed Plato as head of the Academy), employed Aristotle and Theophrastus from 343 to 335, brought the historians Anaximenes, Callisthenes and Theopompus to his court, and hired leading actors to compete in the dramatic contests which were a part of the Festival in honour of the Muses. That Philip was a man of culture and a patron of the arts was admitted even by his critics. So too was at least one of his entourage; for Antipater was a pupil of Aristotle and wrote a history of the Illyrian Wars.

Archaeology came late to Macedonia. It has completely altered our perception of Macedonian culture. The statement of Alexander that Philip left a few gold and silver drinking-vessels did not prepare us for the discovery of almost fifty silver vessels in the unplundered tombs of Philip and Alexander IV. They are of unsurpassed beauty in their varied shapes and exquisite workmanship. The miniature heads at the base of the handles are most skilful. One (Plate 4(b)) represents a young Heracles with the features of Alexander. There was nothing comparable in the city-states, and the recently discovered cache of silver vessels at Rogozen in northwest Bulgaria has shown us that the Thracian versions, though imitating Macedonian forms, were inferior in workmanship. Nor were these silver vessels a monopoly of the royal court. Equally lovely specimens have been found, for instance, at Derveni (in Mygdonia), Sevaste (near Dium), and Nikisiani (near Kavala). Gold work was no less fine. The two gold coffers in which the cremated remains of Philip and his Queen were placed are of pure gold and beautifully decorated with the bursting star, rosettes and lotus flowers, which were associated with a belief in the after-life (see Plate 5(a)). Coloured glass-paste is used for the rosettes. Equally remarkable are the gold wreaths (see Plate 5(b)). Similar wreaths have been found in tombs of the period throughout Macedonia. Skill in working precious metals was of long standing in Macedonia, as we know from the finds of the archaic period at Sindos, Aegeae and Aeane and from discoveries of silver-gilt fittings and gilded iron at Katerini early in the fourth century. The gilded silver diadem in Philip's Tomb is decorated with the snake-skin pattern, suggestive of immortal life.

The miniature ivory heads, only an inch high, are realistic portraits of members of Philip's family and of his close Friends. Those representing Philip's parents, Philip, Olympias and Alexander lay together with their limbs of gold and ivory on the floor of his Tomb where they had fallen. They were miniatures of the gold-and-ivory statues of the same persons, which were dedicated in Philip's circular shrine at Olympia as a thanksgiving to Zeus. The artistry of the ivory heads is beyond compare. See Plate 1(b).

The frescoes on the walls of the Tombs of Amyntas and of Eurydice, and on the façade of Philip's Tomb are far superior in artistic skill, use of shading and understanding of perspective to any paintings elsewhere in the Greek world. Under the patronage of the kings the school of Zeuxis set a fashion in painting which was to inspire Hellenistic and Roman painting (as at Pompeii and Herculaneum). Alexander chose the subject of the fresco which was painted below the cornice in honour of his father (see Plate 2). The subject is a Royal Hunt with the royals on horseback and the Pages on foot. Philip is shown as a bearded man of mature age about to despatch a mountain-lion, on which the gaze of his left eye is fixed (for he was blind in the right eye). The conspicuous royal in the centre (Plate 15) is Alexander, laurel-wreathed, rushing with poised spear to help his father. He is young, clean-shaven, with slightly protruding eyes. The third royal, seen from behind and naked, is treated with less honour. He was probably Amyntas, the son of Perdiccas. The composition of the figures in motion and the trees in the background is masterly.

A related art was that of mosaic, not with flat tesserae but with rounded pebbles, which reflect the light in a more lively manner. The mosaic floors of the houses at Pella, which date from the last quarter of the fourth century, are highly sophisticated with representations, for instance, of Dionysus riding a panther and of a lion-hunt, in which the hunters were probably Alexander and Craterus as young men (Plate 6(a)).

'Pella, previously small, was enlarged by Philip who was brought up there. It has a fortified headland in Lake Loudias. The outlet of this lake is the river Loudias, and the lake is fed by an offshoot of the Axius.' Excavation has revealed a large city with rectangular building-plots

47 m square, bounded by streets 9 m wide and 6 m wide. There were two paved roads with sidewalks which led from the harbour to a central avenue 15 m wide. Most houses had one or two inner courtyards, surrounded by a colonnade. The harbour is of great interest, because it is the first riverine harbour to be mentioned in literature. The canal from the Axius to the lake basin and the outflow-channel must have been maintained by artificial banks and locks. Some remains of the Palace date to the reign of Philip; its area of 60,000 square metres was entered through a monumental Propylon. The city was fortified with a circuit-wall of brick on a stone base. Philip encouraged the Macedonian cities to build such walls. He planned many new cities in the enlarged kingdom and in Thrace. As we have seen (above, p. 6), Alexander founded one in the Strymon valley.

The building of temples was encouraged by Philip. At Pella there were small temples to Aphrodite-and-Cybele near the Agora and to Darron, a local god of healing with an attached sanatorium. A circular pit, like one in the sanctuary of the Cabiri in Samothrace, was associated with fertility cults and local deities, and there was worship of Artemis, Pluto and Athena as protectress of cattle. The people of Pella, as of Dium, worshipped not only the deities of the Greek pantheon but also many others which were native to the varied peoples of the enlarged kingdom. One form of architecture in which Macedonia led the way was that of built tombs. The line of development is clear from the cist-tomb of Amyntas III, *c.* 370, through a larger two-chambered cist-tomb near Katerini to the very large, vaulted, two-chambered Tomb of Eurydice, set within a framework of parallel walls, which were

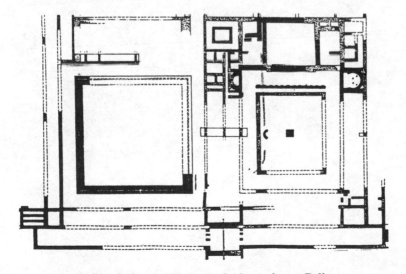

6. The Palace of Philip and Alexander at Pella

designed to help to carry the weight of a tumulus of soil. The vaulted Tomb of Philip dispensed with that framework, and it therefore developed the fine façade with the fresco of the Royal Hunt. The addition of a classical façade to a functional building of different shape, and the building of a vaulted crypt in honour of a deity, or a dead hero, have had a long and distinguished history in European architecture.

Finally we have learnt from excavation that Macedonian craftsmen excelled in the making of weapons and armour, whether of iron or bronze. Philip's cuirass and helmet were made of iron. They were such as Alexander put on before the Battle of Gaugamela – 'gleaming like polished silver' (evidently a form of mild steel). He and his Queen were equipped for the after-life with a variety of weapons (pike, spear, javelin, sword, bow, arrows and quiver-case of gold) and fine armour (greaves with gold engraving, and a gilded iron gorget). It was Macedonian armourers who equipped and maintained the army of Alexander in Asia with the weapons and the armour which played a major part in their victorious advance to the Hyphasis in Pakistan.

CHAPTER VI

The crossing of the Hellespont and the first victory

1. Arrangements in Europe and calculations for Asia

Alexander made the arrangements which he judged necessary for a long absence in Asia. He appointed his senior Friend, Antipater, to be 'General with full powers' as his deputy 'in the affairs of Macedonia and the Greeks'. Within Macedonia Antipater exercised the military command (*hegemonia*) over 12,000 phalangites and 1,000 Companion Cavalry of the king's men, 500 light-armed cavalry and some light-armed infantry, and he was able to call up the militia of the cities in case of need. He was the acting headmaster of the School of Pages, and he handled the finances of the state for military and naval purposes. As Macedonian commander he was in charge of 'Triballi, Agrianes, Illyrians' (including the Dardanians as 'Illyrians'), and 'Epirus up to the Ceraunian mountains' (from the Macedonian point of view the northern part only of Epirus). In regard to the Greek Community Antipater as deputy *Hegemon* exercised the powers which had been laid down in the agreement between the Common Council and Alexander. These powers included command of the security forces and of any other forces, military and naval, which might be raised by the Greek Community within its orbit of authority. Antipater had the right to appoint his own deputies to positions of command.

There were other aspects of the monarchy. The most important was the religious activity of the king both as head of state and as the representative of the Temenid royal house, and this involved daily sacrifice, leading processions, organising festivals, providing sacrificial victims and so on. An acting head of the royal family in Macedonia had to administer the royal estates and manage the finances of the royal house, which included the receipt of taxes and much routine expenditure. In addition there were some departments of civic administration which were directed by the king. The responsibility for all these matters in the absence of the king was laid upon the holder of an office called the 'Protectorship of the Monarchy' (*prostasia tes basileias*). This office was held in the highest esteem among the Macedonians. Alexander conferred it on Olympias, the Queen Mother. We know that during his absence she 'conducted sacrifices on his behalf' (*prothuetai*) and was expert in the traditional sacrifices of the Argeadae (the royal tribe) and in those paid to Dionysus.

In some matters Antipater and Olympias were to act together, for instance in dealing with Athens over the arrest of a deserter. But in general it seems that each had a clearly defined sphere of activity. Even so friction was likely to develop between these two strong characters, and in that event Alexander would have to make the decision between them. It seems unlikely that Antipater was authorised to hold an assembly of the 13,000 King's Men under his command and treat it as an assembly of state. The situation was rather that the Macedonian state operated wherever the king and the King's Men happened to be, and it was clear in spring 334 that for some years he and they would be in Asia. The arrangements which Alexander thus made for Macedonia were on the whole wise. It is important to notice that the military command of Thrace was entrusted not to Antipater but to a separate 'General of Thrace', answerable directly to Alexander and responsible for maintaining the vital line of communication from the Hellespont to the eastern frontier of the Macedonian kingdom at the river Nestus. To this responsible post Alexander appointed his namesake, Alexander Lyncestes, who had been the first to acclaim him as king.

The obvious criticism of Alexander's arrangements was that 13,000 King's Men was a tiny force in relation to its responsibilities. But at the same time one might equally well have claimed that to undertake the conquest of Asia with 13,800 King's Men under his own command was wellnigh absurd. Alexander must have assessed the risks in each case with extreme care. He evidently relied on the acceptance of the Macedonian system of control by the Balkan tribes and on the loyalty of the Balkan troops which he took to Asia in 334 and later. Similarly he must have reckoned that the majority of the city-states and Athens in particular would honour the charter of the Greek Community during his absence, and that the fleet and the soldiers with him in 334 would be eager to liberate the Greek city-states from Persian rule and to take revenge on Persia for past acts of sacrilege.

At the beginning of spring in 334 the Macedonian contingents (1,800 Companion Cavalry, 12,000 phalangite infantry and some light-armed troops, both cavalry and infantry) and the Balkan contingents (Illyrian, Triballian, Agrianian and Odrysian, totalling 7,500 men) mustered in Amphaxitis. From there they marched through the Kumli valley, past Lake Cercinitis to Amphipolis, where they met Parmenio in command of 2,300 cavalry and 7,000 hoplites of the Greek Community and of 5,000 Greek mercenaries. Thus the total of fighting troops was 5,100 cavalry and 32,000 infantry, of which those provided by the Macedonian kingdom were considerably less than a half. The army was accompa-

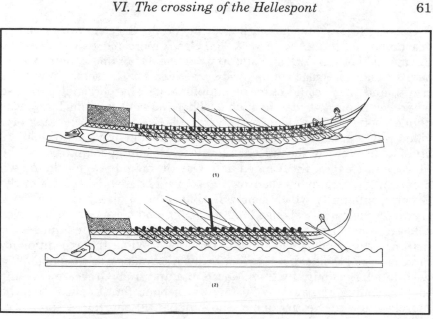

7. The penteconter

nied by various services and specialists. The march from Amphaxitis to
Sestus on the Hellespont, a distance of some 350 miles, took 20 days, so
that if we allow for some three days of rest the daily march was one of
20 miles more or less.

The fleets met at Amphipolis. The Macedonian fleet consisted of 22
triremes and 38 smaller warships (penteconters and triaconters), with
crews totalling perhaps 6,000 men, and the Greek fleet, provided by the
Greek Community, numbered 160 triremes with crews of some 32,000
men. In addition to the warships there were merchant ships which
carried equipment and supplies, the latter sufficient for one month only.
The entire force may be estimated at 90,000 men. At least half of these
men came from the Greek Community and from centres of mercenary
recruitment in Greece, and only a quarter at most came from within the
Macedonian kingdom. They were all under the supreme command of
Alexander as king and *Hegemon*, and he appointed the commanders of
the various contingents and flotillas.

Of the financial commitments we know very little. The King's Men
must have received pay during the lengthy campaigns of Philip, and
they were to do so for the campaigns in prospect now. The rate of pay
may have been a drachma a day for a first-line infantryman, as it seems
to have been for one in the security forces (see Tod no. 183), and three
drachmae a day for a cavalryman. The Greek hoplite was paid probably

five obols (the drachma having six obols) and the Greek cavalryman two drachmae and three obols a day. The Greek mercenaries were paid by the month, both cavalry and infantry, but we do not know their rates of pay. In addition basic rations were provided for the soldiers and the crews, and these could often be supplemented by personal purchase wherever a market was available. The financial responsibility was divided between Macedonia and the Greek Community. The king provided wages and maintenance for the Macedonian and Balkan soldiers and for the crews of the Macedonian fleet. He equipped and armed the Macedonians, but the Companion Cavalrymen brought their own horses and presumably their own grooms. The member states of the Greek Community which sent a flotilla of ships manned them with crews at their own expense (Tod no. 192), and those which provided soldiers must have seen to it that they were properly equipped, for instance with cavalry mounts and remounts. When the expeditionary forces were in the field, it is evident that Alexander was the paymaster with funds sent initially from Macedonia and from Greece. According to Aristobulus he had only 70 talents in hand for supplies when he marched towards Sestus, and by the summer the shortage of funds was one reason for his decision to disband the Greek fleet. In this department too we can see that Alexander's calculations were finely drawn.

2. The crossing of the Hellespont

The crossing of the Hellespont was fraught with religious associations. The ancestors of Alexander, Heracles on his father's side and Achilles on his mother's side, had fought against Troy on different campaigns. 'The Achaeans', the ancestors of the Greeks in Alexander's army, had conducted the siege and capture of Troy, celebrated by Homer. When the army reached Sestus, Alexander was 'fired with incredible exaltation of spirit' by the sight of Asia. There, at Sestus, he set up twelve altars, which were dedicated to the twelve Olympian gods for the impending war, and he made sacrifices for victory in that war, for which he had been appointed commander as avenger of Persian wrongdoing in Greece. The Persians had ruled for long enough, and better rulers would take their place. This account comes ultimately from Cleitarchus, whose interest was primarily in the Greek part in the expedition. After the sacrifices Parmenio was ordered to oversee the transportation of all non-Macedonian trooops from Sestus to Abydus on the Greek fleet and a number of merchant ships.

Alexander marched with his Macedonians to Elaeus at the tip of the peninsula. He sacrificed there at the tomb of Protesilaus, who had been 'far the first to leap ashore' but had been killed by a Trojan; for Alexander hoped his landing would be more successful. He and his men then embarked on the Macedonian fleet of 60 warships and sailed for

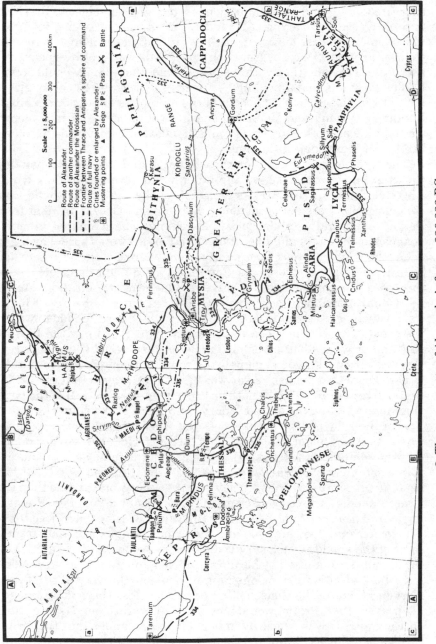

8. The movements of Alexander's forces, 336-333 BC

'the harbour of the Achaeans'. Halfway across the Hellespont Alexander sacrificed a bull and poured libations from a golden goblet to Poseidon and the Nereids. On arrival Alexander, fully armed, was the first of the Macedonians to cast his spear into the ground and to leap ashore with the declaration: 'I accept from the gods Asia won by the spear.' He sacrificed there and then with the prayer that 'those lands would accept him as their king not unwillingly'. For his safe landing he set up altars both at Elaeus and at the harbour of the Achaeans in honour of Zeus of Landings, Athena and Heracles. These accounts came from Ptolemy, Aristobulus and others such as Callisthenes and Onesicritus, who had been with Alexander at the time.

The ceremonies at Sestus on the one hand, and those accompanying the crossing from Elaeus on the other hand reveal the aims which Alexander had for the war. As *Hegemon* of the Greeks he would take vengeance for Persian wrongdoing, liberate the Greeks in Asia from Persian rule and establish a better regime. These limited aims, of vengeance on Persia and liberation from Persia, were those which had been stated by the Greek Community from the time of Philip. There had been no mention of the Greek Community acquiring land in Asia or incorporating the liberated Greeks in its own organisation. As an individual Alexander had his own additional aims: to become King of Asia, which he accepted from the gods and which he intended to win by the spear. Thus his purpose was not merely to overthrow the Persian rule and provide a better regime for Persia's subjects; it was to accept 'Asia' as his own kingdom, namely the continent bounded in the east by Ocean. From that moment 'Asia' was his, and he prayed that the Asians would accept him willingly as their king. That was the will of the gods. Once again we see the extraordinary confidence of the young king.

Alexander loved the *Iliad* beyond any other literary work. To him it was a record of historical persons and actions. He laid a wreath on the tomb of Achilles, and Hephaestion laid one on the tomb of Patroclus; for Hephaestion was Alexander's 'trusted friend', just as Patroclus had been Achilles' trusted friend. They and the other Companions then ran a race naked, in the customary manner, in honour of Achilles. Proceeding inland from the tomb of Achilles to Troy, Alexander sacrificed to the Trojan Athena, dedicated his armour in her temple, and took from it some of the shields which survived from the Trojan War. He atoned for the sacrilege committed by his ancestor, Neoptolemus, the son of Achilles, who had killed Priam, the king of Troy, at the very altar of Zeus Herkeios (Zeus of the Household). For he sacrificed there to Priam, and he prayed that Priam would not vent his wrath on Neoptolemus' descendants. It was evidently important to Alexander that the Trojan Athena as goddess of war and the potent spirit of Priam should be won over to his side. He was said to emphasise his connection through Olympias with Andromache, a granddaughter of Priam; for she bore to

Neoptolemus a son Molossus, after whom the Molossian royal house was named. We see here the depth of Alexander's belief in his own descent, in the power of the gods wherever their shrines might be, and in the power of a king centuries after his death.

An unknown artist portrayed the moment when Alexander fixed his long pike (*sarissa*) into the soil of Asia. The painting, a copy of a Hellenistic original (Plate 7), survived under the lava of Mount Vesuvius at Boscoreale. Alexander is shown as a young man, wearing the traditional cap (*kausia*), and beside him there is a Macedonian shield with a star at its centre. He is on one side of the blue water of the Hellespont, and the personified figure of Asia on the other side returns his intent gaze with a look of acceptance. To the spectator's left, the philosopher Aristotle watches from a distance.

3. The battle of the river Granicus

From Troy Alexander rejoined the main army. He paraded and numbered the forces which had crossed with him to Asia. A record was made in the *Journal*, but different figures were released to deceive the enemy. Most of the record has come down through Diodorus from Ptolemy (above, p. 64). Alexander had been able to make the crossing in peace, because the vanguard which Philip had sent was in control of the Asiatic coast of the Hellespont, and because the Persian fleet had not yet entered the Aegean. During the last eighteen months Alexander and the Greek Community had not reinforced the vanguard, which had been driven back by the Persian commander-in-chief, Memnon (above, p. 25). In the Greek cities there were partisans for each side. Parmenio enslaved the population of Gryneum, a city in the south which had evidently joined Memnon, but he failed to take Pitane by siege. On this front the Persian forces reached Rhoeteum in the Troad. To the north Memnon and his officers, wearing the Macedonian cap (*kausia*), nearly tricked the people of Cyzicus into opening their gates, but he then ravaged their land with a force of 5,000 Greek mercenaries. Alexander arrived just in time to save the holding force of Macedonians, Greek mercenaries and probably Greek troops from the Greek Community, whose commander-in-chief then was Calas.

As we have seen, Alexander needed a speedy victory to obtain supplies. Memnon probably realised this, for he advised a strategy of retreat leaving scorched earth; but the Persian satraps refused to sacrifice their lands and concentrated their forces near Zelea, inland to the east of Abydus. Their intention was to attack Alexander's base at Abydus, if he should advance southwards; or to draw him eastwards and block his advance there. They adopted a strong defensive position on the east bank of the river Granicus, placing their excellent cavalry 20,000 strong on the level ground facing the river and their 20,000

Greek mercenary infantry on the hillside above the level ground. It was a position which could not be turned on either flank, and it blocked the approach to the 'Asian Gates', a narrow pass through which a Persian road ran eastwards.

Alexander acted with characteristic speed and confidence. Three days after completion of the landing he advanced into the Granicus plain not with his full army but with the Macedonian forces, the Agrianians and the Greek cavalry. They numbered some 13,000 infantry and 5,100 cavalry. Alexander will have learnt from Calas the strength of the Persian army, and he was sure that his élite forces could defeat the superior numbers of the enemy. It was after midday when his scouts galloped back to tell him of the Persian position on the far side of the river. Alexander halted to consult his commanders. Some record of the discussion was preserved in the *Journal* which Ptolemy was able to consult, and we probably owe to him a summary of what Parmenio advised. He was opposed to a frontal attack (presumably proposed by Alexander), because the river was deep in places and the far bank was steep and high, and because if some troops did force their way onto the level ground they would be swamped by the enemy cavalry. He proposed camping where they were and deciding next day how to make a crossing. Alexander's comment in reply included the remark: 'I am ashamed if, after crossing the Hellespont easily, this little stream will stop us from crossing as we are.' He then issued his detailed orders. These had to envisage the development of the action and provide for tactical moves, because he himself as 'a mighty fighter' would be immersed in combat.

Alexander formed his line for a frontal attack as follows. On the left, which Parmenio commanded, the units were from the left the Greek cavalry (1,800 Thessalians and 600 from other states), a squadron of Thracian cavalry (150) and three brigades of phalangites (4,500). On the right, which Alexander commanded, the units were from the right the Agrianians (500), the Archers (500), the Companion Cavalry (1,800), a squadron of Paeonian cavalry (150), the Lancers (600), the Hypaspists (3,000) and three brigades of phalangites (4,500). The numbers of cavalry were the same in each part of the line, but the infantry were more numerous in the right part and the Archers and the Agrianians formed an extension on the extreme right. If the cavalrymen were ten horses deep and the infantry eight men deep, as was normal, the length of the line was some two and a half kilometres. It matched the length of the Persian line of cavalry with a depth of some sixteen horses, of which the rear ranks had plenty of room to manoeuvre on level ground.

The Persian commanders stayed in the position which they had initially adopted and which had been reported to Alexander. If the Macedonian infantrymen had been armed like Greek mercenaries with seven-foot spears, they would have had no chance of fighting their way up and over the bank in the face of the Persian cavalrymen's missiles and against the weight of the horses. But the twelve-foot range of the Macedonian pike was another matter; for a pikeman could strike a horse or its rider from below with deadly effect, and once engaged he was no longer an easy target for missiles. Alexander, on the other hand, counted on his infantry pinning down and gradually defeating the opposing cavalry, and he planned in the meantime to make a break-through with massed cavalry at one point and by extending his line to the right to outflank the enemy. He attacked at once, in order to exploit the folly of the Persian commanders in immobilising their Greek mer-cenaries.

Alexander, wearing white plumes on his helmet, was a conspicuous figure at the front of the Royal Cavalry Guard. The Persian command-ers moved to face him with their finest cavalry. At Alexander's order the trumpets blew and the army went down into the wide, shingly riverbed. The initial assault was delivered to the left of Alexander's position by one Companion Cavalry squadron, the Paeonian cavalry, the Lancers and the Royal Brigade of Hypaspists. While the attack pinned down the opposing cavalry, Alexander did not engage but was extending his line on his side of the riverbed to his right, so that the Archers and the Agrianians outflanked the opposition. By then the Companion Cavalry squadron which had led the assault and inflicted casualties was being driven back. At that moment Alexander ordered the general attack. At the head of the Royal Cavalry Squadron he charged into the enemy group which had repulsed the weakened squad-ron.

In ferocious hand-to-hand fighting Alexander and his entourage prevailed thanks to their 'strength, experience and lances of cornelwood against javelins'. Alexander's lance had broken; so too had that of his groom. But Demaratus gave him his own lance. Alexander and those with him were on top of the bank but not in formation, when a wedge of enemy cavalry, led by Mithridates, began to charge. Alexander rode out ahead, struck Mithridates in the face and unseated him, just as Rhoe-saces charged Alexander and smashed part of his helmet with his scimitar. As Alexander struck Rhoesaces in the chest with his lance, Spithridates was raising his scimitar to kill Alexander when his right arm was hacked off by Cleitus. The Persians were now losing ground all along the line. On the right the Archers and the Agrianians, attack-ing the cavalry in the flank and mingling with their own cavalry, were rolling up the enemy's left wing, and the squadrons of the Companion Cavalry fought their way onto the top of the bank. To the left of Alexander the Hypaspists and the phalangites used their pikes to good effect. 'When the Persian centre had given way, the cavalry on each wing broke and fled precipitately.'

Alexander regrouped his men and surrounded the phalanx of the 20,000 Greek mercenary infantry, which had stood still 'more in astonishment at the unexpected turn of events than from tactical considerations'. They were a formidable force, because they outnumbered Alexander's phalangites by a large margin and were experienced fighters. But when they stayed still and were surrounded, they had little chance of survival; for the Macedonian phalanx would deliver a frontal charge and the cavalry and the light-armed infantry would attack their exposed flanks and rear. According to Plutarch, who was probably following Aristobulus, the commander of the mercenaries asked for terms of withdrawal under oath, but Alexander refused; for he knew they would then fight again in Persian service. He himself on horseback led the attack 'more in passion than in reason', and his horse was killed under him by a sword-thrust. But the outcome was as it had been with the Sacred Band at Chaeronea; for the pikemen in formation shattered the Greek phalanx. The surrender of 2,000 was accepted.

The total defeat of the enemy was due to the military genius of Alexander. His immediate grasp of the tactical situation, his coordination of all arms in a coordinated attack, and his ingenuity in combining the initial assault with the extension of his line upstream to the right were all brilliant. His speed in deliberation and in action left the Persian commanders no chance of reorganising their forces and enabled him to defeat the cavalry and then the infantry separately. The cavalry battle caught the public eye. For the Persian cavalry was an élite force recruited from as far afield as Bactria and commanded by members of Darius' family and entourage, known as 'The Kinsmen' (*syngeneis*). 'The meed of valour' (*aristeia*) went to Alexander in person; and 'the mighty warrior' must have felt that he bore a charmed life, as any young man is apt to do in battle.

The 2,000 Greek mercenaries were sent to Macedonia to labour in chains for life (corpses so chained have been found recently in Chalcidice), because 'being Greeks they had fought against Greece in violation of the decisions of the Greeks'. The Greek mercenaries who had fallen in battle and the Persian officers were given an honourable burial. The loss of the Persian cavalry was put at 1,000 men; for there had been no pursuit. Of the Macedonians the twenty-five dead of the Companion Cavalry squadron which had led the assault were treated as heroes. Alexander commissioned Lysippus to make bronze statues of them, which were to be set up at Dium, alongside the statues of the Temenid kings. Of the other cavalry sixty and of the infantry some thirty had fallen. All were buried with their arms and equipment, and 'remission of taxes on land and property, and of personal services' was granted to their parents and their children. The wounded were visited by Alexander, who listened to the accounts of their exploits and examined their wounds. The spoils were collected for Alexander. He sent 300 sets of Persian armour to be dedicated to Athena on the Acropolis of Athens with the inscription: 'Alexander son of Philip and the Greeks except the Lacedaemonians from the barbarians living in Asia.' Similar dedications may have been made in other states; for Alexander 'wished to make the Greeks partners in the victory', rightly since the Greek cavalry had won on the left wing and the Greek fleet had mounted the invasion of Asia. The bulk of the spoil, notably drinking vessels and purple robes, was sent to Olympias.

We owe our information mainly to Arrian, using Ptolemy, who was himself a combatant and had access to the *Journal* in which Alexander's orders and acts were recorded. A less accurate account, that of Aristobulus, was used by Plutarch who reported the fallen as twenty-five cavalrymen and nine infantrymen; and it was evidently Aristobulus who criticised Alexander for acting 'in passion' and understood his wish to make the Greeks partners in the victory. An entirely different account has survived in Diodorus, who used Cleitarchus. It is complete with omens in advance, huge figures (100,000 Persian infantry, 20,000 prisoners), a crossing next day at dawn, separate battles of cavalry against cavalry and then of infantry against infantry, and 'chance' pitting Alexander against 'The Kinsmen'. This account is as worthless as that of the capture of Thebes in Diodorus (above, p. 46). One deduction of interest is that Aristobulus must have published his account of the Macedonian casualties before that of Ptolemy, which rested on the *Journal* and was clearly correct.

CHAPTER VII

The winning of Asia Minor

1. Alexander's policy and advance to Ephesus

The morale of the satraps was shattered. Their leader, Arsites, committed suicide, the others fled each to his satrapy, the large force of Persian cavalry disintegrated, and Parmenio occupied Dascylium, the capital of Hellespontine Phrygia, without opposition; for its garrison had fled. The weakness of the Persian imperial system in this western area was apparent. Each satrap governed his own satrapy (analogous to a Roman province) with full powers, and he recruited his own armed forces, which consisted primarily of the native aristocrats as cavalrymen and of Greek mercenary soldiers as infantrymen. When infantry was recruited from the indigenous peoples, it was of poor quality and reluctant to fight in support of Persia's oppressive rule. So far from recruiting Greeks the satraps often had to supply garrisons to buttress the rule of dictators or juntas imposed on the Greek cities by Persia. Moreover, the satraps were often at odds with one another. The Great King, living at Susa in Iran, exercised a remote control in that he appointed and deposed members of his own family or of his entourage as satraps, and he was informed of the situation in each satrapy by his agents, known as the King's Eyes. But that control was loose; and when he appointed Memnon to be commander-in-chief of the resistance to the Macedonians, Memnon was unable to impose his will on the satraps. After the defeat at the Granicus Memnon received little or no support from the satraps and relied on the garrisons in the Greek cities to slow down the advance of the Macedonians.

Alexander was able to publicise his own policy in these early days. It was not that which Isocrates and Aristotle had advised, namely the subjection of the barbarians as slaves to their Greek and Macedonian masters. The self-declared King of Asia, he regarded the land as his possession and the peoples of Asia, whether Greek or native, as his subjects. His aim was to overthrow the oppressive Persian rule and to introduce his own rule, under which the native peoples would be respected and fairly treated. Thus when he reviewed his army after the landing, he placed a ban on looting and ravaging, because 'his own property was to be spared'; and when hillsmen came to make their submission, expecting slavery, he told them 'to return each to his own property'. The Greek city Zelea had served as the Persian base. On capturing it Alexander did not punish the people by enslaving them as Parmenio had done at Gryneum (above, p. 65). He pardoned them on the grounds that 'they had been forced to fight on the side of the barbarians'. He showed respect for the Persian officers who had so nearly killed him; for he gave honourable burial to those who had fallen, and he took into his service any Persian cavalrymen who wished to join him. Immediately after the battle he made dedications to the Trojan Athena and he declared Troy a free city, i.e. exempt from paying tribute; for this Asian goddess had accepted and supported him. It was indeed said that one of the shields which he had taken from her temple saved his life during the hand-to-hand fighting at the Granicus.

The wisdom of Alexander's policy appeared as he approached Sardis, the satrapal centre of Lydia. 'He was met by the chief citizens of Sardis (Lydians) and by Mithrenes (the Persian commander), who surrendered the city and the treasury ... he kept Mithrenes by his side, according him honourable rank, and he granted to the Lydians the use of their ancestral laws and he left them to be free' – 'free' in the sense that they were to govern themselves in their own way. He retained the satrapal system and the payment of tribute to which the Asians were accustomed, and he appointed Calas, a Macedonian, as satrap of Hellespontine Phrygia. He made an important reform in the case of Lydia and elsewhere thereafter: for Pausanias was put in charge of a garrison of Argive troops at Sardis, Nicias in charge of assessing and collecting tribute, and Asander in charge of civil affairs with some troops 'for the time being'. Each officer was responsible directly to Alexander. Their names are known to us from Arrian, whose source, Ptolemy, drew on the *Journal* in which their appointment and their responsibility to Alexander were recorded. The separation of military, financial and civil duties was a measure which Rome was not to take in Asia until the time of Augustus. Another innovation was made now or soon afterwards in Lydia, namely the training of young Lydians for service in the king's forces; some four years later Lydian troops joined his field army (below, p. 123).

The liberation of the Greek cities was undertaken by a number of task forces which Alexander sent out under Macedonian commanders. He marched with the rest of the army from Sardis to Ephesus, which he reached on the fourth day. He overthrew the pro-Persian oligarchy, brought back the exiles and set up a democracy. He himself was fortunate in having no political ideology. So when the democrats began to kill their political opponents, Alexander put a stop to 'further interrogation and reprisal, realising that if permission was given the people would kill the innocent as well as the guilty, from personal hatred or in order to seize their property'. His prevention of the excesses of party-strife (*stasis*) was highly praised at the time. It was to be characteristic of all his dealings with Greek city-states.

After his action at Ephesus he passed a general order that all liberated Greek cities were to replace oligarchies with democracies, again with an insistence on amnesty, and to re-establish their own legal procedures. He dealt with the Greek cities in person, not through the local satrap, and he exempted them from the payment of tribute. Thus they were granted a favoured status within the kingdom of Asia. But they were still subject to the orders of the king, and for the prosecution of the war he required payment for the time being of a financial contribution (*syntaxis*). At Ephesus he asked not for a contribution but for the payment of the assessed Persian tribute to the authorities of the temple of Artemis, perhaps in gratitude for their action in setting up a statue of Philip in the temple. His concern to win the favour of the Greek deities was apparent also at Sardis, where he planned to build a temple to Zeus and was guided by a violent thunderstorm to the divinely revealed site. While political changes were being made in many of the liberated cities, Alexander stayed in Ephesus, offered a state sacrifice to Artemis, and mounted a grand procession in which the army under arms was drawn up as for battle. He had good reason to thank the deities. For his anxiety over finance and supplies was a thing of the past, he now ruled over two-thirds of the western coast of Asia Minor, and he had publicised his policy as King of Asia towards his new subjects.

2. The war at sea and the siege of Halicarnassus

While he was still at Ephesus, Alexander must have known that a Persian fleet was about to enter Aegean waters. When it did so, he would face the problem which Agesilaus, king of Sparta, had faced in 396. He had already avoided the mistakes of Agesilaus which Xenophon had revealed in his *Hellenica*. For Agesilaus had made excessive demands on the 'liberated' Greek cities, had treated the indigenous peoples as enemies, and had ravaged far inland in pursuit of booty. In the Greek mainland and in the islands the oppressive rule of Sparta had led to a rising by states which hoped for Persian aid in gold and in troops. Sparta had recalled the bulk of Agesilaus' army and left the Greek navy under Spartan command to face the Persian fleet. The result had been the defeat of the Greek navy, Persian support of the Greek rising against Sparta, and the Peace of Antalcidas in 386, under which Persia took over the Greek cities in Asia and guaranteed the autonomy of the Greek states elsewhere. In 334 Alexander knew that the Persian fleet would be formidable; for Persia was in control of Egypt, Cyprus, Phoenicia and all the coast up to Ephesus, and it was from these areas that Persia now conscripted triremes with their native crews of trained oarsmen.

On the day after the procession at Ephesus Alexander marched towards Miletus. He invested the inner city and brought the Greek fleet of 160 triremes to the offshore island of Lade, where they were beached and protected by a large force of his Balkan troops. A Persian fleet of 400 triremes appeared three days later and sailed northwards for some fifteen kilometres to establish a base on Cape Mycale. Should the Greek fleet offer battle? Alexander consulted his staff. According to Arrian Parmenio wished to engage the enemy and offered to go on board himself. He thought a Greek victory probable, particularly because an eagle had been seen on the beach astern of the Greek fleet and its appearance there was, he thought, a presage of victory sponsored by Zeus. Alexander was not willing to engage. He judged the Phoenician and Cyprian crews to be better trained than those of the various Greek contingents, and in the event of defeat by such superior numbers he would lose the lives of the Macedonians acting as marines and increase the danger of a rising by some Greek states of the mainland. The omen he interpreted differently. The fact that the eagle was on the land meant that 'he would master the Persian fleet from the land'.

A leading Milesian offered to open the city to both sides. Alexander told him to expect an attack at dawn. During the siege the entry to the harbour was blocked by a line of Greek triremes, so that the Persians were unable to intervene. The city fell with considerable losses among the Greek mercenaries and the Milesians. Alexander pardoned the other Milesians and declared them to be 'free', in the sense that they would govern themselves. He took into his own service 300 Greek mercenaries who had been prepared to fight to the death. During the siege the Persians were prevented from landing at Mycale by a detachment of Macedonian cavalry and infantry, and they ran so short of supplies and water that they withdrew to Samos. They returned only to see the fall of Miletus, the strongest city of the west coast.

Alexander now sent the bulk of the Greek fleet to home waters. There the crews were not demobilised but were to be ready for recall. He knew that his Greek fleet was no match at sea for the Persian fleet, and he was able to shift the payment of its wages from his own funds in Asia to those of the Greek Community. His plan now was to follow the indication given by the eagle, the bird of Zeus, namely to capture all the bases of the Persian fleet on the Mediterranean coast, prevent it from obtaining replacements of crews and equipment, and so force it to surrender. The plan was extraordinarily bold. For its success was dependent on a number of factors: the ability of his army to capture the bases, the ability of the Macedonian fleet to hold the Hellespont, and the unwillingness of most city-states and especially of Athens to desert the Greek Community and join forces with Persia. To many that boldness may have seemed a gamble. To Alexander it was a matter of precise calculation and of faith in the divine will as it was revealed in the omen of the eagle.

For the rest of the sailing season Darius appointed Memnon to take command of 'lower Asia (southern Asia Minor) and the entire fleet'. It might have been expected that he would sail unopposed across the Aegean in the hope of raising a revolt in Greece. However, he decided to hold Halicarnassus (Bodrum) with the pick of his Persian troops, many Greek mercenaries and a part of the fleet, stationed inside the harbour. The defences of the city were exceptionally strong: a deep, wide moat to make approach difficult, a masonry wall six feet thick, high masonry towers, battlements and sally-ports, and two inner citadels. There was a large stock of missiles for catapults, and supplies of every kind could be brought in by sea. If the city should hold out, the Persian fleet would have an impregnable base within the Aegean basin and the advance of Alexander might be halted.

During the march from Miletus Alexander won over the cities 'by his kind treatment' and granted self-government and freedom from tribute to the Greeks. The deposed ruler of the Carians, Ada, came as a suppliant to meet him and to surrender her stronghold, Alinda; for his part Alexander accepted adoption as her son and entrusted Alinda to her. His chivalry won the approval of the Carian cities, which sent missions to crown him with golden crowns and promised to cooperate with him. This welcome was of great importance, since the Carians were a warlike people and had fought for their freedom in the past. He was now able to concentrate all his forces outside Halicarnassus. During the inactivity of the Persian fleet his small Greek fleet, led by the Athenian flotilla of twenty triremes, brought from Miletus the scaling ladders and the siege-engines (battering-rams, wheeled towers, mantlets and catapults), many of which had been made in sections and were re-assembled on arrival. Some ships carried supplies of food for the army, and these were supplemented by contributions from friendly cities. After an abortive attempt to capture Myndus nearby Alexander settled down to what was certain to be a long and difficult siege.

Two accounts of the siege have survived, each in an abbreviated version. That of Diodorus, drawing on Cleitarchus, was written from the point of view of the defenders and magnified their successes in an epic manner; it is of little worth. That of Arrian, drawing on Ptolemy and Aristobulus, who had written for participants, portrayed actions mainly from the Macedonian standpoint and derived some details from the *Journal* (e.g. the numbers of Macedonians killed and of Macedonians wounded when the defenders made a sortie at night). It did not omit successes by the defence; but it named only Memnon, Orontobates (satrap of Caria) and a Macedonian deserter on the Persian side, whereas a number of Macedonian officers were named as commanders and as casualties, no doubt as in the *Journal*.

It is enough here to describe the final stage of the siege. The attackers had brought down two high towers and the intervening wall, but the defenders had built a crescent-shaped brick wall behind the gap and manned high towers, one at either end, so that the missiles from their catapults enfiladed those who attacked the brick wall. When Alexander in person led a second attack on this wall, the entire force of the defenders made two coordinated sorties and came near to success. But in the end they were driven back with great loss, and the Macedonians might have forced an entry, had not Alexander halted his forces in order to spare the Greeks of Halicarnassus from the horrors of street-fighting. During this operation we have the first mention of engines firing 'great stones' and of more powerful bolt-shooting catapults, which relied on the torsion of twisted horse-hair. These were invented by Diades and Charias, pupils of Philip's Thessalian expert, Polyidus. The stone-throwers could smash a doorway or a masonry face, and the improved catapults could drive defenders from towers and parapets.

Orontobates and Memnon now decided that they could not withstand another assault. They therefore set fire to their own equipment and to the houses near the walls that night, and they withdrew their troops into the two citadels. Entering the city, Alexander ordered that Halicarnassian citizens should be spared and the fires extinguished. Next day he decided not to lay siege to the citadels. He moved the population elsewhere, since he could not protect them, and he razed the buildings of the city. He appointed Ada to be satrap of Caria, confident that she would be loyal to him, and a Macedonian officer to command 200 cavalry and 3,000 Greek mercenaries. They were to keep the Persians at Halicarnassus under observation, but they were a small force for such a task. For the Persians held the harbour and could bring in reinforcements. Alexander must have known that he was leaving a dangerous centre of resistance and a base for the Persian fleet in 333 (for the sailing season was ending). But he decided to go ahead with his plans elsewhere.

3. The division of forces and the advance of Alexander to Pamphylia

In the autumn of 334 Alexander had a fair idea of what Persia intended to do the following year. The decision of Orontobates and Memnon to keep control of the citadels and the harbour of Halicarnassus was a clear indication that the Persian fleet hoped in the spring to use Halicarnassus as a base and to advance through the Aegean either to raise revolt in the Peloponnese and/or to wrest the Hellespont from the Macedonians – things which it had failed utterly even to attempt in 334 because Memnon had concentrated all his forces on the defence of Halicarnassus. Then on land it was surprising that after the defeat at the Granicus Darius had not sent a part of his imperial army from Persia into Asia Minor to attack Alexander's lines of communication or to face him in battle. The explanation could only be that Darius intended to do so with a very large army in the spring or summer of 333. He was planning presumably to advance along the Royal Road through the centre of Asia Minor towards the coast, or to engage Alexander in a set battle in Cilicia or in Syria. In either case he would be in a very strong position if he was able to meet his fleet and conduct a coordinated offensive.

Alexander knew from the experience of Philip in Macedonia and Thrace that possession of a coastal strip alone was precarious and that it was essential to control the hinterland. This was particularly true in Asia Minor; for the valleys of the great rivers (Caïcus, Hermus, Caÿster and Maeander) provided easy routes to the coast, and Alexander did not have sufficient forces to block those valleys. The best defence therefore was to take possession of the very extensive Anatolian plateau from which these rivers flowed. That plateau was very suitable for cavalry, and its enormous resources of grain and fodder would supply his army throughout the winter. Concurrently he intended to continue his policy of 'mastering the Persian fleet from the land' by gaining control of the harbours on the southern coast of Asia Minor – a major undertaking because the mountainous terrain was suitable only for infantry and the native peoples were warlike. If he was to pursue both policies, he would need to divide his army and increase, if possible, the number of his troops.

After burying those who had been killed during the final night at Halicarnassus Alexander sent those of the Macedonians who were recently married to Macedonia, so that they could spend the winter with their wives – an act of compassion which won him much popularity. The officers in charge of them were ordered to 'enlist as many as possible from the countryside, both cavalry and infantry' and to bring them on their return. Another officer was sent to the Peloponnese to hire mercenaries with money which Alexander was now able to spare from his winnings in Asia. The Thessalian and other Greek cavalry, 'a hipparchy of the Companions' (perhaps half of the squadrons with the exception of the Royal Squadron), the Greek infantry, the siege-train and the baggage-train were sent under Parmenio via Sardis to capture the northern part of the Anatolian plateau, known as 'Greater Phrygia'. This task was completed during several months. We know nothing of how it was done, because the actions of Parmenio were not recorded in the *Journal* and so were not known to Ptolemy, on whose account Arrian was largely drawing. Alexander set off with the rest of the army 'towards Lycia and Pamphylia to gain control of the coastal region'.

The Lycians were a warlike people both on land and at sea. They had become partly Hellenised, as we know from a bilingual inscription of 337/6 at Xanthus, and they had been ruled by the satrap of Caria. Alexander's army captured at the first attack the city of Hyparna, and Alexander let the mercenary garrison of its acropolis depart under terms. All the cities of southwest Lycia joined Alexander 'by agreement' or 'by surrender'. He attacked the mountaineers of the interior, probably to benefit the coastal cities, and envoys came to him from the coastal cities of southeast Lycia to offer 'friendship'. Alexander ordered them to put themselves in the hands of his representatives. This they did. Alexander benefited them and in particular the Greek city Phaselis by joining forces with them and destroying a garrisoned strongpoint inland, from which the Pisidians had launched raids on the coastal peoples. Arrangements were made for the training of young Lycians in the Macedonian manner. The first draft of them reached Alexander in 329 (below, p. 123).

As Alexander advanced into Pamphylia, one part of his army used a mountain road, which had been made by his Thracian infantry, and the other part followed the seashore, which was passable when a north wind was blowing. Alexander was with the latter group. When he drew near, a southerly wind fell and a strong north wind blew, so that the passage became 'easy and swift', 'not without divine aid, as Alexander and his retinue used to explain'. The belief that the gods were on his side suited Alexander. He himself did not make any such claim in his *Letters*. But he allowed Callisthenes as his official historian to suggest that the sea 'bowed down' to Alexander. In Pamphylia he made Perge, a Greek city, his base. Envoys from another Greek city, Aspendus, came to surrender the city but asked that it should not be garrisoned. Alexander agreed, but he required Aspendus to contribute 50 talents to the expeditionary force and send him the horses they were breeding for the Great King as a form of tribute. The envoys accepted these conditions. Alexander continued along the coast to Side, a city Greek in origin but of mixed population, as bilingual inscriptions reveal. He garrisoned Side and went on to Syllium, a strongly fortified city which had a garrison of mercenaries and Pamphylians. But he turned back on a report that Aspendus had refused entry to his envoys and was preparing to withstand a siege.

Aspendus, beside which the river Eurymedon entered the sea, was an ideal base for a Persian fleet, as it had been in *c.* 467. Alexander found the population concentrated on the naturally strong, well fortified acropolis, and he did not have the equipment to mount what was likely to be a long siege. Negotiations therefore followed, during which the Aspendians offered to accept the same terms as before. These would have left their city ungarrisoned. Alexander made his own demands, which were accepted: the payment of 100 talents, the provision of the horses, the surrender of the leading men as hostages, payment annually of tribute to 'Macedonians', acceptance of an adjudication about some disputed territory, and obedience to the orders of a satrap appointed by Alexander. These terms were no doubt recorded in the *Journal*, from which Arrian obtained them through the medium of Ptolemy's history. When we consider the original terms and those now imposed on Aspendus, we can see that a liberated Greek city-state in Asia was required to make an *ad hoc* contribution to help the army, exempted from payment of annual tribute, not garrisoned normally, not subject to the orders of a satrap but dealing directly with Alexander. Aspendus was now penalised in that its contribution was doubled, it had to pay annual tribute to 'Macedonians', it was made subject to the orders of the satrap, it had to accept an adjudication by an outside body, and it had to give hostages as a guarantee of future conduct. There is no doubt that Alexander garrisoned the city in order to keep control of the harbour.

The payment of tribute to 'Macedonians' is of particular interest. Alexander did not ask that the money be paid to himself either as King of Macedonia or as King of Asia; for he did not wish the conquest to be regarded as a personal one – similarly Philip had made the Thracians pay a tithe to the Macedonians –, and he did not wish as King of Asia to make a departure from his practice in dealing with the Greek city-states in Asia. Aspendus was thus placed in a separate category, being subject to the Macedonian Assembly in financial matters and subject to Alexander's satrap in local matters.

From Aspendus and Perge Alexander went inland. Before we follow him, we must mention a plot, of which he heard when he was near Phaselis. A Persian agent, called Sisines, was arrested by Parmenio (then invading Phrygia) and forwarded to Alexander. His story ran thus. He had been sent by Darius nominally to meet the Persian satrap of Phrygia but actually to make contact with Alexander Lyncestes, who was then in command of the Thessalian cavalry with Parmenio (above, p. 77). For this Alexander had sent a letter to Darius by the hand of a Macedonian deserter, Amyntas, and in response to that letter Sisines was to say that, if Alexander Lyncestes would assassinate Alexander, Darius would make him king of Macedonia and add a bounty of 1,000 gold talents. Sisines had been arrested before he could reach Alexander Lyncestes.

Alexander convened his Friends and sought their advice. They judged Alexander Lyncestes to be guilty of treason on the evidence of Sisines' report. They were influenced also by an omen. During the siege of Halicarnassus, when Alexander was enjoying a siesta, a chattering swallow flew over his head, landed here and there on his bed, persisted even when it was brushed aside, perched on his head, and so woke him up. At the time Alexander had consulted his diviner, Aristander, who had said that it portended a plot by one of Alexander's Friends and that the plotter would be revealed. Alexander now reported this matter to his Friends in council. They advised Alexander to 'put Alexander Lyncestes out of the way speedily' in case he made himself more popular with the Thessalian cavalry and rebelled with them. A Macedonian officer, wearing local dress and accompanied by guides from Perge, reached Parmenio and delivered a verbal order for him to arrest Alexander Lyncestes. This was done successfully. Alexander kept Alexander Lyncestes under guard for some four years (below, p. 134).

Arrian's account, which we have summarised was based on the versions of Ptolemy and Aristobulus, and Ptolemy could have consulted accounts of the swallow's behaviour and the discussion by Alexander and his Friends which were recorded in the *Journal*. Scholars have generally inferred from the epithet 'Lyncestes' that this Alexander was a member of the disestablished royal house of Lyncus. But the epithet was simply the indication of his residence and so of his citizenship in Lyncus. Everything indicates that he was a member of the Temenid royal house; for he was the first to declare in favour of Alexander in 336, he was said to have succeeded to the command on the supposed death of Alexander in 335, he was given top-ranking appointments by Alexander, and he was a suitable person for Darius to put on the Macedonian throne. His father Aëropus was probably the grandson of Aëropus II, who had been king c. 398-395. Why did Alexander not bring the prisoner before the Macedonian Assembly on a charge of treason? The evidence which had convinced the Friends would certainly have convinced the King's Men. It may be that Alexander had an affection for his cousin. There may have been a public reason. Alexander risked his life frequently. If he were to be killed, who was competent to succeed? Arrhidaeus was half-witted. As a gifted and popular commander Alexander Lyncestes might be a suitable successor.

4. Anatolia and Gordium

Winter was well advanced when Alexander turned inland from Perge to force his way through the land of the Pisidians, renowned fighters, and to reach the Anatolian plateau. The first city to resist was Termessus. On approaching a precipitous defile which was held by the Termessians, Alexander encamped to give the impression that he would not attack. As he anticipated, most of the enemy went home, leaving a few guards in position. Alexander then made a rapid attack with a light-armed force, captured the defile, and encamped near the city. A rival of Termessus, Selge, sought and obtained Alexander's friendship with instructions to keep Termessus in check. He was thus able to pass on and attack Sagalassus, reputedly the most formidable of the Pisidian cities. The Sagalassians and some Termessians manned a steep hill in front of the city. Alexander led a frontal assault with 7,500 phalangites, whose flanks were protected by light-armed troops, Archers and Agrianians on the right and Thracian javelin-men on the left. Since the light-armed went ahead, the Archers in particular suffered some casualties but by then the phalangites began to engage the enemy who had no defensive armour and were felled by the pikes. In the battle some 500 were killed and the rest fled, so that Alexander was able to take the city by storm. His own losses were some twenty men. He quelled the rest of the Pisidians by capturing some forts and accepting the surrender of others. He could claim that he had imposed his rule; but he made no appointments and pressed on into Phrygia. 'On the fourth day' he reached Celaenae (now Dinar), a central point in the communications within Anatolia.

The satrap of Phrygia had been defeated and driven south by Parmenio. He had fled from the satrapy, but he had left 100 Greek mercenaries and 1,000 Carian soldiers under orders to hold the impregnable citadel of Celaenae. They were to be reinforced on a specified date. On the arrival of Alexander they offered to surrender the citadel on that date, if no reinforcements should reach them. Alexander accepted the offer, left 1,500 troops to guard the approaches, and in due course the citadel was surrendered to him. He spent ten days in southern Phrygia, during which the army had a well-earned rest and he made his administrative arrangements. He appointed Antigonus Monophthalmus ('One-eye') satrap of Phrygia, and led his army to Gordium (near Ankara), where he was joined by the forces under the command of Parmenio and by the reinforcements and the Macedonians who had wintered at home. These reinforcements were 300 Macedonian cavalry, 3,000 Macedonian infantry, 200 Thessalian cavalry and 150 Elean cavalry. It is probable that they more than made good the losses incurred in action and through illness during the last twelve months. For it was now late in April 333.

The achievements of Alexander's army in the one year of unremitting action since it set out from Macedonia in April 334 almost exceed belief. It had added to its control an area larger in extent and richer in resources than the whole of Thrace. It had rendered the Persian fleet ineffective through its own ability and daring in siegecraft. It had anticipated any movement of Persia's imperial army into Anatolia by the rapidity of its own movement. The greatest credit was due to the King's Men and the Greek cavalry in battle. But their advance was made possible only by the support system of the Greek fleet until its departure from Asia, the Greek and Balkan infantry, the engineers of the siege-train, and the organisers of the baggage-train. Because Alexander banned ravaging and looting, it was only rarely that he 'lived off the enemy land', as he did for instance in Pisidia, when the baggage-train was with Parmenio. Otherwise he relied on capturing enemy dumps and on contribution or purchase of supplies. It was his mastery of logistics which enabled the spearhead of the army to move with such speed.

His genius as a commander was apparent in his ability to inspire his men by his own bravery in every action and to obtain a heroic response to his commands. His bold strategy was justified by its success. His policy of liberation and favoured treatment for the Greek cities won their cooperation. As King of Asia he freed native peoples from Persian oppression and obtained the support, for instance, of Lydia, Caria and Lycia. Where he met opposition, as in Pisidia, he proved his superiority in war but did not impose garrisons or exact reprisals. There was no period of 'military government' of the modern kind. For he took over the existing form of satrapal government, made important improvements in it, and began the training of some young men in the Macedonian manner.

CHAPTER VIII

The battle of Issus and the capture of the Mediterranean coast

1. War at sea and the advance to Tarsus

On the acropolis of Gordium there was a wagon which, it was believed, had been dedicated to Zeus the King by Midas, a Phrygian king. Alexander was told of the local belief that anyone who untied the elaborate knot binding the yoke to the pole 'must rule over Asia'. He tried in vain; but then he took out the yoke-pin and so separated the yoke from the pole. That night thunder and lightning showed the approval of Zeus, and Alexander sacrificed next day to 'the gods who made the signs manifest and revealed the way to undo the binding'. Such was the account of Aristobulus, who saw that Alexander was actuated by a 'yearning' (*pothos*) in tackling the knot. Other authors said that Alexander lost his temper and cut the knot with his sword. Since Aristobulus may well have been present and wrote for contemporaries, his version is to be preferred. The incident was important in that Alexander's words at the Hellespont 'I accept Asia from the gods' were now confirmed by the deities. He knew beyond a doubt that he would be the ruler of Asia.

Between April and August Alexander consolidated his authority and extended it towards the Black Sea. Paphlagonia accepted his rule, provided hostages, and was added to the satrapy of Hellespontine Phrygia. It was exempted from paying tribute. The Greek cities on its coast were ordered to install democracies, as we know in the case of Amisus, east of Sinope. Alexander then led the recruits from Macedonia into Cappadocia, east of Paphlagonia, brought much of the region to his side, and appointed a Macedonian to be satrap of Cappadocia, which controlled the entry from Armenia into Asia Minor. He prolonged his stay in Anatolia for strategic reasons. From it he could move readily to the Hellespont, to the west coast or southeastwards into Cilicia, and his choice would depend on the outcome of the war at sea.

In March 333 Memnon sailed unopposed into the Aegean with 300 triremes and an abundance of money. He had a strong force of Greek mercenaries, which overpowered Alexander's supporters in Chios and in Lesbos except at Mytilene, where Greek mercenaries sent by Alexan-

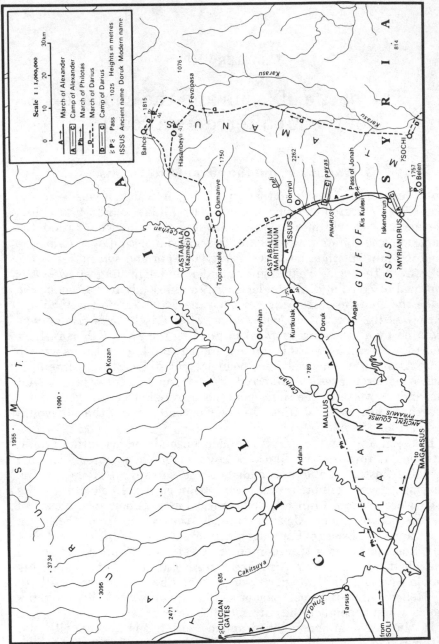

9. Cilicia

Scale 1:1,000,000

30 km
20
10
0

A →   March of Alexander
A ━━ C Camp of Alexander
Ph →   March of Philotas
D ‑‑‑‑→ March of Darius
D ━━ C Camp of Darius
⋛ P ⋚   Pass   • 1025 Heights in metres
ISSUS Ancient name Doruk Modern name

A
M
A
N
U
S

S Y R I A

• 814

Karasu

1076 •

Bahçe
• 1815
Se?
Hasanbeyli ·?
Fevzipaşa

Karasu

Karasu

?SOCHI

• 1750
Osmaniye

Deli

Dörtyol
2262
payas
Pass of Jonah
1757
Belen

Ceyhan

CASTABALA
(Kazmacı)

Toprakkale

CASTABALUM
MARITIMUM
ISSUS

PINARUS

GULF OF
Kis Kulesi
Iskenderun
?MYRIANDRUS

ISSUS

M
T.

1090 ·

1955 ·

Kozan

C
I
L
I
C
I
A

• 789

Ceyhan

Kurtkulak

Doruk

Aegae

P

MALLUS

ANCIENT COURSE
PYRAMUS

N

to
MAGARSUS

Adana

635

Çakıtsuya

CYDNUS

A →

A →

C
A
L
E
I
A
N
P
L
A
I
N

• 3734

• 3095

2471 •

?CILICIAN
GATES

A →

Tarsus

from
SOLI

der strengthened resistance. From late April until June Memnon maintained a blockade of Mytilene, thus losing the initiative at sea. Meanwhile Alexander had ordered the Macedonian fleet in the Hellespont to take the offensive, Antipater to recruit naval forces and hold the western Aegean, and the Greek Community to call up the Greek fleet 'in accordance with their treaty obligations as his allies' and hold the Hellespont. He sent 1,100 talents to the Macedonian commanders and to Antipater, and a letter to Athens, which with her stock of some 350 triremes (she could man half herself) held the balance at sea. The Greek Community stayed loyal. At Athens 'the orators' proposed refusal but the good sense of Phocion and others prevailed. Alexander's earlier confidence in 'The Greeks' was justified. The fleets were at sea when Memnon died in June. Thereafter the Persians stayed at Mytilene under the command of a Persian Pharnabazus, whose appointment was not confirmed by Darius for a month or so.

In July Alexander learnt of Memnon's death, and soon afterwards of the departure of Memnon's force of Greek mercenaries, who had been summoned to Syria by Darius. It was Alexander's belief that the Greek and Macedonian fleets would hold the Hellespont and the western Aegean. He therefore chose now to invade Cilicia and to encounter Darius' large army, which was evidently on the way to the Syrian coast. The Cilician Gates, a narrow cliff-bound pass, was held by Persian forces. Alexander encamped far off, and in person led a force of Hypaspists, Archers and Agrianians on a night march, hoping to surprise the enemy at dawn. In fact the Persians were on the alert, but when they saw that Alexander was leading the attack, they fled and the pass was open. When cavalry and other light-armed infantry came up, Alexander led them so fast that they covered the fifty-seven miles to Tarsus before dark. The Persian satrap had planned to plunder the city, but he fled, leaving it intact.

Alexander collapsed, either from sheer exhaustion or after a plunge into the icy waters of the Cydnus at Tarsus, and the doctors despaired of his life, except one, Philip, an Acarnanian. He was preparing a potion when Alexander was informed by a despatch from Parmenio that Philip was in the pay of Darius. Alexander handed the despatch to Philip and drank the potion, 'demonstrating his trust to Philip and his complete confidence to his friends – and also his strength of will in the face of death'. Such is Arrian's account, derived from Aristobulus. Other versions were even more sensational. The illness persisted from July into October. During that time Pharnabazus reinforced the Persians at Halicarnassus, and he captured Mytilene, Tenedos and Samothrace, from which he threatened the Macedonian hold on the Hellespont. Other Persian ships sailed to the Cyclades and an advance force of ten triremes reached Siphnos. There they were surprised at dawn by a Macedonian commander with fifteen warships, and only two escaped.

The defence of the Hellespont and the western Aegean was still holding when Alexander recovered his health.

By early October Alexander knew that Darius was on his way towards the coast. He sent Parmenio in command of the Thessalian cavalry, Greek and Balkan infantry, and some Greek mercenaries with the task of expelling the satrapal forces from the coast as far south as the Pillar of Jonah, where a narrow pass divided Cilicia from Syria. He himself led the rest of his army westwards into Cilicia Tracheia ('Rough'), where there was some support for Persia. He fined Soli, a Greek city, for that reason and placed a garrison in it, and he took a flying column into the mountains, where he won over some communities and expelled others, all in a week. Alexander's aim in sending Parmenio so far and himself reducing Cilicia Tracheia was to prevent the fleet of Pharnabazus and the army of Darius operating together on the Mediterranean coast; for if they should do so, they would be able to land troops in his rear and cut his line of communications and supply. As it was, after his and Parmenio's success, no port of call was available for Persian warships south of Halicarnassus and Caunus. On his return to Soli the news arrived that the satraps of Lydia and Caria had won a victory over the Persian forces of Orontobates near Halicarnassus. Alexander now celebrated the Macedonian state festival in honour of Olympian Zeus and the Muses, as he had done in 335, with a procession by the whole army, a torch-race and competitions. He made a sacrifice to Asclepius who had restored him to health.

Alexander then began the march to join Parmenio. He halted at Mallus, a Greek city, where he put a stop to a *stasis* among the citizens, and he was still there when news came that Darius was encamped at Sochi in Syria, a march of some two days inland from the Pillar of Jonah, which was held by Parmenio's force. It seemed that Alexander's strategy was succeeding. For he expected to engage the army of Darius, when it was inland and out of reach of the Persian fleet. See Plate 10.

2. The campaign of Issus

Alexander consulted his close Companions. They urged him to lead them into action forthwith. He thanked them, met Parmenio en route, placed his baggage-train and his sick at Issus, passed the Pillar of Jonah and encamped by Myriandrus on the coast (near Iskenderun). A night of storm and rain caused him to stay in camp and rest his army all day. A report came early on the following day that Darius was behind him on the far side of the Pillar of Jonah. Incredulous, Alexander embarked some Companions on a triaconter. They sailed back, entered the bay by the mouth of the river Pinarus (Payas), and came back with some information about Darius' position. It was only too true. Darius had cut Alexander's line of supply; and if he could stand firm, he would starve Alexander's army into surrender. How had it happened? Darius had waited for many days at Sochi, where a wide plain suited his superior numbers and his fine cavalry. He knew that Alexander's army was split, and he assumed from Alexander's delay that Alexander would stay at Tarsus. He therefore marched his army north, crossed the Amanus range by the Bahce pass, and reached the coast at Issus. Had his assumption been correct, he would have camped between the two enemy forces, dealt with each separately and probably been helped by his fleet. By sheer chance Alexander had marched from Tarsus to Myriandrus during the very days when Darius was on his way to and from the Bahce Pass. On reaching Issus Darius mutilated and then killed the Macedonian sick. He then moved his huge army — several times as numerous as that of Alexander – to a defensive position on the right bank of the river Payas.

When the triaconter returned, Alexander convened his commanders, exhorted them and received their enthusiastic support. He sent some cavalry and archers to ascertain if the pass at the Pillar of Jonah, six kilometres away, was occupied by the enemy. It was not, to Alexander's relief, for the route was along a narrow beach which was flooded when winds were adverse and which was flanked by cliffs on the landward side. The army was told to take its evening meal. It then marched to the pass, which it reached about midnight. Sentries were posted on the cliff-tops, and the men had a few hours of sleep. Alexander sacrificed in thanksgiving to the deities of the sea (Poseidon, Thetis, Nereus and the Nereids), because the beach was not flooded. At dawn the march began towards the Payas river, six kilometres away, and as the army, deploying from column into line of battle, began to descend slowly towards the low ground, Alexander was issuing his orders to his commanders.

The army numbered 5,300 cavalry and 26,000 infantry. Parmenio was to command the left-hand part of the line, which consisted from left to right of the squadrons of Greek cavalry but not the Thessalians, then the Cretan Archers and the Thracian javelin-men, and then three brigades of phalangites, the last under the command of Craterus. Parmenio was told to keep close to the coast, in order not to be outflanked. Alexander commanded the right-hand part, of which the units from right to left were Lancers and Paeonian cavalry, then Macedonian Archers and Agrianians, then Thessalian cavalry, Companion Cavalry, Royal Infantry Guard, Hypaspists and three brigades of the phalanx, which was eight men deep. There was a second line behind and shorter than the phalanx; it consisted of Balkan, Greek and Greek mercenary infantry. He changed some of these dispositions during the slow descent. The Thessalian cavalry was transferred to the left wing. Because his right was outflanked by a Persian force on a spur of the mountain (see Fig. 10), he detached 300 cavalry to keep it at bay and extended his own line to the right by bringing up Greek mercenaries from the second

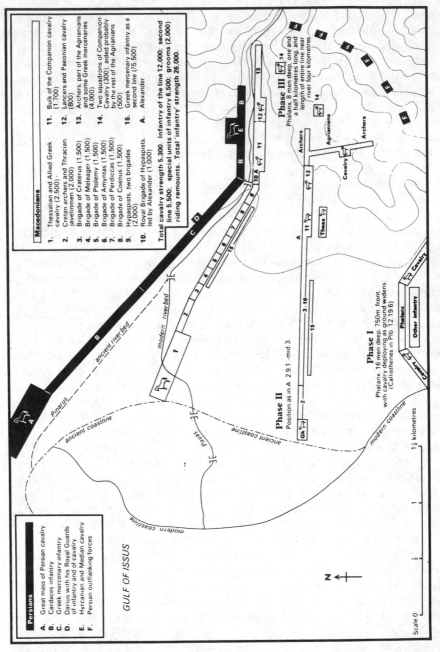

Persians

A. Great mass of Persian cavalry
B. Cardaces infantry
C. Greek mercenary infantry
D. Darius with his Royal Guards of infantry and of cavalry
E. Hyrcanian and Median cavalry
F. Persian outflanking forces

GULF OF ISSUS

Macedonians

1. Thessalian and Allied Greek cavalry (2,500).
2. Cretan archers and Thracian javelinmen (2,000)
3. Brigade of Craterus (1,500)
4. Brigade of Meleager (1,500)
5. Brigade of Ptolemy (1,500)
6. Brigade of Amyntas (1,500)
7. Brigade of Perdiccas (1,500)
8. Brigade of Coenus (1,500)
9. Hypaspists, two brigades (2,000)
10. Royal Brigade of Hypaspists, led by Alexander (1,000)
11. Bulk of the Companion cavalry (1,700)
12. Lancers and Paeonian cavalry (800)
13. Archers, part of the Agrianians and some Greek mercenaries (4,000)
14. Two squadrons of Companion Cavalry (300), aided probably by the rest of the Agrianians (500)
15. Greek mercenary infantry as a second line (75,500)
A. Alexander

Total cavalry strength 5,300. Infantry of the line 12,000; second line 5,500; special units of infantry 6,500; grooms (2,000) riding remounts. Total 'infantry' strength 26,000.

Phase II
Position as in A 2.9.1–mid 3

Phase I
Phalanx, 16 men deep, 750m front, with cavalry deploying as ground widens (Callisthenes in Plb 12.19.6)

Phase III
Phalanx, 8 men deep, one and a half kilometres long, and length of entire line near river four kilometres

Scale 0

kilometres

10. The Battle of Issus

line. When these dispositions were completed, he halted the four-kilo-metres-long line. He rode along it, exhorting his men, returned to his position at the head of the Royal Infantry Guard, and ordered the final advance in perfect line 'step by step'.

Although the army of Darius was much larger, there were no more men in his front line than in Alexander's front line, so that his superiority in numbers was of little value. The position he had chosen was exceptionally strong. On emerging from the steep mountainside the Payas today has a boulder-strewn bed some 35 metres wide, and shelving banks, sometimes eaten into by flood water. A little below the first bridge (Fig. 10) the river enters a channel, cut long ago through the conglomerate rock, with a cliff-like right bank some three to seven metres high but with occasional breaks. Below the second bridge the river flows through gravel and sand and has low banks. Its course was different here in antiquity, but the terrain was the same. Darius placed his best infantry on the top of the bank between the positions of the two modern bridges and strengthened any gaps with stockades. The infantry were Greek mercenaries, flanked on each side by Persian 'Cardaces', equipped like the mercenaries but having also bow and arrows. They were in an unusually deep phalanx. Behind them was Darius and his Royal Cavalry Guard, 3,000 strong. This part of the line was designed solely for defence. Between the second bridge and the coast Darius placed beyond the Cardaces a great mass of cavalry, which, he hoped, would break through the enemy and attack their flank and rear. Above the first bridge there were Cardaces and a relatively small force of cavalry, and in advance of them on a spur of the mountain a mixed force, which Alexander managed to isolate during his advance, as we have mentioned. The plan was sound, if the defensive position down to the second bridge should hold firm and the cavalry could break through.

As his line advanced from higher ground, Alexander could see the enemy's dispositions in increasing detail. When the righthand part of his line was some eighty metres from the enemy, Alexander led the Royal Infantry Guard 'at the double' through the riverbed just above the first bridge, charged the Cardaces and broke through their formation. On his left the Hypaspists and the phalanx-brigades entered the channel and engaged the enemy. On his right the Companion Cavalry and beyond them the infantry crossed the riverbed, outflanked and broke the enemy position. Alexander now joined the Royal Cavalry Guard and attacked the flank and rear of the Cardaces and then of the Greek mercenaries, for he was followed by the victorious troops of his right wing (Plate 3(b)). Meanwhile the phalangites, trying to storm the defensive position of the mercenaries and the Cardaces, suffered considerable casualties but maintained the pressure with extraordinary courage. On the left the Persian cavalry charged time and again. However, the Thessalian and other Greek cavalry managed to hold their ground.

The impetuous advance of Alexander towards Darius decided the issue (Plate 12). As the infantry of the right wing attacked the flank of the Greek mercenaries, and behind them Alexander and the Cavalry Guard forced their way towards Darius, the king turned his chariot around and fled, followed by his Cavalry Guard. Alexander pressed on towards his left wing, where the Persian cavalry joined the general rout. Only then did Alexander order the pursuit by his cavalry, which covered a distance of 37 kilometres until nightfall and inflicted very heavy losses on the Persian cavalry. The surviving Greek mercenaries escaped into the hills and some of them later rejoined Darius. Alexander's losses were 150 cavalry and 300 infantry, and he was one of 4,500 wounded. The victory and the small number of killed were due to Alexander's planning, to superior weapons and armour, and to fighting in formation. The defeat of the imperial army was total. Its numbers were no doubt inflated in the official reports by Callisthenes, and so also its losses (110,000 being the standard figure). Whatever the true numbers were, the full strength of the Persian Empire failed utterly on the banks of the Payas. Alexander expressed his thanksgiving by erecting altars there to Zeus, Heracles and Athena.

There was a considerable fall-out of the defeated forces. One large group, led by Persian officers, escaped to Asia Minor where they recruited some Cappadocian and Paphlagonian troops and then invaded Lydia. Alexander did not pursue them. He relied on the capable satrap of Phrygia, Antigonus Monophthalmus – justifiably, for Antigonus defeated the Persians in three battles. Another group, which included 4,000 Greek mercenaries and was commanded by the Macedonian deserter Amyntas, son of Antiochus, fled southwards to Tripolis, from which they sailed to Cyprus and then to Egypt. There Amyntas claimed to be the new satrap appointed by Darius. His mercenaries defeated the Persian garrison of Memphis but were then annihilated when they scattered on a spree of looting. A third group of 8,000 Greek mercenaries made their way eventually to Taenarum in the Peloponnese.

3. The winning of the coast and the siege of Tyre

To capture Susa and to pursue Darius before he had a chance of recruiting another imperial army may have been a tempting prospect after the total victory at Issus. But Alexander persisted in the strategy of mastering the Persian fleet from the land, and of controlling the Mediterranean coast, although he would thereby give Darius the opportunity to recruit an even larger imperial army. His decision was to be epoch-making.

Darius fled so precipitately that he abandoned his mother, wife and children and some ladies-in-waiting who were in his advanced camp. When Alexander heard of their capture and their mourning for Darius, whom they supposed to be dead, he sent Leonnatus to tell them that Darius was alive, and that they were accorded by Alexander the status and the title of their royal rank; for 'the war was not one of enmity towards Darius but had been conducted lawfully for the rule over Asia'. Such was the account of Ptolemy and Aristobulus, said Arrian, and it is without doubt correct. There was also a statement, derived not from these two Macedonians but probably from Cleitarchus, that next day, when Alexander and Hephaestion paid them a visit, the mother of Darius mistakenly made obeisance to Hephaestion and in her embarrassment was consoled by Alexander who said 'Hephaestion too is Alexander'. True or not, this statement inspired a splendid painting by Paolo Veronese (Plate 11). Some weeks later a request for the restitution of the royal family was made by Darius. The substance of his letter and the reply of Alexander, both as reported by Ptolemy from the *Journal* and then transmitted by Arrian, help us to understand why Alexander was treating the family of Darius as royalty.

After accusing Philip and Alexander of unprovoked aggression Darius offered 'friendship and alliance' on terms which would be arranged by negotiation. In reply Alexander accused Persia of aggression in the past 'against Macedonia and the rest of Greece' – citing the Persian Wars, interference at Perinthus, and invasion of Thrace by Artaxerxes Ochus; of organising the murder of Philip; and of urging 'the Greeks' to attack Macedonia and destroy the (Common) Peace, 'which I organised'. Alexander certainly had the stronger case. He evidently felt it important to justify his action in the sight of men and of the gods. In his letter he represented himself as legitimate king of Macedonia, ruler of Thrace and *Hegemon* of the Greeks, whereas he accused Darius of being responsible for the murder of his predecessor Arses and of having seized the throne 'unjustly and not in accordance with the law of the Persians'.

'Now it is I who possess the land, since the gods gave it to me; and I take care of those of your soldiers who have joined me of their own will. Come then to me as I am the Lord of all Asia ... You shall have your family and anything which you persuade me as King of Asia to grant to you.' He here repeated the claim he had made on landing in Asia, that he accepted Asia as the gift of the gods, and he now required Darius to recognise him as Lord of all Asia. The suggestion which was implicit in his treating the family as royalty and in offering whatever Darius could persuade him to give was surely that this family would continue as the royal family of the Medes and Persians and Darius would continue as their king, provided that they and he recognised Alexander as their overlord, the King of all Asia. 'But if you refuse in the matter of the Kingship, stand and fight for it.' At the time Darius made no reply.

Meanwhile Alexander had overcome any financial difficulties. For he had acquired 3,000 talents in the advanced camp of Darius and a much greater quantity of gold in the Persian base at Damascus. He began to issue a prolific coinage in silver and in gold on the Attic standard for circulation primarily in Asia. The silver tetradrachm portrayed the head of a youthful Heracles and on the reverse Zeus seated on a throne, holding an eagle on his right hand and a sceptre with his left hand. For the Macedonians Heracles was the ancestor of the royal house, and his youthful aspect might be associated with the youthfulness of Alexander himself; and for the Asiatics Heracles was a familiar deity under other names. Zeus the King ruled far and wide, and his eagle had guided Alexander in the decision to defeat the Persian fleet on land. For the Asiatics the seated figure was Ba'al, even as he had appeared on the Persian coins minted at Tarsus. Now Ba'al was represented as the sponsor of Alexander. The victory at Issus was commemorated on the gold coinage with the head of Athena and on the reverse Nike, holding a wreath and a *stylis* (used for the outlook-post on a warship). The Athena here was the goddess of war, both Alcidemus for the Macedonians and Trojan for the Asians, and the *stylis* recalled the daring of the Companions who sailed to the mouth of the Pinarus in order to observe the dispositions of Darius.

The success of Alexander's propaganda was apparent as he advanced along the coast. Those in power at Aradus, Byblus and Sidon accepted the rule of Alexander over themselves and their dominions. Thereafter they and their successors issued only the coinage of the King of Asia with a monogram of the ruler or of the city in Aramaic. Envoys from Tyre met him on his march and reported the decision of the Tyrians 'to do whatever Alexander may order'. Alexander expressed his commendation and said that he wished to enter Tyre and to sacrifice to Heracles (worshipped as 'Melkart' by the Tyrians). The Tyrians replied that they would obey Alexander's other commands but would not admit any Persians or any Macedonians into their city. Alexander's request had been the acid test of Tyre's submission, deliberately made because Tyre was the leading sea power in Phoenicia and her flotilla the strongest in the fleet of Pharnabazus. The Tyrians thought of their strongly fortified city on its island as impregnable; their fleet could bring in supplies; and they hoped for help from Carthage. Alexander convened a meeting of Companions and Commanders and made a speech of which Arrian gave his own version, derived from Ptolemy, who had read a report of the speech in the *Journal*.

Alexander's arguments were concerned with strategy. To advance into Mesopotamia in pursuit of Darius and to leave the Persian fleet at sea with Tyre, Cyprus and Egypt as its bases would be an act of folly; for that fleet with reinforcements, with Sparta's collaboration and with Athens wavering would 'transfer the war into Greece', quite apart from recapturing harbours on the Mediterranean coast. Nor would it be reasonable to advance towards Egypt with the fleet and Tyre endanger-

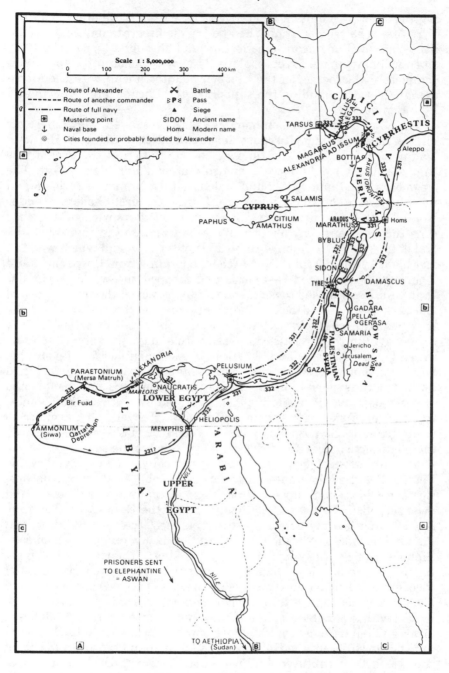

11. The movements of Alexander's forces, 333-331 BC

ing the lines of communication. It was essential, therefore, to capture
Tyre first. The results would then be the disintegration of the Persian
fleet through Phoenician disaffection and through Cyprus changing
sides willingly or perforce; a relatively easy invasion of Egypt; and a
complete thalassocracy of the Eastern Mediterranean with the Macedonian fleet commanding the support of the Phoenician, Cyprian and
Egyptian navies.

The Companions and Commanders were persuaded. Alexander was
all the more confident because he dreamed that night of Heracles
leading him into Tyre. Aristander's interpretation of the dream was
that Alexander would succeed but only after a Herculean effort. The
siege began in January 332 and ended in July. Immense heroism and
ingenuity were shown on both sides. During the first phase Alexander
worked with his men and rewarded their best efforts with gifts as they
constructed a causeway about half a mile long into the bay. When the
end of the causeway came within range of the city-wall which was 150
feet high, Tyrian catapults and archers operating from the parapet and
from triremes inflicted casualties and stopped the work. Alexander
then built two-wheeled towers, 150 feet high, moved them to the end of
the causeway, and attacked the enemy on the city-wall and on the
triremes with catapult fire, while work continued on extending the
causeway. But the Tyrians countered with a huge fire-ship, which was
towed to the causeway-end, where it was set alight with a favourable
wind and burnt both towers, while supporting troops landed and
burned all the siege-equipment. Alexander ordered his men to make the
entire causeway wider and his engineers, led by a Thessalian Diades,
to build more siege-equipment and towers. He went off to collect as
many triremes as possible, 'since the conduct of the siege appeared
more impracticable with the Tyrians in control of the sea'.

The situation at sea was altering radically. In autumn 333 the
Persian fleet had dominated the Aegean with bases at Halicarnassus,
Cos and Chios, held advanced positions at Siphnos and Andros, and
even established a base at Callipolis within the Hellespont. The time
seemed ripe for any dissident states on the Greek mainland to join
Persia. Pharnabazus brought his finest flotilla of a hundred triremes to
Siphnos. But he was joined only by Agis, king of Sparta, with a single
trireme, who asked for men, money and ships to promote a rising in the
Peloponnese. During their discussion the news arrived that Darius had
been utterly defeated at Issus (in November). Pharnabazus turned back
to deal with a possible rising in Chios. Agis was given thirty talents of
silver and ten triremes, but he chose now to operate not in the Peloponnese but in Crete. In the Hellespont a Macedonian fleet and a flotilla of
the Greek fleet captured Callipolis and destroyed the Persian force
there, probably in December. Operations lapsed for the rest of the
winter, but news reached the Phoenician and Cyprian crews that their

cities apart from Tyre were in Alexander's hands and were being treated liberally. With the start of the sailing season the Persian fleet began to disintegrate. By midsummer 332 some eighty Phoenician warships and one hundred and twenty Cyprian warships made their submission to Alexander, who 'let bygones be bygones'.

Thus Alexander was able to muster at Sidon a large fleet, which included also ten triremes each from Rhodes and Lycia. While it was being equipped for action, he campaigned inland to the Antilebanon, in order to safeguard the supply of timber from Mount Lebanon. He then opened the second phase of the siege of Tyre by bringing up his fleet and confining the Tyrian ships to their harbours; for the Cyprians and the Phoenicians, who had suffered at the hands of Tyre, were eager for revenge. Great efforts were made to breach the wall facing the new causeway, but the Tyrians had dropped rocks into the sea by the foot of the wall and Alexander's ships were unable to reach the wall. These rocks were eventually dragged away and ships carrying siege-engines attacked the wall. The Tyrians made a successful sortie against the Cyprian fleet off one of the harbours, but Alexander intercepted the Tyrian ships and destroyed most of them. Having complete control by sea, Alexander now tested various parts of the circuit-wall and planned the assault for a day of calm weather.

Three attacks were delivered at the same moment. The Phoenicians broke the booms blocking one harbour and destroyed the Tyrian ships. The Cyprians captured another harbour and forced their way into the city. The Macedonians brought up ships carrying siege-engines and towers and breached the wall. These ships were replaced by ships carrying the Hypaspists and a phalanx brigade, gangways were lowered onto the fallen wall, and the assault began. The first man to land, Admetus, was killed, and after him Alexander and his Companions drove back the enemy and secured the landing-place, from which they led the way into the city itself. There those Tyrians who had retired under the attack of the Cyprians joined the other troops and faced the Macedonians, but to no avail; for they were surrounded on all sides. 'The Macedonians went to all lengths in their anger; for they were enraged by the length of the siege and by the Tyrian slaughter of Macedonians taken prisoner and the throwing of the corpses into the sea in front of the Macedonian camp.' It was estimated that 8,000 Tyrians were killed during the siege, and of the survivors 30,000 were sold into slavery, while others were smuggled out by Phoenicians. The Tyrian king, his nobles and some Carthaginian envoys on a sacred mission were pardoned as suppliants at the altar of Heracles. The Macedonian dead were reported as some 400 by Arrian, and the wounded probably exceeded 3,000 (see above, p. 90, for the proportion of dead to wounded).

Alexander now paid honour to Heracles. The army paraded under arms, the fleet mustered for review, and games and a torch-race followed within the precinct of Heracles. The successful siege-engine and the Tyrian sacred ship were dedicated by Alexander to Heracles. Thus the interpretation by Aristander of Alexander's dream was confirmed, and Alexander's faith in that interpretation and in the favour of Heracles was justified.

4. The advance to Egypt and the estabishment of thalassocracy

The way to Egypt was blocked by Gaza. Alexander's engineers said that it was impossible to take by assault the fortified city; for it stood on a mound 250 feet high and had a strong circuit-wall. But Alexander was not to be deflected. He set the entire army and the local people to build an equally high mound around the city, and when it reached the height of the point in the circuit-wall which seemed weakest, Alexander brought up his siege-engines and made sacrifice. As he did so, 'a carnivorous bird flying over the altar dropped a stone onto his head'. Aristander gave his interpretation: 'O king, you will capture the city but you must take care for yourself today.' At first Alexander stayed out of range. But when the first wave of the assault failed he led the Hypaspists into action and was hit by a catapult-bolt which went through his shield and cuirass into his shoulder. He lost much blood and was healed with difficulty; but he rejoiced in his belief that the first part of the interpretation was also to prove true.

The ruler of Gaza, called Batis, had hired a force of Arab mercenaries who fought with fanatical courage. Alexander's siege-engines were brought by sea from Tyre, moved with difficulty through sand and erected on the mound. The wall was pounded by stone-hurling catapults and battering rams and undermined by sapping, until it collapsed at several places. Three assaults failed. Then as a great stretch of wall came down the phalanx-troops crossed on gangways with much rivalry in courage. The prize of valour went to Neoptolemus, a member of the Molossian royal house. 'The men in Gaza all died, each fighting at his post.' Women and children were sold into slavery, and the city was repopulated with people of the locality. This is the account of Arrian, based on Ptolemy and Aristobulus. On the other hand Curtius had Batis taken prisoner, taunted by a furious Alexander and dragged round the walls by Alexander in his chariot, in imitation of Achilles dragging Hector round the walls of Troy – a finale probably drawn from the account of Cleitarchus. It is to be rejected; for Alexander always honoured the brave.

In December 332 fleet and army proceeded together from Gaza to Egypt in seven days, averaging some twenty miles a day – a fine example of planned logistics. The fleet entered Pelusium (Port Said) unopposed, the army was welcomed by the priests and the people, and the Persian commander surrendered to Alexander at Memphis. The fleet sailed on the waters of the Nile, and a naval base was soon established at Alexandria. By now the Persian fleet was indeed 'conquered on land'. For reports were reaching Alexander that the Macedonian fleet and the Greek fleet, helped by risings in the islands, had driven the remnants of the Persian forces and their supporters at sea, 'the pirates', from the Aegean islands, and that fighting continued only within Crete.

At Tyre Alexander had envisaged a Macedonian thalassocracy. It was rapidly achieved. The Phoenician cities and the Cyprian kings placed their navies under Alexander's command, and they were treated with due honour by him. In the summer of 331, when trouble was brewing in the Peloponnese, a Macedonian fleet was reinforced there by 100 Phoenician and Cyprian ships. The fleet of 'The Greeks', numbering 160 triremes, operated mainly within the Aegean. The constituent parts of the multiracial fleet under the control of Alexander as King of Macedonia, *Hegemon* of 'The Greeks' and King of Asia were all commanded by Macedonian officers, and their orders for 331 were to free Crete and 'above all to clear the seas of the pirate fleets'. In 331 a thalassocracy extending from the Black Sea to the shores of Egypt was established for the first time in history. Alexander intended that thalassocracy to be the basis of a maritime intercontinental trade which would bring an unparalleled prosperity to all the coastal peoples of the area. That intention was indeed fulfilled despite the later division of the Macedonian world into warring kingdoms. This achievement by Alexander ranks with his organisation of the Kingdom of Asia in the East. Its effects were to be even more longlasting; for they underlay the prosperity of the Roman Empire and its successor, the Byzantine Empire.

CHAPTER IX

Advance to the East and the battle of Gaugamela

1. Events in Egypt in early 331

With the opening of communication by sea between Greece and the southeastern Mediterranean fifteen envoys from the Council of the Greeks came to greet Alexander. As they sailed up the Nile, some may have recalled the attempt of Athens and her Allies to control Egypt which had ended in the disaster of 454. Now they bestowed on Alexander a golden crown in recognition of his services as Hegemon 'for the safety and freedom of Greece'. In the Aegean islands the supporters of Alexander and the Greeks were now in power. They arrested some pro-Persian leaders and sent them to Alexander in Egypt. He sent them back for trial by their fellow-countrymen, except for those of Chios, a member of 'The Greeks', who were to be tried by the Council of that body. He rewarded Mytilene for its stalwart resistance to Persia with a gift of territory on the Asian coast, which he had won 'by the spear'. He granted the requests of embassies from mainland Greece, one being the release of Athenians captured in the Battle of the Granicus. His purpose was to encourage loyalty to the Common Peace and resistance to Sparta, which was at war on the side of Persia.

To the Egyptians Alexander was 'Pharaoh'. Hieroglyphic inscriptions reveal that they gave him the traditional titles: 'Son of Ra' (the supreme god) and 'King of Upper Egypt and King of Lower Egypt, beloved of Ammon and selected of Ra'. As Pharaoh he sacrificed 'to the gods (of Egypt) and especially to Apis'; for Apis was the god against whom Cambyses and Artaxerxes Ochus had committed gross sacrilege. Thus Alexander showed his respect for the Egyptians and his acceptance of their religious beliefs. At the same time he sacrificed and held athletic and musical competitions in the Macedonian manner, for which athletes and artists came from the Greek mainland. There was no inconsistency; for in the belief of the polytheist there were innumerable gods. From Memphis he and a select force sailed down the western branch of the Nile. There he decided to build a city on an isthmus between the sea and Lake Mareotis which could be connected by a canal to the Nile, so that the city would have two harbours. He was seized by a longing (*pothos*) to start work at once. So he marked out the circuit-wall fifteen kilometres long, the city-centre, and the sites of temples to Isis (analogous to Demeter) and to Greek gods. The deities smiled on the enterprise; for a sacrifice proved favourable, and the barley with which Alexander marked the ground was devoured by flocks of birds. Aristander said this portended 'prosperity especially in fruits of the earth'. The date was probably 20 January 331, and the city was to be named Alexandria.

From the start of his campaign Alexander had foreseen the importance in his Kingdom of Asia of cities, whether native, Greek or mixed. After the first battle he declared Troy, then a native village, to be a city 'free and exempt from paying tribute', and he left instructions for its buildings to be erected. He gave the same status to the liberated Greek cities, and he played an important part in the building of Priene near the mouth of the Maeander. The most southerly of the Greek cities were Magarsus, where he sacrificed to its goddess Athena, and Mallus, founded by Amphilochus, to whom he sacrificed as a hero. He put a stop to faction (*stasis*) at Mallus, as he had done at Ephesus (above, p. 72). Thereafter he founded mixed cities: Aegae and Alexandria on the coast of the Gulf of Issus, Bottia on the Orontes, and inland Arethusa in Syria, and Gadara, Pella and Gerasa in eastern Palestine and in Jordania. In these cities he placed Macedonians no longer fit for his very active service, Greeks and native peoples; and it was the Macedonians who gave the cities and the districts their Macedonian names. Alexandria was his only foundation in Egypt.

These cities were of economic importance, those on the coast as terminals of trade from inland and as exporters of goods in the Eastern Mediterranean, and those inland as key-points on caravan routes from the interior. For instance, Alexandria was to be the outlet for the produce of Egypt, of the coasts of the Red Sea and of Aethiopia (Sudan), and a centre of exchange with Cyrene (Libya) and the countries of the East Mediterranean; and Gerasa was to be a market for the spices and unguents of Arabia. If Alexander had stayed west of the Euphrates, as Parmenio was said to have advised, he would already in 331 have ensured a rapidly growing prosperity within the area of his conquests in Asia, the Balkan peninsula, the Black Sea and the Aegean basin. That was the result of three years of forward planning, and it was now guaranteed by the establishment of the thalassocracy which he had foreseen at Miletus in 334. The cities spread Greek skills in agriculture, land reclamation and capitalism, and a knowledge of the Greek language, which was the official medium in all cities. That language, known as the *koine*, was based on the Attic dialect and modified by Alexander and his staff.

The cities were centres of culture and education. Each had its theatre and its Odeum for the production of plays and music of the traditional kind; for Alexander studied the writings of Homer, Pindar and the tragedians, and he was deeply interested in 'philosophy', which covered ideas in the arts and the sciences. The form of education in the mixed cities was Macedonian. The curriculum seems to have resembled that of the Royal School of Pages (above, p. 5), lasting from the age of fourteen to the end of the seventeenth year. It was an early form of state-education, organised and paid for by Alexander as King of Asia, and the lessons in Greek and the military training were given in a standard form of building, known as the 'Gymnasion' (excavated for instance at Priene). Manuals for the teaching of Greek as a foreign language and for the study of Greek literature and philosophy have been found in Egypt. Thus Alexander was laying the foundations of what has been called 'Hellenisation'. But it was in a Macedonian form; for training in hunting, horsemanship and the pikeman-phalanx was included, and the graduates were sufficiently skilled to enter the King's Forces. We gain some idea of the numbers from a statement that '6,000 King's Boys on the order of Alexander the Macedonian were practising thoroughly the arts of war in Egypt'. The intake was at least 1,500 a year. 'The order of Alexander' was no doubt given by him in Egypt early in 331, and the place of education was to be Alexandria.

Politically the model for the cities in Asia was the Macedonian city and not the Greek city-state. For although the liberated Greek cities passed decrees as if they were free democracies with their own magistrates, council and assembly, and although they dealt directly with the king and not with his satrap, they had to accept the foreign policy and the orders of the King of Asia. This loss of sovereignty was offset by certain advantages: they were exempt from tribute, had no expenses for defence, provided no troops to the King's Forces, and devoted their energies to economic progress. Violent party-strife (*stasis*) was banned. Respect had to be shown for the law, as in the rules governing the Common Peace. The cities south of Magarsus and Mallus were like those founded by Philip in Thrace, in that they had a mixed population and were in direct contact with the king.

The organisation of a mixed city is best known to us at Alexandria. The city was divided into wards, called 'demes'. The citizens were the Greek-speakers of two origins: soldiers drafted by Alexander, and Greek settlers. The former alone carried arms, maintained law and order, and had a deme-membership. The citizens of both grades conducted the administration with an Assembly, Council and Magistrates. The Egyptians were subject to the laws of the city; but they retained their own customs, practised their own religion and were subject to Egyptian law, administered by Egyptian judges. They had no say in the administration of the city. But if they should learn Greek and become 'Hellenised', as the 6,000 King's Boys were to do, they could be admitted to the citizen class. Thus the boundary between citizen and non-citizen was not as rigid as it was in a Greek city-state.

Alexander's arrangements for the administration of Egypt were as follows. A Macedonian admiral with a fleet of thirty triremes, two Macedonian generals in command of 4,000 troops, and commanders of garrisons at Pelusium and Memphis were each answerable directly to Alexander. Their soldiers, mainly Greek mercenaries, were under strict control and regular inspection. Alexander appointed two Egyptians to conduct the administration, including the taxation, of Upper Egypt and Lower Egypt according to the traditional system. All revenues were sent to Alexander's finance officer, a Greek called Cleomenes. The frontier areas – 'Arabia' (Suez) and 'Libya' (adjoining the western desert) – were administered each by a Greek with civil powers. These administrators were all answerable directly to Alexander. Throughout the country the daily life of the Egyptians was regulated only by their own civil governors, and they were free to live in accordance with their own traditions.

Although Alexander was not affected by Egyptian religion, he led his select force from Alexandria via Mersa Matruh to the shrine of Zeus Ammon in the oasis of Siwah. The gods favoured the journey by sending rain and then two crows to guide them, when they lost the way in dust-storms. Alexander wished to emulate his ancestors Perseus and Heracles, who had visited the shrine. He was greeted by the priest as 'Son of Ra', that is as the reigning Pharaoh (this was translated as 'Son of Zeus'). Alexander entered the shrine alone. The utterances of the god were not divulged. Such was the gist of the official account, written by Callisthenes and approved by Alexander. Moreover, in a *Letter* to Olympias Alexander wrote that he had received 'secret prophecies' from the god, which he would tell her, and her only, on his return to Macedonia. There was of course speculation by others. Ptolemy and Aristobulus thought 'he was trying to some extent to trace his birth to Ammon', and they reported Alexander as saying that he had heard 'what was to his liking'. Other writers, led by Cleitarchus, invented questions and answers to delight their readers.

To Alexander Zeus Ammon was a Greek god, who had a shrine at Aphytis in Chalcidice and was revered at Dodona. Alexander's faith was such that he believed those 'secret prophecies' would come true. One of them had probably proved correct on the occasion when on beginning the voyage down the Hydaspes Alexander sacrificed to Ammon. Later, in the estuary of the Indus, Alexander sacrificed to the gods, to whom, he said, he had been ordered by Ammon to sacrifice. It seems likely that one of Ammon's prophecies was concerned with Alexander reaching the bounds of Asia. Whatever the priest of Ammon really said, the belief which developed in the rank and file of the Macedonians was that Alexander had been encouraged to regard Ammon as his father and that in the end Alexander came to think so. While he was still in Egypt, it was reported that Apollo of Didyma, whose oracle had been silent since the conquest by Persia, had declared Alexander to be 'born of Zeus', and that the Sibyl at Erythrae had spoken of 'his exalted birth' (*eugeneia*). These reports were published by Callisthenes with the approval of Alexander. It is not a necessary conclusion that Alexander believed himself to be 'born of Zeus'. For he may have encouraged the idea for propaganda purposes.

For some four months in Egypt the army enjoyed a respite from combat. It was not idle but engaged in building the city of Alexandria, undertaking expeditions and regular training. One expedition was up the Nile. Alexander himself had a 'longing' (*cupido*) to go into Aethiopia 'almost beyond the limits of the sun', but he was represented by Callisthenes, who reported that the flooding of the Nile was due to enormous rainfall. This satisfied Aristotle. The expedition was halted by 'the blazing zone of parched sky'. The strength of the King's Forces had been maintained by reinforcements of 300 cavalry and 3,000 infantry from Macedonia which had arrived in 333. From Gaza Alexander sent an officer in late 332 to Macedonia 'to enlist young men suitable for campaigning'. A year was to pass before these young men reached Alexander near Susa. He had received 350 Greek cavalry in 333, but he relied mainly on recruiting Greek mercenaries, 3,300 who had been in Persian service and 4,400 from Greece. He was joined at Memphis by 500 Thracian cavalry.

As spring approached, Alexander held a festival in honour of Zeus the King, which corresponded to the Xandica at home. The army under arms paraded in the procession, contests in athletics and in the arts were held, and sacrifices were made on a lavish scale. The Nile at Memphis and the canals had been bridged for the departure of the army. The fleet and the army set out at the beginning of spring and they met again at Tyre.

2. The campaign and the battle of Gaugamela

Tyre had been refounded with a Phoenician population, and it was securely held by a Macedonian commander who was in charge of the region. Alexander had planned in advance a splendid festival with sacrifices to Heracles, athletic contests and competitions in the arts. It was an occasion to celebrate the winning of the sea by Alexander and the Greeks. The kings of Cyprus equipped and trained the choruses for the plays, actors came from Athens, and the judges of the dramatic competition were the leading Macedonian generals. When an actor to whom Alexander was devoted did not obtain first prize, Alexander said he would have given up part of his kingdom to have it otherwise, but nevertheless he accepted the verdict. He was deeply moved by the music

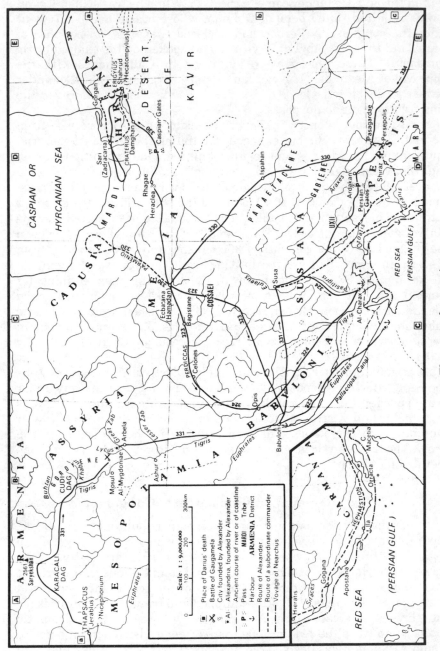

12. The central satrapies

Scale 1 : 9,000,000

0   100   200   300 km

■ Place of Darius' death
✕ Battle of Gaugamela
● Al. City founded by Alexander
● Al: Alexandria, founded by Alexander
        Ancient course of river or of coastline
MARDI Tribe
ARMENIA District
P: Pass
↓ Harbour
——→ Route of Alexander
- - - → Route of a subordinate commander
- - - - - Voyage of Nearchus

of the lyre; when a favourite player was killed in battle beside him, he dedicated at Delphi a bronze statue of the player with a lyre and a spear in his hands. The state-ship of Athens and probably those of other mainland states came to the festival, both to congratulate the *Hegemon* and to make their requests.

Alexander stayed in Phoenicia and Syria for at least three months. During them the harvests were garnered, and supplies were dumped on the route to two bridges which he was having built at the Euphrates. He made some changes in his administrative service. The satrap of Syria, for instance, was replaced, because he had failed to collect the necessary supplies. The Jews of Samaria rebelled and burnt the Macedonian satrap of that area alive. Alexander executed those responsible, expelled the population and made Samaria a mixed city, like Gerasa. He may have hoped that Darius would bring his army to the far side of the Euphrates for a decisive battle, in which case Alexander's supplies were close at hand. When it became apparent that Darius would fight in Mesopotamia, Alexander decided to advance in late July 331. At about that time Antipater sent off from Macedonia the reinforcements which had been demanded, and Alexander ordered a fleet of Macedonian, Greek, Cyprian and Phoenician warships to sail towards the Peloponnese, where a danger of risings in support of Sparta was reported.

On the far side of the Euphrates a Persian commander, Mazaeus, with 3,000 cavalry, 2,000 Greek mercenaries and other infantry held a defensive position. But on the advance of Alexander he withdrew on the main Persian road down the Euphrates, probably in the hope that Alexander would pursue and run short of supplies. Alexander completed his two bridges, brought his troops and supply-train across, and waited for some days, perhaps misleading Mazaeus about his intentions. Then he marched northeastwards along the Armenian foothills to obtain pasture for his horses, use local supplies and avoid the great heat; for he had to feed some 47,000 men and perhaps 20,000 horses and mules. The two armies were completely out of touch with one another for some six weeks, during which the Macedonians made incursions into Armenia. Alexander was the first to capture some opponents, who revealed that Darius' plan was to hold the Tigris. 'Alexander went in haste towards the Tigris'; he crossed its fast-flowing waters with difficulty at an undefended point, for he was higher up river than Darius had expected. While the army waited for the supply-train, the moon was eclipsed on the evening of 20 September 331. Alexander restored confidence by sacrificing to the deities who caused the eclipse – Moon, Sun and Earth – and Aristander announced that the eclipse portended victory over Persia in the present month. Moving south through fertile country Alexander captured some Persian cavalrymen and learned that Darius was in a prepared position not far off. He halted for four days 'to rest his men', fortified a base camp with a ditch and a palisade, and placed in it his sick and the supply-train.

Alexander's scouts reported that the army of Darius was eleven kilometres away, on the far side of low hills. In order to avoid the heat Alexander set off during the night with his army ready for action, crossed over the hills, and at dawn halted his army on seeing the enemy drawn up for battle some five kilometres away on the plain. He had already discussed his advance with some commanders. Now he consulted all his commanders. The majority advised him to engage at once, but 'Parmenio's advice prevailed': to carry out a thorough reconnaissance. When this was done, Alexander reconvened his commanders, exhorted them to fight 'for the rule of all Asia', and insisted on the importance of obeying orders immediately, precisely and in silence. A camp was made for the baggage-animals which carried such essential supplies as barley for the cavalry mounts. The army took its evening meal, and the units slept in the positions which they would take for battle. Towards midday Alexander started the march into the plain.

Darius had mustered in their ethnic units the finest cavalry of the empire from Cappadocia to Pakistan, and the Sacae from beyond its border. He had armed some units with lances and swords, but most were to fight in their traditional manner with archery, javelins and scimitars. They 'were said', wrote Arrian, to total 40,000. He had fifteen Indian elephants, but he left them in his camp, probably because the Indian horses alone had been trained to act with elephants. His élite infantry consisted of some 6,000 Greek mercenaries and 1,000 Persian Guards. Other infantry supported their cavalry units or formed a general reserve. The lowest estimate of the infantry was 400,000, no doubt an inflated figure. Darius had also a new weapon, 'the scythed chariot' with razor-sharp blades attached to the turning wheels, the chassis and the yoke-pole. He reckoned that a charge by 200 such two-horse and four-horse chariots would break up the phalanx-formation and expose the pikemen to close combat, in which the pike would be more of a hindrance than a help.

Darius was the first to reach his desired battle-ground, a stretch of flat pastureland and ploughland. He cleared three fairways for the scythed chariots, and he laid caltrops (spikes) in some places to maim the enemy's horses. On learning that Alexander had set off from his base camp at night (on 29 September), Darius deployed his army and kept it under arms, in case Alexander should attack at or soon after dawn. The huge army stayed in battle-positions throughout 30 September and the next night and on into 1 October towards midday, whereas the Macedonian army had rested one day and slept one night in camp.

On 1 October Darius was pinned to his prepared ground. The centre of his line consisted from front to rear of 50 scythed chariots; four ethnic units (two of cavalry, two probably of infantry); the Royal Cavalry

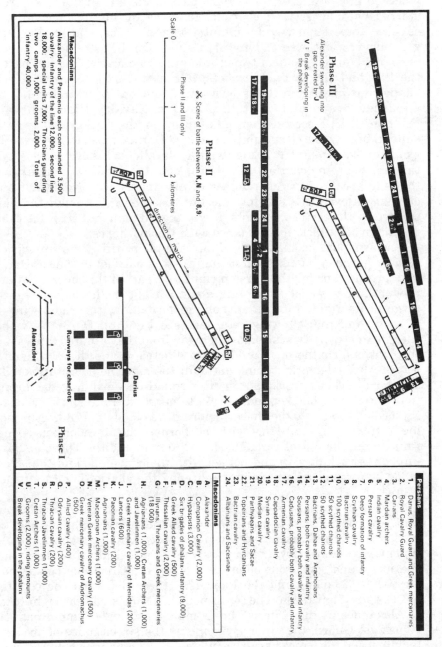

13. The phases of the Battle of Gaugamela

Phase III

Alexander swinging into gap created by **J**

V = Break developing in the phalanx

⚔ Scene of battle between **K,N** and **8,9**.

Phase II and III only

Scale 0   1   2 kilometres

Phase II and III only

Phase II

direction of march →

Runways for chariots

Alexander

Darius

Phase I

Macedonians

Alexander and Parmenio each commanded 3,500 cavalry. Infantry of the line 12,000; second line 18,000; special units 7,000. Thracians guarding two camps 1,000; grooms 2,000. Total of infantry 40,000.

Persians

1. Darius, Royal Guard and Greek mercenaries
2. Royal Cavalry Guard
3. Carians
4. Mardian archers
5. Indian cavalry
6. Persian cavalry
7. Deep formation of infantry
8. Scythian cavalry
9. Bactrian cavalry
10. 100 scythed chariots
11. 50 scythed chariots
12. 50 scythed chariots
13. Bactrians, Dahae and Arachotians
14. Persians, both cavalry and infantry
15. Sousians, probably both cavalry and infantry
16. Cadusians, probably both cavalry and infantry
17. Armenian cavalry
18. Cappadocian cavalry
19. Syrian cavalry
20. Median cavalry
21. Parthyaeans and Sacae
22. Topeirians and Hyrcanians
23. Bactrian cavalry
24. Albanians and Sacesinae

Macedonians

A. Alexander
B. Companion Cavalry (2,000)
C. Hypaspists (3,000)
D. Six brigades of phalanx infantry (9,000)
E. Greek Allied cavalry (500)
F. Thessalian cavalry (2,000)
G. Illyrians, Thracians and Greek mercenaries (18,000)
H. Agrianians (1,000), Cretan Archers (1,000) and Javelinmen (1,000)
I. Greek mercenary cavalry of Menidas (200)
J. Lancers (600)
K. Paeonian cavalry (200)
L. Agrianians (1,000)
M. Macedonian Archers (1,000)
N. Veteran Greek mercenary cavalry (500)
O. Greek mercenary cavalry of Andromachus (500)
P. Allied cavalry (400)
Q. Odrysian cavalry (200)
R. Thracian cavalry (200)
S. Thracian Javelinmen (1,000)
T. Cretan Archers (1,000)
U. Grooms (2,000), riding remounts
V. Break developing in the phalanx

Guard; Darius in his chariot flanked by all the élite infantry; and finally a second line of infantry. The right part of his line in the same order started with 50 scythed chariots, followed by nine ethnic units of cavalry, some supported by infantry of their race, and in the background a part of the second line of infantry. On the extreme right there was an advanced group of two ethnic units of cavalry. The left part of the line had 100 scythed chariots; five ethnic units of cavalry with supporting infantry of their own race; and on the extreme left an advanced group of two ethnic units of cavalry (Bactrians and Scythians). The second line of infantry in the background was in support of only one ethnic unit of cavalry. Darius hoped that Alexander would make a frontal attack with a line parallel to his own, as at Issus; that the charging chariots would break up the infantry phalanx; and that the greatly superior number of his fine cavalry would not only outflank Alexander's shorter line but also charge through the gaps created by the scythed chariots. It was a good plan, but only if Alexander made his attack in accordance with Darius' hopes.

The army of Alexander moved into the plain with perfect precision, as on a parade ground. At first the line was parallel to that of Darius and advanced facing the Persian right and part of the centre, but at a predetermined moment the line made a right incline and advanced towards its right front in an oblique formation, the right wing in advance and the left wing retarded (see Fig. 13). Darius saw that Alexander's army was now moving away from the prepared fairways of the chariots. He therefore ordered the Bactrians and the Scythians to attack Alexander's right flank and halt the movement. But Alexander counter-attacked with squadron after squadron, each in wedge formation, and meanwhile kept advancing to his right front. Darius sent his scythed chariots into the charge before it was too late. But they proved ineffective; for in accordance with their orders the Macedonians opened ranks to let them pass through, the Agrianian and the Thracian 'javelin-men' struck drivers and horses with their javelins, and the troops made a tremendous din which frightened the chariot-horses off their course.

At this point the disposition of Alexander's forces becomes important. In front of and to the flank of his advanced right he had the Agrianians, the Thracian javelin-men, Macedonian archers and 'old-timer Greek mercenary infantry' – some of these dealt with the scythed chariots – and squadrons of cavalry, being the Greek mercenary cavalry, the Paeonians and the Lancers – these delivered the counter-attacks as we have seen. The continuous line consisted from right to left of Alexander at the head of the Companion Cavalry squadrons, the Hypaspist Guard, the other Hypaspists, the six brigades of the phalangites, and the Greek cavalry of which the Thessalians held the wing. On the left there was a flank-guard consisting of Greek mercenary cavalry in front; then some Greek cavalry, the Odrysian cavalry, and the Thracian cavalry; and in support of them Thracian javelin-men and Cretan archers. Behind the main phalanx there marched a second phalanx of the same length, consisting of Greek mercenary infantry, Illyrian infantry and Thracian infantry. This second phalanx was to face about if Persian cavalry should come at it from the rear.

While the scythed chariots were making their attack, Darius ordered a general advance and at the same time sent some Persian cavalry to support the defeated Bactrians and Scythians. Alexander ordered the last unit of his flank-guard, the 600 Lancers, to charge into the Persian cavalry at the point where it was leaving the Persian main line. When the Lancers broke through and created a gap, Alexander turned his line ninety degrees to his left, formed 'a wedge of the Companion Cavalry and the infantry there' (Hypaspists), charged with a resounding battle-cry through the gap, and swung left 'in the direction of Darius himself'. In fierce fighting the long lances of the Companion Cavalry and the bristling pikes of the Hypaspists prevailed, and as they drew near Darius panicked and fled. The impetuous charge of Alexander's wedge had been delivered at the moment when the attacking cavalry of the Persian right was bringing the left part of the Macedonian phalanx to a halt. A gap inevitably arose between that part of the phalanx and the brigades which were advancing in line with Alexander's wedge.

The gap was exploited by Indian and Persian cavalry. But instead of wheeling and attacking, they rode to the camp which was guarded only by a small force of Thracians. Part of the second line of the halted phalanx turned about 'as they had been ordered to do' and defeated the enemy in the camp. But the whole of the left wing, which was under the command of Parmenio, was hard pressed by attacks from all sides. A request for help reached Alexander. Although he must have been tempted to pursue Darius, now in flight, Alexander turned the squadrons of Companion Cavalry to his left and fought his way through the cavalry of the Persian right centre which met him head on in formation. Sixty Companions fell. 'But Alexander overcame these enemies also.' He was about to attack the cavalry of the extreme right, when it broke and fled under the brilliant charges of the Thessalian squadrons. The whole of the huge army was now in flight.

Alexander and the Companions led the pursuit, and they were followed by the troops of Parmenio. The aim was to break the morale of the enemy cavalry. When light failed, Alexander camped until midnight. Meanwhile Parmenio captured the Persian camp. Thereafter Alexander carried the pursuit to Arbela, where he captured the treasure and the possessions of Darius. The pursuit over 110 kilometres cost the lives of 100 men and 1,000 horses, but the casualties of the enemy ensured that Darius would never again raise an imperial army. At Arbela Alexander made sacrifices of thanksgiving to the gods and distributed rewards. He was acclaimed 'King of Asia' by the Macedonians, who in the flush of victory undertook to win all Asia for their king. He himself proclaimed his triumph in a dedication to Athena of Lindus in Rhodes in his own words: 'King Alexander, having mastered Darius in battle and having become Lord of Asia, made sacrifice to Athena of Lindus in accordance with an oracle.' He saw the defeat of Persia as a preliminary to the winning of all Asia.

CHAPTER X

The advance to Persepolis and the situation in Greece

1. Babylon, Susa and military reorganisation

It is important to realise that Gaugamela was the victory of the Greeks as well as of the Macedonians. During the slow advance into the plain Alexander addressed the Greeks on his left wing. Raising his right hand in appeal to the gods he prayed, as Callisthenes says: 'If in truth I am descended from Zeus (*Diothen gegonos*), guard and strengthen the Greeks.' He was referring to the oracles which Callisthenes had made known from two Greek cities that he was 'a son of Zeus' and 'of exalted birth' (above, p. 103). He was addressing Greeks, not Macedonians, and he was also addressing his own faith – which must have seemed later to be justified by the victory. He now reported to 'The Greeks' (of the Common Peace) that liberation (from Persia) was complete and the liberated cities were autonomous; and he paid special tributes to Plataea and Croton for their part in the Great Persian Wars. His attention to the Greeks was timely, because he knew that there was a danger of a rising in the Peloponnese (above, p. 105). But communication was slow. It took perhaps two months for a courier, and three months or more for troops to proceed from Pella to Susa. Thus the first news of a double rising, in Thrace and in the Peloponnese, was not to reach Alexander until late November or early December 331.

The firstfruit of victory was Babylonia, the wealthiest satrapy in the Persian empire. The satrap, Mazaeus, who had commanded the Persian right wing at Gaugamela and had fought with distinction, came to meet Alexander and surrendered the city of Babylon to him. As Alexander approached at the head of the army, the priests and the people welcomed him, bearing gifts and covering his path with flowers. For the Babylonians it was the end of two hundred years of Persian occupation, during which their temples had been violated for instance by Xerxes. Alexander acted as he had done in Egypt. He sacrificed under the direction of the priests to their supreme god, Belus (Ba'al), carried out their recommendations in regard to the temples in Babylon, and ordered the people to repair the damage done by Xerxes. He was accepted by the Babylonians as a liberator and as a king approved by Belus.

In his arrangements for the administration of Babylonia Alexander made different officers responsible for military, financial and civil duties. At the outset Apollodorus commanded 700 Macedonians and perhaps 1,300 Greek mercenaries, and Asclepiodorus was in charge of the collection of tribute. As civil governor, 'satrap', Alexander appointed the Persian holder of the office, Mazaeus. This must have astounded the Macedonians; for they were at war with Persia. It was as if King George VI had appointed Rommel after the Battle of El Alamein to be his Viceroy in India. What was the motive of Alexander? He had always honoured any Persians who of their own volition joined his service – and he had made a point of this in correspondence with Darius – and he had treated them 'in a manner worthy of their rank', which implied that they were Persians of some distinction. A case in point was Mithrenes, who had surrendered Sardis (above, p. 72). Now Alexander appointed him satrap of Armenia, thus indicating that Mazaeus was not exceptional. This policy led to the peaceful taking of Susa; for on his march towards Susa, he was met by a son of the Persian satrap of Susiane, Abulites, offering surrender. That was no small gain; for at Susa Alexander took over treasure worth 50,000 talents of silver. Alexander continued Abulites in his position as satrap. For their part Mazaeus, Mithrenes and Abulites must have accepted the rule of Alexander as King of Asia. At this time too the captured women of the Persian royal family were still being treated as royalty. We shall consider the significance of this later (below, p. 116).

While the army was recuperating for a month in winter quarters near Babylon, Alexander distributed a bounty of 600 drachmae a head to Macedonian cavalrymen, 500 to Greek cavalrymen, 200 to Macedonian infantrymen, two months' pay to Greek mercenaries, and analogous payments to Balkan cavalrymen and to Greek and Balkan infantrymen. When he led the army on the long march towards Susa, he met Amyntas with the reinforcements which he expected (above, p. 105). These numbered 500 Macedonian cavalry, 6,000 Macedonian infantry, 600 Thracian cavalry, 3,500 Thracian infantry, and 'from the Peloponnese' 380 Greek mercenary cavalry and 4,000 Greek mercenary infantry. The total of some 15,000 men may be compared with those who crossed the Hellespont in 334, some 37,000 men.

The number of Macedonian infantry is of particular interest. Philip's vanguard in Asia included at the most 3,000 such infantry in two brigades; Alexander entered Asia with 12,000; and he received 3,000 at Gordium. With the new 6,000 he was able to fill his complement of 12,000 (in three Hypaspist brigades and six phalanx-brigades) and add a new phalanx brigade of 1,500 men. Thus the loss from front-line service was 4,500. Those killed in battle were in hundreds rather than thousands. A large part of the 4,500 were stationed in the new cities from Aegae to Alexandria. Occasionally active Macedonians were placed in a garrison, but when danger passed they were recalled to active service. On receiving his last reinforcement Alexander was able to place 1,000 over-age Macedonians (*aetate graves*) as a garrison of the citadel of Susa. The corresponding figures for Companion Cavalrymen, if we assume that there was one squadron in Philip's vanguard, are 200, 1,800, 300 and 500, totalling 2,800. Here the loss from front-line service was 1,000 or so.

Had Alexander taken too many men from Macedonia? He must have asked himself that question when news reached him at Susa that Agis, king of Sparta, with his own army and some 10,000 mercenaries hired with Persian gold, had defeated a Macedonian force in the Peloponnese and had then gained the support of Elis and of most of Arcadia and Achaea. There had also been a rising in Thrace, for which the General in Thrace, Memnon, was held responsible, but Antipater, mustering all his forces, had overawed him and made an agreement. All Alexander could do at Susa in December 331 was to send off 3,000 talents which would not reach Antipater until late February at the earliest; and to let the Athenians know that he was sending them the statues of Harmodius and Aristogeiton which Xerxes had removed. Antipater had probably been able to maintain the army of 12,000 phalangites and 1,500 cavalry which Alexander had left him in 334. For Alexander had taken for reinforcements not any of Antipater's troops but specifically 'young men', i.e. from the militia.

At Susa Alexander held a traditional festival with a sacrifice, a torch-race and athletic events for his Macedonians. He left the mother of Darius, his daughters and his son at Susa and appointed teachers to instruct them in the Greek language. They were still being treated as royalty in the Persian capital. The fighting which lay ahead in Persis and Media would take the form of mountain warfare rather than of set battle. With this in mind, and with the transfer of 1,000 older Macedonians to garrison duty, Alexander made promotions of men who distinguished themselves in tests of courage, and he formed new units which were alternatives, not substitutes for the traditional units: namely Companion Cavalry companies of 75 to 100 troopers, and eight Infantry Commandoes of 1,000 men each (but not taken from the Royal Guard and the Hypaspists). They were trained in the use of the appropriate weapons and tactics for mountain warfare. The Commandoes were first deployed against the Uxii, to the southeast of Susa, with such devastating effect that the Persian commander, Medates, capitulated and was pardoned, and the Uxii submitted and thereafter paid as tribute 600 horses and mules and 30,000 cattle, goats and sheep a year. In the reorganisation of the cavalry it seems that the Paeonian and the Thracian squadrons, originally of 150 men each, were disbanded, and the men were allocated to the Lancers; for these light-armed units must have had heavy losses in the Battle of Gaugamela.

Together with the reinforcements Antipater sent to Alexander 'fifty grown-up sons of Alexander's Friends to act as his bodyguards'. These were one intake of Royal Pages (above, p. 5). They were now to spend their last year under instruction from Callisthenes and other philosophers at court and were to be in close attendance on the king; and Alexander probably let it be known that their successors each year would come likewise to his court. To Macedonians this made an important issue more acute. Where was the centre of their society to be? At Pella or at a moving court in Asia? There was already a dichotomy, in that Alexander was 'King of Macedonians' and 'King of Asia'; and in addition his position as King of Macedonians was fragmented in that his deputy acted in Macedonia as Head of State and he acted as Head of State wherever he happened to be in Asia. The transfer of Royal Pages to Asia must have seemed to tip the balance; for on graduation these ex-Pages and their successors each year were to start their career not in Macedonia but in Asia. Why did Alexander make the transfer? Presumably he felt the need to strengthen his constitutional position in Asia as King of Macedonians and to exert his influence on those who would be leading men later in his reign. But he endangered the close relations he had at the time with the Macedonians in Asia and especially with the Friends and Companions.

2. Persepolis and the future of Persia

The direct route to Persepolis was blocked by a very large Persian force, which held 'the Persian Gates', a narrow defile ten kilometres long between high mountains. A frontal attack failed with some casualties. Alexander withdrew his force which consisted of the Companion Cavalry, the Lancers, the majority of the Macedonian infantry, the Agrianians and the Archers – in fact the élite of the army – and mounted a most daring night operation. Craterus held the camp with a small force and bluffed the enemy by keeping many camp-fires alight. Alexander took the main body through forested country on a circuitous route. Around midnight he divided it into two parts: one consisting of most of the cavalry and part of the infantry was to bridge the river Araxes (Pulvar) between the Persian position and Persepolis, and the rest under Alexander's command was to reach the Persian position before dawn. Everything depended on surprise. Alexander captured or dispersed three Persian guardposts, fell unobserved on the Persian camp, and summoned by bugle the force under Craterus which, as prearranged, delivered a frontal attack. The Persian force in complete disarray was shattered between the hammer and the anvil. A race to Persepolis between Alexander's Companion Cavalry and the survivors of the Persian force was won by Alexander, who entered the city at the head of his men and took over the citadel and the treasury intact. The whole

1. (a) Gold medallions of Olympias and Philip

1. (b) Ivory heads of Olympias (left) and Alexander

2. Fresco of a Royal Hunt

3. (a) Phalanx of pikemen

3. (b) Alexander in action

4. (a) Silver oenochoe with the head of a Silenus

4. (b) Head of a young Heracles on a silver amphora

5. (a) Gold larnax

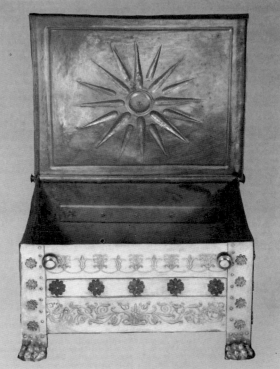

5. (b) Gold wreath

6. (a) Mosaic of a lion hunt

6. (b) Mosaic of Dionysus riding on a panther

7. The right-hand half of the Boscoreale fresco

8. (a) Satellite photograph of the Pelium area

8. (b) The plain beside Pelium

9. Alexander in action

10. Satellite photograph of Cilicia

11. The family of Darius before Alexander

12. The Alexander Mosaic

13. The Porus medallion (left) and the Indian archer

14. The Derveni crater

15. A young Alexander riding Bucephalus

16. A mature Alexander, somewhat idealised

operation was brilliant, and the prize was the heart of the Persian Empire, the capital of Darius I and Xerxes.

On arriving at Persepolis in January 330 with his Macedonians (for the main army and the baggage-train, using a slower route, were still on the way) Alexander sent a force to capture the treasury at Pasargadae, the early capital; appointed a Persian to be satrap of Persis; and convened a group of Friends and Commanders to discuss what course he should pursue at Persepolis. Arrian, following the accounts of Ptolemy and Aristobulus, reported a difference of opinion between Alexander and his leading Friend, Parmenio. Alexander proposed to burn the Palace of Darius and Xerxes in retaliation for their acts of sacrilege against the Greek gods (the same motive was mentioned by Strabo). It is obvious that such a burning would be a striking demonstration that 'The Greeks' had triumphed. When the news would reach Greece, in March 330, it would encourage the loyal Greek states to hold firm against Sparta and the rebels in the Peloponnese. Parmenio opposed the proposal. He thought it would alienate the Persians, who would regard the Macedonians merely as conquerors and ravagers.

Alexander put his proposal into effect. Having removed the treasure, he rewarded the Macedonians for their hard fighting by letting them loot the Palace, the Throne Room and the Treasury, and he then fired the Palace which was reduced to a heap of burnt mud-brick and debris. Excavation has revealed two facts: the looting was so hurried that many small objects of gold and of precious stone were left on the floors, and the firing was so immediate that these objects were not retrieved but buried under the burnt debris. When the Greek troops arrived, the deed had been done. But Cleitarchus invented a sensational story to delight the Greeks, that at a drunken party an Athenian prostitute, called Thaïs, proposed the burning and applied the torch, followed by an inebriated Alexander. The excavation has shown beyond doubt that the burning was not a random, unpremeditated act.

The main army rested for some four months at Persepolis (the city not being affected by the burning of the Palace), but in March Alexander led a select force into the mountains south of Persepolis, where he subjugated the Mardi and other tribes in Arctic conditions. The campaign lasted for a month, with Alexander often in the lead. He continued in office the Persian strap of Carmania, who accepted his authority after the expedition against the Mardi.

In May, when he led his army northwards, he left a garrison of only 3,000 Macedonians at Persepolis. He was evidently confident that the Persians would not rise and create a second front, while Darius had an army in Media which Alexander was now entering. The reasons for that confidence deserve consideration. From the fall of Sardis onwards Alexander had welcomed into his entourage any Persian satraps and governors who surrendered and accepted his regime. They and their retinue were given the status they had had under Persian rule, whether as cavalrymen or courtiers or administrators. In 332, when the wife of Darius died, Alexander gave her a lavish funeral with Persian rites, which were conducted by the leading Persians of his court. Alexander's relations with Darius' mother, Sisigambis, were particularly respectful – indeed he was said to have treated the Uxii leniently at her request. When he accorded royal status to Darius' family, whether on the campaign or at Susa, he was treating it as the royal house of Persia; and in arranging for the education of Darius' eight-year-old son, Ochus, at Susa he was regarding him as the heir presumptive to the throne of Persia. And the tomb of Persia's national hero, Cyrus the Great, at Pasargadae was restored on the order of Alexander.

These actions showed that Alexander did not intend to disestablish the royal family and the leading statesmen of Persia. His appointment of Persians as satraps of the defeated areas, Susiane and Persis, showed that Persia was to be a self-governing state within Alexander's Kingdom of Asia, no less than Egypt and Babylon. More remarkable still was his appointment of Persians as satraps of Babylonia, Armenia and Carmania on their liberation from Persian rule. For this could only mean that he intended that Persians should participate in the administration of his Kingdom. Moreover, he chose to implement this policy when Darius was still at war and in command of an army in Media.

Alexander's policy is to be contrasted with that of Rome after the defeat of Macedonia at the Battle of Pydna, which may be summarised as ruthless plundering, partition and impoverishment, the parading of the royal family in chains in Rome, and the lingering death of Perseus in prison. The only precedent in past history for an enlightened policy towards a defeated state or states was that of Philip after the Battle of Chaeronea. Subsequent history, whether in Europe or Asia, provides no analogy.

3. The situation in Greece

While Alexander wintered at Persepolis, he learned that only Arcadia and Elis had defected from the Greek Community, and that their forces under Sparta's command had not advanced into Central Greece but were laying siege to Megalopolis in Arcadia. In the attitude of the Greek Community the decision of Athens was of crucial importance. If she stayed loyal to the Common Peace, she would be able with her fleet to reinforce the thalassocracy of Macedonia in the Aegean Sea, and with her army to enfilade any army advancing from the Isthmus into Central Greece, where Sparta could rely on support from some states. On the other hand, if she joined Sparta, by manning 200 warships and providing vessels for any naval allies she could challenge the Macedonian fleet, as she was to do after the death of Alexander, and her army could join the Spartan coalition and invade Macedonia. In the Assembly Aeschines and Demades advocated loyalty. Demosthenes wished to join Sparta and bring out the fleet. Had he had his way, Alexander might have been compelled to halt his advance in Persia and send reinforcements from his army to Macedonia. However, the Assembly decided to take no action, as Alexander had foreseen; for 'he had favoured Athens beyond all other Greek states'. Once Athens' decision was known to Antipater, he could assure Alexander that, in view of the huge subsidy which had reached him, it was only a matter of collecting sufficient forces to crush Sparta and her allies. That assurance may have reached Alexander at Persepolis and encouraged him to advance into Media in May.

Although it was not known to Alexander at the time, Antipater marched unopposed into the Peloponnese in late April or in May. His army, reported as 40,000 strong, consisted of at least 1,500 Macedonian cavalry and 12,000 Macedonian infantry, the contingents of those states which actively supported the Common Peace (but none from Athens), Balkan troops and perhaps some mercenaries. Agis, king of Sparta, commanded 2,000 cavalry, 20,000 citizen hoplites and 10,000 Greek mercenaries, hired with Persian gold. The decisive battle was fought near Megalopolis. In one account the losses of Sparta and her allies were 5,300 and of Antipater more than 1,000 with very many wounded. Macedonia's losses were said to have excited the comment of Alexander that it had been 'a battle of rats'; for his battles had cost few Macedonian lives. But Antipater had calculated well. His enemies capitulated without terms. Would they be enslaved as Thebes had been enslaved in 335? Having commanded the joint forces as the deputy-*Hegemon* of 'The Greeks', Antipater asked 'the Common Council of the Greeks' to decide on the terms. He was acting as Alexander had done in 335. The Council imposed on Arcadia and Elis an indemnity of 120 talents, which was to be paid to Megalopolis, and arrested their leaders for violating the charter of the Common Peace. No doubt they were put on trial later. It is a sign of the Council's independence that it granted such moderate terms without waiting for the opinion of the *Hegemon*.

Sparta had not been a member of the Common Peace. She had consistently opposed Macedonia, and on this occasion she had tried to create a coalition under her own leadership on the lines of what we call the Peloponnesian League. The Council of the Common Peace was therefore correct in referring the decision on Sparta's fate to Macedonia. Antipater had already taken fifty leading Spartans as hostages, and now in summer 330 he sent them and a Spartan delegation to Alexander. It would be a matter of four months before Alexander's decision would be known in Greece. Meanwhile at Athens the Assembly elected Phocion general and passed proposals by Demades, which both implied acceptance of the Common Peace and of the alliance with Macedonia.

But two verdicts in the Law Courts showed that the People hankered after the days of unlimited sovereignty, which entailed withdrawal from the Greek Community. When Lycurgus prosecuted Leocrates for having left Athens after the defeat at Chaeronea and demanded the death sentence, the votes of the jury were equally divided. Probably in August Aeschines revived the prosecution of Ctesiphon, who had proposed early in 336 to crown Demosthenes for his services to Athens but had been accused of illegal procedure. Aeschines tried now to take advantage of the current situation. 'In a few days,' he said, 'the Council of the Greeks will meet ... and if you crown Demosthenes it will be seen that you are of the same mind as those who are violating the Common Peace.' But Demosthenes in his speech 'On the Crown' defended his entire political career. Aeschines failed to obtain even a fifth of the jury's votes and left Athens, never to return.

It was probably soon after the trial that the forces of the Greek Community which had defeated Persia came home and boasted of their victories and of the generous pay and bounty which they had received from Alexander. They also publicised the opportunities for Greeks to develop trade and to settle in the cities founded by Alexander. The gulf which had existed between the homeland and what Aeschines called 'the ends of the world' was closed. The returning warriors are likely to have strengthened support for the Greek Community in their individual states. Alexander could be confident that the Council of the Greek Community would control the situation on the mainland of Greece in the coming years.

CHAPTER XI

The death of Darius and the decision to advance to the east

1. The advance to Ecbatana and the pursuit of Darius

For seven months Darius had been undisturbed in Media, which was a considerable part of the Persian homeland, and he had been in contact with his subjects from eastern Armenia to Bactria. Yet he failed to raise an army comparable to that which had fought at Gaugamela, partly because defeat had undermined his authority, and partly because Alexander's liberal policy, for instance in Babylonia and in Persis, offered an acceptable alternative to Persian domination. Alexander, however, was unaware of that failure, when he advanced in May from Persis with his entire army. Opposition in Paraetacene was overcome, and a Persian was installed as satrap. When he was twelve days' march from the border of Media, a report reached him that Darius had decided to stand and fight, his army being reinforced by Scythian and Cadusian allies. Alexander advanced in readiness for battle, while the wagons of the baggage and supply trains were to follow with their guards. But the report proved false. Darius' allies had not arrived, and he was withdrawing from Media. 'Alexander advanced all the more rapidly' towards the capital city, Ecbatana (Hamadan). He was met on the way by Bisthanes, a son of Artaxerxes Ochus (the predecessor of Darius on the Persian throne). His submission was an indication that the Persian aristocrats were accepting the rule of Alexander as King of Asia. Moreover, he reported that Darius had fled with 7,000 talents and an army of only 3,000 cavalry and 6,000 infantry.

Alexander knew now that he did not need his entire army for a set battle in the near future. On entering Ecbatana, the last of the three Persian capitals, Alexander as *Hegemon* brought to an end the war of the Greek Community against Persia; for the Greek forces had attained their objectives – the liberation of the Greek cities in Asia and the taking of revenge on Persia (above, p. 64) – and had no interest in winning the Kingdom of Asia for Alexander. In addition to full pay until they should reach Euboea in Greece, being conveyed from Cilicia by trireme, each cavalryman received a bounty of one talent and each infantryman one sixth of a talent. Alexander gave presents to all of them, and they were escorted on their way to the coast. Cavalrymen who volunteered to serve in the Macedonian forces received a donative. The total outlay was said to be 12,000 talents. The gap in his forces may have been partly met by the hiring of 6,000 mercenaries, who had come from the Aegean area via Cilicia under the command of an Athenian mercenary general.

Alexander moved his base of operations from Persepolis to Ecbatana. The palace there was not destroyed, but much of the silver tiles and of the gold and silver plating of the woodwork was looted by 'Alexander and his Macedonians'. Harpalus was to be the financial officer in charge of the accumulated treasure, which was said to amount to 180,000 talents and would be stored in the citadel. The garrison was to be 6,000 Macedonians (3,000 of these coming on from Persepolis), and at first Parmenio was to be in command. Alexander planned three operations. A force of Thracians, mercenaries and light-armed cavalry under Parmenio's command was to campaign in Cadusia and Hyrcania. At a later date the 6,000 Macedonians were to follow the Persian road into Parthyaea, where they were to meet Alexander. This force was to be under the command of Cleitus, who had been left sick at Susa and was to come to Ecbatana. Alexander set off at once in pursuit of Darius. He took the Companion Cavalry, the Scouts, the mercenary cavalry, the Hypaspists, the rest of the phalangites, the Archers and the Agrianians.

Alexander set off at such a pace that infantrymen collapsed and horses died of exhaustion during the first ten days. He had hoped to catch Darius west of the Caspian Gates (the defiles of Sialek and Sardar), but Darius kept ahead and entered the Gates. Alexander stopped short at Rhagae (near Teheran), where his troops rested for five days. He appointed as satrap of Media a Persian, Oxydates, who had been imprisoned at Susa by Darius and liberated by the Macedonians. From Rhagae he passed through the Gates and paused in Choarene at the edge of the desert. There Bagistanes, a distinguished Babylonian, and Antibelus, a son of Mazaeus, came from the camp of Darius to report that Darius had been arrested – in other words deposed – by three leading Persians (Nabarzanes, Bessus and Barsaentes). It might have been thought that Darius was no longer of any significance and that the three Persians were the enemy and could be pursued at leisure (as was the case months later). But Alexander made a superhuman effort to get possession of Darius.

Taking the Companion Cavalry, the Scouts and the fittest infantrymen, lightly armed, and rations for two days, he travelled at speed all night and next day till noon, and again that evening until next day, when he came to an abandoned camp and learnt that the enemy had split into two groups – Artabazus with his sons and the Greek mercenaries taking to the hills, and Bessus in command of the remainder, including Darius under arrest. 'Already his men and his horses were exhausted by the continuous hardship, but he led them on, covering a great distance that night and next day till noon.' He was now in the camp which Bessus had occupied the preceding night, and he learned from the villagers that there was a short cut ahead through waterless country. He selected the 500 fittest men, mounted them on cavalry horses, and had them take their infantry weapons. The rest were to follow the route taken by Bessus. At the head of his select force Alexander covered 74 kilometres that night, and at dawn he came upon the enemy marching without weapons. Only a few resisted his attack. Bessus and his party tried to escape with Darius in a closed wagon, but when Alexander was in pursuit Satibarzanes and Barsaentes drove their spears into Darius and fled with 600 cavalry. Darius was dead when Alexander reached the wagon, on a July day in 330.

This account by Arrian, following Aristobulus and Ptolemy, is far preferable to those of other writers; for Ptolemy drew on the day-to-day record of Alexander's doings in the *Journal*. Why did Alexander make this supreme effort to capture Darius alive? The probable answer is that he wished Darius and his family to continue as the royal house ruling over the Medes and the Persians but within the authority of Alexander as King of Asia. Darius was said to have had great personal charm, and he could have been accepted by the Persian nobles of Alexander's entourage. No other explanation has been put forward. As it was, Alexander did everything possible to conciliate Persian opinion. Darius was accorded a royal burial at Persepolis. The obsequies were conducted by Sisigambis, and Alexander mourned his death. Moreover, Sisigambis and her family continued to be treated by Alexander as the royal house of the Medes and the Persians. For Alexander never laid claim to their throne: 'He did not proclaim himself King of Kings.' His Kingdom was 'the whole of Asia'.

2. Alexander's concept of 'Asia' and the preliminaries to the advance eastwards

Alexander derived his concept of 'Asia' from the teaching of Aristotle, for whom 'the inhabited earth' was surrounded by 'the Great Sea', Ocean, and was divided into three areas – 'Europe, Libya and Asia'. Thus the earth was not round but flat, and 'Asia' was limited on the west by the Tanais (Don), the inland sea and the Nile, and on the east by 'India' and 'the Great Sea' (see Fig. 15). The basis of Aristotle's knowledge and his idea of scale are apparent from the following passage:

> To judge from what is known from journeys by sea and land, the length [of the inhabited earth] is much greater than the width; indeed the

distance from the pillars of Heracles [at Cadiz] to India exceeds that from
Aethiopia [Sudan] to Lake Maeotis [Sea of Azov] and the farthest part of
Scythia in the proportion of more than five to three (Aristotle, *Meteorologica* 362b19-23).

When Aristotle wrote this passage, he may have benefited from
Alexander's early journeys by land, especially from the expedition to
Aethiopia (above, p. 103); for the surveyors (*bematistai*) and scientists
whom Alexander took into Asia sent reports on distance, climate, flora,
fauna and human and animal oecology to the School of Aristotle in
Athens. However, Aristotle did not yet know that he was mistaken in
supposing that from the ridge of the Parapamisus (Hindu Kush) one
would see 'the outer sea' and that 'India' was a small peninsula running
east into that sea. We may therefore date the passage which I have
quoted to a time before Alexander's invasion of the Indus valley. Thus
it gives a fair picture of Alexander's beliefs in July 330, when he had to
decide whether to accept Parthyaea as his eastern frontier or to conquer
the rest of 'Asia'.

By July 330 Alexander knew that Antipater had defeated Sparta and
confirmed the authority of the Council of the Greek Community on the
Greek mainland, and that the Macedonian thalassocracy in the Eastern
Mediterranean and the Black Sea was unchallenged. His rule as King
of Asia had been accepted in Egypt and western Asia, and his policy of
cooperation with the ruling class in Persis and Media seemed to be
succeeding. His Macedonian forces were available for further conquest;
for they were not required to serve as 'armies of occupation' or as
garrisons in support of imposed governments, either in Europe or in
Asia. Thus as Alexander looked back at what had been achieved in four
years in Asia, there was nothing to deter him from the feeling that his
hands were free for further adventure.

Practical considerations were not the only factors in Alexander's
thinking. At the outset he had accepted the gods' gift of Asia to be won
by the spear (above, p. 64), and his advance had been marked by
expressions of the gods' favour at Sardis, Gordium, Erythrae, Didyma,
Siwah and Gaugamela. Thus his faith required him to become 'Lord of
Asia', as he had foretold in the dedication which he had made at Lindus
in Rhodes (above, p. 110), and he had no doubt that with the continuing
favour of the gods he would succeed in whatever lay ahead in 'Asia'. It
was this conviction which was to carry him through several crises in the
years ahead.

The willing cooperation of the Macedonians was the first requirement for his plans to succeed. In the flush of victory at Gaugamela they
had elected him 'King of Asia', and he intended to keep them to their
word. When the Greek troops returned home from near Ecbatana, the
Macedonians may have entertained hopes of homecoming for them-

selves. Certainly those hopes came to a head when the pursuit of Darius ended and the Macedonians with Alexander – 2,000 Companion Cavalrymen, 3,000 Hypaspists and 2,000 phalangites – rested near Hecatompylus in Parthyaea. But Alexander addressed them in an Assembly. A summary of his arguments was given in a *Letter* to Antipater which was read by Plutarch (*Alex.* 47.1-3). To go home would be to abandon Asia to confusion, and to expose themselves to counter-attack by the Asians. Let any who wished desert their king now, when he was winning the inhabited world for his country, and he would go ahead with his friends and a force of volunteers. The response was immediate: let him lead them to anywhere in the inhabited earth that he desired.

The replacement of the troops of the Greek Community was another requirement. The 2,000 or more cavalry and in particular the Thessalians had a superb record. Alexander could not have won his three set battles without them. The 7,000 infantry, together with the cavalry, had carried out important operations under the command of Parmenio, for instance in the Anatolian plateau and on the coast from Tarsus to the Pillar of Jonah. Because they had served as garrison-troops and support-troops, all the Macedonians had been able to fight in the first line. As usual, Alexander had foreseen the need to provide replacements for these Greek troops by training young Asians in Lydia, Lycia, Syria and Egypt. In autumn 330 he was joined by 300 Lydian cavalry and 2,600 Lydian infantry, and in the winter of 329-328 by 1,000 cavalry and 8,000 infantry from Lycia and Syria, all fully trained in Macedonian weaponry. The cavalry lacked any experience of battle, but Alexander had been bringing into his entourage and so into his cavalry a steady flow of Asiatic aristocrats, mainly Persian, who had been the élite cavalrymen of the Persian army. It was probably now or soon afterwards that he formed a Cavalry Guard of Persians, called 'the Euacae', which was of the highest quality.

Advance to the east was possible only if the Medes and the Persians accepted his regime and cooperated in matters of supply and communication. There had been no disarmament after victory and no dislocation of the internal administration, so that a concerted rising might be organised without difficulty and cut Alexander off from the west. He continued with his policy of partnership in the top level of civil administration; for he appointed Persians as satraps of Parthyaea and of Mardia-Tapuria, and a Parthyaean as satrap of Hyrcania. At his court he now had a large number of distinguished Asiatics who were accorded the high honours they had enjoyed in the past. Among them were a brother of Darius, a son of Artaxerxes Ochus, Darius' second-in-command, a leading statesman (Artabazus) and commander (Mazaeus). Alexander decided to adopt a version of Persian ceremonial in his audiences with the Asiatic courtiers. Whereas he called his leading Macedonians 'Friends', he called the Asiatics 'Kinsmen' and let them

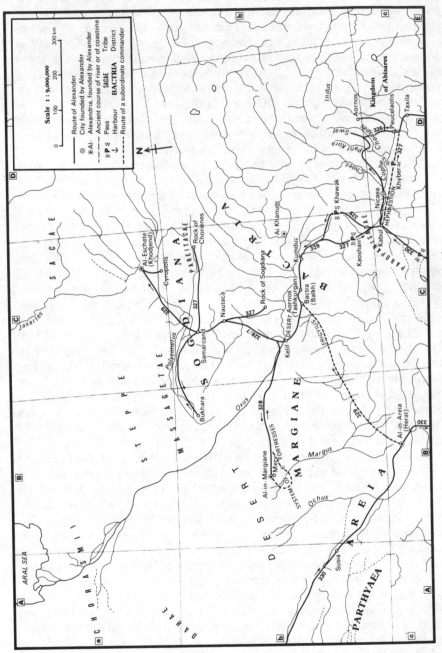

14. The northeastern satrapies

Scale 1 : 9,000,000

0   100   200   300 km

— Route of Alexander
◎ City founded by Alexander
◉Al- Alexandria, founded by Alexander
-- - Ancient course of river or of coastline
SACAE Tribe
BACTRIA District
ᴮ P ↓ Pass
↓ Harbour
- - - - Route of a subordinate commander

N

kiss him in the Persian manner, and they did obeisance to him (*proskynesis*). In these audiences he wore an idiosyncratic form of dress which combined Median and Persian features and did not include the attributes of a Persian king, and he was attended by mace-bearers in the Asiatic style. He instituted this form of ceremonial first in Parthyaea in mid-August 330. No doubt he consulted his Friends at this preliminary stage and was aware of opposition.

In preparation for the advance to the east Alexander divided his forces into three after the death of Darius, led that which followed the most dangerous route and subdued the Tapurians in the high country of Mount Elburz (18,550 feet). Further operations reduced the Mardi. Alexander made his base at Zadracarta (probably Sari) on the edge of the fertile plain betwen Mt Elburz and 'the Great Sea' (Arrian. 3.23.1); for at this time Alexander accepted the belief of Aristotle that the Hyrcanian (Caspian) Sea was an inlet of Ocean. The 1,500 Greek mercenaries who had served with Darius put themselves in Alexander's hands. He let those go free who had entered Darius' service before 'the peace and alliance (of the Greeks) with Macedonia' in 337. The others were required to serve under Alexander. Some Greek envoys also gave themselves up. Those from Sparta and Athens were arrested, but he let the envoy from Sinope (on the south coast of the Black Sea) go free, because Sinope was not a member of 'the Community of the Greeks' (Arrian 3.24.4). At Zadracarta he celebrated a traditional Macedonian festival with the customary sacrifices and with a competition in athletic events for fifteen days. He then returned to Parthyaea in mid-August. He was now in full control of the corridor between the Caspian Sea and the Kasht-i-Kavir desert.

It was at this point that the crucial choice between two policies had to be made in practice. One policy was to adopt a defensible frontier, running from the southeast corner of the Caspian Sea through the Elburz Mountains, across the corridor, along the west side of the two great deserts of Kavir and Lut, and through Kerman to the mouth of the Persian Gulf. Since Alexander could count on the support of Egypt and Babylon and on the cooperation of the Medes and the Persians, he would be in control of a huge and prosperous area of which the centre woud be Cilicia with its ports giving access to the Aegean Sea and to Macedonia. He would be able to extend that control by campaigning in Arabia on the one hand and in the area between the Caspian Sea and the Black Sea on the other hand. At an early stage Parmenio had advised Alexander to accept the upper Euphrates as his eastern frontier, and then at Persepolis he had warned Alexander that it was dangerous to give the Asians the impression that he was 'merely going ahead conquering'. In mid-August 330 Parmenio was in command at Ecbatana; but there must have been Friends and Companions in

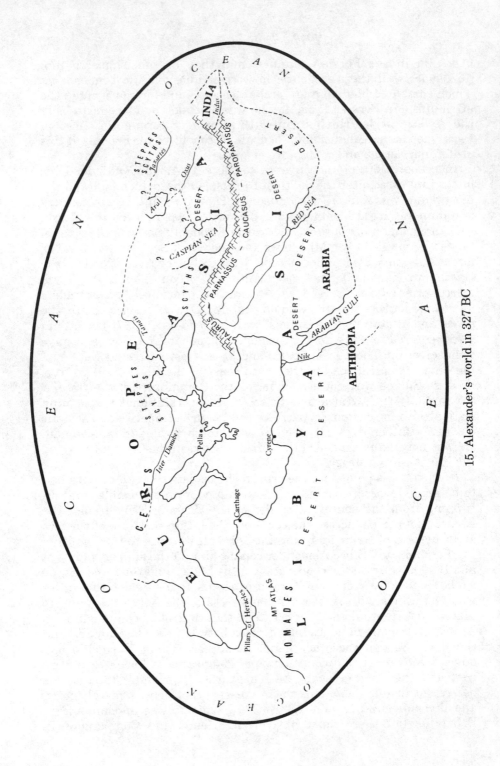

15. Alexander's world in 327 BC

Parthyaea who would have preferred to stop there and to consolidate a clearly defensible kingdom in Asia.

The other policy was to advance eastwards into areas which were beyond the range of Greek mercenaries and so little known to Greek thinkers. But they were familiar to many of the Asian courtiers of Alexander, who will certainly have warned him that it was a vast region of difficult terrain with high mountains and extensive deserts, and that its warlike peoples would be determined fighters in defence of their lands. He had seen at Gaugamela how formidable their cavalry was when they were serving under Darius as subjects or as allies – Parthyaeans, Bactrians, Arachosians, Sacae, Dahae, Massagetae, Scythians and Indians. How far to the east was it necessary for Alexander to go? The answer is related to Aristotle's concept of the inhabited earth (see Fig. 15). Aristotle had proved correct up to date. For at the edges of the earth there were areas of steppe country and desert facing Ocean in the north between the Black Sea and the Caspian and beyond the Caspian by hearsay as far as the Jaxartes river, and in the south in Libya, Arabia, Carmania and Gedrosia; and it was evident that a great range of mountains which Aristotle called 'Taurus-Parnassus-Caucasus-Parapamisus' divided northern Asia from southern Asia. What lay east of Parapamisus was not known even to the Asian courtiers of Alexander; for it seems that the Indian cavalry and the Indian elephants with their mahouts had come to Gaugamela from the westernmost region of Indian settlement. Alexander and his followers therefore believed that Aristotle was correct also in his description of 'India' when seen from the ridge of the Parapamisus as a small triangular promontory projecting eastwards into Ocean. Thus it was reasonable for Alexander to envisage the conquest of 'all Asia' as feasible in two stages, up to the Parapamisus ridge (our Hindu Kush) and then beyond it to Ocean. Once this was achieved, the Kingdom of Asia would be bounded by steppe and desert and by the waters of the Great Sea, and it would be easily defended against any enemies.

Alexander had long ago decided in principle in favour of the second policy, and he had persuaded his Macedonians in an Assembly at Hecatompylus to accept it (above, p. 123). It was a policy which he could have abandoned in mid-August, when he saw how strong a frontier could be drawn with the corridor as its central feature. Instead, he pressed on with the policy which he believed the gods had forecast for him: the winning of all Asia.

Scientific exploration was also a part of Alexander's plans. He was already in a part of the world which was largely unknown to Greek scientists. Thus he had been able to investigate the strange behaviour of the river Stiboetes (now Chesmeh-i-Ali) which flowed in and out of underground channels in Hyrcania and to send back to Greece a report, of which a summary is preserved in accounts by Diodorus and Curtius.

There is no doubt that he and his scientists and surveyors were in regular correspondence with Aristotle. It was probably in 330 that Alexander sent to him the huge sum of 800 talents, with which Aristotle was able to found in Athens for the first time in history a great library of literary texts on papyrus and to make the first collection of specimens for teaching (especially in the field of zoology). The advance eastwards was to provide a wealth of new discoveries.

CHAPTER XII

From Parthyaea to Kabul in Afghanistan

1. Forward planning by Alexander

Alexander showed his usual foresight during the summer of 330. Because the peoples between Parthyaea and the Parapamisus excelled in cavalry warfare, Alexander trained two new groups of light-armed cavalry: mounted javelin-men and mounted infantrymen. The personnel of the first were Medes and Persians, and that of the second group were Europeans. These units, together with the Scouts, who were armed with the lance, were to be deployed against the light-armed cavalry of the enemy and also to keep order in partially subjected districts. In addition he had considerable numbers of light-armed Thracian and Greek mercenary cavalry, which had been trained to act as flank-guards to the heavy cavalry in battle. They would now operate as independent light-armed units. The heavy cavalry, consisting of the Companion Cavalry and the Persian Euacae (above, p. 123), fought in formation against comparable cavalry and attacked infantry formations in the flank or in pursuit. Their task now would be to act in small numbers in support of the light-armed cavalry. He expected reinforcements – they reached him in the autumn at Artacoana on the border of Afghanistan – namely 130 Thessalian cavalry as allies, 500 Greek mercenary cavalry and 300 Lydian cavalry trained in the Macedonian manner.

For operations as far as the Parapamisus Alexander seems to have considered that his infantry forces, together with those he was expecting, namely 3,000 Illyrians and 2,600 Lydians, would be sufficient. He relied on the superb quality of his own experienced Macedonians, Agrianians and Archers, on his artillery and on his siege-train for attacks on enemy armies and strongholds, and he had an adequate number of Greek mercenaries and Balkan infantry to support them. He knew that he would not face any Greek mercenaries; for they preferred now to seek employment with him. In late spring 329 he sent orders for reinforcements, and these were brought by officers stationed in coastal areas of western Asia to Zariaspa (Balkh) in Bactria in early winter 329. They were as follows: 1,600 Greek mercenary cavalry, 11,400 Greek mercenary infantry, 500 Lycian cavalry, 4,000 Lycian infantry, 500 Syrian cavalry and 4,000 Syrian infantry.

The Lydian, Lycian and Syrian troops which have been mentioned were the first products of a training course which Alexander had established for selected boys in those countries, as also in Egypt (above, pp. 72, 78 and 101). He could now look ahead to a time when the Kingdom of Asia would be complete and he would have need of an army of Asian infantry. It was to this end that in late 330 and early in 329 he set up 'in his newly-founded cities and in the rest of the spear-won land' a complete system of training. Plutarch wrote as follows: 'He selected 30,000 boys (*paides*) and gave orders that they should learn Greek letters and be trained in Macedonian weaponry, and he appointed many supervisors.' In other accounts we are told that the boys when selected were 'utterly young', and that when the first draft of 'the new genera-tion' (*Epigonoi*), 30,000 in number, paraded before Alexander in 324 they were already men, i.e. had reached manhood at twenty. It follows that the course started with boys aged fourteen and continued for four years until their eighteenth birthday. Alexander appointed teachers and trainers as well as supervisors to serve at his expense, so that he was providing what we may call a subsidised system of state-education for the brightest Asian boys in his kingdom. On completing the course they were to serve as soldiers under the command of the satrap of their region.

2. Campaigning in Afghanistan

Alexander's march from Parthyaea into Areia was unopposed. For the Persian satrap, Satibarzanes, came to meet him at Susia (near Meshed) and on behalf of himself and the Areians accepted his rule. Alexander continued Satibarzanes in the office of satrap, and sent to him a Companion with forty mounted javelin-men, whose task was to prevent any pillaging by the Macedonian army on the march. This is the first indication in the surviving accounts that Alexander's order on crossing into Asia that there was to be no pillaging might not be obeyed. As he marched on towards Bactra (in northernmost Afghanistan), he was met by some Persians. They reported that Bessus, a relative of Darius, was wearing royal dress as King of the Medes and Persians, renaming himself 'Artaxerxes', and claiming also to be 'King of Asia' as a direct challenge to Alexander; that he had a following of Persians and of Bactrians; and that he was expecting Scythians to come as his allies. Soon afterwards Alexander was joined by some of the troops who had been with Parmenio at Ecbatana and were sent forward by Parmenio (above, p. 120). The army, perhaps now of some 45,000 men, was proceeding on the line of the Persian royal road, which was itself being used by the wagons of the siege-train, baggage-train and supply-system. The great advantage of the road was that it was routed through fertile areas in which supplies could be purchased or requisitioned.

Alexander was still on the way to Bactra, when it was reported that Satibarzanes had killed the javelin-men and their commander, was calling the Areians to arms in support of Bessus, and was about to concentrate the rebel forces at Artacoana (near Herat), the capital of the satrapy. This was the first instance of rebellion after submission and acceptance of Alexander's rule as King of Asia. How was that acceptance ratified at the time? In Egypt Alexander was received into 'the cities and the country' and on his route 'the inhabitants put their places in his hands'; so too in Babylon he was welcomed by the Babylonians *en masse*, their priests and their magistrates, and 'each section of the inhabitants brought gifts and surrendered the city, the citadel and the treasure'. It is to be assumed that each unit of society within the satrapy not only made formal surrender, as these details in Arrian's account indicate, but also took formal oaths of loyalty to Alexander as their king and undertook to pay an annual sum as tribute and provide services. Rebellion thereafter meant the breaking of formal oaths and was punishable with justifiable severity.

Rebellion was in some ways more dangerous for Alexander's forces than open warfare. For once a satrapy had submitted, any troops in the satrapy were either acting as relatively small garrisons or operating in the countryside. They might easily be taken by surprise and liquidated, as presumably in the case of the forty mounted javelin-men. The risk too was that rebellion might spread rapidly, if the first outbreak was not nipped in the bud, and a widespread rebellion would cut the communications between the army with Parmenio and that of Alexander.

For such reasons Alexander acted with extraordinary speed. Taking the Companion Cavalry, the mounted javelin-men, two brigades of phalangites, the Agrianians and the Archers, he covered the 110 kilometres to Artacoana in two days. Satibarzanes fled, for he had not yet concentrated the troops of Areia. He escaped with 2,000 cavalry to join Bessus in Bactria. Alexander used the Persian road as the base from which operations were conducted against the insurgents by several detachments for a period of a month. Alexander commanded one such detachment. The ringleaders of the Areians were executed, and many of their followers were sold as slaves. The last city to be laid under siege was Artacoana. When the defenders saw the siege-towers coming up to the walls, they surrendered and asked for mercy. Alexander pardoned them and left them in possession of their property. He also made arrangements for the future. For he founded not far from Artacoana a new city, Alexandria-in-Areia, with a mixed population of Macedonians, Greeks and Areians, and he arranged for the teaching and training of selected Areian boys. The satrapy, comprising much of Afghanistan, was of great strategic importance, since routes radiated from it to Bactria in the north, 'India' in the east, and Drangiana in the south. Despite his experience with Satibarzanes Alexander appointed a Persian to be satrap of Areia.

3. The trial of Philotas and others

With the army reunited Alexander followed the Persian road southwards for 295 kilometres, according to his surveyors, and he made his headquarters at Phrada (Farah), the capital of Drangiana. The satrap had fled towards the Indians; for he was Barsaentes, one of those who had arrested and wounded Darius, and later, when the Indians sent him to Alexander, he was executed for that act of treason. While the army rested at Phrada for nine days, in October 330, a plot against the life of Alexander was reported.

One of the plotters was a Macedonian soldier of no particular distinction, named Dimnus. He boasted of the plot to his boy-lover, forced him to take an oath of secrecy, and named some leading Macedonians who were planning with him to kill Alexander. The boy told his brother Cebalinus, who went at once to Alexander's headquarters. He waited outside, as he had no authority to enter, and he accosted Philotas, a son of Parmenio, who came out alone from an audience with the king. Cebalinus told Philotas of the plot and asked him to report it at once to Alexander. On that evening and again next day Cebalinus asked Philotas if he had made the report, and Philotas put him off with excuses. This made Cebalinus suspect that Philotas was privy to the plot. So he approached one of the Royal Pages, who smuggled him into the armoury of the headquarters. There he told Alexander what he knew of the plot and of Philotas' failure to pass on his report of it.

As Alexander had done when Alexander Lyncestes was suspected of treason (above, p. 79), he now convened his Friends and sought their advice. They thought that the case should be submitted to trial. Alexander gave orders for the arrest of those under suspicion. Dimnus managed to commit suicide. Philotas did not resist. Next day the Macedonians were summoned to assemble under arms as judges. They were the Companion cavalrymen, the Hypaspists and the phalangites, and of them some 6,000 were present. Ptolemy, a participant at the time and writing when some other participants were still alive, gave an account which Arrian summarised as follows:

> Philotas was brought before the Macedonians. He was prosecuted vigorously by Alexander, and he made his own defence. Those who had reported the matter came forward and convicted Philotas and those with him with clear proofs, and particularly with the fact that Philotas himself agreed that he had heard that some plot against Alexander was being prepared and that he was convicted of saying nothing of it to Alexander,

although he visited Alexander's headquarters twice daily. Philotas and all who took part in the plot with him were shot down by the javelins of the Macedonians. ... At the same time four sons of Andromenes were accused of complicity in the plot, but they were acquitted by acclamation.

The centre of interest in this account was Philotas, because he was the Commander of the Companion Cavalry and a son of Parmenio. 'Those with him' were serving officers, for whom the form of execution was by javelin rather than by stoning. The 6,000 Macedonians, being full citizens of the Macedonian state, formed what may be called a 'People's Court'; they decided the verdicts, whether condemnation or acquittal. A People's Court was not unusual in Greek city-states. In contemporary Athens cases of treason were tried by the Assembly in which for some items of business a quorum of 6,000 was required, and Athens was proud of her system of law and justice.

Other writers – Diodorus, Strabo and Justin – had both Philotas and Parmenio (*in absentia*) undergo trial and Parmenio be condemned as an accomplice. There is no reason to doubt that this was so; moreover, it was customary that male relatives of a man condemned for treason were also put to death (Curtius 8.6.28 *Macedonum more*). In Arrian's summary of Ptolemy's account the executions of Philotas and others were coupled together in one sentence as results of the trial. At the time Parmenio was at the base at Ecbatana in command of a force of 6,200 Macedonians and 5,600 Greek mercenaries and in charge of 180,000 talents. If he should hear of the verdict of the Assembly in time, he might rebel and carry the army with him. Accordingly, an officer disguised as an Arab and with an Arab escort went on fast camels by the direct route through the desert and gave Alexander's written orders for the execution of Parmenio. He was killed without being aware of his son's trial and death. A statement by Alexander was read out to the Macedonians, who were about to mutiny. Arrangements were made for them to march the 2,000 kilometres to Arachosia and join their compatriots there.

Alexander had had a narrow escape. Had Cebalinus not been so persistent, Alexander would have been killed on the day when in fact the trial took place, and the conduct of affairs would have passed into the hands of Philotas as commander of the Companion Cavalry and of Parmenio as senior general. Alexander commemorated his escape by founding a city in Drangiana and naming it 'Anticipation' (Prophthasia). Further enquiries led to the execution of Demetrius, a Bodyguard, as a conspirator. The whole experience had a lasting effect on Alexander. He knew now that he could not trust even his closest Macedonian Friends. He never again placed so large a force of Macedonian soldiers under a separate commander, and he split the command of the Companion Cavalry between two officers, one being his friend from youth

Hephaestion and the other an older man, Cleitus. Alexander must have realised that what had prompted Philotas, Parmenio, Demetrius and other officers was opposition to his policy of partnership with Asians (for he had appointed only Asians as satraps since the Battle of Gaugamela), of dressing up as an Asian and holding an Asian court, and of advancing farther and farther eastwards.

In his account Ptolemy noted what he himself speculated were Alexander's inner thoughts on the subject of Parmenio. 'Possibly he thought it incredible that Parmenio was not a partner of Philotas in the plot; possibly too, if Parmenio had not participated, he was too dangerous to survive his son's execution' in view of his position and his popularity. This speculation had nothing to do with any arguments which Alexander had advanced as prosecutor. It is rather an indication that Ptolemy himself had an open mind on the question of Parmenio's innocence or guilt, and that Ptolemy could see, he thought, two ideas which had 'possibly' influenced Alexander.

According to Arrian, who cited Ptolemy and Aristobulus as his sources, Philotas had been suspected of plotting against Alexander in Egypt, i.e. in 331, but Alexander had not thought it credible at the time. Plutarch, drawing probably on Aristobulus, added the interesting point that Alexander did not reveal that suspicion for 'more than seven years'. It follows that when Alexander was prosecuting Philotas in 330 he did not mention this earlier suspicion, although it would have strengthened the case against Philotas. Plutarch added the just comment that Alexander made 'the fairest and most kingly use of his authority' in this case.

While the Assembly was in session, it was proposed by Atarrhias, a Commander, that Alexander Lyncestes should be brought in for trial; for he had been under arrest for some four years by the order of Alexander but had not been tried (above, p. 80). The Assembly approved. Alexander Lyncestes was prosecuted on a charge of treason, presumably by the king. He failed to muster words in his own defence, and he was killed by the Assembly's javelins. It is unlikely that he received any sympathy; for the Friends of Alexander had judged him guilty of treason in 333, and the evidence of the letter carried by Sisines (above, p. 79) was still available.

The knowledge that there was opposition among his Friends and Commanders to his policy seems to have made Alexander more anxious to gain the support of his Asian courtiers. He therefore developed at this time his use of Asian dress and ceremonial by appointing the most distinguished Asians to be his personal guards – corresponding to the seven Macedonian Bodyguards – and by giving to some of his Companions Persian cloaks to wear and Persian harness for their horses. Hephaestion was one who willingly supported Alexander in this policy. Then it was noted that Alexander used 'his ancient seal-ring' for correspondence sent to Europe, and that of Darius for correspondence within Asia. The wearing of a seal-ring was a general practice among Macedonians of some standing, and in Alexander's case he wore the traditional seal-ring which had been handed down in the Temenid dynasty; for that is the meaning of 'ancient' (*veteris anuli*) in the context. Now within Asia he began to use the traditional seal-ring of the Achaemenid dynasty for correspondence within Asia (especially correspondence with his Asian satraps), because that seal had long been recognised and accepted. The fact that he was drawing an official distinction between his position as King of Macedonia and his position as King of Asia may have given offence to those Macedonians who disliked the sharing of power with the Asians.

4. Operations in Afghanistan and Baluchistan

During three or four months into January 329 Alexander conducted extensive operations, of which his historians tell us little. We know that he founded two cities in this period, Alexandria probably at Kandahar and Alexandropolis at Kalat-i-Ghilzai. From Drangiana he advanced south into the very fertile land of the Ariaspi (Sistan), famous for its lakes and its production of cereals. These people were called 'Benefactors', because they had saved the starving army of Cyrus the Great by sending to him 30,000 wagon-loads of grain from their country. They accepted the rule of Alexander, and he treated them with generosity, adding land to their territory and giving them presents. His base camp was established there for some sixty days, during which stocks were accumulated for the winter months. The people of Gedrosia (Makran) made their submission, recognised Alexander's rule and were given presents by him. Alexander made sacrifice to Apollo, and he appointed a Persian to be satrap of Arimaspia and Gedrosia.

Meanwhile another rebellion in Areia threatened his line of communications; for Satibarzanes with his 2,000 cavalry had returned and raised an army of Areians in the name of Bessus. Alexander sent a force mainly of cavalry under the joint command of the Persian Artabazus and of Erigyius and Caranus, and he ordered the Persian satrap of Parthyaea to invade Areia at the same time. There was fierce fighting, which was brought to an end when Erigyius killed Satibarzanes in hand-to-hand combat, probably in November. While the rising in Areia was being suppressed, Alexander campaigned in Arachosia where he forced the people to submit. Because this satrapy in eastern Afghanistan was of great strategic importance, he departed from his usual practice and appointed a Macedonian to be satrap with a force of 600 cavalry and 4,000 infantry. In Arachosia he was joined by the army which had marched from Ecbatana (above, p. 133). It consisted of 200 Companion Cavalry, 6,000 Macedonians, 600 Greek mercenary cavalry and 5,000 Greek mercenary infantry. Then, if not earlier, the Spartan envoys and hostages arrived from Greece and made their appeal for clemency after their defeat (above, p. 117). Alexander pardoned them but required Sparta to become a member of the Greek Community and thus his ally.

He now advanced northwards with his united army on a route along a high flank of the mountain which the Macedonians called the Caucasus (Hindu Kush). It was now midwinter and there was deep snow and intense cold which caused frostbite and snow-blindness. Supplies were short for the troops, and there were casualties among them and among the camp-followers, who were not on the ration-strength but managed their own affairs. The native people lived in huts under the snow and had stocks for the winter months, and the Macedonians were saved from disaster by identifying the villages from the smoke and obtaining shelter and food from them. When they crossed the Sher-Dahan pass, they saw the crag where Prometheus had been chained and the cave in which the eagle nested that fed on his liver. On the northern side of the pass the weather was less severe, and the army spent the rest of the winter near Kabul where supplies were available. Alexander 'sacrificed to the gods to whom he usually did', and he founded Alexandria-in-Caucaso near Begram and some other cities in this region. The settlers near Begram numbered 7,000 Asians of the locality, 3,000 camp-followers and any volunteers among his Greek mercenaries, of whom many had Asian concubines and children. In these cities selected boys were enrolled in the four-year course. Alexander appointed a Persian to be satrap of the area, which was called Parapamisus. Routes from it led to Parthyaea, Bactria and 'India'.

The scale of these operations may be measured by the fact that they covered an area comparable to Asia Minor in extent and mountainous in character. The ethnic groups had a strong nationalistic feeling; they fought not for a continuation of Persian rule but for their own independence. Some he won over to his Kingdom of Asia by persuasion and with a courteous exchange of gifts. Others he had to overcome by force, and he succeeded mainly through the skilful deployment of his excellent cavalry in rapid sweeps. Whether he prevailed by persuasion or by force, he applied his usual principle, that the land was 'spear-won' and in his possession. Generally he gave it to the current inhabitants to cultivate on payment of a tax, which we call 'tribute'. Where there was a reason, he might confer additional territory, e.g. on the Ariaspi, or take territory away, as he did from the Areians. The peace on which he insisted brought economic advantages. In the six or more cities which he founded there was a prospect of collaboration between Europeans and Asians, and in particular the schools for selected Asian boys were evidence of Alexander's desire for the Asians to share in the future administration of the Kingdom. There was a danger of interference by outside powers. Bessus might try to stir up trouble again, and that was one reason for Alexander leaving so strong a garrison force in Arachosia. The other danger was that the Indians might invade. Alexander had made contact with the most westerly Indians who were neighbours of the Areians. It seems from a passage in Strabo 724 that Alexander annexed a border area between the two peoples and planted in it some military settlements (*katoikiai*) presumably of Greek mercenaries with their families.

CHAPTER XIII

The advance to the river Jaxartes

1. The system of supply and the crossing of the Hindu Kush

The Alexander-historians tell us little of Alexander's system of supply. It may be considered as having two departments: the maintaining of a central reserve and the provision of rations and fodder for forays. The Macedonians, like the Spartans, had a supply company or 'commissariat'. Its commander or director had the title 'Skoidos' according to Pollux, a late lexicographer. He had to purchase or requisition a huge stock of basic supplies, which were transported on four-wheeled wagons, drawn by horses, mules or oxen. He therefore needed all-weather hard-surfaced roads. The Macedonians and the Thracians had a long tradition of road-making, and there was probably a pioneer-brigade of Thracians who made and maintained roads. It was fortunate for Alexander that the Persians also were famous builders of roads. Thus the supply-column, like the baggage-train and the siege-train, followed the Persian roads as far as Arachosia and Areia. So also did the camp-followers, who made a living by selling food and goods to the soldiers and travelled with their families on their own wagons.

The provision of rations and fodder from the central reserve for expeditions into enemy country was much more difficult. The amounts had to be calculated in advance, even when the duration of an expedition was very uncertain. Philip trained his infantrymen to carry a month's supply of flour (bread being the staple diet), and Alexander ordered each man to carry four days' supply of water in desert country – these in addition to weapons and equipment. They were physically tougher than any modern soldier of the western hemisphere. A cavalryman had a groom, who also had to be mounted on a cavalry expedition and presumably carried the rations for two men and oats for two horses. Fresh fodder was most desirable for warhorses and was usually obtained by foraging, as near Pelium (above, p. 37). The most remarkable achievement was the feeding of men and horses during Alexander's racing pursuit of Darius, when two days' rations had to be spread over four days.

A new problem faced Alexander in the Hindu Kush. For there was no road from Kandahar over the Sher-Dahan pass to Kabul, and again from Kabul to Kunduz. At Kandahar Alexander must have learned through interpreters of the difficulties he would face in crossing the Sher-Dahan pass in the winter; but he overcame them thanks to 'the customary boldness and endurance of the Macedonians'. The description of the crossing which was given above (p. 136) applied to the vanguard which went ahead and chose a route for the main body and the baggage-train and siege-train, which would follow later. Alexander commanded that vanguard, and there were stories of him helping men who fell by the wayside. The supplies of the vanguard were carried by the men, their horses and pack-animals. When he was at Kabul, Alexander was aware that the crossing to Kunduz would be even more difficult under wintry conditions. Nevertheless, he undertook it in March 329 in order to anticipate any attempt by Bessus to defend the Khawak pass, which attains some 3,300 metres. Accounts of the hardships suffered by Alexander and the vanguard stem from Aristobulus. During the crossing, which took some sixteen days through thick snow, supplies ran short and the order was given to kill the pack-animals and season the raw meat (for there was no kindling) with the 'silphium' (possibily asafoetida) which grew abundantly in the spring. To this the soldiers added herbs and trout as they descended the north face of the mountain. 'Even so Alexander continued to advance.'

Bessus had never thought that Alexander would cross the mountain and invade Bactria so early in the year. He was beginning to lay waste the countryside on the Bactrian side of the mountain with a force of 7,000 Bactrian cavaly and a group of Dahae cavalry when the news of Alexander's approach reached him. Although the Bactrians were said to have 30,000 cavalry, Bessus had failed to muster them, and he now added to his incompetence by taking flight precipitately. He crossed the river Oxus (Amu-Darya) and burnt every boat in the hope that Alexander would be unable to pursue. As Bessus was abandoning their country, the Bactrian cavalry went home. Bessus depended now on the Sogdians and their allies, the Dahae.

2. The crossing of the Oxus, the Branchidae and the failure of Bessus

For some weeks Alexander made his base at Drapsaca (Kunduz) at the foot of the Hindu Kush. During this time the main body, the baggage-train and the siege-train were making the crossing from Kabul in improving weather. The country ahead of Alexander consisted of two satrapies which formed the northeastern frontier of the Persian empire, and beyond them lived the numerous nomadic peoples of the steppe country. The Bactrians, the Sogdians and the Areians were interrelated and had a common language with local variations, and for that reason the Bactrians had supported the risings in Areia. The territory of the

Bactrians and the Sogdians consisted of extensive, fertile plains and arid deserts. There were few cities but very many villages, mountain fastnesses and nomadic tribes in desert regions. Society was organised on an aristocratic basis. The barons and their retinues were superb cavalrymen in a countryside famous for horse-breeding, and it was they who organised resistance to the raids of the mounted Scythian tribesmen or entered into alliance with them.

When he had sufficient troops, in April or May, Alexander attacked the two greatest cities of Bactria, named Aornus and Bactra, and he captured them at the first assault. Whether there were other operations we do not know. Arrian was very brief: 'He left a garrison in the citadel of Aornus ... and as satrap over the rest of the Bactrians who readily came over to him he appointed Artabazus the Persian.' The surrender of the Bactrians will have involved the recognition of Alexander as King of Asia, the taking of oaths of loyalty by the barons and other magistrates, and the preliminary assessment of tribute. When these arrangements were complete, Alexander led a select force across an arid desert towards the river Oxus. In the intense heat of early summer he marched mainly at night, guided by the stars, and the men suffered great distress from the scarcity of water. When a cup of it was offered to Alexander by a soldier, Alexander told him to give it to his sons. On reaching the Oxus he encamped for some days, during which he selected the oldest Macedonians, now unfit for active service, and he sent them homewards, together with some Thessalians who had been serving as volunteers. He gave to all of them a generous bounty, and he urged them to beget children. In view of their departure Alexander convened an Assembly of the Macedonians in his force, and 'they promised that they would serve for the remainder of the war'.

Because he was afraid of a renewal of trouble in Areia, he sent Stasanor, a Companion of Cypriote origin, to be satrap in place of the Persian Arsaces, who in Alexander's judgement had been remiss in dealing with the revolt. The army crossed the Oxus, a huge river a kilometre wide, in five days on rafts buoyed up by the soldiers' leather tent-covers, which were filled with chaff and sewn up to be watertight. Soon after the crossing the army came upon a little town occupied by people who were bilingual in Greek and Persian and called themselves Branchidae. Their ancestors had been the priests and guardians of Apollo's oracular shrine at Didyma near Miletus, a shrine as famous then as those of Delphi and Dodona. But in 479 'the Branchidae had handed over the monies and the treasures of the god' to Xerxes, who had burnt the temple, and then they had 'willingly' accompanied him to Persia, where they had been given a new home. 'Their sacrilege and their treason' were heinous and infamous. Moreover, although the oracle was consulted after their departure, the god was silent until Alexander freed Miletus and Didyma. Then Apollo declared that Alexander was 'born of Zeus' and forecast events of his future career (above, p. 103).

How were the Branchidae of the little town to be treated? Whereas Arrian and Plutarch did not even mention the place, Curtius gave a highly sensational account. In it Alexander referred the question to the Milesians in the army as Didyma was in their territory; and when they disagreed among themselves, Alexander himself decided to destroy the place. Since the writer on whom Curtius relied for his account was Cleitarchus, and since ancient critics condemned Cleitarchus as 'notoriously untrustworthy' (above, p. 46), most scholars have rejected Curtius' account. However, Strabo in writing of places in Bactria and Sogdiana made the statements which are quoted in the previous paragraph, and he added that Alexander 'destroyed the town of the Branchidae in his disgust at the sacrilege and the treason' of their ancestors (Strabo 518; cf. 634 and 814). Strabo's sources were Callisthenes at 814 and most probably Aristobulus at 518 and 634, both participants in the campaign writing for contemporaries. As they cannot have been mistaken, it is evident that Alexander did destroy the town, killing the adult males and probably enslaving the remainder, as Curtius following Cleitarchus reported.

Why should Alexander have destroyed the place? He attached great importance to the sacrilege of the Persians in the wars of 499-479 and to his role as avenger of the gods and the Greeks for the Persian atrocities. His destruction of the palace of Xerxes at Persepolis was such an act of vengeance. The guilt of those Greeks who took the side of Persia was inherited by their descendants; for in the discussion about the treatment of the Thebans in 335 the treason of their ancestors was advanced as a reason for destroying Thebes (above, p. 48). So too the Branchidae in 329 were still polluted by the infamous conduct of their ancestors, which so disgusted Alexander. Moreover, in his role as champion and avenger of Apollo he was bound to punish these polluted Branchidae. We may recall that Philip as champion and avenger of Apollo of Delphi had drowned 3,000 prisoners of war, who as mercenaries had accepted money stolen from the god (above, p. 17). Alexander may well have had that precedent in mind when he killed the adult male Branchidae.

Alexander's aim was to engage the forces of Bessus. He therefore marched at speed, but he slackened his pace, when a message came that the arrest of Bessus was being planned by his associates, Spitamenes and Dataphernes, and that they would hand him over to a Macedonian officer in command of a small force. Alexander selected Ptolemy for this mission but gave him a considerable force of élite cavalry and infantry. Arrian's account follows that of Ptolemy. In four days of very rapid marching they reached the camp which Spitamenes had occupied a day before, and they learned that there was some doubt about the intentions of Spitamenes and Dataphernes. So Ptolemy pressed on with his cavalry and came to a village where Bessus was in the custody of a few soldiers. After negotiations with the villagers Ptolemy took possession of Bessus, and in accordance with instructions from Alexander placed him, bound, naked and wearing a wooden collar to the right of the road which the army was about to take. When Alexander came up, he questioned Bessus about the murder of his king Darius, and Bessus replied that he was only one of several who had intended to please Alexander. Then Bessus was scourged, while Alexander had a herald announce the crimes which he had committed.

'The king handed Bessus over to the brother of Darius and the other Kinsmen for punishment.' One of Alexander's principles was that offenders should be tried by their own nationals in accordance with their laws. Thus he had handed over the captured tyrants to the Greek islanders, and the Branchidae to the Milesians according to Curtius. The Persian courtiers met under the presidency of Alexander as King of Asia, and they decided to mutilate Bessus in the Persian manner by cutting off his nose and ear-lobes. Alexander sent him under escort to Ecbatana, where 'the Council of the Medes and Persians' would decide on the form of execution. When Arrian reported the treatment of Bessus, he censured Alexander as if it was he and not the leading Persians who made the decisions.

The history of Bessus illustrates the success of Alexander's policy in relation to Persia. We have seen that Alexander appointed Persians or at least Asians as satraps in almost every area east of the Euphrates as far as Bactria, and that after the death of Parmenio he left very few troops in Persis and Media. His confidence that the Medes and Persians would not rise against him was justified. Yet it is very surprising. No one was better qualified to lead resistance than Bessus, a member of the ruling house and satrap of Bactria, who brought to Gaugamela the forces of Bactria and Sogdiana and the Indians neighbouring Bactria. In the battle they had done him great credit, and it was the Bactrian cavalry which covered the escape of Darius. When Bessus disposed of Darius and declared himself King of the Medes and Persians, he must have hoped for a national rising; but nothing of the sort occurred. It was only the Areians, being related to the Bactrians and Sogdians, who rebelled with help from Bessus. When he too failed, some Persians in the northeast area fought on, but the future of Media and Persia lay with the Council of the Medes and the Persians and with the members of the royal family whom Alexander had left at Susa. It is doubtful if any conquered people in medieval or modern history has shown to any similar degree not only acceptance but also collaboration; for some leading Asians entered at once into the service of the conqueror, the Persians formed a Cavalry Guard to protect him, and the Persian mounted javelin-men played their part in the extension of the Kingdom of Asia.

3. Risings in Sogdiana and Bactria in 329

Alexander made good his losses in horses and advanced unopposed to the capital of the satrapy, Samarcand, where he placed a garrison of 1,000 men in the citadel, and then to the river Jaxartes, which formed the frontier of the Persian empire. In Aristotle's geography (see Fig.15) this river was thought to be the upper part of the Tanaïs (Don), which separated Europe from Asia. Alexander saw that it did indeed flow in a westerly direction, and one theory was that it flowed through the Caspian Sea, left the Caspian with the name Tanaïs, and entered the Maeotid Lake (Sea of Azov). Whatever was the truth of the matter (and Alexander planned to explore the Caspian Sea), he accepted the Jaxartes as the border between Asia and Europe, and he regarded the steppe country north of it as the edge of 'the inhabited earth'. He realised how extensive the steppe country was when he entered into diplomatic relations with two groups of Scythians, the Abii south of the river and the Sacae on the far side of the river. As a precaution against the Scythians he placed garrisons in the Sogdian cities south of the river.

The ease with which Alexander had taken possession of Bactria and Sogdiana was to prove misleading. The spirit of independence was first shown when some Macedonians who were foraging were seized and killed by members of a large tribe which mustered 30,000 men and occupied a mountain fastness. Alexander, leading the attack against them, was struck by an arrow which broke part of his fibula, and many others were wounded by missiles, before the summit was captured. Of the Sogdians 8,000 escaped; the others were killed in the fierce fighting or committed suicide by throwing themselves over the cliffs. While his wound was healing, Alexander began to draw up the plans of a new city at Khodjend on the Asian side of the Jaxartes, which was to be called Alexandria Eschate, that is Alexandria of the frontier. He intended also to establish his authority more firmly in the two satrapies, and he sent instructions to the leading men to attend a meeting which would be held at Bactra (Balkh).

'At this point the native people captured and killed the soldiers who had been placed as garrisons in the cities', i.e. in those which lay south of the river. Most of the Sogdians rose in sympathy; some of the Bactrians, instigated by Spitamenes and Dataphernes, joined the in-surrection; and the Scythians on the north side of the Jaxartes began to muster an army for an invasion. If they had time to coordinate their actions, they would pin down the army of Alexander and encourage the peoples west of the Hindu Kush as far as Media to rise against the

Macedonians. Alexander realised that the very existence of his army
was at stake. An immediate example must be made of the insurgents
near at hand. Five cities were captured by assault in two days; for their
defensive walls of mud-brick were pounded by catapults, while slingers,
archers and javelin-men cleared the walls of defenders. On Alexander's
orders all the men were killed and the women and children were part
of the loot which was given to the troops. The largest city, called
Cyropolis, had stronger defences, but Alexander led a select group
through a dry torrent-bed into the city and opened some gates from the
inside. The defenders concentrated their attack on Alexander's group.
Alexander himself was struck on the neck by a stone and fell unconscious, and many officers were wounded; but they rallied and captured
the market-place, while the rest of the army was coming through the
gates. In the fighting 8,000 Sogdians were killed, and the remaining
7,000 surrendered. The seventh city surrendered, according to Ptolemy
as cited by Arrian, and the men were deported to another part of
Sogdiana.

These measures checked any would-be insurgents in the vicinity. But
it was reported that the garrison at Samarcand was being besieged by
Spitamenes. Alexander sent to its relief a force of 60 Companion Cavalry, 800 mercenary cavalry and 1,500 mercenary infantry, and he
himself stayed to face the greater menace, a large army of Scythians on
the far bank of the Jaxartes. During twenty days his army built the
circuit-wall of Alexandria Eschate, which was twelve kilometres in
length, and he planted as settlers some Macedonians who were unfit for
active service, some Greek mercenaries and local Sogdians who volunteered. He purchased the liberty of some Sogdians whom his soldiers
held as slaves, and he made them free settlers in the city, an act of
kindness which was long remembered. The foundation of the city was
celebrated by competitions in horsemanship and athletics, and Alexander sacrificed to the usual gods.

He made plans to cross the river on rafts buoyed up by tent-covers
and attack the Scythians, but the omens when he sacrificed were
pronounced adverse by Aristander. A second sacrifice was little better;
for Aristander said that the omens portended danger to Alexander, and
he refused to change the interpretation. Alexander mounted an attack
nevertheless: his catapults drove the Scythians back from the far bank,
his first rafts crossed with him and the archers and slingers, who
covered the crossing of the phalangites, and then the cavalry followed.
He had had experience in Europe (above, p. 19) of the dreaded Scythian
horsemen, who withdrew, encircled their pursuers and rode round them
while firing their arrows. He therefore made a series of attacks in quick
succession. The first group, numbering perhaps 1,500 cavalry, charged
the enemy who withdrew and surrounded them in a wide circle. Then
a second force of cavalry intermingled with Archers, Agrianians and

javelin-men and led by Alexander attacked at a point in the circle and stopped the encircling movement, whereupon two groups of his cavalry, one on either side of the second force, charged the Scythians as they were turning back. Alexander took command of one group and attacked with his squadrons each in column formation. The Scythians fled in confusion. They lost 1,000 men killed, 150 taken prisoner and 1,800 horses, whereas the losses of Alexander were 60 cavalry, 100 infantry and 1,000 wounded. During the pursuit Alexander drank dirty water, had violent diarrhoea, and was carried back to the camp. 'Thus the prophecy of Aristander came true.'

This brilliant victory brought an apology from the Scythian king and an offer to comply with Alexander's wishes; and Alexander gained some goodwill by releasing the prisoners without ransom. The Sacae sent envoys to offer submission, and Alexander opened negotiations with them. But he was distracted by bad news from Samarcand. The force which he had sent raised the siege of the citadel and then pursued Spitamenes, who led them into Scythian territory. There Spitamenes was joined by some 600 Scythian mounted archers and went into the attack. 'Riding round and round the phalanx, the archers fired volleys of arrows.' The cavalry of the Macedonians tried to drive them off, but since their horses were jaded and lacked fodder they made little impact. Spitamenes' cavalry returned to shoot at the infantry, which changed its formation into a hollow square and withdrew towards the river Polytimetus, where cover might be available. It was the duty of the cavalry to protect the flanks and rear of the infantry, and especially when it was crossing the river; but the cavalry commander tried to get his own men across the river first. This left the rear ranks of the infantry at the mercy of the enemy archers, and all the infantrymen rushed in disorder into the river. There they were surrounded and destroyed. Any prisoners were killed. Only 40 cavalry and 300 infantry escaped.

When Alexander learned of the disaster, he set off at once with half the Companion Cavalry, the Archers, the Agrianians, and some commando infantrymen, and he covered 278 kilometres in a little over three days to approach Samarcand at dawn. But Spitamenes who had the citadel under siege fled in time and could not be overtaken. Advancing to the river Polytimetus Alexander 'ordered the bones of the dead to be covered with a mound and made sacrifice in their honour in accordance with ancestral custom'. He then turned back and captured the strongholds in which Sogdians who had attacked the Macedonians had taken refuge. Those who survived the assaults were put to death as rebels. The main body of the army under the command of Craterus joined him at Samarcand. He made a show of strength by traversing all the area watered by the Polytimetus. It was now late in 329, and the army went into winter quarters at Bactra. There Alexander received larger reinforcements than ever before, 2,600 cavalry and 19,400 infantry (above, p. 129).There was no doubt that he would need them for the double task of putting down rebellions and defeating Spitamenes in the next campaigning season.

CHAPTER XIV

The subjugation of the northeastern area in 328-327

1. Operations against rebels and the Cleitus episode

During the winter the Persian satrap of Parthyaea, Phrataphernes, and the Cypriote Stasanor brought under arrest Arsaces, whom Stasanor had superseded as satrap of Areia, and the leaders of the Areians who had supported Bessus. They were able to assure Alexander that his communications with the west were now secure from danger. The negotiations, which the king of the Sacae had opened after Alexander's defeat of the Scythians, bore fruit. Ambassadors came with gifts to Alexander and with the offer of the king's daughter in marriage as a guarantee of a treaty of friendship and alliance. While Alexander did not take up the offer of marriage or a further offer of marriages between leading Macedonians and leading Scythians' daughters, it is to be assumed that he accepted the treaty; for it would ensure that the Sacae would not cross the Jaxartes and help the rebels in Sogdiana. At this time another Scythian king came in person, accompanied by 1,500 horsemen, to offer collaboration with Alexander in a campaign which he proposed they should undertake from his own kingdom, Chorasmia, which lay east of the Caspian Sea, towards the Black Sea. A summary of Alexander's reply, which Ptolemy probably consulted in the *Journal*, was given by Arrian. 'My concern at present is with India. If I reduce the Indians, I shall indeed possess all Asia, and with Asia mine I shall return to Greece and march from there via the Hellespont and the Propontis into the region of the Black Sea with all my naval and military forces. Your proposal should be reserved for then.' He made a treaty of friendship and alliance with the king (his name was Pharasmanes) and commended him to Artabazus, the satrap of Bactria, and to the other satraps whose provinces neighboured Chorasmia. On the other hand there were no envoys from the Scythian tribes between the Jaxartes and Chorasmia, of which the most dangerous were the Massagetae.

At the beginning of the campaigning season Alexander deployed his forces against the rebels in Bactria and Sogdiana, who relied on speed

of movement as cavalrymen and on the strength of the forts which
formed their bases. Because the rebels did not combine but were
widespread, Alexander had to divide his army into separate detachments. He left four commanders of such detachments in Bactria, led
another detachment into Sogdiana, and put four other detachments
there under the command respectively of Coenus and Artabazus together, and of Hephaestion, Ptolemy and Perdiccas. The detachments
had some success in capturing forts by assault and killing the defenders, and also in granting terms to those rebels who surrendered, but
their tasks were far from completed when Alexander recalled them to
meet him at Samarcand and made new plans. He commissioned
Hephaestion to found new cities in settled parts of Sogdiana. He himself
attacked and reduced some parts of Sogdiana which the rebels still
held. And he sent Coenus and Artabazus to his northern border, because there were reports that Spitamenes had taken refuge with the
Scythians.

Spitamenes moved first. With a company of fugitives from Sogdiana
and 600 Massagetae he took a fort in Bactria by surprise, killed the
garrison and carried off the commandant. A few days later they raided
the countryside round Bactra and acquired much booty. The small
garrison of Bactra made a bold sortie, recaptured the booty, but were
ambushed on the way back and suffered losses. On hearing of this
Craterus, being in command of a detachment, marched with great
speed and intercepted the troops of Spitamenes, which had been reinforced by 1,000 more Massagetae. Craterus defeated them. But the
Scythians escaped into the desert with the loss of only 150 men.

It was autumn 328, when Alexander returned to Samarcand for a
respite from warfare. The Sogdians, like the Macedonians, were keen
hunters, and they had a safari park full of wild beasts near Samarcand.
So Alexander mounted a great hunt, during which he personally killed
a lion and his soldiers were said by Curtius to have slaughtered 4,000
animals. Another diversion was a banquet to which Alexander invited
his leading Macedonians. Such banquets were a traditional feature of
the Macedonian court, and they provided an occasion for the king and
his guests to drink neat wine and to engage in frank discussion. Women
were not present. The king and his guests were not armed, but the king
was under the protection of armed men, namely his seven Bodyguards
and some soldiers of the Macedonian Guard. The banquets were held in
the palace at Aegeae, for instance, and on this occasion in the palace
inside the citadel of Samarcand. The Royal Hypaspists were stationed
outside the palace but within the citadel.

One of the most distinguished guests was Cleitus. He had saved the
life of Alexander during the Battle of the Granicus (above, p. 67), and
he had been in command of half of the Companion Cavalry since 330.
At Samarcand he was nominated to be satrap of Bactria and Sogdiana

in succession to Artabazus, who had just resigned on account of his advanced age. Cleitus too was a generation older than Alexander; for his sister had nursed Alexander as a baby, and she was much loved by Alexander. Thus there was trust and affection between the two men. However, during the heavy drinking a singer ridiculed the Macedonian officers who had fallen in the recent disaster near Samarcand (above, p. 146). This gave offence to the older men, but Alexander and those with him encouraged the singer to continue. Then contention arose between the older men, who judged the achievements of Philip to be the greater, and the younger men who flattered Alexander and put him on the same level as Heracles. This led to further recriminations in which Cleitus as the chief spokesman of his generation denounced the Asian policy of Alexander and mocked his pretension to be the son of Ammon. Personal insults followed. Alexander then threw an apple at Cleitus, tried to find his dagger which one of the Bodyguards removed, and shouted in the Macedonian dialect for the Hypaspists to come to his aid. He also ordered a trumpeter to sound the alarm, and he struck the man when he refused to obey. Cleitus was still blustering; but Ptolemy and others pushed him outside, took him over the ditch of the citadel, and deposited him beyond it.

When Cleitus was alone, he could not bear it but went back. He met Alexander just when Alexander was calling out 'Cleitus'. As Cleitus said 'Here I am, Cleitus, Alexander', he was struck by Alexander's pike and fell dead. Alexander saw that Cleitus was unarmed. He was immediately appalled at what he had done and tried to turn the pike against himself. But the Bodyguards disarmed him and carried him off forcibly to his room, where he lay lamenting for the rest of the night and next day.

The account which I have given is taken mainly from the narrative of Plutarch. His source in my opinion was Aristobulus, who was particularly interested in Alexander's personality and conduct. There is no doubt that fear of assassination was always in Alexander's mind (for he had seen his father killed by a Bodyguard), and that was why he called for the help of the Hypaspists and struck the trumpeter. He thought that there was a plot, and that he was acting in self-defence when he killed Cleitus. It was the sight of Cleitus unarmed that brought him to his senses. According to Aristobulus, as cited by Arrian, the fault which led to the tragedy (the *hamartia*) was that of Cleitus in returning to the banqueting-room – not that Alexander was thereby exonerated. Plutarch recorded his own opinion that the killing was not a matter of deliberation (*apo gnomes*) but due to an unfortunate chance (*dystychia*), when the king's passion and drunkenness provided the opportunity for the evil destiny (*daimon*) of Cleitus.

The terrible remorse and the despair of Alexander lasted for three days, during which he fasted and paid no attention to his bodily needs.

His Friends were alarmed and brought philosophers and diviners to argue with him. The most successful was Aristander, who argued as follows. It so happened that the day of the banquet was the day dedicated to Dionysus, and on that day each year Macedonians made sacrifice to Dionysus. Alexander for some unknown reason sacrificed instead to the Dioscuri. Cleitus began to sacrifice to Dionysus, but he answered a summons from Alexander and failed to complete it. When he was going to join Alexander, three sheep on which libations had been poured as a preliminary to the sacrifice followed after Cleitus. This was reported to Aristander and another diviner, who interpreted it as a bad omen. Alexander accordingly ordered them to sacrifice for the safety of Cleitus. But the banquet started, and instead of completing his sacrifice to Dionysus Cleitus went to the banquet. Aristander argued that the tragedy was due to 'the wrath of Dionysus', who had not been honoured by Alexander and Cleitus, and that it had been predetermined by the god (*katheimarmenon*). Alexander was convinced by Aristander. He sacrificed to Dionysus and began to take food.

The whole episode revealed the tensions between the older Friends and the younger Friends, and their respective feelings towards Alexander. The older men felt that they had been slighted by Alexander's promotion of young men over their heads. For instance, of the exact contemporaries of Alexander, Hephaestion had been put in command of half of the Companion Cavalry at the age of 26 and was now being given important commissions, and Leonnatus had been promoted to be a Bodyguard at an equally young age. Alexander's friends whom Philip had exiled were given military and administrative posts (Ptolemy, Nearchus, Erigyius and Harpalus), and Alexander's policy of appointing Asians to be satraps deprived the older Macedonians of advancement in the administrative field. It seems too that it was the older men who particularly resented Alexander's granting of a military command to an Asian. Thus it could be argued that the disaster at Samarcand had been due to Alexander's appointment of a Lycian rather than a senior Macedonian officer such as Caranus to be commander of the detachment.

During the banquet Alexander was made rudely aware of dissension among his Friends and of the hostility of the older men towards his Asian policy. It was within his power to appease his older Friends by giving them promotion and by modifying or abandoning his Asian policy. Compromise, however, was not in Alexander's nature. He was determined rather to pursue his Asian policy, and, if need be, to depend less on his Macedonians and more on the Asians. The killing of Cleitus would always be a terrible memory for Alexander, and he must have blamed himself for his heavy drinking and his passionate anger. But he probaby came to see, as Aristobulus did, that the death of Cleitus was largely due to accident in human circumstances, and that it had been predetermined on the divine plane.

2. Operations in the northeastern area

During the summer of 328 Alexander was able to recruit Bactrian and Sogdian cavalrymen. This was a sure sign that many leaders preferred the law and order which Alexander was imposing to the raiding tactics of Spitamenes with his Bactrian and Sogdian refugees and his Scythian allies. Alexander had been able to seal off the desert to the west of Bactria by founding Alexandria-in-Margiana in the Merv oasis and by linking it to a line of hill-forts which he garrisoned. The effect was that Spitamenes could direct his raids only into Sogdiana. For winter quarters Alexander settled with his main body at Nautaca in central Sogdiana, and he posted Coenus with a select force near the Sogdian frontier facing the Massagetae. His order to Coenus was to intercept any raiders. Early in the winter Spitamenes invaded with his Bactrian and Sogdian followers and with 3,000 Massagetae as allies, and Coenus advanced to meet him with 400 Companion Cavalry, the mounted javelinmen, the Bactrian and Sogdian cavalry, and two phalanx-brigades. In a fierce battle Spitamenes lost 800 cavalry, whereas Coenus lost only 25 cavalry and 12 infantrymen, and the Bactrians and the Sogdians deserted to Coenus, when their baggage was plundered by some Massagetae. Spitamenes and his allies fled into the desert. But when it was rumoured that Alexander himself was coming up from Nautaca, the Massagetae killed Spitamenes and sent his head to Alexander. The Dahae handed over Dataphernes, the partner of Spitamenes, and themselves recognised the rule of Alexander.

In midwinter Alexander concentrated all his forces at Nautaca. He made some new appointments. As Mazacus had died, Stamenes became satrap of Babylonia; Stasanor was moved as satrap from Areia to Drangiana; and Atropates was sent to Media to replace the satrap Oxydates, who had been slack in administration. The trusted satrap of Parthyaea, Phrataphernes, was sent to arrest Autophradates, the satrap of Mardia and Tapuria, who had failed to answer Alexander's summons; and these two areas were taken over by Phrataphernes. Three officers were sent to Macedonia with orders to bring out reinforcements.

Early in 327 Alexander decided to attack the so-called 'Sogdian Rock', in which many rebels and their families had taken refuge, because it was thought to be impregnable. If he could take that, no refuge would be safe. The rock was precipitous on all sides, and heavy snow had just fallen. The defenders refused to negotiate, and they laughed at Alexander, saying that he needed winged soldiers to succeed. 'In his passionate pursuit of glory' Alexander offered immense rewards, ranging from twelve talents down to three hundred gold darics, to any who could reach the top of the rock. Many Macedonians were experienced rock-climbers, and three hundred men now volunteered to climb the rock at night. They chose the most precipitous face because it was not guarded, drove iron tent-pegs into frozen snow or clefts, and pulled themselves up on ropes. Thirty fell to their death, but by dawn most of the rest were on the top and unfurled the flags which they had worn. Alexander's herald proclaimed that he had found 'the winged soldiers', and that they were there to see on the summit of the rock. The enemy, thinking that the men on the summit were very numerous and fully armed, panicked and surrendered themselves and their families.

In the family of one of the Sogdian leaders, called Oxyartes, there was a young girl second in beauty, it was said, only to the wife of Darius. Her name was Roxane. Alexander fell in love with her at first sight. 'Despite his passion his wish was not to ravish her as a prisoner of war; rather he thought it not unseemly to marry her' (the marriage was later). This was the observation made at the time by those close to Alexander. They may have been surprised by his self-restraint; but it was in keeping with the respect he had shown for the wife of Darius. The love-life of Alexander was no doubt of interest to them. In the past Alexander had neglected the advice of Parmenio to marry and beget an heir before leaving Macedonia. In Asia he had formed a liaison – on the advice again of Parmenio according to Aristobulus – with Barsine, a daughter of Artabazus and the widow of Memnon, a mercenary captain from Rhodes who had served under Darius. This relationship started in 332 and resulted in the birth of a son, Heracles, probably in this year, 327. Alexander did not regard the child as an heir to the throne, since he was born out of wedlock, and he must have realised the need now to beget an heir. His choice of Roxane as his future wife was not only timely. It was politically appropriate; for it was in line with his Asian policy, and his chivalry towards Roxane won the approval of his Asian subjects. Alexander took Oxyartes into his entourage and treated him with suitable honour.

Alexander turned next to the vast and precipitous 'Rock of Chorienes', held by Chorienes and other local rulers. As an outer defence it was surrounded by a deep ravine. It seemed impossible to take it, but that only made Alexander more determined. He directed operations all day, and Leonnatus, Ptolemy and Perdiccas did so at night; for the entire army worked in shifts despite heavy snow and a shortage of provisions. Ladders were made from felled pine-trees and lowered into the ravine; the workers went down and drove stakes into the sides of the ravine at the requisite height; and on these stakes they constructed a bridge of wicker-work and soil on top of it. As they were within the range of enemy missiles, screens were erected for protection.

But when the bridge was completed and carried higher, they themselves were able to bring their arrow-firing catapults into action. Astounded by the Macedonians' progress, Chorienes asked Alexander to send Oxyartes to give him advice. That advice was to surrender; for Alexander and his army were irresistible, and Alexander was a man of good faith and integrity. So Chorienes surrendered. Alexander left the Rock in his hands and continued him as the local ruler. In gratitude Chorienes issued to the victors enough wine, grain and dried meat to feed them 'tent by tent' for two months.

A separate operation with a large force was carried out by Craterus in mountainous country. He killed or captured all the rebel leaders, who lost 120 cavalry and 1,500 infantry, and he then joined Alexander who had advanced to Bactra. The northeastern area was now pacified after two years of fighting under difficult conditions. The eight newly-founded cities were in operation, and the training of selected boys was under way. The peoples of the plains enjoyed an unparalleled freedom from raids by the hill-tribes and by the Scythian nomads, and agriculture and commerce developed rapidly as the peoples of the hills adopted a settled life. For his next campaign Alexander took large forces of cavalry from the Bactrians, Sogdians, Massagetae and Dahae; and he left behind with Amyntas, the satrap of Bactria, an unusually large garrison force of 3,500 cavalry and 10,000 infantry.

3. The conspiracy of the Pages

It was while he was at Bactra that an old friend of Alexander, Demaratus of Corinth, came to pay a visit and died a natural death. In his honour Alexander had a great mound built, 40 metres high. It was a cenotaph; for the corpse was cremated and the ashes were carried by a magnificent four-horse chariot on the long journey to his home. In Greek eyes such a cenotaph was an example of Asiatic extravagance.

At Bactra too a plot against the life of Alexander was discovered. According to Arrian it originated in the punishment of a Royal Page, Hermolaus, for breaking a rule of the Royal Hunt. He had killed a boar which Alexander was about to despatch, and for that offence he had been caned in the presence of the other Pages and had been deprived of his horse. Bitterly incensed, Hermolaus persuaded his lover and four other Pages to join him in seeking revenge. The plan was that one of them, whose duty it was to guard the king on a particular night, would admit the others and they would kill him in his sleep. The night came. But Alexander did not return. Some said that he stayed all that night at a drinking-party, but Aristobulus gave a fuller account, which has the ring of truth. There was at the court a Syrian woman, who sometimes went into ecstasy and was thought then to be possessed by a god; for she made prophecies which came true. Alexander had faith in her, and he allowed her access to him at any time. During this particular night Alexander was returning to his bedroom when she met him and begged him to go back and make it an all-night party. He did so and thus escaped assassination.

Next day one of the Pages, Epimenes, told his lover about the plot, and the lover mentioned it to Epimenes' brother, who went at once to Ptolemy and made a report. Ptolemy as a Royal Bodyguard had immediate access to the king. He therefore informed Alexander, who ordered the arrest of the Pages who had been named as conspirators. They were subjected to torture, admitted the plot, and gave the names of certain others. The Macedonians among them (for one Page was a Thracian) were prosecuted by the king before the Assembly of Macedonians, found guilty and stoned to death in accordance with Macedonian custom. The account I have given comes from Arrian, who was drawing on Ptolemy and Aristobulus, and it is confirmed as accurate by statements in two *Letters* of Alexander which mentioned the confession of the Pages (*paides*) under torture and the stoning of them by the Macedonians. On the other hand, Curtius provided a much longer account, which included speeches allegedly delivered during the trial by Hermolaus and by the king. His version is clearly fictitious; it was written to please his own contemporaries on the theme of liberty and tyranny.

It was clear at the time, as it is to a reader today, that the Pages in the conspiracy cannot have been motivated solely by a desire to seek revenge for the punishment of one of their number. They knew that caning was usual in the School, and that the removal of Hermolaus' horse was not permanent but temporary. They might well have sympathised with Hermolaus, but not to the extent of risking almost certain death themselves; for had they succeeded in killing Alexander they would have been the first to be suspected. It was therefore natural to suppose that the Pages had been inspired by others who hoped to benefit by the death of Alexander and proposed to protect his killers from retribution. Who could those others have been? According to Arrian some denounced Callisthenes as having 'participated' (*metesche*) in the plot, and others said that Callisthenes 'incited them (*eperen*) to the plotting'. To Arrian's second group Aristobulus and Ptolemy belonged: for Arrian reported them as agreeing that the Pages said 'Callisthenes incited them (*eparai*) to the daring deed'. There was, of course, a great difference between being a conspirator and being a persuasive figure in the background. Thus what the Pages said at the time of the trial was not sufficient in the judgement of the Macedonians for them to condemn Callisthenes.

After the trial there was further investigation, as there had been after the trial of Philotas (above, p. 133). This led to the arrest of Callisthenes, the court historian and philosopher. In the second *Letter* of Alexander, written to Antipater in Macedonia, Alexander wrote as follows, according to Plutarch: 'I shall punish the sophist and those who sent him out and those who accept in the cities the men who are plotting against me.' He was himself confident that Callisthenes had been involved as a conspirator; but because Callisthenes was not a Macedonian, he was to be tried not in the Assembly of Macedonians but 'in the presence of Aristotle in the Council' (of the Greek Community), the quotation being from Chares, a Greek courtier. This procedure was as it had been for some Chians (above, p. 99). In fact Callisthenes died seven months later 'of a disease', according to Chares and Aristobulus. The version of Ptolemy, that Callisthenes was tortured and hanged, is to be rejected; for the case of Callisthenes was still *sub judice*. It seems that Ptolemy, as a Macedonian, was less interested in the fate of the Greek philosopher.

We do not know the grounds on which Callisthenes was arrested. There are, however, 'stories' about him which may provide clues. As the philosopher who taught the Pages, Callisthenes was said to enjoy a particularly close relationship with Hermolaus. The story went that when Hermolaus asked Callisthenes how he might become most famous Callisthenes replied, 'By killing the most famous man.' The fact that exactly the same story was reported by Diodorus in reference to Philip's assassin does not add to its credibility. Other 'stories' showed Callisthenes giving offence to Alexander by feeble consolations after the killing of Cleitus and later at a banquet when in response to a challenge he listed the faults of the Macedonians only too freely. More to the point were the 'stories' of Callisthenes leading the opposition to Alexander over the matter of prostration (*proskynesis*). One of them, as reported by Arrian, gave Callisthenes a clearly fictitious speech in which he described it as a characteristic of oriental despotism and as anathema to freedom-loving Greeks and Macedonians.

There may be some truth in the 'story' that Alexander held a banquet for some courtiers who had agreed to prostrate themselves and then exchange kisses with Alexander, and for a number of leading men who would be asked only at the banquet to follow suit. Callisthenes was one of the first group. But because Alexander was talking to someone else, Callisthenes did not prostrate himself but went forward for the kissing. Alexander, however, was told of Callisthenes' misconduct and would not kiss him. Whereupon Callisthenes exclaimed in a loud voice: 'Well, then, I shall go away the poorer for a kiss.' His mockery, it seems, brought the experiment in prostration to an end.

After his death Callisthenes was portrayed by philosophers of Aristotle's 'Peripatetic' School as a martyr who had defended liberty against oriental despotism. At the time Alexander saw Callisthenes as a leading figure in a network of conspirators which included 'those who sent him out' (presumably Aristotle and other philosophers) and malcontents in Asia who later found shelter in cities of the Greek mainland. That at

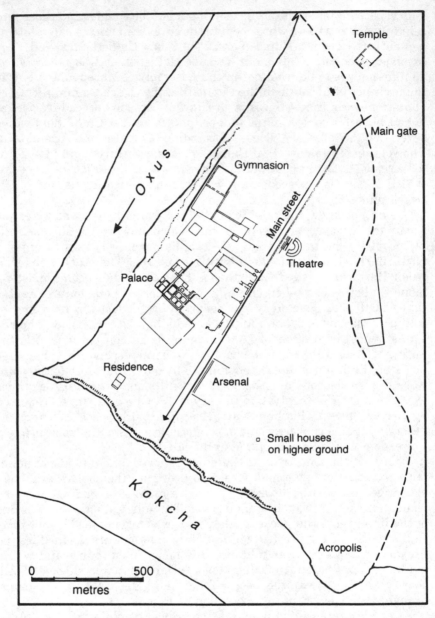

16. The Alexander-city at Ai Khanoum

least was what he wrote subsequently to Antipater. He must have realised that there was growing opposition to his Asian policy among representatives of the Greek city-states, both in Greece and in Asia, and among the leading Macedonians and among the Pages.

One cause of discontent was a change in the composition of the Companion Cavalry. After the death of Darius Alexander had recruited very large numbers of Asian light-armed cavalry in the area from Parthyaea to Sogdiana. Most served in their own ethnic units, but the best were incorporated into the Companion Cavalry, which had hitherto, apart from a few Asians, been the preserve of the Macedonians. The new Companion Cavalry consisted of eight 'hipparchies', each 500 strong and composed probably of one almost entirely Macedonian squadron and two light-armed squadrons (mainly of Asians but including the Scouts, for instance). Thus a Companion hipparchy was well fitted to act against light-armed enemies, whether Bactrian or Scythians. However, this large-scale adulteration of the Companion Cavalry offended nationalist Macedonian feeling.

When Alexander decided to cross the Hindu Kush, he left Amyntas in Bactria with 10,000 infantry and 3,500 cavalry, the latter perhaps including a Companion hipparchy. Alexander's allocation of forces between the control of the northeastern region and the invasion of the Indus valley was justified by the results. For in Bactria and Sogdiana trade and urbanisation developed under settled conditions. Two centuries later it was reported by Chinese invaders that they found men living there in a thousand walled cities. The excavation at Ai Khanoum has revealed one of them.

CHAPTER XV

The Indus valley

1. The advance to and the crossing of the river Indus

For two years Alexander had campaigned continuously winter and summer alike. Now, in 327 as 'spring was on the way out', the army had to make the arduous crossing of the Hindu Kush and return to Alexandria-in-Caucaso. The weather was less harsh and Alexander had discovered 'shorter routes' than in March 329, but even so the army had to climb as high probably as 14,300 feet over the Kaoshan Pass. It was therefore important to reduce the size of the baggage-train, which had been swollen by loot acquired during the sack of rebel centres. Alexander and his Companions set the example by burning some of their possessions, and the Macedonians destroyed what was superfluous to the needs of themselves and their families (for most of them were accompanied by Asian concubines and their children). The leading troops crossed in ten days, but the transportation of heavy material continued through the summer months. Meanwhile Alexander was training his multiracial army. He enlarged Alexandria by adding unfit soldiers and local people, and he replaced an incompetent administrator with one of his Companions. On his departure he left a garrison; for it was to be his advanced base. The satrap of the region 'Parapamisus' was Tyriespis, a Persian, and Alexander added land in the upper valley of the river Kabul to his satrapy.

In winter 327 Alexander sacrificed to Athena and embarked on the conquest of 'Indike', the land of the Indus and its tributaries, which constitutes today Pakistan and Kashmir. Aristotle had stated (above, p. 127) that 'India', being the region east of the Indus (Arrian *Ind.* 2. 5), was a peninsula pointing eastwards into the outer Ocean, an area so small that from the ridge of the Caucasus a man could see the Ocean on a clear day. Alexander knew now that 'Indike' was much larger, but his trust in Aristotle led him to direct his campaign continually eastwards in order to reach the Ocean. If he should acquire this 'India', he would possess 'all Asia', as he had told Pharasmanes (above, p. 149). The peoples of the region, called collectively the 'Indi', were known to be excellent fighters. Their infantry was armed with exceptionally long and powerful bows, javelins or sometimes long spears, and they all had swords. The cavalry attacked with javelins. Infantry and cavalry alike carried small shields of hide and had little or no protective armour. Fortunately for Alexander the 'Indi' were disunited; for tribe fought against tribe, and king against king. Where the caste-system prevailed, the soldiers were a separate class, father being succeeded by son, and they did not attack the caste of cultivators. Alexander had still to learn that the population within his 'Indike' was extremely large.

During the summer Alexander's emissaries had gone ahead and secured the submission of the tribal communities west of the Indus and of one community east of the river, and their rulers – mostly kings – had given sureties of allegiance. Now he summoned them, and they came bringing gifts and promising to hand over their war-elephants. But Alexander was not deceived. Taking a large striking force under his own command he entered the mountainous area which was to be the Northwest Frontier of British India. The first group of tribes, the Aspasians, defied him. When they took to their fortified cities, Alexander captured one after another by assault; and when they concentrated their forces, Alexander defeated them, taking 40,000 prisoners and carrying off 230,000 oxen according to Ptolemy. The next group, the Guraei, accepted his rule. The Assaceni mustered an army of 2,000 cavalry, 30,000 infantry and 30 elephants, but on his approach they dispersed to defend their cities. They resisted into the early months of 326. The fighting was as fierce as it had been in Bactria and Sogdiana, and Alexander employed the same methods, destroying the first centres and the inhabitants as rebels, then pardoning others, and in the final stages establishing new cities (e.g. at Arigaeum and Bazira), garrisoning some existing cities and setting up guardposts at strategic points.

Alexander owed his success to his speed of movement with cavalry forces (for he used mounted archers, mounted javelin-men and infantry called 'dimachae'), his artillery and his assault troops in sieges, and the skill of subordinate commanders such as Craterus and Ptolemy. Set battles were rare, and then the phalanx in formation was unstoppable. The number of Macedonians killed was small, but very many, including Alexander twice, were wounded by arrows. The toughest resistance was at Massaga, where the Assacenians were reinforced by 7,000 mercenaries from east of the Indus. When the Assacenian commander was killed by a catapult-bolt, his widow opened negotiations, during which the 7,000 mercenaries came out and camped close to the Macedonians. In the night a breach of the agreement occurred – Ptolemy and/or Aristobulus attributing it to the mercenaries, and other writers to Alexander – and the result was that the mercenaries were surrounded and killed. Finally, in order to show that resistance could never succeed, Alexander attacked the 'Rock Aornus' (Pir-Sar), which Heracles, it was said, had twice failed to take. Alexander felt a 'longing' (*pothos*) to outdo Heracles. Alexander and Ptolemy, commanding separate forces, captured a way up by a pincer movement; then a ravine was bridged, as at the rock of Chorienes, and from the bridge a peak was captured 'with incredible audacity'; finally of two climbing parties at night seven hundred men reached the top (Alexander arriving first) and routed the enemy. As Sir Aurel Stein commented, success was due to 'Alexander's genius and the pluck and endurance of his hardy Macedonians'. For in all these operations the King's Men and their traditional support-troops played the leading part.

In the course of this campaign Alexander and his Macedonians believed that they had been preceded not only by Heracles but also by Dionysus. The Indians themselves promoted the idea by claiming that Dionysus had founded a city of theirs called Nysa, and that Dionysus had planted the ivy which grew there and in no other Indian land. The Macedonians were delighted to see the ivy and other supposed signs of Dionysus' presence, and Alexander himself was seized with a 'longing' to visit the sacred places. Sacrifices were made to Dionysus; Alexander declared Nysa to be a free city; and 300 cavalrymen from Nysa served with the Macedonians until the autumn of 326. Thus the idea took root that Dionysus and Heracles had fought in the area west of the Indus, but that they had never crossed the great river. Alexander and his Macedonians planned to surpass them.

At Aornus Alexander was close to Kashmir, the realm of Abisares, who had helped the Assacenians and now gave refuge to survivors from Aornus. Alexander did not pursue them. He turned south, captured a number of war-elephants, found suitable timber and built ships which were floated down the Indus. As satrap of the whole area Alexander appointed a Macedonian, Philippus, and as guardian of the Rock Aornus a loyal Indian, Sisicottus. They proved dependable; for when a rising occurred in Assacenia late in this year, Alexander was informed by Sisicottus, and Philippus and Tyriespis restored order. As elsewhere, Alexander imposed peace and provided promise of progress in his new cities.

On setting out from Nicaea near Alexandria-in-Caucaso Alexander had sent the bulk of the army, commanded by Hephaestion and Perdiccas, on the direct route via the Khyber Pass to the Indus. They took over by surrender or captured by assault all inhabited centres (for they were to be on Alexander's main line of communication); and they fortified and garrisoned one of these, Orobatis. When the Indian ruler of the district Peucelaotis rebelled, his city fell after a siege of thirty days. An Indian was appointed governor of the city. Hephaestion had been instructed to bridge the Indus, and he therefore built boats which could serve as pontoons. These were made with local timber in sections, which could be transported overland and reassembled, and the largest were a pair of triaconters. When Alexander arrived in the spring of 326, the united forces held a great festival with athletic and equestrian games. Alexander sacrificed to the usual gods, and sacrificial offerings for the soldiers were provided by an Indian ruler, Taxiles, to the number of 3,000 cattle and above 10,000 sheep. The omens in the sacrifices were favourable. At dawn Alexander himself crossed first into 'India', a land totally unknown to the Greek world.

The army which crossed the Indus numbered some 75,000 combatants, of whom the bulk were infantry from Macedonia, the Balkans and Western Asia. Of the cavalry the Companions were so reconstituted that the four hipparchies accompanying Alexander consisted predominantly of Macedonian Companions; for he would need them to attack as heavy cavalry in any set battles. The ethnic units of light cavalry were highly trained. Our sources mention the mounted javelin-men who were Persians, the Dahae mounted archers, the Bactrians and the Sogdians, and there were certainly other units, for instance the Thracians.

2. The Battle of the Hydaspes

The rule of Alexander had been accepted in advance, and gifts had been exchanged on the most lavish scale between Alexander and Taxiles, on whose death at this time his son took the same dynastic name. This younger Taxiles placed his capital, Taxila (Bhir), at the disposal of Alexander, and he provided 5,000 soldiers to serve with Alexander. At Taxila Alexander received envoys and gifts from lesser rulers in the vicinity and from Abisares, ruler of Kashmir. He sacrificed to the usual gods, celebrated a festival with athletic and equestrian contests, and made his administrative arrangements. Philippus, a Macedonian, was appointed satrap over the region. Taxiles was rewarded with additional territory. A Macedonian garrison was placed in Taxila; unfit soldiers were left there; and the boats of the Indus bridge were transported in sections to Alexander's next objective, the Hydaspes. For no envoys had come from the ruler beyond that river, an enemy of Taxiles called Porus.

The army which advanced to the Hydaspes numbered some 75,000 soldiers, drawn from many parts of Alexander's dominions, and it was spearheaded by not more than 15,000 Macedonian citizen troops. The problem of supply was eased by the extraordinary fertility of the alluvial plains, which produced reserves of grain. On the far side of the river an army of some 35,000 men and 200 war-elephants had been assembled by Porus. It was not possible for Alexander to cross the river and force a landing, as he had done at the Jaxartes, because the sight and the smell of the elephants would make his cavalry horses unmanageable. By several masterpieces of deception Alexander masked his preparations for a crossing at a point some 27 kilometres upstream from his own camp. Then, despite many difficulties during a stormy night in May, Alexander landed 5,000 cavalry and 6,000 infantry on the

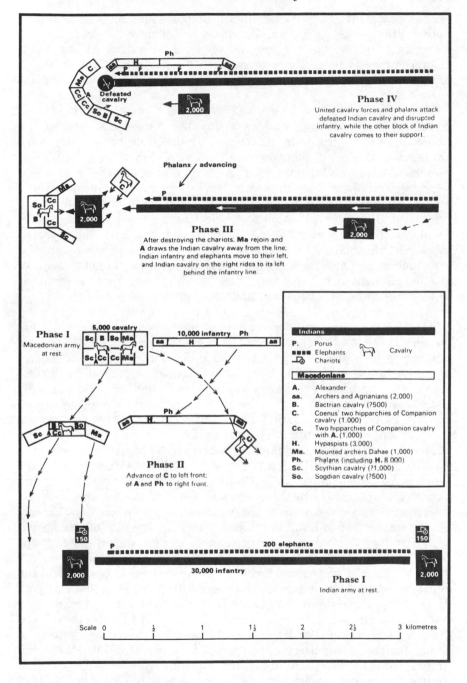

Phase IV

United cavalry forces and phalanx attack
defeated Indian cavalry and disrupted
infantry, while the other block of Indian
cavalry comes to their support.

Phalanx / advancing

Phase III

After destroying the chariots, **Ma** rejoin and
A draws the Indian cavalry away from the line;
Indian infantry and elephants move to their left,
and Indian cavalry on the right rides to its left
behind the infantry line.

Phase I

Macedonian army
at rest.

Phase II

Advance of **C** to left front;
of **A** and **Ph** to right front.

Indians

P.   Porus
■■■■ Elephants   Cavalry
Chariots

Macedonians

A.   Alexander
aa.   Archers and Agrianians (2,000)
B.   Bactrian cavalry (?500)
C.   Coenus' two hipparchies of Companion
      cavalry (1,000)
Cc.   Two hipparchies of Companion cavalry
      with **A.** (1,000)
H.   Hypaspists (3,000)
Ma.   Mounted archers Dahae (1,000)
Ph.   Phalanx (including **H.** 8,000)
Sc.   Scythian cavalry (?1,000)
So.   Sogdian cavalry (?500)

Phase I

Indian army at rest.

Scale   0   ½   1   1½   2   2½   3 kilometres

17. The Battle of the Hydaspes River

far bank soon after dawn. Detachments of troops had taken up positions between the crossing-point and the camp, and their orders were to cross when they should see the Indians engaged in battle. At the camp Craterus was to be ready to cross with his force, but only if 'Porus should take all his elephants with him against me'. Those were Alexander's words.

When the landing was reported by scouts, Porus sent his son in command of 120 chariots and 2,000 cavalry to meet the enemy. The chariots were bogged down on the wet ground, and the cavalry were routed with the loss of their commander and 400 men. Porus left some elephants to deter Craterus from crossing, and deployed his army on sandy ground away from the bank. His 30,000 infantry formed a line ten men deep and some three kilometres long. In front 200 elephants were posted at intervals of 50 feet, and on each wing 150 chariots in front and 2,000 cavalry behind them were in column. He expected Alexander to make a frontal attack with forces which he knew would be outnumbered on foot. As Alexander advanced, he was joined by some of the detachments from the other bank and he gave them a breather before launching his attack not frontally but against one wing.

Alexander sent 1,000 cavalry under Coenus towards the right wing of Porus' line in order to deceive Porus and make him keep his 2,000 cavalry there. At the same time the mounted archers (1,000 Dahae) attacked the chariots on Porus' left wing and caused confusion, whereupon Alexander with 1,000 Companion Cavalry appeared on the left flank of the column of Indian cavalry which wheeled left to face him. By attacking and retreating, squadron by squadron, he drew the Indian cavalry away from the infantry line. That was the moment for Coenus, in accordance with his orders, to change direction and charge the flank and rear of the Indian cavalry. Attacked on every side, the Indian cavalry fled to the protection of the elephants (to which their horses were accustomed). Meanwhile Porus had ordered his elephants and infantry line to move to their left and support the cavalry, but the movement was slowed down by the elephants and some confusion arose. As Alexander had ordered in advance, his infantry in phalanx formation (Hypaspists, Phalangites, Agrianians, Archers and others, perhaps 10,000 strong) attacked the left part of Porus' line, using pikes against the mahouts and arrows and javelins against the elephants. At first the battle hung in the balance; for the elephants trumpeted and charged, the cavalry now reinforced by those from the right wing attacked, and the Macedonians' horses were terrified by the elephants. It was the infantry which prevailed by forming close order, advancing with bristling pike-points and driving the stampeding elephants onto their own troops, while the Macedonian cavalry attacking from behind Porus' line routed the Indian cavalry. The defeated troops and elephants collided with the rest of Porus' line, which all broke and fled. Craterus meanwhile had crossed the river and joined in the pursuit, during which the Indian losses of killed and captured were estimated at two-thirds of their total force.

Porus and his mahout fought on despite wounds until an Indian persuaded him to dismount and meet Alexander. 'Treat me, Alexander,' said Porus, 'like a king.' Alexander let Porus retain his kingdom as a vassal-king and gave him additional territory; and later he persuaded Porus and Taxiles to end their enmity towards one another. Of the force which had made the original crossing 80 Macedonian infantry were killed and 20 Companion Cavalry; and of the other troops 720 infantry and 280 cavalry. Alexander sacrificed to the usual gods and to the Sun-God, who had granted 'the conquest of the lands towards his rising'. He told an Assembly of his Macedonians that the wealth of India was theirs and that they had only to advance 'to the farthest East and the Ocean'. The Assembly promised to complete the task; for they too thought that the Ocean was not far away to the east.

Alexander rested his army for a month. During it he drew up plans for two new cities which he later named Nicaea and Bucephala – the latter in memory of his war-horse, which died of old age soon after the battle. In celebration of his victory Alexander issued silver medallions of decadrachm size. In that which is shown in Plate 13 Alexander, wearing cavalry uniform and diademed, holds a lance in his left hand and a thunderbolt in his extended right hand, and Nike is about to crown him with the wreath of victory. On the obverse side Alexander mounted attacks Porus and his mahout on an elephant which is withdrawing. The diadem proclaimed Alexander as King of Asia, and the thunderbolt implied that Alexander was the vicegerent of Zeus.

3. Advance to and halt at the Hyphasis

For Alexander and his scientists there were two routes to the Ocean. One was southwards down the Indus. It had been thought that the Indus was the upper Nile because the flora and fauna of the rivers were the same, but the Indians then reported that the river flowed into the sea, presumably the Ocean. The other was eastwards to the tip of Aristotle's peninsula. While the army rested, Alexander began to build the fleet for the southwards voyage. But his first choice was to go eastwards to 'the end of the land mass' (*finem terrarum*).

At first the numerous tribes surrendered or were easily subdued by Alexander and Hephaestion in command of advance-detachments, while the main body followed. Lives were lost in crossing the Acesines (Chenab), swollen by the monsoon rains which had just started. It was beyond the next river, the Hydraotes, that he met well-organised forces at Sangala (near Lahore). The siege cost him 100 killed and 1,200 wounded, but the enemy losses of 17,000 killed and 70,000 captured soon ended all opposition, and he reached the bank of the last river, the Hyphasis (Beas). Beyond it Alexander and his Macedonians had been led to believe that they would find 'the end of Asia and the Ocean'.

The truth was reported by the local Indians, that farther east was the populous valley of the Ganges and the greatest number of elephants 'remarkable for size and courage'. Bitter disillusion set in among the Macedonians, who were suffering from exhaustion and the effects of seventy days of continuous rain; for they had been misled and 'the end of Asia' was not at hand. They made it clear by their behaviour that they intended to go no further. On the other hand, Alexander was determined to advance and to reach, as he believed, the Ocean beyond the Ganges valley. He therefore consulted a meeting of the regimental commanders. His appeal was heard in silence. Then Coenus, a senior general, spoke 'on behalf of the majority of the army': their desire was to return home. The anger of Alexander was apparent. Next day he reconvened the meeting and announced his intention of going forward with those who were willing to follow; others could go home and say they had deserted their king. He stayed incommunicado in his tent for three days, hoping that the mood of the army would change. When silence persisted, he emerged to make sacrifice as for a crossing of the river. The omens were unfavourable. Through his Friends he announced that 'he had decided to turn back'. The soldiers shouted for joy, and some went to his tent and blessed him. Alexander had failed to impose his will. But he had avoided a confrontation, and he emerged with the goodwill of the Macedonians. The *anabasis*, the drive eastwards, was at an end.

On the bank of the Hyphasis 'he divided the army regiment by regiment and ordered them to set up twelve altars as high as the highest towers ... in thanksgiving to the gods who had brought him so far victorious and as memorials of his own labours'. The altars were dedicated to the twelve Olympian gods of the Greek pantheon, for they had guided the army, and Zeus had given Alexander the victory, as he had claimed on the Porus medallion. The mention of his labours invited comparison with Heracles, who had commemorated his labours by erecting at the western limit of the world 'the Pillars of Heracles'.

CHAPTER XVI

Southern Asia

1. To the delta of the Indus

It was characteristic of Alexander that as he advanced to and returned from the Hyphasis he made his arrangements for the governance of the territory. After the victory at the Hydaspes he extended the realm of Porus to the north into Kashmir, where the Glausae surrendered their thirty-seven cities and very numerous villages with a total population of something like half a million. Beyond them was the realm of Abisares, who after much prevarication finally submitted and sent lavish gifts and thirty elephants. Alexander confirmed him in his rule and made a neighbouring ruler subject to him. The region between the Acesines and the Hydraotis, and then most of the territory between the Hydraotis and the Hyphasis were added to the realm of Porus, who had loyally served with 5,000 Indians and many elephants under Alexander's command and had supplied the army. That realm was said finally to include more than 2,000 cities, which implied a population in excess of ten million. The area round Sangala was entrusted to some Indians who had come over voluntarily. The new cities which he founded, two by the Hydaspes and one by the Acesines, were on lines of communication. Thus he relied almost entirely on the native rulers to control the large and populous region up to the foothills of the Himalayas. His bond with them was personal and he treated them as 'allies', provided that they accepted his overall rule and paid to him the financial tribute which he assessed. For Alexander realised that he did not have the manpower to exercise direct rule over this northeastern area, and his trust in the native rulers was justified at the time.

The area of the greatest strategic importance was the kingdom of Taxiles, who had shown as staunch a loyalty as Porus had done. Alexander gave him additional territory, treated him as an 'ally', and expected him to cooperate with his neighbour, Philippus; but to make doubly sure Alexander maintained a garrison in Taxila, which Taxiles had entrusted to him (above, p. 164). Philippus as satrap controlled the areas through which communications with Macedonia ran, namely the route of the Khyber pass, the valleys of the Kabul, Cophen and Choaspes (Swat), and an enclave east of the Indus. Thus the entire hinterland was under control, and he could advance southwards with safety.

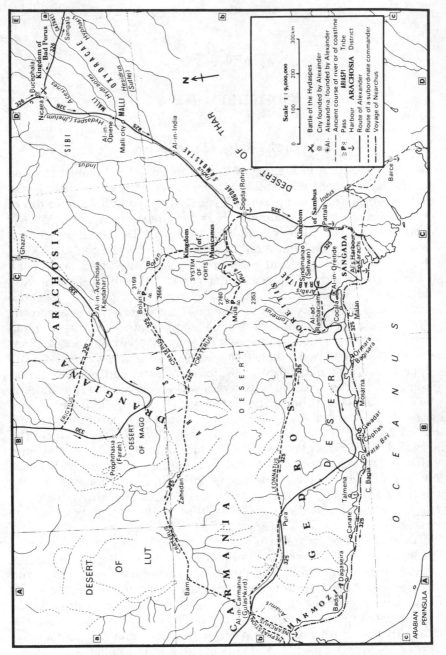

18. The southeastern satrapies

Moreover, for the new venture he was joined by large reinforcements: 6,000 cavalry from Greece and Thrace, 7,000 Greek mercenary infantry, and 23,000 infantry from his allies in Greece and in Asia (i.e. from the Greek cities). Together with them came two and half tons of medical supplies and 25,000 panoplies (sets of armour) inlaid with gold and silver – the product of Macedonian workshops. The total of combat troops available for the advance southwards was about 120,000 men, according to Nearchus. We may estimate the constituent numbers as follows: 13,000 cavalry; 55,000 front-line infantry of which the King's Men, Agrianians and Archers numbered about 15,000; and 50,000 supporting infantry, of which 15,000 were Indian troops. The fleet which awaited him on the Hydaspes was very large (the numbers in our texts vary widely). There were 80 triaconters and all sorts of other vessels, specially designed for the transportation of the army, its equipment and supplies.

Alexander's plan of campaign was unprecedented. He intended to use the Hydaspes, Acesines and Indus not only to carry the supplies which Taxiles and Porus had assembled but also to provide the base for military operations; for troops could be moved faster downstream than on land, and any opposition could therefore be outmanoeuvred. Expert crews were needed to cope with the rapids and other hazards. These were found among the soldiers from the Aegean islands and the Greek cities of Western Asia, and among camp-followers who hailed from Phoenicia, Cyprus and Egypt; for the Indians ventured on the rivers only for local fishing. Alexander had his own ship and helmsman, Onesicritus, and he appointed as his senior naval staff thirty-four leading officers – Macedonians, Greeks, Cypriotes, and one Persian. The role of most of them was honorary, and their title 'trierarch' did not involve an actual command.

On the eve of departure in November 326 a festival was held with competitions in the arts and in athletics, and victims for sacrifice were issued to the army. Alexander himself sacrificed then to his ancestral gods, the gods whom the diviners enjoined, the three river gods, Poseidon, Amphitrite, the Nereids and Ocean. At dawn on the day of departure he sacrificed on shore to his usual gods and to Hydaspes, and on shipboard to the three river gods, Heracles, Ammon and his usual gods. Then the bugle sounded, the fleet set out in formation, and the riverbanks rang with the cheers of the oarsmen. Alexander sailed in command of the Hypaspists, the Archers and the Royal Squadron of the Companion Cavalry. Two detachments of the army had started in advance, the larger with 200 elephants on the left bank under Hephaestion, and the other on the right bank under Craterus; and a third detachment under the satrap Philippus was to follow. The fleet and the detachments met at prearranged points. Most of the Indian tribes surrendered, and the others were subjugated as far as the confluence of the Hydaspes and the Acesines. There in the troubled waters some oared ships were damaged and lives were lost, but those vessels which went with the current came to no harm.

Alexander had early intelligence that the two largest and most warlike tribes in the central region, the Malli and the Oxydracae, were preparing to join forces and engage him in set battle. That was a daunting prospect; for their huge numbers would be effective, and a single defeat for the Macedonians might be disastrous. He must be first in the field, before they could combine. While the fleet sailed down to the border of the Malli, Alexander raided the country of their northern neighbours. On rejoining the fleet he made his dispositions. Craterus, proceeding down the right bank, was to be in command of the elephants. Hephaestion on the left bank was to move five days ahead of Alexander's own force, and Ptolemy was to follow three days behind Alexander's force, so that they could deal with any fall-out following on Alexander's attack. Alexander himself in command of the Hypaspists, one phalanx-brigade, the Agrianians, the Archers, half the Companion Cavalry and the mounted archers (totalling 6,500 infantry and 2,000 cavalry), marched through desert country deep into Mallian territory. In a day and a night he covered over 90 kilometres.

The attack by his cavalry at dawn was a complete surprise. Many Mallians were killed defenceless in the fields, and when the infantry came up they forced their way into the city and drove the enemy into the citadel. 'Alexander appeared here, there and everywhere in the action.' The citadel was captured by assault, and the 2,000 defenders were killed. The inhabitants of a nearby city fled, but many were overtaken and killed by the cavalry. After another night march he overtook a force of Mallians which was crossing the Hydraotes, killed many and took some prisoners, and then captured their stronghold. The survivors were enslaved. Another city was strongly held by Mallians and by Brahmans, members of a fanatical religious sect. The Macedonians gave covering fire with their catapults while the sappers undermined the walls (as elsewhere in the plains, these were of brick), and Alexander was the first to mount the wall of the citadel, in which some 5,000 Mallians fought to the death. 'Such was their courage that few were captured alive.' Other cities were abandoned. Alexander ordered a detachment to comb the woods and 'to kill all who did not voluntarily surrender'.

The heavy losses of the Mallians were due partly to the fanatical resistance of their soldiers and partly to the killing of refugees on Alexander's orders (e.g. in Arrian 6.8.3, derived through Ptolemy from the *Journal*). Since panic was now widespread, the only organised army of the Mallians, 50,000 strong, left their main territory and crossed the Hydraotes, intending evidently to join the Oxydracae. In close pursuit Alexander forded the river with his cavalry only and halted the Mal-

lians by riding round them until his infantry appeared. At the sight of
the phalanx the Mallians fled to a strongly fortified city, and next day
when the Macedonians attacked they took refuge in the citadel. Alexander as usual was in the forefront. As he thought his soldiers to be
slow, he himself propped a ladder against the citadel wall and led the
way up, being followed by Peucestas, who was carrying the sacred
shield of Athena of Troy, and by Leonnatus, a Bodyguard. Another
ladder was raised alongside, and the first man up was Abreas. Behind
them both ladders broke under the weight of the troops. The leaders
were alone. Alexander forced the defenders off the top of the narrow
wall and was joined there by Peucestas, Leonnatus and Abreas. Since
he was a standing target, he jumped to the ground inside, killed some
who attacked him, and was joined by the other three. Abreas was killed
by an arrow fired at short range. Alexander was struck by another
arrow which pierced his lung. He collapsed, but Peucestas and Leonnatus protected him with their shields. Now the Hypaspists arrived,
some scaling the walls and others breaking down a gate, and in the
belief that Alexander was dead the army killed everyone inside the
citadel.

Alexander survived with much loss of blood. When he showed himself
to the army, they shouted for joy and wreathed him 'with such flowers
as India was then producing'. All the forces were now united at the
confluence of the Hydraotes and the Acesines. While Alexander conva-
lesced, the terrible losses he had inflicted on the Mallians had the
effects he had foreseen. Mallians, Oxydracae, Sogdae and other tribes
and communities as far as the confluence of the Acesines and the Indus
sent envoys and gifts and accepted his rule. The only tribe which
refused was reduced by Perdiccas. At the confluence he set the southern
limit of the satrapy of Philippus, to whom he gave a garrison force which
included all the Thracians, and a new city, Alexandria-in-Opiene, was
to be built with dockyards. For Alexander foresaw the importance of the
many navigable rivers for a water-borne trade which the disunited
Indian tribes had never developed. Territory west of the Indus which
Craterus overran was added to the satrapy of Arachosia.

Continuing down the Indus he received the submission of the tribes
and founded another city with dockyards near the capital of the Sogdae
(at Rohri). The river flowed not far from the desert of Thar, and the
fertile country was to the west. There Musicanus reigned over what was
said to be the richest kingdom of the Indus valley. Because Musicanus
had sent no envoys, Alexander embarked a force on his now enlarged
fleet, sailed swiftly downstream, and reached the kingdom before Musicanus even heard of his departure. Astounded, Musicanus came to
meet Alexander. He brought lavish gifts and all his elephants, and he
placed himself and his people at the service of Alexander. Pardon was
granted, Musicanus was confirmed as vassal-king, and the citadel of his

capital was garrisoned by the Macedonians. A neighbouring king, Oxicanus, had not negotiated. Sailing with a picked force to his realm, Alexander captured Oxicanus and two of his cities by assault. He gave all the plunder to his troops; but he kept the elephants. The ruler of the next kingdom to the south, Sambus, fled but his relatives surrendered the capital and the elephants.

Alexander was now close to the head of the Indus Delta. But behind him there broke out a mutiny, inspired by the Brahmans and led by Musicanus, and the danger was that the mutiny would spread. Alexander acted with his usual speed. The satrap he had appointed for southern 'India', Peithon, invaded the kingdom and captured Musicanus, while Alexander attacked the cities which were subject to Musicanus. 'Of some cities he enslaved the inhabitants and razed the walls, and in others he placed garrisons and fortified the citadels.' Any Brahmans who were captured and Musicanus were taken to their place of residence and were hanged as instigators of the rebellion. Another revolt occurred in the realm of Sambus (mentioned not by Arrian but by other writers). Alexander treated the cities in the same way, except that he pardoned those who surrendered, most notably at the chief city of the Brahmans, Harmatelia.

The king of the Delta, Soeris, came to Alexander, accepted his rule and was ordered to prepare supplies for the army. As the subjugation of 'India' seemed to be complete, Alexander prepared for the next phase by sending Craterus on the route through Arachosia and Drangiana to Carmania, which adjoined Persis. Craterus took any Macedonians who were unfit for active service, three phalanx-brigades, some of the Archers, all the elephants, and a baggage-train together with the families of the King's Men. His task was to confirm or extend Macedonian control of the areas through which he would pass. It was clear that Alexander intended to lead a more mobile army into unconquered territory, which had therefore to be south of Craterus' route.

After the departure of Craterus in June 325 Alexander sailed rapidly to Pattala at the head of the Delta, because Soeris was said to have fled with his tribesmen. It was true, but most of the tribesmen came back on the assurance that they would work their own lands (see above, p. 71, for a similar assurance). Alexander enlarged the cultivable area by having wells dug in the desert. At Pattala he planned his chief naval base: a large basin was excavated for the bulk of the fleet; dockyards were built; and both were included together with the citadel in a fortified complex. From Pattala he explored both arms of the Indus. He lost some ships through a storm from the sea and then a powerful ebb tide, of which he had had no experience. He found the eastern river to be more navigable. He arranged for the building of another basin and dockyards there, with a fort for a garrison, which would mark his eastern frontier. No doubt he hoped to develop trade by sea eastwards.

During his first voyage he landed on a river island and then on an island in the sea, and at each of them he sacrificed not to the usual gods but to special gods with special rituals, as he had been instructed to do by Ammon at the oracle of Siwah (above, p. 102). He then sailed out to sea, sacrificed bulls to Poseidon, and as a thank-offering cast vessels of gold upon the waters. He was confident that he had reached the Ocean – something which Ammon had presumably forecast – and he set up altars to Oceanus and to Tethys.

The conquest of 'India' south of his cities on the Hydaspes within seven months was an amazing example of Alexander's audacity, originality and planning and of his leadership of a multiracial army. His Macedonians were at the peak of their form. Because Arrian wrote of Alexander and the King's Men, we know little or nothing of the achievements of his Greek and Asian troops, of whom the Persian, Bactrian, Sogdian, Scythian and Indian cavalry must have played a leading part. Alexander was undeterred by the vastness of the plains, the huge populations, the elephants and the war-chariots; and his use of the rivers gave him a speed of execution which prevented his enemies, traditionally disunited, from combining their forces. Nor was it merely a matter of conquest. He had brought about acceptance of his rule. Polyaenus, a military commentator who drew on Ptolemy's account, observed that Alexander's mixture of the harshest methods as at Sangala and then of pardon and clemency to the neighbouring tribes (above, p. 167) had the effect that the reputation for clemency 'becoming current persuaded Indians to accept Alexander willingly' (4.3.30). Alexander later remarked that he had left Indians 'to maintain their own forms of government in accordance with their own customs' (Arrian 7.20.1). What he brought to Indians who had been split into warring communities was peace and with it the promise of economic development. We have seen the new use of the rivers, the digging of wells and the excavation of harbours. In Alexander's cities Indians had new opportunities, and their sons were eligible for a Greek form of education. Greek scientists and Greek adventurers with Alexander had much to teach the Indians in practical matters such as the mining of salt and the smelting of metals. The conditions were set for a new age.

2. The conquest of the southern regions

When Alexander sacrificed at sea, he prayed 'that Poseidon would escort safely the naval force which he intended to send with Nearchus to the Persian Gulf and the mouths of the Euphrates and Tigris'. This force would sail through uncharted seas. Indeed it was not known whether such a voyage was possible; for little credence was given in 325 to the report by Herodotus, which Alexander will have read, that almost two centuries earlier the Greek captain of a merchant ship, dependent on sail only, had voyaged from the Indus to the Red Sea in thirty months (4.44). It was thus an open question whether the sea off the Indus was an inner sea, like the Mediterranean Sea, or was the Ocean which in Aristotle's belief encircled the inhabited land mass. The voyage of Nearchus would solve that question.

The fleet was selected from the three classes of warships which were fastest under oar: triaconters (open boats with fifteen oars a side), *hemioliai* (light ships with one and a half banks of oars), and *kerkouroi* (skiffs). These ships had the advantage over merchant ships that they were faster under most conditions, were not held up by lack of wind, and could land on open beaches. Their disadvantage was that they could carry very little water and food. What alarmed Alexander was the danger of disaster during a voyage of unknown length (in fact some 1,200 miles), if the coast was harbourless, uninhabited, or deficient in natural foodstuffs. Indeed he had reason to think that some of the coast would be uninhabited, because Ocean was believed to be fringed by desert or steppe country. Nearchus made the shrewd comment that Alexander's apprehensions 'were overcome by his desire to achieve something new and extraordinary always'.

The voyage of the fleet was to be helped by an army which would start two months earlier, dig wells or mark water-points, dump supplies where they would be needed, and subjugate any hostile tribes. The army would soon be marching through unknown country. There was merely a tradition that an Assyrian queen, Semiramis, and Cyrus the Great had emerged from that country with only a handful of men, because it was deserted and difficult to traverse. Nearchus said later that Alexander had been aware of the tradition and intended to succeed where they had failed. The nature and the scale of the difficulties were not known. Alexander set off in August with an army of perhaps 20,000 men and four months' supply of grain; for he had sent home most of the numerous Asian cavalry and the Indian infantry. The first two tribes, Arabitae and Oreitae, planned resistance but capitulated. Alexander founded two cities, appointed Apollophanes as satrap, and left Leonnatus in command of the Agrianians, some of the Archers, and cavalry and infantry who were mainly Greek mercenaries. After the departure of Alexander Leonnatus put down a rising in a set battle, when the enemy losses wee 6,000 and his were trivial but included Apollophanes. He welcomed the fleet on its arrival, provided substitutes for some of the crews, and gave Nearchus supplies for ten days.

With some 12,000 soldiers, mainly Macedonians, the supply-train and the camp-followers, who were traders with their families, Alexander entered Gedrosia in October, the month during which the fleet had been ordered to start. The first shortage was water, and Alexander was forced to go inland; but he still managed to send to the coast some supplies, which were reaching him from Apollophanes; but these dwindled with his death. Alexander then faced an agonising choice: either to take his army inland on an easy route to the capital, Pura, or to march near the coast through what was reported to be desert. He chose the latter course, in order to provide help for the fleet where it might need it most.

The army suffered dreadfully from intense heat, shortage of water and exhaustion. Where the sand was soft, it was impossible for the animals and men to drag the wagons uphill. To supplement their rations the troops killed the animals, broke up the wagons and used the wood to cook the flesh. With no means of transport the sick and the exhausted were left to die. When it rained inland, a flash flood at night swept away 'most of the women and children of the camp-followers, the king's property and most of the surviving transport animals'. Alexander's leadership held the troops together. He walked in front, and when he was given some water he poured it on the ground to show that he would drink only when they all could drink. Finally the native guides lost the way in the featureless desert. It was Alexander who reached the sea and discovered fresh water in the shingle. The army followed the coast for a week, drinking this water. It then turned inland into inhabited territory and headed for Pura, the capital of Gedrosia. It is to be noted that during the crossing of the desert food supplies, though short, were maintained for the army. It was the camp-followers who suffered most, for they were not on the ration strength.

After resting at Pura the army marched into Carmania, and there it was joined by the army of Craterus, who had carried out his task (above, p. 174). The reunion was an occasion for a festival of the arts and of athletics, and Alexander made 'sacrifices of thanksgiving for the victory over the Indians and for the salvation of the army in Gedrosia'. His anxiety now was for the fleet. On learning that Nearchus and a few others were being brought to him, he thought the fleet had been lost and they were the sole survivors. So when they appeared, he asked, 'How were the ships and the men lost?' Nearchus replied, 'Your ships and your men are safe, and we have come to tell you of their safety.' Alexander wept with relief. He mounted another festival of the same kind and made 'sacrifices for the salvation of the fleet to Zeus the Saviour, Heracles, Apollo averter of evil, Poseidon and other gods of the sea'. He was right to do so; for where we might say that luck was on his side he knew that the gods had saved him.

The fleet too had had a hard passage, which lasted from early October into January. During it, in accordance with Alexander's orders, Nearchus listed the inhabitants, anchorages, water supplies, and fertile and barren parts of the coast, and this information was the basis of a *Mariner's Guide* for what was to be a regular route for traders. After Alexander's death Nearchus published an account of the adventures of himself and his crews, which makes excellent reading in the version abbreviated by Arrian. In it he paid little attention to the army's support. Yet without it there is no doubt that the fleet would either have been lost or would have turned back for lack of food or water.

Nearchus had left his fleet in Harmozia near the entry to the Bay of Hormuz. He continued his voyage of exploration, moving mainly from island to island, and was able to rest and restock at the mouth of the river Sitaces (Mand), where Alexander had deposited a large quantity of grain. From there he sailed to the mouth of the Euphrates, which Alexander had set as his goal (above, p. 175), and then turned back to the mouth of the Pasitigris. On this part of the voyage also he recorded information for a *Mariner's Guide*. He then joined Alexander at a bridge over the Pasitigris in February 324. A festival was held with sacrifices for the safety of the ships and men, and Alexander placed crowns of gold on the heads of Nearchus for his services to the fleet and of Leonnatus for his victory in Oreitis (above, p. 176). It was a triumphant conclusion to a large-scale operation in which the four divisions of Alexander's forces had conquered the southern provinces and opened communication by sea between India and Persia.

3. Southwestern Asia

The success of Nearchus opened up new vistas for Alexander. Was there a route by sea from the Persian Gulf to the Egyptian Sea (our Red Sea), or if the Egyptian Sea was an internal sea was there a route by sea round the southern side of Libya to the Pillars of Heracles? During the next twelve months three expeditions, each in a triaconter, worked their way down the east coast of the Arabian peninsula, and the last reached Cape Macetia, a good Macedonian name for the Oman peninsula. Another expedition set out from Suez and reached Yemen; for that was 'as far as the water in their ships permitted'. Had Alexander lived longer, he would have completed, in the opinion of Arrian, the circumnavigation of Arabia.

From the Pasitigris Alexander marched to Susa where there was another reunion, and he then sailed with a select force down the river Eulaeus to the sea. With the fastest ships he explored the coast to the mouth of the Tigris. The Persians had built weirs on the Tigris, in order to prevent any enemy from coming upriver. Alexander had them removed and proceeded to Opis. The Euphrates on the other hand had not been blocked by the Persians and was navigable very far inland to Thapsacus. Aristobulus wrote of Chaldaean traders, settled at Gerra on the Arabian coast, who sent cargoes of Arabian spices on rafts to Babylonia, whence they went by river to Thapsacus and were then distributed overland. Alexander appreciated the importance of this route. He assembled a great fleet at Babylon. To the ships of Nearchus were added Phoenician naval vessels, from quinqueremes (in which the upper and middle oars were each rowed by two men, the lower by one man) to triaconters, which had been transported in sections from Phoenicia to Thapsacus, were reassembled there, and then sailed down to Babylon. Other ships were being built from local cypress in dockyards there. To accommodate the fleet a basin was excavated to hold 1,000 warships, and naval personnel were recruited from the Mediterranean area, some voluntarily, some hired in advance, and others 'bought', i.e. redeemed from slavery and liberated. Moreover, 'Alexander intended to found settlements on the coast and the islands of the Persian Gulf, since he thought it would become as prosperous as Phoenicia'.

The prosperity of Babylonia was due to a system of irrigation, which Alexander personally investigated and improved. A particular problem was posed by the control of the flood water of the lower Euphrates, which was carried off by the Pollacopas canal and formed marshlands on the coast; for during most of the year the water had to be diverted away from that canal and used for irrigation. The Persians had achieved this by employing 10,000 labourers for two months each year to dam the outlets from the river into the canal. Alexander discovered a deposit of boulder clay, constructed a permanent dam, and used sluices to control the flow from the Euphrates into the canal. The head of the Persian Gulf has altered greatly since ancient times, but its general nature is the same. The marshlands, extending towards what is now Kuwait, were regarded as part of the natural defences of Arabia. Alexander visited them and founded a city, in which he settled Greek mercenaries, in Kuwait, before he returned to Babylon in 323. There the fleet had been under constant training with competitions in oarsmanship and helmsmanship and between ships. Alexander intended to command it himself and to join the main army in Kuwait for the invasion of Arabia. He was planning the details of the voyage and the Arabian campaign during his final illness. Had he lived, there is no doubt that he would have conquered at least part of Arabia.

CHAPTER XVII

The Kingdom of Asia and the Macedonians

1. The organisation of the Kingdom of Asia

We have seen that in the central provinces Alexander appointed Asians, mainly Persians, to be satraps. Four of these had commanded large contingents in the Battle of Gaugamela: Mazaeus, Phrataphernes, Atropates and Satibarzanes. The first three were outstandingly loyal to Alexander. Satibarzanes rebelled and led an actual revolt in 330. Thereafter Alexander spent five years in Bactria and India, during which it was not possible for him to supervise the conduct of his administrators, both European and Asian, in the area from the Hellespont to Parthyaea. As in Macedonia, every subject of the King of Asia had the right of appeal, but this was an effective safeguard against maladministration only when the king was within range. This was so in 325 when complaints were lodged against the satrap of Parapamisadae, Tyriespis, and he was brought to south 'India', put on trial and executed for peculation and oppression of his subjects; his satrapy was transferred to the Sogdian Oxyartes, the father of Roxane. But when he returned from India, a number of complaints reached him. In Carmania, the satrap, Astaspes, came under suspicion; an inquiry was held and on being found guilty he was executed. Advancing from Carmania to Persis, Alexander learned that the satrap of Persis, Phrasaortes, had died a natural death, and a Persian, Orxines, who had been a commander at the Battle of Gaugamela, had taken control of the satrapy 'for Alexander', then in India. Complaints were now made by Persians against Orxines for misgovernment; he was tried, found guilty and was hanged. At Susa Alexander arrested on charges of maladministration Abulites, satrap of Susiane since 331, and his son Oxyartes, satrap of Paraetacene since 330 (he had been a commander at Gaugamela), and both were executed.

Arrian, drawing on Ptolemy and Aristobulus, wrote that the satraps of the region (i.e. Astaspes, Abulites, Oxyartes and the self-appointed Orxines) did not believe that Alexander would survive, particularly in the Gedrosian desert, and that this belief led them to misgovern. The implication, and probably the fact, was that these Persian satraps had

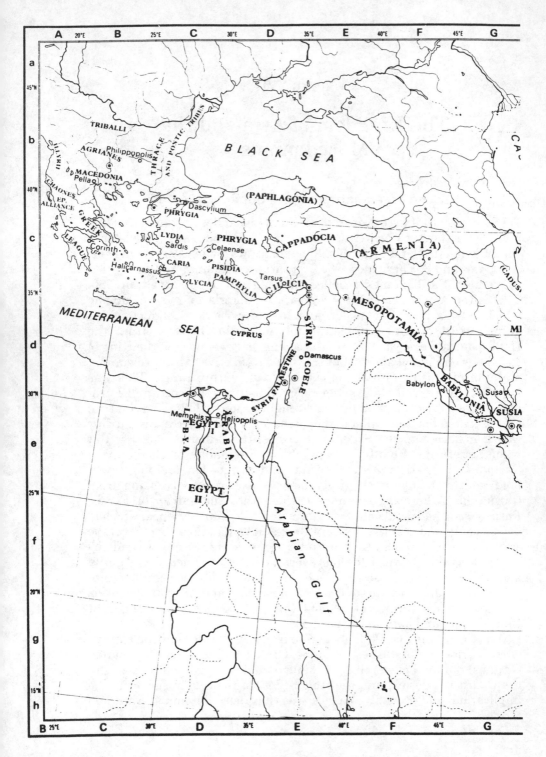

19. The administrative divisions of Alexander's territories.

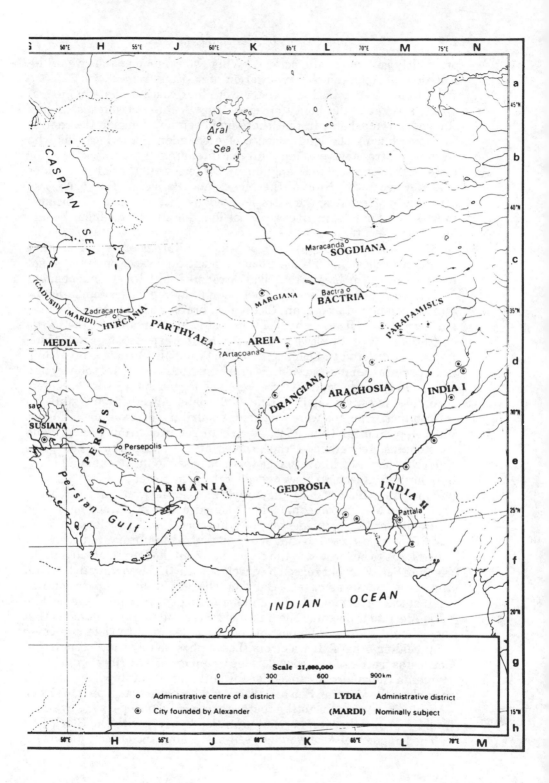

CASPIAN SEA

Aral Sea

(CADUSII)
(MARDI)
Zadracarta

HYRCANIA

MEDIA

PARTHYAEA

?Artacoana

MARGIANA

Maracanda   SOGDIANA

Bactra
BACTRIA

AREIA

PARAPAMISUS

DRANGIANA   ARACHOSIA   INDIA I

sa
SUSIANA

PERSIS

Persepolis

CARMANIA   GEDROSIA   INDIA II

Pattala

Persian Gulf

INDIAN OCEAN

Scale 21,000,000

0   300   600   900 km

o   Administrative centre of a district   LYDIA   Administrative district

⊙   City founded by Alexander   (MARDI)   Nominally subject

previously governed satisfactorily. When we remember the size of the Kingdom of Asia and the installation of satraps from 334 to 325, we should not be surprised that there were four cases of maladministration. As regards the policy of appointing Asians as satraps, it had succeeded remarkably in that there had been no risings in the central satrapies during the long absence of Alexander. Some Persians who were not satraps were found guilty of intending to start rebellion, for instance two arrested in Drangiana by Craterus, but the only pretender who claimed to be 'King of the Medes and Persians', Baryaxes, was arrested by Atropates, the satrap, and delivered with some associates to Alexander in 324. In all cases those found guilty of rebellious behaviour were executed.

Misconduct by European troops was on a larger scale. As we have mentioned (above, p. 72), the troops in a satrapy were commanded not by the satrap (in Media the loyal Atropates) but by an independent officer. Thus a force of some 10,000 men in Media was commanded by a distinguished Macedonian, Cleander a brother of Coenus, and on his staff were two officers, who like him had held commands at the Battle of Gaugamela – Sitalces and Agathon. In response to complaints, Alexander ordered these officers to bring the bulk of their army to him in Carmania. Asians and soldiers laid numerous charges of robbery and rape, and Cleander and Sitalces, being held reponsible, were executed. After an investigation in Media 600 soldiers were found guilty of misconduct. They too were executed. So striking an example of justice did more than anything else, as Arrian reported from Ptolemy and Aristobulus, to persuade 'the peoples of the spear-won lands to be orderly ... for they knew that it was not possible in Alexander's Kingdom for his subjects to be wronged by those in power'.

Since Alexander was looking forward to campaigning in Arabia and then in the Mediterranean, he had to ensure that the Kingdom of Asia would be 'orderly' during his long absence. Most of his actions in 324-323 were directed to that end. The centre of military and economic control was to be located in the region between the Persian Gulf and the Caspian Sea. For that reason he developed the thalassocracy in the Gulf and made the fleet's base at Babylon. His only military operation was against the tribesmen who lived in high villages and raided the lowlanders. Alexander defeated them in the winter and founded cities 'so that they should no longer be nomads but become agriculturists and cease from raiding others'. It was from these tribes, led by the Cossaei, that Peucestas recruited a considerable number of warriors in 323. In Hyrcania Alexander arranged for the building of warships, which were to explore the Caspian Sea and discover whether it was a part of Ocean – in which case on Aristotle's theory there would be a passage by sea to 'India' – or whether it had communication by river with the Black Sea.

The Kingdom of Asia would be self-sustaining and orderly during his absence in the West only if the policy of cooperation with the Asians and particularly with the Persians were to continue successfully. Hephaestion was to be his deputy as King of Asia with the title 'Chiliarches' (Arrian *Succ.* 1a 3), and Peucestas was to be satrap of Persis. Both men were close friends, entirely loyal and in sympathy with Alexander's policy. Unfortunately Hephaestion died in 324, and Alexander did not appoint anyone in his place before his own death. 'Peucestas alone of the Macedonians adopted Median dress, learned the Persian language and in all respects assimilated himself to Persian ways ... to the gratification of Alexander and to the delight of the Persians.'

For the defence of the Kingdom and for the maintenance of law and order within it Alexander's deputy would need a large army which could not be provided by Macedonia. Greek mercenaries were unsuitable for this purpose. They were willing to serve any paymaster, and they had been recruited by some satraps who had thought that Alexander would not return from 'India'. Moreover, they were unruly and even fought among themselves, for instance in Bactria in 325. Nor were the Thracians dependable; for example, they assassinated the satrap Philippus in 'India' in 325. Alexander therefore created in May a mixed army of Macedonian and Persian infantry, 26,700 strong, in which each file contained four Macedonian pikemen and twelve Persian archers and javelin-men (the latter from Cossaea and Tapuria). Each file was commanded by a Macedonian, and there was higher pay for the Macedonians. It was shortly before his illness that Alexander presided at the integration of these Persians and Macedonians. At the same parade he allocated Lydian and Carian troops which had arrived as reinforcements. He had for some years had units of cavalry in which Macedonians, Persians and other Asians fought alongside one another. He intended to leave a considerable number of these in Asia. He was joined probably by a reinforcement of Companion Cavalry who came from Macedonia under the command of Menidas.

'Alexander thought that Asia could be held together by an army of modest size, because he had posted garrisons at many places and because he had filled the newly founded cities with settlers who were eager to maintain the *status quo*.' The garrisons were stationed at strategic points in the web of all-weather roads which enabled troops to move rapidly. The new cities numbered seventy, each starting with at least 10,000 male citizens, and it was in these cities that 'boys' were trained in Greek literacy and in Macedonian weaponry. In addition there were militias in the towns which would resist raiders. One should think therefore of the mixed army, consisting of Macedonians and Asians, as a mobile force which could move rapidly to defeat any considerable rising and so hold Asia together. The defence of the Kingdom of Asia against outside enemies hardly figured in Alexander's calculations; his frontiers were mainly desert and steppe, the Scythian tribes had entered into alliance, and his fleets ruled over the waves of the Indian Ocean, the Red Sea, the Eastern Mediterranean and the Black Sea.

The greatest threat to peace within Asia came from unemployed Greek mercenaries. During Alexander's long absence many of these mercenaries had been hired by ambitious satraps and military commanders, who hoped to carve out a kingdom for themselves if he should be killed. On his return they were dismissed on his order, and they joined the huge number of mercenaries who had lost their employment with the defeat of Darius and his satraps. Before he fell ill Alexander was planning to settle 50,000 of them together with their Asian women and their children in Persis, and no doubt to train their 'boys' to be his soldiers later. It is probable that his plan became known at the time; for a considerable number preferred to move to Greece, where there was still hope of employment. He must have been glad to see them go.

As a military area Persis was second to Media. For the overland communications between east and west all ran through Media; it had provided the best soldiers of the Persian Empire; and its pasturelands bred the finest horses in Asia. The dependable satrap Atropates had kept the Medes loyal during Alexander's absence, and many of them were serving in his Companion Cavalry. According to Polybius, 'it was on the initiative of Alexander that Media was ringed round with Greek cities'. The process probably began before his death (it was completed by his general Seleucus). It seems that these foundations were not mixed in population, but that city-populations were transplanted from the Greek mainland or islands; and their place there was taken by Asian city-populations. For in the plans which were made known after his death Alexander intended 'to establish cities and transplant populations from Asia to Europe and conversely from Europe to Asia'.

The other factor which was to hold Asia together was economic growth and prosperity. Alexander encouraged the transition from pastoralism to agriculture by creating urban centres for native peoples, for instance the Cossaeans and the subjects of Musicanus, and Greek methods of intensive agriculture were introduced by the settlers of his new cities. His concern is seen in flood-control, irrigation and the digging of wells in barren land. Trade expanded rapidly with secure, peaceful conditions and no tariffs over the entire area from the Greek mainland to the river Hyphasis. Overland communications were eased by the maintenance of all-weather roads and bridges, the siting of the Alexander-cities, and the suppression of brigandage. The carriage of goods on a large scale on the great rivers of Mesopotamia and of Pakistan, and the development of sea-borne trade between the Persian Gulf and the Delta of the Indus were innovations which added enormously to inter-regional exchange and the distribution of surplus foodstuffs. Whereas Persia had made only limited use of coined money,

Alexander issued a gold and silver coinage of real value which was valid throughout the Kingdom of Asia and beyond its eastern frontier. The chief mint was at Babylon, 'the metropolis' as the M on its coins indicated. Alexander was able to stabilise the relationship between gold and silver and to avoid inflation by his control of the output of coinage. The change from barter to capitalism was rapid and effective.

Some have suggested that if Alexander had lived longer he would have reorganised the system of government in Asia. This seems not to be so. The only alternative was the representational system of the Greek Community. But that system could not have succeeded in Asia; for whereas the members of the Greek Community had a common language and lived close to one another, the Asians spoke innumerable languages and were widespread. The combination of an autocratic king with an improved satrapal system and full local self-government was in Alexander's lifetime effective and acceptable. For his purpose was understood, as we see in a passage of the *Alexander Romance*, in which after the death of Darius Alexander was represented as saying to the Persians as follows:

> You are each to observe the religions and customs, the laws and conventions ... which you observed in the days of Darius. Let each stay Persian in his way of life, and let him live witin his city ... for I wish to make the land one of widespread prosperity and employ the Persian roads as peaceful and quiet channels of commerce.

Such a prospect of peace, prosperity and progress is lacking in many parts of the modern world.

2. Macedonians and Asians

A decisive factor in the policy of Alexander was the small number of Macedonian citizen troops in Asia. The only firm figures we have are for 324, when the infantry totalled 23,000 and the cavalry more than 2,000, and there were in addition perhaps 1,400 Macedonians unfit for active service in the Alexander-cities. An army of this size would have been swamped by the forces of Darius. From the start Alexander had to add Balkan troops, Greek allies, Greek mercenaries and after his first victory Persians and other Asians, and for the future he set up the training of young Asians for service with Macedonian weapons. The recruitment of Asians and particularly Persians was possible only if they accepted Alexander's rule willingly (as he had prayed in 334; above, p. 64). In consequence, the policy of cooperating with Asians and of treating them as equals was essential for Alexander and became a *sine qua non* with the expansion of the Kingdom of Asia. The process began with the drafting of Persians into the Companion Cavalry and the ranking of the Persian Royal Cavalry Guard on a par with the Companion Cavalry Guard. The adoption of Median dress and Persian ceremonial in audiences for Asians was a mark of respect for them, even if very few Macedonians followed Alexander's example.

Alexander's chivalry towards the Persian Queen Mother and towards the Sogdian princess, Roxane, whom he did not rape but married, made a great impression on the Asian aristocracy. In 324 at Susa he arranged the weddings of more than eighty Persian, Median and Bactrian aristocrats to the leading Macedonians. A daughter of Darius and a daughter of his predecessor, Artaxerxes Ochus, were taken in marriage by Alexander. The weddings were conducted in the Persian manner, in which the bridegroom kissed the bride. Also at Susa Alexander converted into official marriages the liaisons which some 10,000 Macedonian soldiers had formed with Asian women; and he gave them wedding presents. It was known that many Macedonians owed money to Asian traders, who had little hope of recovering it. Alexander paid the money *in toto* without requiring the soldiers in debt to reveal their identity. In all these ways Alexander was treating his Macedonians and his Asians as equals in status and in obligation.

He was still at Susa in February 324 when 'the satraps came to him bringing from the newly founded cities and from the rest of the spear-won land 30,000 boys (*paides*) already reaching maturity and all of the same age'. These were the 'Epigonoi' (above, p. 130), whose training Alexander had started in 330/329. They were now in their twentieth year. 'They were equipped with Macedonian weapons and they were practised in the arts of war in the Macedonian manner.' When they were paraded before the king, 'they showed amazing dexterity and agility in their manoeuvres'. Trained as pikemen and serving as a parallel unit to the Macedonian phalanx, they were superior in number and bound to outlive the ageing Macedonians. That was why 'Alexander called them Epigonoi' – the next generation, the successors. He needed them for the campaign in Arabia, for which he would have few Macedonian phalangites; and he was also implementing his policy of placing Asians and Macedonians on the same level of respect.

The Macedonian phalangites, however, took a very different view. They were the acknowledged élite of Alexander's army, and they had held that position through many years of devoted and exacting service. They resented the arrival of the Epigonoi, and they were alarmed by the fear that they would ultimately be replaced by them. Their anger was focussed on Alexander. He had already offended Macedonians by his Median dress, his Persian ceremonial, his staging of the massed marriages, and his integration of Asians into the Companion Cavalry and even into the Cavalry Guard and the arming of them with the Macedonian lance. There was little that Alexander could do to placate them. He held many assemblies but found them unruly.

The crisis came at Opis in summer 324. Alexander had decided to send to Macedonia those Macedonians who were unfit for active service on account of their age or their injuries. They would number several thousand (in the event 10,000 went), and apart from some cavalrymen they would be phalangites rather than Hypaspists, who seem to have remained with him as a unit. He convened an assembly of the Macedonians and announced his decision. The reaction of those he had in mind was not pleasure at going home, as he may have expected, but fury that they were being despised as unfit and treated with contempt; and the reaction of those who did not feel themselves threatened was anger that Alexander was insulting his Macedonians once again and would replace them with Asians. In the general outcry Alexander was told to send them all home and go campaigning 'with his father', meaning Ammon. He and the commanders beside him leapt down from the dais into the crowd and ordered the arrest of the ringleaders by the Hypaspist Guards. Thirteen men were marched off to be executed for mutiny.

In the silence which ensued Alexander made a speech, of which the substance, not the words, was preserved by Arrian. In brief, he recounted the services of Philip and more especially of himself in raising the Macedonians from obscurity and poverty to be the leaders of the world, the conquerors of every land and sea, the owners of Persia's treasure and of India's good things. He had not exalted himself above his men; he had been wounded as often as any of them, lived more humbly than most, and had won everlasting glory for them and for those who had died in action. His intention had been to send home those unfit for war. Now they could all go home and report there that they had abandoned their king to the mercies of those who had been conquered.

After his speech he shut himself off from any Macedonian for two days, and on the third day he summoned the leading Persians and conferred on them the command of Asian troops which were not only brigaded in the Macedonian manner but were given the Macedonian names: Foot-Companions, Town-Companions, Companion Cavalrymen and so on. The Persian commanders were to be his 'Kinsmen' and they alone had the right to kiss him. He had turned his back on the Macedonians. But they could not bear it. They threw down their weapons at his door in supplication and begged him for mercy. He came out quickly, and 'seeing them so humble ... he too shed tears'. A leading Companion complained that Alexander was calling some Persians 'Kinsmen' and letting them kiss him but was not according that privilege to Macedonians. Alexander cried out: 'You are all my Kinsmen,' and the Companion and anyone else who wished kissed Alexander. The Macedonians went to their camp rejoicing and singing the victory song. 'Alexander thereupon sacrificed to the usual gods.'

At the start of the narrative which Arrian derived from Ptolemy and

Aristobulus it was clear that Alexander misjudged the situation. He thought that in announcing his decision 'he would of course please the Macedonians', and the reaction of the Macedonians was 'not unreasonable'. Ptolemy and/or Aristobulus realised that Alexander was out of touch with the Macedonians' feelings about the latest developments of his Asian policy. Their embittered and angry mood broke out into an uproar, which Alexander quelled by treating it as an act of mutiny. One dimension of the impasse was the Asian policy. The other dimension was the splitting of the Macedonian State. For throughout the campaign Alexander and the Assembly of Macedonians had acted as the Macedonian State in matters of policy, trials for treason and celebrations of festivals in honour of the gods. If the Macedonians went home and he stayed, the Macedonian State would be torn apart. Alexander exploited this fact. By showing that he would stay, he virtually forced them to stay with him. The emotional tension was understood and was shared by him, as his tears showed. Despite their singing the victory lay not with the Macedonians but with the King. They would stay with him, and they would accept such Persian customs as being 'Kinsmen' and 'kissing the king'.

Alexander did not let his victory dwindle. He staged a banquet of reconciliation for 9,000 guests. The Macedonians sat with him; and next to them were the Persians and representatives of the other races in Asia. The Greek diviners and the Persian Magi pronounced the omens favourable. Alexander 'prayed especially for concord and for the sharing of the rule between Macedonians and Persians'. All who were present poured the same libation and sang the victory song. It was the triumph of Alexander's Asian policy. Macedonians and Asians were to share as equals in the administration of the Kingdom of Asia.

CHAPTER XVIII

The plans and personality of Alexander

1. Arrangements affecting the Macedonians and Macedonia

After the reconciliation in late summer 324 Alexander offered his terms for any Macedonians who might volunteer to go home. They would be paid the normal wage up to their arrival in Macedonia, and each man would receive a gratuity of one talent. They were ordered to leave their Asian wives and children in Asia, where Alexander undertook to bring up the boys 'in the Macedonian manner in other respects and in military training'; and he said he would send them thereafter to their fathers in Macedonia. He made provision also for orphans of Macedonian soldiers in Asia. Some 10,000 Macedonians accepted these terms. 'He embraced them all, with tears in his eyes and tears in theirs, and they parted company.' They were being released from the campaign in Asia, not from military service. In summer 323 they reached Cilicia, where Alexander intended that they should winter. In spring 322 they were to be transported to Macedonia by his newly built fleet. By then Alexander expected to have completed his Arabian campaign and to be in Egypt or Cilicia. He was to be joined there by 10,000 Macedonians 'in their prime', who would be replaced in Macedonia by the returning veterans.

In summer 324 arrangements were made to change the representatives of the king's authority in Macedonia. Olympias had held the *prostasia*, which comprised the religious affairs of the state and the financial management of the royal property (above, p. 59); and Antipater had been 'General with full powers'. The two had become increasingly incompatible, and each of them accused the other of exceeding their powers in letters to Alexander. In 324 he moved Olympias to Molossia and brought their daughter Cleopatra from Molossia to hold the *prostasia* in Macedonia. At that time Molossia was almost a dependency of Macedonia. From 334 to 331 the Molossian king, Alexander, the husband of Cleopatra, had conducted his own campaign in Italy, and after his death Cleopatra held the office of *prostasia* in the Molossian state, which was a member of the newly formed 'Epirote Alliance'. As a member of the Molossian royal house Olympias was well qualified to take the place of Cleopatra. In recognition of Olympias' services in Macedonia Alexander announced that on her death she would be 'dedicated to immortality' (*immortalitati consecretur*), that is to receive worship at her grave as a deity.

Antipater had been entirely loyal to Alexander. In 324 he became seventy-three years of age, and Alexander decided to replace him. The commander of the returning Macedonians was Craterus, the most trusted and respected general of those who had served under Philip, and he was instructed to take over the duties of Antipater on reaching Macedonia in 322. Antipater was then to have the honour of commanding the 10,000 Macedonians 'in their prime' who were to join Alexander. 'No public act or statement by Alexander was reported which might have implied that Antipater was not as highly regarded as ever by Alexander.'

His other representative in Europe was the 'General of Thrace', Zopyrion, who exercised authority also over the Black Sea. It was no doubt on Alexander's order that he embarked on a major campaign by land and by sea against the Getae and then the Scythians of South Russia in 325. His large army, reported to be 30,000 strong, must have consisted mainly of Thracian troops. His fleet was destroyed in sudden storms, the army suffered a crushing defeat, and Zopyrion was killed. Thereupon the most powerful tribe in Thrace, the Odrysians, rose in revolt. 'Thrace was almost lost.' That it was recovered must have been due to an agreement at the time with the Odrysian king, Seuthes III.

2. Arrangements affecting the city-states

Alexander respected the sovereignty of the Greek Community in the settlement of affairs after the defeat of Agis and his allies (above, p. 117), and he continued to do so, for instance by sending captured works of art to the states in the Greek Community. His conduct in these years indicates that the allegations of exceeding his powers as *Hegemon*, which were made in a speech 'On the Treaty with Alexander' in 331, were groundless. Within the Greek Community only one breach of the charter was reported in our sources, the expulsion of the people of Oeniadae from their city by the Aetolians. It happened perhaps in 325; for Alexander said that he himself would punish the Aetolians, presumably on his return to the West. In the years of peace a large number of Greek allies went east to serve in Alexander's army (above, p. 171), and no doubt others emigrated to trade or settle in Asia. At Athens Phocion was re-elected general repeatedly as the advocate of compliance with the Charter, and Lycurgus used the prosperity which Athens enjoyed under the peace to complete the construction in stone of the auditorium of the theatre of Dionysus and to improve the naval shipyards.

In June 324, when Alexander was at Susa, one of his financial officers, Harpalus, fled to Greece in order to escape punishment for misconduct. He came to Cape Sunium with 5,000 talents, 6,000 mercenaries and 30 ships, and as an Athenian citizen (for he had been honoured earlier by a grant of citizenship) he proceeded to Athens and asked for asylum and in effect alliance against Alexander. The Assembly rejected his request. He and his forces went on to Taenarum in the Peloponnese, but he returned as a suppliant with a single ship and a large amount of money. The Assembly then granted him asylum as an Athenian citizen. Although he gave bribes freely in Athens, he did not win over the leading politicians. Meanwhile Antipater and Olympias made the demand that Athens as Macedonia's ally should extradite Harpalus; and envoys from Alexander came from Asia with a similar demand. On the proposal of Demosthenes the Assembly voted to arrest Harpalus, confiscate his money, and hold him and his money 'for Alexander'. During the debate Harpalus said he had brought 700 talents to Athens, but when his money was confiscated it amounted only to 350 talents. While the Council of the Areopagus was enquiring into the missing talents, Harpalus escaped, collected his forces at Taenarum and sailed to Crete, where he was assassinated. The attitude of Alexander was conciliatory. He did not demand the return to him of the 700 talents. Six months were to pass before the Areopagus Council delivered its report. During those months two general issues were raised by Alexander, as follows.

When his forces were assembled at Susa, Alexander announced to them that all exiles, except those under a curse and those exiled from Thebes, were to be recalled and reinstated. He chose this method of letting his intention be known, because he was acting on his own authority and not in collaboration with the Council of the Greek Community; for he was addressing a larger number of states than those of the Greek Community. An official announcement in the form of a letter was made by his envoy at the Olympic Festival in July, when 20,000 exiles were among the audience. The wording was as follows: 'Alexander to the exiles from the Greek cities ... we shall be responsible for your return ... we have written to Antipater about this, in order that he may compel any states which are unwilling to restore you.' This announcement to the exiles was not an order to the Greek states. We may assume that a separate statement was sent to them in the form of an 'ordinance' (*diagramma*), which could lead to a discussion between a state and Alexander. We see this in an inscription from Tegea in the Peloponnese. The purpose of Alexander was twofold: to resettle the floating population of exiles (we may call them refugees today), which caused instability and often led to mercenary service; and to reconcile the parties which had fought one another and caused the vicious circle of revolutionary faction (*stasis*; above, p. 10).

Such an act of statesmanship was and is unparalleled. It affected almost all Greek city-states to varying degrees, and it hit Athens and Aetolia hardest. For Athens had expelled the population of Samos in 365 and occupied the island herself; and now, forty years later, she would have to restore the island to its proper owners. And Aetolia had to hand back Oeniadae to the Acarnanians she had expelled. At the time Alexander could not be accused of restoring his own partisans; for the bulk of the exiles had been opponents of the pro-Macedonian regimes in power. According to Hieronymus, an objective historian born around 364, 'people in general accepted the restoration of the exiles as being made for a good purpose'. In many states the restoration had taken place at the time of Alexander's death, but Athens and Aetolia were still making objections.

Alexander addressed the Greek states individually with two other requests in 324: the granting of heroic honours to Hephaestion, who had died in October, and the granting of divine honours to himself. The distinction between the two forms of honours was basically one of a person's achievement in life being worthy of a hero or of a god. In the case of Hephaestion, Alexander consulted Zeus Ammon at Siwah, and he accepted the response that Hephaestion should be worshipped as a hero. In answer to his request many states, including Athens, set up cults honouring Hephaestion as a hero; for there were many precedents in the city-states. 'Divine honours' were on a different plane, and the request in this case was to grant them to a living man. In Macedonian practice the worship of a king or queen after death was a mark of special distinction, and the granting of divine honours to Philip II in his lifetime (above, p. 25) was exceptional and perhaps unique. Alexander felt himself to be in competition with his father. He therefore asked the Assembly of Macedonians in Asia to grant him 'divine honours' (*caelestes honores*), but they refused. On the other hand some city-states of the Aegean islands and on the Asian coast had already in 334/333 granted divine honours to Alexander and had set up a shrine, games and sacrifices to him. These had been spontaneous acts of gratitude for liberation from Persian rule. Neither in Macedonia nor in the city-states was a man so honoured thought to be literally a god on earth.

Alexander's request was granted by most, perhaps by all, of the city-states individually which he addressed. Athens, for instance, dedicated a shrine, an altar and a cult-image to him. A general act of recognition was staged at Babylon in 323, perhaps at the traditional spring festival of the Macedonians. 'The envoys from Greece came to Alexander, wearing crowns themselves, and they crowned him with golden crowns; for they had come indeed on a sacred mission to honour a god.' The analogy of the honours paid to Philip must have been in people's minds; for then 'not only distinguished individuals but also the majority of the important city-states, including Athens, crowned him with golden crowns'. Alexander himself must have felt that he had attained the same pinnacle of glory and was the equal of his father. The motives of the city-states were no doubt mixed. But it is evident that the majority in the democratic assemblies recognised that they owed to Alexander the stability of the Greek Community, the liberation of the city-states overseas, the overthrow of the Persian empire, the thalassocracy in the Eastern Mediterranean and the Black Sea, the opening of Asia to Greek enterprise, and the consequent peace and prosperity. The most bitter enemy of Alexander, Demosthenes, was found guilty by the Areopagus Council of embezzling money deposited by Harpalus. Unable to pay an enormous fine, he was imprisoned; but he escaped and went into exile.

When embassies came to Babylon, Alexander heard first those concerned with religious matters. Because the Olympian gods had granted victory to Macedonia and the Greek Community, Alexander planned to build magnificent temples to Apollo at Delos and Delphi, Zeus at Dodona and at Dium, Athena Alcidemus at Cyrrus (in Macedonia), Artemis at Amphipolis, and Athena at Troy. He intended also to pay a special honour to his father, Philip: 'to build a mound of proportions equal to the tallest pyramid in Egypt.' He did not live to achieve it, but one of his generals – probably Lysimachus – built the Great Mound over the tomb of Philip at Vergina. Thanks to the plan of Alexander the tomb survived intact until it was excavated in 1977 by Manolis Andronicos.

3. Preparations for the Mediterranean campaign

Alexander must have let it be known at Susa in 324 that he intended to campaign in the West; for envoys came to Babylon early in 323 from that area. The Libyan envoys congratulated Alexander on winning 'the Kingdom of Asia', and those from Italy – Bruttians, Lucanians and Etruscans – honoured him for his achievements. This information was transmitted from Ptolemy and Aristobulus by Arrian, and is to be accepted. The Libyans thought he would march along the African coast; the Italian peoples expected him to follow the example of his namesake, the king of the Molossians, and invade South Italy from Epirus. The plans which were made public after Alexander's death were more specific: to build a thousand warships larger than triremes in Phoenicia, Syria, Cilicia and Cyprus for the expedition which was to be undertaken against Carthage, the coastal peoples from Libya to Spain, and those of the coast from Spain to Sicily; to build a coastal road from Libya to the Pillars of Heracles; and to build harbours and dockyards to accommodate so large an expeditionary force. These were, of course, provisional plans which Alexander sketched out for an expedition two years ahead, and they are chiefly of interest in revealing the scale of his ambitions. It seems from a passage in Justin 13.5.7 that Alexander issued orders before his death for the construction of the thousand warships.

If the expedition had materialised, the forces at Alexander's disposal would have been of the following order. If he should leave the Macedonian fleet and that of the Greek Community to maintain order in the Aegean Sea, he could count on the fleets of Phoenicia, Cyprus and Egypt in addition to his thousand new warships. If he should conquer Arabia with small casualties, he would have some 16,000 Macedonian pikemen, 20,000 Asian pikemen, the Persian Infantry Guard, plenty of light-armed infantry, the Companion Cavalry and units of Asian cavalry. There is no doubt that he would have defeated Carthage, and that he would have advanced to the Pillars of Heracles.

4. Events leading to the death of Alexander

In October 324 at Ecbatana Alexander suffered a terrible blow in the death of Hephaestion, his closest friend from childhood days and his constant sympathiser and supporter. He lay in a paroxysm of grief for two days, fasting and inaccessible. The funerary games were on an unprecedented scale with 3,000 artists and athletes, and the ashes of Hephaestion were taken to Babylon, where work began on a ziggurat of colossal size (its completion was still on order when Alexander died). The place and the form of this memorial were chosen because Hephaestion had been appointed *chiliarches*, i.e. the second-in-command in the Kingdom of Asia, and if he and Alexander had survived long enough he would have ruled the kingdom from Babylon as its metropolis. Mourning in the Persian manner was ordered throughout the Kingdom. The Macedonians instituted a cult of Hephaestion as 'a hero', which lasted for centuries as an inscription from Pella reveals. Special tributes were paid to Hephaestion as Commander of the Royal Hipparchy of the Companion Cavalry, many Companions dedicated themselves and their weapons to his memory, and Hephaestion's standard continued to be carried in front of the Hipparchy. The city-states too were asked by Alexander to pay heroic honours to Hephaestion, and many did so (above, p. 194). Alexander did not appoint a successor to Hephaestion either as chiliarch or as Commander of the Royal Hipparchy; but in practice Perdiccas became second-in-command, and it was he who took the initiative when Alexander died.

The death of Hephaestion and the immoderate grief of Alexander were the subject of many sensational accounts, which Arrian judged to be often untrue. Writers critical of Alexander, for instance, said that he razed the temple of Asclepius at Ecbatana, and that he ordered worship of Hephaestion 'as a god'. Arrian cited from the account by Ptolemy a letter from Alexander to Cleomenes, in which memorials were to be erected to Hephaestion in Alexandria and on the offshore island,

Pharos, and Alexander promised Cleomenes pardon for any offences in the past and in the future, 'if I shall find the shrines in Egypt in good condition'. It was Ptolemy who added that Cleomenes was 'a bad man' (so Arrian), in self-justification because he executed Cleomenes in 322. Did Ptolemy invent and insert the promise of Alexander? Some have thought so. Let us summarise the little we know. Cleomenes had been appointed in 331 as the senior financial officer in Egypt, and during Alexander's absence he took control of Egypt under unknown circumstances. That may have been one offence which Alexander would pardon. The pardon for future offences was only until Alexander should arrive in Egypt, probably early in 322. It is thus possible that the letter is genuine, and that it is an indication of Alexander's passionate desire to commemorate Hephaestion in grand style.

'After the funeral of Hephaestion ... the divine power began to indicate the end of Alexander himself, for many strange omens and signs occurred.' Most of the prognostications were inventions of the numerous authors who wrote about the end of Alexander. The omens ranged from a donkey kicking to death the finest lion in Alexander's menagerie to an escaped convict sitting on the king's vacant throne. There was, however, one prognostication which did affect the march of Alexander and his army after the campaign against the Cossaei. As he crossed the Tigris on his way to Babylon, he was met by Chaldaean diviners who warned him not to enter Babylon from the east but to do so from the west. According to Aristobulus Alexander wished to comply with the warning and did march the army round to the Euphrates on the west side of the city, but he was then thwarted by coming upon marshes and open water and so he entered from the east side. 'Thus willy-nilly he disobeyed the god', i.e. Belus (Ba'al); for Aristobulus believed the Chaldaeans had been inspired by Belus to give the warning. During his stay in Babylon Alexander set the army to work on clearing the site for a temple to Belus (the earlier one having been destroyed by Xerxes). He himself sailed down the Pollacopas canal (above, p. 179), and on his return through the marshlands he entered Babylon from the east side, confident in the fact that nothing disastrous had occurred since his first entry.

Soon afterwards, in May 323, the preparations for the Arabian campaign were complete. As usual before embarking on a new enterprise (above, p. 51), Alexander sacrificed to the gods for their blessing and distributed sacrificial victims and wine to the army, unit by unit; and he entertained the Friends at a banquet far into the night. He prolonged the drinking as the guest of a Friend, Medius, and slept by day, as was probably usual in the heat of summer in Iraq. He did the same the following night and day, and it was on that day that the fever started. 'However, he was carried out on a bed to perform the sacrifices, as custom prescribed for each day, ... and as darkness fell he issued orders to his commanders for the march and the voyage'. This is Arrian's abbreviation of a fuller account in the *Journal* (Plutarch had provided his own abbreviation). Alexander acted in this way day by day until he lost the power of speech. The Macedonian soldiers forced their way into his room in their longing to see him. 'The *Journal* says that as the men filed past he was unable to speak but greeted them severally, with difficulty raising his head and indicating with his eyes.' Death came to him that night, on 10 June 323, at the age of thirty-two. All the symptoms suggest that he died of *malaria tropica*. Later allegations that his death was due to poisoning or the result of alcoholism are untrue, for they are not consistent with the detailed report in the *Journal*.

5. Alexander's beliefs and personal qualities

Alexander grew up in a kingdom which was continually at war, and he saw it as his duty to lead the Macedonians in war not from a distance but in the forefront of the fighting. He saw the destiny of Macedonia as victory in war, and he and his men made military glory the object of their ambitions. Thus he spoke of the victorious career of Philip as conferring 'glory' both on him and on 'the community of Macedonians'. His own pursuit of glory was boundless. As he declared to his Commanders at the Hyphasis, 'I myself consider that there is no limit for a man of spirit to his labours, except that those labours should lead to fine achievements.' He made the same demand on his Commanders and his men. They had committed themselves to following him when they had sworn the oath of allegiance (*sacramentum pietatis*), to be loyal and have the same friend and enemy as their king. If a man should be killed in his service, Alexander assured them that his death would bring him glory for ever and his place of burial would be famous.

Life was competitive for boys in the School of Pages and for boys being trained for the militia in the cities, and thereafter in civilian affairs and in the services. No Macedonian festival was complete without contests in such arts as dramatic performance, recitation of poetry, proclamation as a herald, and musicianship, and in athletic events which on occasion included armed combat. Alexander was intensely competitive throughout his life. He would be the first to tame Bucephalus, to attack the Theban Sacred Band, to mount a city wall or climb an impregnable rock. He was the inspirer and often the judge of competition in others. He alone promoted soldiers and officers, awarded gifts for acts of courage, bestowed gold crowns on successful Commanders, and decided the order in the hierarchy of military rank up to the position of Senior Friend and Leading Bodyguard. Competitions between military units and between naval crews were a part of training and of battle. Alexander himself believed that he must compete with

Philip, Cyrus the Great, Heracles and Dionysus and surpass them all, and as Arrian remarked, 'if he had added Europe to Asia, he would have competed with himself in default of any rival'.

His belief in the superiority of Greek civilisation was absolute. His most treasured possession was the *Iliad* of Homer, and he had the plays of the three great tragedians sent to him in Asia, together with dithyrambic poems and the history of Philistus. They were his favourite reading. He admired Aristotle as the leading exponent of Greek intellectual enquiry, and he had a natural yearning (*pothos*) for philosophical discussion and understanding. His mind was to some extent cast in the Aristotelian mould; for he too combined a wide-ranging curiosity with close observation and acute reasoning. His belief in the validity of the Greek outlook of his time was not modified by his acquaintance with Egyptian, Babylonian and Indian ideas. One mark of Greek civilisation was the vitality of the city, both in Europe and in Asia, and Alexander believed that the best way to spread Greek culture and civilisation was by founding cities throughout Asia. At the outset the leaders in these cities were the Macedonians and the Greek mercenary soldiers, who conducted the democratic form of self-government to which they were accustomed. At the same time the future leaders were being educated 'in Greek letters and in Macedonian weaponry' in the schools which Alexander established. The process was already well under way before Alexander died, as we see from a passage in Plutarch's *Moralia*: 'When Alexander was civilising Asia, the reading was Homer and the boys (*paides*) of the Persians, Susianians and Gedrosians used to chant the tragedies of Euripides and Sophocles ... and thanks to him Bactria and Caucasus revered the Greek gods'. Egypt has yielded a teaching manual of the late third century, which was designed to teach Greek as a foreign language and included selections from Homer and the tragedians. The excavations at Ai Khanoum in Afghanistan have revealed Greek temples, theatre and odeum (for music) alongside a very large Asian temple in the late fourth century (see Fig. 16). Alexander was the standard-bearer of Greek civilisation. His influence in education and so in civilisation has been profound, extending even into our own age.

Faith in the orthodox religion of Macedonia was deeply implanted in Alexander's mind. He sacrificed daily, even in his last illness, on behalf of himself and the Macedonians and on innumerable other occasions. He organised traditional festivals in honour of the gods in the most lavish fashion. He believed as literally as Pindar had done in the presence in our world of the Olympian gods, in the labours of heroes such as Heracles and the exploits of Achilles, both being his ancestors. The deities made their wishes or their warnings manifest to men through natural phenomena and through omens and oracles, which were interpreted and delivered by inspired men and women. It was an advantage of polytheism that the number of gods was not limited, and Alexander could see Zeus in the Libyan Ammon and in the Babylonian Belus, and Heracles in the Tyrian Melkart or the Indian Krishna. His special regard for Ammon was probably due to the prophetic oracles which he received at Siwah and which were evidently fufilled *in toto* when Alexander reached the outer Ocean. He gave thanks time and again to 'the usual gods' (the twelve Olympians) for the salvation of himself and his army, and he must have thought that he owed his charmed life to them. Even in his last illness he believed that his prayers in the course of sacrifices would be heard and that he would live. For he died without arranging for the transition of power.

Of the personal qualities of Alexander the brilliance, the range and the quickness of his intellect are remarkable, especially in his conduct of warfare. At Gaugamela and at the Hydaspes he foresaw precisely the sequence of moves by his own units and the compulsion they would place on his enemies. As Ptolemy, himself a most able commander, observed of the first campaign, 'the result was as Alexander inferred that it would be', and after the last campaign 'not a one of the operations of war which Alexander undertook was beyond his capability' (*aporon*). In generalship no one has surpassed him. Arrian wrote that Alexander had 'the most wonderful power of grasping the right course when the situation was still in obscurity'. Thus he knew on his landing in Asia that he must set up his own Kingdom of Asia and obtain the willing cooperation of his subjects. Already at Sardis he began the training of boys who would become soldiers of that kingdom. The originality of his intellect was apparent in his development of the Indus, the Tigris and the Euphrates as waterways of commerce and his reorganisation of the irrigation of Mesopotamia. The boldness of his calculations was rewarded with success in many engagements and especially in the opening of navigation between the Indus Delta and the Persian Gulf.

His emotions were very strong. His love for his mother was such that one tear of hers would outweigh all the complaints of Antipater. He sent letters and gifts to her constantly, and he said that he would take her alone into his confidence on his return to Macedonia. His loyalty to the friends of his own generation was carried sometimes to a fault, and his passionate grief for Hephaestion was almost beyond reason. He loved his soldiers and they loved him; he and his veterans wept when they parted company; and he and they acknowledged that love in his last moments. When he killed Cleitus, his remorse was desperate. His compassion for the Theban Timoclea and for the family of Darius and his love for Roxane were deeply felt and led to actions which were probably unique in contemporary warfare.

As King of the Macedonians and as King of Asia he had different roles to fill. His way of life was on the same level as that of the Macedonians on campaigns and in leisure. As he said at Opis, his rations were the same as theirs and he shared all their dangers and hardships; and he enjoyed the same festivals and drinking parties as they did. He led them not by fiat but by persuasion, and a crucial element in that persuasion was that he should always tell them the truth, and they should know that he was telling them the truth. Thus he respected the constitutional rights of the Macedonians, and his reward was that he was generally able to convince them in their Assemblies that they should accept his policies. His role as King of Asia was almost the opposite. His court, like that of the Persian King of Kings, was the acme of luxury and extravagance. He gave audience in a huge pavilion which rested on fifty golden columns, and he himself sat on a golden chair, surrounded by so many richly-dressed guardsmen that 'no one dared approach him, such was the majesty associated with his person'. He accepted obeisance, and he ruled by fiat. The wealth at his command was beyond belief; for he had taken over the accumulated treasure of the Persian monarchy, and he received the fixed tribute which was paid by his subjects over a huge area. His expenditure was extraordinary by Greek standards, for instance on memorials commemorating Hephaestion, but it was in proportion to his wealth as King of Asia. The strength of his personality was such that he was able to keep the two roles separate in his mind and in his behaviour, and Ptolemy and Aristobulus were correct in seeing the real Alexander as Alexander the Macedonian.

Alexander combined his extraordinary practicality with a visionary, spiritual dimension which stemmed from his religious beliefs. As a member of the Temenid house he had a special affinity with his ancestors Heracles and Zeus, and he inherited the obligation to rule in a manner worthy of them and to benefit mankind. His vision went beyond Macedonia and the Greek Community. When he landed on Asian soil, his declaration, 'I accept Asia from the gods', and his prayer, that the Asians would accept him willingly as their king, were expressions of a mystical belief that the gods had set him a special task and would enable him to fulfil it. This spiritual dimension in his personality created in him the supreme confidence and the strength of will which overrode the resistance of the Macedonians to his concept of the Kingdom of Asia, and which convinced the Asians of the sincerity of his claim to treat them as equals and partners in the establishment of peace and prosperity. The power of his personality was all-pervading. It engaged the loyalty of Persian commanders and Indian rulers after defeat in battle and the loyalty of Asian troops at all levels in his service. It inspired *The Alexander Romance* in which Asian peoples adopted Alexander as their own king and incorporated his exploits into their own folk-lore. We owe to Plutarch, drawing probably on the words of Aristobulus, an insight into this spiritual dimension in Alexander.

Believing that he had come from the gods to be a governor and reconciler of the universe, and using force of arms against those whom he did not bring together by the light of reason, he harnessed all resources to one and the same end, mixing as it were in a loving-cup the lives, manners, marriages and customs of men. He ordered them all to regard the inhabited earth (*oikoumene*) as their fatherland and his armed forces as their stronghold and defence.

Appendix

The following articles support views expressed in the text, enumerated by chapters.
Abbreviations are as follows:

AG = N.G.L. Hammond, *Alexander the Great: King, Commander and Statesman* (1st edn. New Jersey 1980, London 1981; 2nd edn. Bristol 1989; 3rd edn. Bristol Classical Press 1994)
AJPh = *American Journal of Philology*
CQ = *Classical Quarterly*
GRBS = *Greek, Roman and Byzantine Studies*
JHS = *Journal of Hellenic Studies*
HG = N.G.L. Hammond, *A History of Greece to 322 B.C.* (Oxford, 1st edn. 1959, 2nd edn. 1967, 3rd edn. 1986)
HM = *History of Macedonia*, vol. 1 by N.G.L. Hammond (Oxford, 1972); vol. 2 by N.G.L. Hammond and G.T. Griffith (1979); vol. 3 by N.G.L. Hammond and F.W. Walbank (1988)
MS = N.G.L. Hammond, *The Macedonian State* (Oxford, 1989)
Sources = N.G.L. Hammond, *Sources for Alexander the Great* (Cambridge, 1993)
THA = N.G.L. Hammond, *Three Historians of Alexander* (Cambridge, 1983).

Chapter I. *Sources* 20 ff. (Bucephalus); *Historia* 39 (1990) 261 ff. (Pages).
Chapter II. *HG* 521-32 and 582-95 (Greek states); *HM* 1.59-123 (Upper Macedonia); *MS* 16-36 and 49-70 (Institutions).
Chapter III. *Philip of Macedon* (London, 1994); *HM* 3.471-9 (Greek Community).
Chapter IV. *GRBS* 19 (1978) 343 ff. (trial); *CQ* 38 (1988) 382 ff. (Calindoea); *JHS* 94 (1974) 66 ff. (Balkan campaign).
Chapter V. *Sources* 198-210 and *Historia* 37 (1988) 129 ff. (Sources of information); *AG*[3] 68 f. and *Antichthon* 20 (1986) 74 ff. (Crossing to Asia and Kingdom of Asia).
Chapter VI. *CQ* 30 (1990) 471 ff. (Europe); *Antichthon* 26 (1992) 30 ff. (Macedonian navy); *JHS* 100 (1980) 73 ff. (Granicus).
Chapter VII. *THA* 38 ff. (Miletus); 39 f. (Halicarnassus); 40 and 62 (Marmara).
Chapter VIII. *THA* 97, 120, 184 and *Sources* 47, 217 (Gordium); *AG*[1] 96-110 with Figs. 23-28, *Historia* 41 (1992) 395 ff., and *Prudentia* Suppl. Number, 1993, 77 ff. (Issus); *THA* 124 ff. and *Sources* 56 f. (Gaza).
Chapter IX. *Historia* 39 (1990) 275 ff. (King's Boys); *AG*[3] 132 ff. (Gaugamela); *CQ* 28 (1978) 336 ff. (Pursuit).
Chapter X. *CQ* 42 (1992) 358 ff. (Persepolis); *Historia* 39 (1990) 261 ff. (Pages); *JHS* 109 (1989) 63 ff. (Losses).

Chapter XI. *Sources* 74 f., 233 and *THA* 57, 101, 133 (Darius' death); *Historia* 39 (1990) 275 f. (Epigonoi).

Chapter XII. *Sources* 84 f., 180, 233 and *THA* 59 f., 103, 136 (Philotas).

Chapter XIII. *THA* 141 f. (Branchidae); *Ancient World* 22 (1991) 41 f. (Samarcand).

Chapter XIV. *Sources* 89 f., 180 f., 240 f. and *THA* 103 f., 146 (Cleitus); *Sources* 98 f., 245 f. and *THA* 148 (Pages' Conspiracy).

Chapter XV. *CQ* 30 (1980) 465 f. (Hipparchy); *Sources* 106 and *THA* 52 f., 104, 149 (Massaga); *Sources* 248 ff., 258, 314 (Nysa); *AG*³ 208 ff. (Hydaspes); *Sources* 258 ff. (Coenus' speech); *Sources* 114 f. and *THA* 64, 152 (altars).

Chapter XVI. *Sources* 115 ff., 268 ff. and *THA* 65, 105, 154 (city of Malli); *Sources* 124, 273 ff. and *THA* 68 ff., 155 f. (Oreitis and Gedrosia).

Chapter XVII. *CQ* 30 (1980) 469 f. and *JHS* 109 (1989) 64 ff. (Macedonians in Asia); *Historia* 39 (1990) 275 f. (Epigonoi); *Sources* 134, 287 ff. and *THA* 72 f., 106 f. (Opis mutiny).

Chapter XVIII. *CQ* 30 (1980) 471 f. and *JHS* 105 (1985) 303 f. (Olympias); *THA* 157 (Exiles); *Sources* 136 f. 294 ff., *THA* 73, 75, 107 f. (Hephaestion); *Sources* 140 f., 300 ff. and *THA* 74, 108 (Chaldaeans); *Historia* 37 (1988) 129 ff. and 40 (1991) 382 ff., and *AJPh* 110 (1989) 155 ff. (Journal).

Further articles are forthcoming in my *Collected Studies* IV (Hakkert).

Notes on illustrations

Figures

1. Cavalryman wearing helmet, cuirass and cloak practises with his double-headed lance. A thong attaches the back part of the lance to his wrist, so that if the lance breaks he can use the back part as a spear. He aims at a shield held by a negro groom. The pikemen are indicated by dots. The four front ranks have pikes at the ready, and the four rear ranks hold their pikes upright. See Plate 3(a).

7. The penteconter, about 120 feet long and 13 feet wide, had 25 oarsmen on each side, and the triaconter had 15 oarsmen on each side. Note the steering-sweep and the rigging for the sail, which is to be imagined.

9. See Plate 9 which is on the same scale.

15. The land-mass rested on the underworld and was surrounded by ocean. The length of the land-mass in proportion to its width was estimated by Aristotle to be 5 to 3.

16. Only parts of the site in north Afghanistan have been excavated. The public buildings and the fine residences were generally on the lower ground, and the bulk of the population lived on the higher ground east of the main street. The course of the fortification-wall is shown by the broken line.

Plates

1. (a) Roman gold medallions of Philip wearing the diadem and a cuirass similar to that of Alexander in Plate 3(b), and of Olympias, whose headband is suggestive of a diadem. Diameter 5.4 cm.

2. The Royal Hunt Fresco, 5.56 m long, on the façade of the Tomb of Philip. The central horseman is Alexander, and that on the viewer's right is Philip about to strike the lion with his spear. The page on the right wears the traditional dress which included the *kausia*. The marble door of the façade leads into the antechamber of the built-tomb.

3. (a) A phalanx of pikemen making a charge. The first five ranks present their pikes at the ready, and the other ranks hold their pikes aloft to intercept missiles.

   (b) Alexander in action in the 'Alexander-Mosaic', protraying the Battle of Issus. He holds the lance at the point of balance in his right hand. His cuirass has shoulder-pieces like those of Plate 1.

4. (a) One of twenty silver vessels in Philip's Tomb. The Silenus was associated with the worship of Dionysus. Height 24.5 cm.

   (b) The miniature head on a silver amphora from Philip's Tomb represents Heracles, wearing the lion-skin cap. His features may resemble those of Alexander. Height of amphora 36.4 cm.

5. (a) The gold larnax from Philip's Tomb contained his cremated remains, wrapped in purple cloth.

(b) The gold wreath of oak leaves and acorns in its present state weighs 714 g.

6. (a) The Mosaic of a Lion Hunt from a house in Pella is dated 'a little before 300'. The figures may represent Craterus coming to the aid of Alexander. 4.9 x 3.2 m.

(b) The Mosaic of Dionysus riding on a panther, from the same house, is evidence of the worship of Dionysus. 2.7 x 2.65 m.

7. The Boscoreale fresco is a reproduction of a Macedonian original. A youthful Alexander, wearing a *kausia* (as on Plate 2), plants his *sarissa* across the Hellespont into Asiatic soil, while Asia gazes at him with a look of acceptance. The Macedonian shield is the emblem of a defensive war, which is being waged against Persia. On the lefthand part of the fresco (not shown here) a philosopher, i.e. Aristotle, watches his pupil, Alexander. Other interpretations have been advanced.

8. (a) The photograph shows Lake Little Prespa and just below it the plain of Pelium. To the west of that plain is the plain of Koritsa.

(b) The knoll (right centre) is the site of Pelium, near which the river Eordaicus ran. Alexander's army on parade advanced towards the camera.

9. Alexander, wearing the lionskin cap, in action; from the 'Alexander-Sarcophagus', found at Sidon and dated c. 325-300.

10. The river Payas is visible low down on the right.

11. Paolo Veronese appreciated the remarkable charisma and the perfect manners of Alexander, which won the love of Sisigambis (and the loyalty of Taxiles and Porus).

12. The 'Alexander-Mosaic' (5.12 x 2.71 m) in the National Museum of Naples shows Alexander on the left and Darius on the right at the Battle of Issus. Behind Darius the pikes of the Macedonian infantrymen rise high in the air. This Roman mosaic copied a Macedonian fresco of the late fourth century BC.

13. The 'Porus Medallion' shows a cavalryman attacking Porus and his mahout, who are mounted on an armoured elephant. The Indian archer and the unarmoured elephant perhaps commemorate an elephant-hunt as in Arr. 4.30.8. Another interpretation is given by M.J. Price in *Studia Paulo Naster Oblata* I (Leuven, 1982) 75 ff.

14. The bronze crater from Derveni, dated c. 330, portrayed scenes with Dionysus, Ariadne, Maenads and Satyrs. Worship of Dionysus was associated with life after death for his followers. Height 90 cm.

15. A young Alexander, riding Bucephalus, is hastening to help Philip in the Royal Hunt Fresco (Plate 2 above). This contemporary portrait shows the piercing eyes, prominent nose and narrow face, which are features of the youthful Alexander in the Alexander-Mosaic (Plate 3 (b) above) and the Boscoreale painting (Plate 7 above). See M. Andronicos *V* Fig. 70 on p. 115.

16. A marble copy of a late fourth century original. This and similar portraits show a mature Alexander with deep-set eyes, a full face and hair brushed upwards from the forehead in the style called *anastole*. These features were probably idealised. This head is in the Pella Museum. Height 30 cm.

Chronological table of dates
adopted in the text

336 BC	Spring	Vanguard invades Asia.
	October	Accession of A(lexander).
	Nov.-Dec.	A gains support of Amphictyonic Council; A appointed *hegemon* of Greek forces v. Persia.
335	Spring to Sept.	A campaigns in the Balkans; Memnon counter-attacks in Asia.
	Oct.	Fall of Thebes; arrangements for war v. Persia concluded with the Greek League Council.
	Nov./Dec.	Festivals at Dium and Aegeae.
334	May	A lands in Asia.
	May/June	Battle of the Granicus river.
	Summer	Capture of Miletus and isolation of Persians at Halicarnassus.
334/3	Winter	A conquers Caria, Lycia, Pamphylia and Phrygia.
333	March-June	Naval offensive by Memnon; he dies in June.
	April-July	A is based on Gordium and campaigns in adjacent areas.
	July-Sept.	Pharnabazus conducts his naval offensive.
	Aug.	A enters Cilicia; ill until late Sept.
	Oct.	Parmenio sent ahead to 'Syrian Gates'; A campaigns in Rough Cilicia.
	Nov.	Battle of Issus.
332	Jan.-July	Siege of Tyre; disintegration of the Persian fleet.
	Sept./Nov.	Siege of Gaza; Macedonia supreme at sea.
	Dec.	A enters Egypt.
331	Jan.	A founds Alexandria.
	Feb.	A visits Siwah.
	Spring	Festival at Memphis.
	Early summer	A in Phoenicia and Syria. Reinforcements leave Macedonia in July.
	Late July	A sets out for Thapsacus.
	Aug.-Sept.	A campaigns in northern Mesopotamia and southern Armenia.
	Sept. 20, p.m.	Eclipse of the moon.
	Oct. 1	Battle of Gaugamela; Agis raises a coalition in Greece.
	Dec.	A at Susa learns of Antipater's settlement of Thrace and of Agis laying siege to Megalopolis.
330	Jan.-March	A at Persepolis.

	March-April	A campaigns v. Mardi.
	April/May	Antipater defeats Agis.
	May	A leaves Persepolis.
	Summer	A campaigns in Tapuria, Hyrcania, Parthyaea and Areia. Pursuit and death of Darius in July.
	Oct.	Plot of Philotas.
	Nov.	A in Ariaspia.
	Late Dec.	Armies unite in Arachosia.
329	Jan.	A advances to Kabul and winters there.
	Spring	A crosses the Hindu Kush.
	Summer	A reorganises his cavalry. Crosses the Oxus. Captures Bessus. Advances to the Jaxartes.
	Autumn	Rising of Sogdians and Bactrians.
329/8	Winter	A at Bactra.
328	Spring/Summer	Campaigns in Sogdia and Bactria.
	Autumn	Death of Cleitus at Samarcand.
328/7	Winter	A at Nautaca. In late winter A captures the Sogdian Rock and the Rock of Chorienes.
327	Spring	Forces unite at Bactra. Plot of the Pages.
	Spring/Summer	Army crosses the Hindu Kush.
327/6	Winter	Hephaestion advances to the Indus. A campaigns in Swat, and late in the winter captures Aornus.
326	Spring	Forces unite at the Indus.
	May	Battle of the Hydaspes.
	Summer	A advances to and returns from the Hyphasis.
	Nov.	The fleet starts down the Hydaspes.
326/5	Winter	A campaigns against the Malli; is wounded in an assault on a Mallian city.
325	Feb.	Forces unite at the confluence of the Acesines and the Indus.
	Spring	The Brahman rebellion.
	June	Craterus starts for Carmania.
	July	Other forces unite at Pattala.
	Late Aug.	A starts for Carmania.
	Oct.	Nearchus starts on his voyage. A enters Gedrosia.
	Dec.	A meets Craterus in Carmania.
324	Jan.	A meets Nearchus in Carmania; A advances into Persis.
	Feb.	A's army and Nearchus' fleet meet on the Pasitigris.
	July/Aug.	Recall of exiles announced at Olympic Games.
	Late summer	Mutiny at Opis. Veterans set off with Craterus for Cilicia and Macedonia.
	Autumn	A at Ecbatana; Hephaestion dies there. Perdiccas takes main army to Babylon.
324/3	Winter	A campaigns v Cossaei.
323	April/May	A joins Perdiccas at Babylon.
	May	Final preparations for summer campaign against the Arabs.
	End of May	A falls ill.
	June 10	A dies.

Index

A stands for Alexander and D for Darius III. Place-names include their inhabitants, 'Sparta' for instance including Spartans.